D0752935

Psychological Aspects of
CRISIS
NEGOTIATION

Second Edition

Psychological Aspects of
CRISIS
NEGOTIATION

Second Edition

Thomas Strentz, PhD

CRC Press
Taylor & Francis Group
Boca Raton   London   New York

CRC Press is an imprint of the
Taylor & Francis Group, an **informa** business

CRC Press
Taylor & Francis Group
6000 Broken Sound Parkway NW, Suite 300
Boca Raton, FL 33487-2742

© 2012 by Taylor & Francis Group, LLC
CRC Press is an imprint of Taylor & Francis Group, an Informa business

No claim to original U.S. Government works

Printed in the United States of America on acid-free paper
Version Date: 20111020

International Standard Book Number: 978-1-4398-8005-0 (Hardback)

Visit the Taylor & Francis Web site at
http://www.taylorandfrancis.com

and the CRC Press Web site at
http://www.crcpress.com

Table of Contents

Acknowledgments   xvii
Introduction   xxi

Section 1

BASIC CONCEPTS

1 The American Psychiatric Association (APA)   3

Introduction   3
Multiaxial Evaluation   5
Mental Health Negotiators   6
Types of Disorders Typically Encountered by Crisis Negotiators   8
The Axioms of the Negotiations Process   9
  Listening   9
  Active Listening   9
    The Mechanics of Active Listening Skills (ALS)   10
  Victimization   12
  Tone of Voice   12
  Role Change   12
  Time   13
  No   13
  Defense Mechanisms   13
    Two Defense Mechanisms   14
  Two Typical Symptoms of Psychosis   16
    Delusions   16
    Hallucinations   16
    Excellent Idea   16
Conclusion   16
References   17

**2 Characteristics of Effective Hostage/Crisis
Negotiators**   19

Introduction   19
What Is Past Is Prologue   19
The Way We Were   20

The Way It Should Be   20
Who Talks the Talk So SWAT Does Not Have to Shoot?   21
   Method   23
   Results   23
Conclusion   24
References   25

3   Cross-Trained versus Cross-Qualified   27

Introduction   27
References   30

4   First Responder Guidelines   31

Life and Crime Scene Analogy to the Crisis Scene First
Responder   31
Three Factors   31
   First   32
   Second   32
   Third   32
Our Past Is Our Prologue   32
Some Good Guidelines   33
References   35

**5   Non-Law Enforcement/Correctional Crisis
Negotiators   37**

The Role of Third-Party Intermediaries   37
To Whom Are We Listening?   38
Legendary Linguistic Lapses   38
Potential Problems   39
Time Is on Our Side   40
Typical Third-Party Problems   40
   Some Simple Solutions   41
Professional Models   42
Control of Non-Law Enforcement/Correctional Interpreters   43
   The Interpreter Cannot Be Allowed to Improvise   44
   Third-Party Intermediators Do Not Guarantee Success 44
Conclusion   45
References   46

6   The Crisis Negotiation Team   47

Introduction   47
The Team Concept   49

Downs v. United States   51
The Process of Crisis Negotiations   53
Team Structure   54
The Successful Approach—Teamwork   58
Crisis Negotiations Team   59
References   60
Appendix A: FBI Crisis Negotiations Unit Crisis Site
Assessment II   61

7 Crisis Negotiator Stress   63

Introduction   63
We Have Met the Enemy and He Is Us   63
General Personality Traits of Emergency Personnel   64
Negotiating and Negotiators' Stress   65
    Preincident Precautions and Preparation   65
    Incident   66
    Postincident   67
Critical Incident Stress Debriefings   68
    Debriefings   69
    Defusing   70
    Demobilizations   71
Conclusion   71
References   72
Appendix A: International Critical Incident Stress
Foundation, Inc.   73
Appendix B: Holmes-Rahe Stress Scale   73
Appendix C: Life Change Indicators and Disease Risk
Patrol—School Version   74

Section 2

DEALING WITH THE OTHER VICTIM

8 Negotiating with Normal People   79

Mission Statement   79
Stress Is Personally Defined   79
Every Call for Service Means Stress for Someone   80
Active Listening   81
Negotiating Guidelines   82
References   84
Appendix A: Holmes-Rahe Stress Scale   85

9   Negotiating with the Adolescent Hostage Taker   87

Introduction   87
The Role of the Negotiator   88
Defining Adolescence   88
    Adolescence—Phase 1   88
    Adolescence—Phase 2   89
    Adolescence—Phase 3   89
Normal Adolescents   90
The Crisis Mind-Set   90
Adolescent Crisis Resolution Skills   91
Common Clinical Conditions   91
    Depression   91
    Anxiety/Inadequacy   92
    The Adolescent Criminal—Antisocial Personality   92
    The Psychotic   93
Negotiating Guidelines   93
Guidelines for Negotiating with an Adolescent Hostage Taker   94
References   95

10   Negotiating with the Inadequate Personality   97

Introduction   97
Incidence in Society   97
The American Psychiatric Association Version   98
The Military Version   99
The Movie Version   100
The Law Enforcement Version   101
Conclusion   104
    Negotiating Guidelines and Their Rationales   105
References   106

**11   The Antisocial Personality Disorder (It's All
        about Me!) Hostage Taker   107**

Introduction   107
It's All about Me   108
The Antisocial Personality Disorder   108
    The Movie Version   109
    The Law Enforcement Version   110
American Psychiatric Association (APA)   110
Hostage Takers   113
Negotiating Guidelines and Their Rationales   113
References   115

12 Negotiating with the Paranoid Schizophrenic Hostage Taker   **117**

Introduction   117
Etiology   119
     The Movie Version   120
Definition   120
Incidence in Society   121
     Law Enforcement Exposure   121
Major Symptoms   122
Negotiating Guidelines and Rationale   124
Conclusion   126
References   127

13 The Bipolar Hostage Taker   **129**

Law Enforcement Encounters with Bipolar Hostage Takers   129
The American Psychiatric Association (APA) Multiaxial
Evaluation   131
The Bipolar Disorder and the American Psychiatric Association   132
The Bipolar Disorder and Hollywood   133
Hostage Takers   135
Negotiating Guidelines and Their Rationale   135
References   138

14 The Suicidal Hostage Holder (Also Known as the Solo Suicidal Subject)   **139**

Introduction   139
Asking the Difficult Question   140
The Golden Gate Bridge, Doubt, Alcohol, and Judgment   141
The Less Than Lethal Alternative   142
Police and Solo Suicidal Subjects   143
Depression in the *DSM-IV*   143
Suicide by Police   145
Snakes with and without Venom   145
Civilian Suicide   146
Mental Health Professionals   147
Negotiating Guidelines and Rationale   147
     Evaluate Preincident Behavior   147
     Incident Behavior: Use the CPR Acronym   148
     Suggested Officer (Negotiating Team Activities) Behavior
     and Strategies   148
     Negotiating Techniques   149

Postincident Considerations   149
References   149
Appendix A: Some Web Resources   150
Appendix B   151
Appendix C: Phrases That Work   152
Appendix D: Some Effective Answers   152
Appendix E: Suicide Intervention Flowchart   152

15   Police-Assisted Suicide   157

Introduction   157
Law Enforcement as Mental Health Professionals   160
Snakes with and without Venom   163
The Golden Gate Bridge, Alcohol, Judgment, and Doubt   165
Identification   167
The Less Than Lethal Alternative   168
References   170
Appendix A: Some Web Resources   171
Appendix B: Diagnostic Criteria for Suicide by Cop   172
Appendix C: Suicide-by-Cop Scale   173
Appendix D   174
Appendix E   174

16   Crisis Negotiations in the Correctional Setting   175

Introduction   175
The Street versus the Institution   175
Daily Experience   178
Hostage Survival   179
The Prison Population   180
Some Sieges   180
    Attica, New York; Oakdale, Louisiana; Atlanta, Georgia;
    Talladega, Alabama; Lucasville, Ohio; and Buckeye,
    Arizona: A Review of Some Lessons Learned and
    Implemented   180
        Attica   181
        Oakdale Correctional Facility (OCF) in Oakdale,
        Louisiana   182
        The Federal Correctional Facility in Atlanta (USPA)   182
        The Federal Correctional Institution
        in Talladega, Alabama (FCIT)   182
        Lucasville, Ohio State Prison   183
        Lewis Penitentiary in Buckeye, Arizona   183
        Lessons Learned   184

Institutional Crisis Negotiations   186
Systems Approach to Crisis Management   191
Conclusion   192
References   192

17   Negotiating with the Extremist   195

Introduction   195
Types of Hostage Holders   196
The Extremist   197
The Terrorist Mystique   198
Brief Case Studies from 1980   198
The Role of Third-Party Intermediaries   199
Time Is on Our Side   199
Conclusion   200
References   201
Appendix A: Chart of U.S. Domestic Terrorist Group
Differences   202

18   Terrorism and the Tenets of Islam   203

Introduction   203
The Middle Eastern Mind   203
Past as Prologue?   204
Insurrections and Islam   204
Shia versus Sunni   204
Is the Christian Past Islamic Prologue?   205
Tenets of Islam   207
Thinking   208
External versus Internal   208
Inshallah or Fatalism   209
Internal   209
Practice   210
Jihad   210
Wahhabi Movement   211
Conclusion   211
References   213

Section 3

CRISIS RESOLUTION INDICATORS

19   Indicators of Subject Surrender   217

Introduction   217

The Indicators   218
Crucial Conclusion   221
   Status   222
   Assessment   222
   Recommendations   222
References   222

20   Indicators of Volatile Negotiations   225

Introduction   225
Suicidal Subjects   226
   1. A Depressed Hostage Taker Who Denies Thoughts
      of Suicide   226
   2. No Rapport   226
   3. Age of the Subject   227
   4. No Social Support System   227
   5. Subject Insists on Face-to-Face Negotiations   227
   6. Subject Sets a Deadline for His Own Death   228
   7. Verbal Will   228
History of Violence   229
   8. Subject Has a History of Violence   229
   9. Prior Confrontations   229
   10. Planned Siege   229
Negotiations Process   230
   11. Refusal to Negotiate   230
Subject–Victim Relationship   230
   12. Targeted Hostages   230
   13. Hostage Taker Insists That a Particular Person Be
       Brought to the Scene   232
   14. Isolation and Dehumanization of Hostages   233
Weapon(s)   233
   15. A Weapon Is Tied to the Hostage Holder   233
   16. Excessive Ammunition—Multiple Weapons   234
   17. Explosives   234
Incident Behavior of Subject   235
   18. Postnegotiations Violence   235
   19. Negotiations Are Becoming More Volatile   236
   20. After Hours of Negotiations, the Subject Has No
       Clear Demands, His Demands Are Outrageous,
       or They Are Changing   237
Subject Stress   238
   21. Multiple Stressors   238

22. Alcohol or Drug Use by Subject or Hostage
during the Siege   239
23. Threat Analysis   239
Types of Threats   239
Conclusion   240
Crucial Conclusion   240
Status   240
Assessment   240
Recommendations   241
References   241
Appendix A   243

Section 4
GROUP DYNAMICS

21   Group Think   247

Executive Summary   247
The European Front Fall of 1944   247
Basic Human Nature Is to Go Along to Get Along   248
Group Think   249
A Bridge Too Far   250
Group Think in 1944   250
What Went Wrong at Waco, Phase I   252
What Went Wrong at Waco with the FBI, Phase I   253
FCI Talladega, Alabama, 1991   254
Ruby Ridge, Idaho, 1992   254
What Went Wrong at Waco with the FBI in 1993, Phase II 255
The FBI Studies Their History   258
Avoiding This Disaster   258
References   259

22   Creative Criteria for Constructive Deviation
from Crisis Negotiation Guidelines   261

THOMAS STRENTZ AND RAY BIRGE

Introduction   261
Landover Mall   261
Long Ago and Far Away   262
A New Direction   263
Judicial Hindsight   263

In the Beginning   264
We've Come a Long Way, Baby   265
Making the Decision to Deviate   265
The Decision to Deviate   266
Procedures for Creativity in Deviation   267
Conclusion   269
References   270

Section 5

HOSTAGE ISSUES

23   **Phases of a Hostage Crisis**   **275**

Introduction   275
The United States   275
The Government of Iran   275
Problem   276
Individual Differences in Response to Stress   277
The Role of Hostage   278
    Two Campers   279
London Syndrome   280
Stockholm Syndrome   281
U.S. Marines in Tehran   282
The Hostage Takers   282
    Types of Hostage Takers   283
       The Criminal Subject   283
       The Mentally Ill Subject   284
       The Politically, Socially, or Religiously Motivated Subject   285
Is It Ever Over?   285
Conclusion   287
References   287

24   **The Stockholm Syndrome**   **291**

The Bank Robbery   291
Some History   292
The Phenomenon   292
Domestic Hostage Situations   295
Stages of Hostage Reaction   296
Time   298
Isolation   300
Positive Contact   300

Hostage Taker Reaction   301
Individualized Reactions   303
References   305

25 What Do You Say to a Hostage?   307

Introduction   307
Time   307
Do's   308
Don'ts   308
Have a Plan   309
Who Are the Hostages?   309
A Litany of Legendary Animosity and Misinformation   309
The Role of the Hostage in the Surrender   310
Conclusion   311

26 A Hostage Psychological Survival Guide   313

Introduction   313
Reacting to the Terrorist/Criminal/Inmate Episode   315
  Coping with Abduction   315
  Control   315
  Preparing for Psychological Reactions   316
  Roles for Survivors   317
Sucessful Coping Strategies   317
  Have Faith in Yourself and Your Government   317
  Contain Your Hostility toward Your Captors   318
  Maintain a Superior Attitude   318
  Fantasize to Fill Empty Hours   318
  Rationalize the Abduction   319
  Keep To or Establish Routines   319
  Control Your Outward Appearance   320
  Strive to Be Flexible and Keep Your Sense of Humor   320
  Blend with Your Peers   320
Conclusion   321
References   322

Index   323

Acknowledgments

This book is the result of my long-held dedication to education and the preservation of human life.

I can trace my love of learning to my parents, neither of whom finished high school. In fact, my dad, like my son and I, suffered from dyslexia. Yet, it was my parents' love of education and their encouragement of my brother and me to get a good education that formed this firm foundation. I recall many family conversations around the dinner table that focused on the need for a good education. I remember my parents, who were first-generation Americans, pointing to the emigrants from war-torn Europe who came to this country with "Only the clothes on their backs, all they have is their education. That is something even Hitler could not take away from them. That is why they are successful in this country." My folks spoke those words some 65 years ago. They remain true today and still ring in my ears.

My younger brother earned his doctorate in journalism from Northwestern University, Evanston, Illinois; several years later, I earned mine from Virginia Commonwealth University (VCU).

Because of my dyslexia, and the fact that I attended three high schools, school has never been easy or enjoyable. To this day, when I walk into a school and smell chalk and other odors I associate with classrooms, my stomach tightens. After high school, I went to Fresno City College and then into the U.S. Marine Corps (USMC) where I earned the rank of Sergeant. Because my dad was a Corporal in World War II, I think my USMC experience and achievements helped me mature.

During my predoctorate college years at Fresno City College and Fresno State, all six of them, I was blessed with mature instructors who, for the most part, had served in World War II, earned their degrees via the G.I. Bill, and brought their life experiences to the classroom. Among those most remembered are Dr. Grivas, a former Marine; Dr. Beaty, an anthropologist and former Army Colonel who commanded the local Army Reserve Artillery Unit; Dr. Powell, a clinical psychologist who was his executive officer; Tom Brigham, a World War II Army Medic; Marie Emil and Pat Pickford, who had extensive experience in mental health; and certainly Dr. Barbara Varley, who took my completion of the course and research and thesis challenge to earn a master's degree in social work as a personal challenge to make a silk purse out of a sow's ear. I earned my degree, but I doubt I ever became a silk purse.

Certainly, the most influential male in my life, aside from my father, was Pastor Phillip A. Jordan of Trinity Lutheran Church in Fresno, California. It was his "Common Sense Christianity" that inspired and guided me through my late adolescent years. His personal witness and teachings taught me that our God is not a God of retribution, hell, fire, and brimstone, but a God of love. Because of him, I seriously considered entering the ministry. However, when I was told I had to learn Latin, I knew such a goal was beyond my ability. Yet, the example and teachings of Pastor Jordan contributed mightily to my orientation on, and value for life. The only animals I ever hunted were humans, and I never killed any of them. More recently, the ministerial duo and great team of Pastors Carol and James Kniseley at Resurrection Lutheran Church in Spotsylvania, Virginia, have contributed to my life and this text. The two of them have been the Pastor Jordan of my later years. Thank you for all you have done to continue my spiritual growth and continued development.

When I joined the Federal Bureau of Investigation (FBI) in 1968, I had a bachelor's degree in social science and a master's degree in social work from what is now California State University, Fresno. While serving in the Behavioral Science and Special Operations Units, I went to school at night in Richmond, Virginia, for 9 years to earn my doctorate from VCU. I put myself under so much stress that on several occasions, as I drove north on IH 95 from Richmond back to Fredericksburg, I had to pull off the road with a blinding headache and throw up. Interestingly enough, I have not had a headache since I earned my degree in 1986. As Frank Bolz says of his education, I got my degree "Magna Cum Regularis."

It was during these years, especially the last three, that I met Dr. Stephen Auerbach in the Department of Psychology. I took his class on crisis intervention and met a soul mate. Dr. Auerbach became my mentor. He guided me through the dissertation research process and the writing of my results. I returned the favor by including him in the work we were doing at the FBI Academy where he participated in several of our field training exercises and lectured after my retirement.

The following chapters are, for the most part, revisions of articles I published while serving at the FBI Academy. They appeared in *The Journal of Police Science and Administration, Law and Order, Crisis Negotiator*, and the *FBI Law Enforcement Bulletin*. Others are written versions of lectures I have developed and delivered since my retirement. Both reflect current thinking and practice in our field. I have yet to deliver a lecture from which I have not learned from my students and improved my presentation.

Unlike university professors, many of whom live in a "publish or perish" environment, instructors at the FBI Academy were not so burdened. It is my guess that of the hundreds of instructors who served at our academy over the years, with the notable exception of those in the Office of Legal Counsel, only about a dozen or so ever published an article. Of those dozen, the vast majority were in the Behavioral Science Unit. I will leave it to others to speculate on these phenomena.

Regrettably, there are all too many in law enforcement and corrections who adhere to the crisis resolution mode of "Kill 'em all and let the Lord sort them out." It is this ignorant, arrogant, and "macho" mind-set that crisis negotiations and negotiation instructors fight in every class we teach and in every incident we work. Unfortunately, and all too often, our ignorant adversaries are highly placed administrators who are too busy to attend class, refuse to learn from history, or assume that by the time their errors and killings come to court they will be long gone, dead, or retired.

Clearly, there is a great difference between negotiations and capitulation. Unfortunately, too many law enforcement and correction administrators fail to understand this fact. Our message is simple—you have nothing to lose by trying to talk to a person in crisis.

Therefore, it is the purpose of this book to educate crisis negotiators and continue the fight to impress our commanders with the virtue and value of taking the time necessary to help ensure the preservation of human life.

Last, but not least, I dedicate this book to my wife of over 20 years and our two children. Both of the children are overachievers who earned university degrees within my hopes but beyond my expectations. They did this in spite of, or because of, my absences from home during their formative years of my Bureau career. Their mother, a lifelong and now retired public school teacher, saw to their education and provided the necessary parenting to guide them toward success.

Our first born, Stacey, is a successful attorney in Virginia. She started a two-attorney law firm. Today, she is a senior partner in that firm of a dozen lawyers and a married mother of two children. Our second is Steve. He earned his degree in education but prefers working as a construction supervisor for an international construction company, where he enjoys directing and driving every piece of heavy equipment known to man. They are both blessings beyond what mere words can describe.

A special word of thanks is in order to the many people who reviewed and commented on various chapters in this book.

My old unit at Quantico, The Crisis Negotiations Unit at the FBI Academy, reviewed the entire book and made several recommendations, all of which were implemented. Similarly, Jack Kirsch and Conrad V. Hassel made valuable contributions to this text and to my life.

In alphabetical order, the others include: Sgt. Dave Anderson (retired from the San Bernardino Police Department); Anne Birge (retired homicide detective from the San Bernardino Police Department); her husband, Captain Ray Birge (retired from the Oakland Police Department); Lt. George Bradford (retired from the Washington, DC Police Department); Andrew

A. Downs, son of the slain pilot Brent Downs (the civil case of *Downs v. U.S.* in 1971 launched the FBI hostage negotiations program); now Warden Ron Fraker and Devon Schrum from the Washington State Department of Corrections; Dr. Paul Graff (retired from the Ontario Police Department); Lt. Brenda Herbert (retired from the San Jose Police Department); and Sgt. John Sieh, U.S. Army Special Forces, who reviewed the material on Dependent Personality Disorder and has been a great guy to work with in the United States and overseas.

And finally, special thanks go to the law library staff at Louisiana State University (LSU) and my LSU soul mate and dearest companion, Carole Lindsay Conques, forever in my heart.

Introduction

The Academy

The Federal Bureau of Investigation (FBI) Academy, located some 50 miles south of the Washington, DC metropolitan area, is situated on the west side of the Quantico Marine Base. The Marines have been at Quantico since 1917. The FBI Academy moved in during the mid-1930s. It is here that all U.S. Marine Corps (USMC) officer training and other training missions of the USMC are conducted. Unlike any other Marine base, Quantico is not the home of any fighting force—it is home for the schools of the Corps.

The FBI Academy arrived for firearms training in 1935 and never left. Prior to 1935, all Special Agents of the FBI were unarmed. It was their job to investigate crimes and gather evidence. When enough evidence was gathered, the FBI would call upon the U.S. Marshals and police to make the arrest. This came to an abrupt change when Special Agent Ray Caffrey and three police officers were killed by Baby Face Nelson as he attempted to "free" Frank Nash at the train station in Kansas City, Missouri, on June 17, 1933. Nash, who was killed in the shoot-out, was being transported to the U.S. Penitentiary in Leavenworth, Kansas. He was to take a vehicle from the Kansas City train station to the federal prison (Clayton, 1975).

Director J. Edgar Hoover petitioned the U.S. Congress to allow the FBI to carry firearms. By January 1935, this authorization was provided, and the FBI sought out the best possible firearms training available. The plan was for the USMC, as an interim measure, to train the FBI at its pistol ranges at Quantico, Virginia, while the FBI sought out Special Agents within its ranks to take over this training at a more suitable location. Excellent firearms instructors within the FBI were soon identified, and no other suitable location was ever found. This was the beginning of a special relationship between the FBI and the USMC. It is interesting that although the USMC makes up about 10 percent of the U.S. military, the majority of FBI agents who are former military are former Marines.

I joined the FBI in 1968, and after 3 months of training at Quantico I was transferred to the San Antonio, Texas, division where I worked in headquarters for 2 months. I worked applicant and some criminal cases. I was transferred to the Austin, Texas, resident agency where I had a "road trip" that covered 10 counties. For the next 10 months I worked applicant, criminal, and security cases and had the time of my life. My wife and I hoped the Bureau would forget about us and leave us in Texas. Unfortunately, Bureau policy in those days was to transfer new agents after a year to a second office. Because I opened my big mouth at the wrong time as a "New Agent," I was identified as a potential instructor for the new academy. Therefore, I was transferred to the Washington Field Office. In those days, the Bureau did not have any cost-of-living allowances. We moved from a "no state income tax" location to the Washington, DC metropolitan area. I worked in the Washington Field Office, also known as WFO. and took a substantial cut in salary.

In a very depressed state, we drove across our great nation in the early winter of 1969 to "the dreaded" East Coast with our infant daughter and two dogs, one of whom had diarrhea. Except for ski clothes, we had no winter clothing. We moved to Takoma Park, Maryland. We had some fantastic neighbors, the Holland family who took us under their wing and made this difficult time in our lives much more palatable and, in fact, enjoyable. From our home I walked a few blocks and took the bus to work and thus saved money on gas, parking, and the hassle of the commute. This usually worked well. In fact I made my first arrest, a pickpocket, on my bus. However, on all too many occasions I had to work late. Because the bus service terminated before I was finished, my wife had to drive into Washington, DC, through some rough areas with our infant daughter, two dogs, and a pistol for protection, to pick me up at work. This was not a fun time. Had it not been for the Holland family and our involvement in our church, I am sure we would have left the Bureau.

Among my initial responsibilities was to identify KGB and GRU (Russian military intelligence units) agents and "turn them" or cause them to be returned to the Soviet Union. This really bothered me. As I saw it, I was to identify spies so they would be deported, sent home. All I ever and really wanted from the FBI was to be sent home to California. I requested and received a transfer to work criminal cases. I found the work enjoyable but still checked the office of preference list monthly to chart my progress toward a transfer to a California office. In early 1972, within a month I arrested a neighbor, my wife had an ugly encounter with some local thugs, and I saw a memo listing the qualifications for, and directing interested agents to, apply for an instructor's position at the FBI Academy, Quantico, Virginia. When I applied, I did not know I would also be promoted. I, we, just wanted to get out of the Washington, DC area.

When I joined the Behavioral Science Unit (BSU) in 1972, there were about a dozen of us. Of that number, seven were former Marines. Of the seven, three were former officers, the rest of us were former noncommissioned officers (NCOs). A more complete history of the unit is available in the text written by John Campbell and Don DeNevi (2003) entitled *Into the Minds of Madmen.*

The FBI Academy is a very special place. It is a special place where hundreds of very special people serve their country in silence. Some refer to it as Hoover High. Others call it the Harvard of Law Enforcement. In either case, it is a very, very special place. I met the Congressional Medal of Honor winners, USMC legend Lt. Colonel Archie Vandergrift and later Special Agent, and former Navy Seal Tom Norris at the academy (Anderson, 1983). It was my honor to be one of their instructors. The high quality and caliber of our students served as a constant source of motivation to the staff to do our very best.

The FBI legends who served at our academy are legion. Among them is Pearl Harbor Veteran, Inspector Jim Cotter who ran the FBI National Academy program. The Inspector, as Cotter was known, earned the Bronze Star for his actions at Schofield Barracks. He is credited with downing a Japanese aircraft with his 1903 Springfield rifle. At the academy, he was affectionately known as the *Dancing Bear. Dancing* because of his ability to dance around regulations to ensure the best training experience and program possible and *Bear* because of his stature. Cotter led by example. He could give an instructor an unforgettable "chewing out" and then sit down with that instructor and have a beer and move on with the program.

Jack Kirsch, the father of Behavioral Science, is discussed at length in Campbell's book. He has been characterized by some as a "truck driver with a Ph.D." Like Cotter, Kirsch was a leader of men. When I first met him, Kirsch already had 20 years "on the job" and was an aspiring doctoral candidate at The Catholic University of America (Washington, DC). A member of the FBI Kidnap Response Squad, he had worked as a street agent in five major cities, served as a Supervisory Special Agent in three headquarters divisions, and had been selected by Director Hoover to head up the embryonic behavioral science experiment that would grow into several units.

Kirsch was an aerial gunner, 15th Air Force, during World War II. His proficiency with firearms earned him a berth as a firearms instructor at the Old FBI Academy—"Mainside Quantico"—in 1955. His subsequent assignments as the Police Training Coordinator in the Chicago and Pittsburgh offices gave him 8 additional years to hone his instructional skills. Recalled to the Training Division in 1966, Kirsch waged a rigorous and relentless campaign for the creation of tactical response and the inclusion of additional aircraft in our field operations. He was the seminal force behind the FBI SWAT (Special Weapons and Tactics) and aircraft support programs. He earned the nickname of "Crazy Jack." Clearly, in everything he did, he was well ahead of his time. Kirsch wore two hats. As a tactical firearms expert he planned and trained for the inevitable; as a student of human behavior he knew that words could prevail over force and that power did not necessarily flow from the barrel of a gun. Kirsch was our creator, our mentor, our father–confessor, and our coconspirator as we worked to build the new FBI Academy complex and prepare its staff for the greatest police training effort in history.

During my 20 years with the FBI, I met many men like Jim Cotter and Jack Kirsch. All were from humble beginnings. Most were the first son in their family to complete college. All were overachievers.

The FBI Academy location, some 50 miles south of Washington, DC, is crucial. This bit of geography is very important because FBI Headquarters, like all headquarters operations, has a way of stifling creativity and experimentation in favor of an established and nonthreatening bureaucratic routine and control. In this regard, those 50 miles between Washington, DC and Quantico, Virginia, may as well be an ocean. I learned early in my career, in the USMC, and later as a psychiatric social Worker, then in the FBI, that the farther one was from headquarters the better one could do his or her job.

At the academy we had a special relationship with field agents. We had the freedom to do what had to be done to do the job well. For the most part, we were left alone by headquarters staff to do the research that was necessary to ensure a good product. As an example, I remember an early trip to the field to assist in an investigation. We were in the Lincoln, Nebraska, resident agency when I heard one agent ask another who we were. He answered, they are from headquarters. Another quickly corrected him by saying, "They are not from headquarters, they are from Quantico." Clearly, on the FBI Table of Organization, the FBI Academy, the Training Division is part of headquarters. However, we were not "headquarter types." We actually assisted the field in their investigations and saw our role as doing whatever we could to help agents do their job better. This is, at least within the FBI, a very important orientation and concept of operating.

One of the reasons we did our job so well was that men like Cotter and Kirsch ran interference for us and kept headquarters off our back. We, in turn, provided high-quality instruction, practical and effective consultation with FBI field agents and law enforcement, along with the research and experience to back up our recommendations.

The Unit

The Behavioral Science Unit (BSU) began with about a dozen instructors. With the passage of time and the recognition and broadening of the application of psychology, sociology, and political science to law enforcement, the then fledgling few gradually became many units.

Hostage/Crisis Negotiations

Blessed are the peacemakers for they shall be called the children of God.

(King James, Matt. 5:9)

The goal of crisis negotiations is the preservation of human life. In that pursuit, negotiators try to save as many lives as possible. In so doing, we attempt to bring peace and terminate a conflict without injury to anyone. However, there are those situations where the on-scene commander must make the difficult decision to take a life to save a life. In that endeavor, our efforts focus on saving the lives of the hostages and the tactical team. The tactical team, like the negotiating team, makes every effort to save as many lives as possible. Unfortunately, the reality is there are those who initiate a hostage, barricaded, or suicidal crisis who do not share our priority and in so doing ensure their demise.

I was part of the first break from BSU when Con Hassel and I, under the leadership of "Detroit Smitty," formed the Terrorist Research and Management Staff (TRAMS) in July 1976. The unit has had several names. Our first unit chief was Harold Smith (known as "Smitty"), an accountant who had supervised the FBI Organized Crime Squad in Detroit, Michigan. During World War II, he served in the China Burma India Theater of Operations and was one of the best pistol shots in the FBI. Like Kirsch, he was a field police instructor. Smith was handpicked by Kirsch and had the good sense to clarify our mission and then stand back. Like Kirsch, he ran interference for us. He was then, and remains, a selfless and honorable man who helped us work to our capacity on our mission. He took care of all the petty "stuff" generated by the bureaucracy. Detroit Smith was Kirsch's Executive Officer (XO). When Kirsch retired, Smith took over as Chief of the Law Enforcement Arts Section. Con Hassel was promoted from my partner to my boss as Unit Chief of SOARS (Special Operations and Research Staff), and we still had Smith to take care of us.

Our baptism of fire began at 8:19 P.M. on Friday night, September 10, 1976. Unfortunately, Smith had taken that day off and was out of town when four Croatians, with an American female, Julie Schultz Busic, the wife of the group leader, Zvonko Busic, hijacked TWA Flight 355 as it flew from New York to Tucson, via Chicago. Because the flight originated at Washington National Airport, the Alexandria Field Office of the FBI was the designated office of origin. Their lead agent was a classmate of mine, Jim Siano. Siano, a former USMC Lieutenant, would later join the BSU. On this evening, he was busy coordinating the FBI response. The aircraft, a 727, landed briefly in Montreal, and left bundles of their demands for a free Croatia. They were written in four languages and were to be dropped over Montreal by the police. The police tried to comply. For reasons still unclear, someone forgot to untie the bundles of leaflets. Rather than having their treatise drift down, page by page over the Montreal metropolitan area, the bundles fell into the St. Lawrence River and sunk to the bottom, never to be read by any Canadian.

The leader Zvonko Busic was extremely intelligent. He wrote his treatise in English, French, Italian, and Croatian. However, he lacked common sense.

He picked TWA Flight 355 because the distance from Washington, DC to New York to Tucson, via Chicago, was the same distance as New York to Paris. He had no idea of the difference in the necessary navigational systems and needs for trans-Atlantic flights versus a cross-country flight. The terrorists' plan was to have their treatise published in several U.S. and foreign newspapers. They also wanted their leaflets dispersed over several cities to include London, Paris, and Rome. To complete this journey, they landed in Gander, Newfoundland, took on additional fuel, and released about half of their passengers. The released passengers were thoroughly debriefed by the Royal Canadian Mounted Police (RCMP) and the FBI. It was learned that the terrorists had what appeared to be improvised explosive devices they had carried onboard in flower pots. As proof of their technical skills, they told the New York Police Department (NYPD) of another bomb they left in Grand Central Station in New York City. While disarming this device the police encountered a rather sophisticated time-delay booby trap mechanism. This explosion killed one NYPD officer and seriously injured several others. The explosion gave immediate credibility to the hijackers' claim of having explosives on the aircraft.

When the aircraft landed in Paris, the FBI advised the French of the hijackers' demands, identities, and the explosion in New York. While refueling in Paris, the French learned that there were no French citizens on board. They cut all communications with the FBI and demanded that the terrorists surrender. Although they claimed to have several bombs on the aircraft, they eventually surrendered and were immediately extradited to the United States. They were tried and convicted for their crimes and, today, some 35 years later, the last of them was released from prison. All five, as a condition of their release after some 30 years in federal custody, are living in Croatia. Good riddance.

This hijacking gave TWA a scare because they had a flight attendant named Julie Schultz. For a few very anxious hours, until they located their employee, they feared that one of their own had aided and abetted this hijacking. One response to this event was the development of a very close liaison between the Federal Aviation Administration (FAA), the airline industry, and the FBI. To prevent some of the errors that occurred during this incident, we designed, developed, and directed an instructional program for the airline industry known as "The Common Strategy" that remains in use today.

It was our mission at the academy to identify terrorist activity and develop countermeasures. Con Hassel is an attorney with a master's degree in criminology who served as a Marine Sergeant in Korea where he won the Purple Heart. After he retired from the FBI, he worked for the Central Intelligence Agency (CIA) where he earned their highest award for bravery, the Intelligence Star. He is the only FBI agent to be so honored. He was my partner and remains my friend, and was also my boss for many years. When we formed TRAMS, Hassel and I were from Behavioral Science, and we were joined in this endeavor by additional agents from The Range.

We brought with us the BSU practice of active support for, not supervision of, field operations. In this regard, we assisted the Washington, DC field office of the FBI and the Washington, DC Metropolitan Police during the 3-day Hanafi Moslem siege in March 1977. In August 1978, I went to Chicago to assist that field office during the Croatian siege of the German Consulate. Since those early days, the unit, now known as the Crisis Response Unit, has provided negotiators for every major FBI hostage incident to include the prison riots and hostage takings in federal correctional institutions at Oakdale, Louisiana; Atlanta, Georgia; Talladega, Alabama; and many state prison incidents too numerous to mention. Other more infamous responses included Ruby Ridge, Idaho, and Waco, Texas (Strentz, 1997).

The formation of the new unit included several agents from The Range, including two bomb technicians, Ed Kelso (former Marine) and Bo Johnson. In addition to these two firearms instructors, we had Jim Adams, Tas Bailey, Tom Riley, John Simeone, and Bob Taubert (all former Marines) along with Don Bassett and Fred Lanceley (both U.S. Air Force veterans). Roger Nisley and Jim DeSarno joined our ranks accompanied by Chin Ho Lee, a former Korean Marine. The nickname for our unit was "The Wild Bunch" (Coulson and Shannon, 1999). We were charting new waters and were more concerned with results than our careers. Only two of us were ever promoted to a position that made use of our experience. John Simeone was the first assistant team leader of the Hostage Rescue Team (HRT), and Roger Nisley was found to be well qualified to become a field supervisor, an Assistant Special Agent in Charge (ASAC), and a Special Agent in Charge (SAC) of a field office. Just after the disaster at Waco, Texas, in Spring 1993, he ended his career back at Quantico by taking over the coveted position of the head of the HRT. Later in our development, Jim DeSarno joined our unit as a negotiator. DeSarno eventually became the SAC in New Orleans, Louisiana, and retired from the FBI as a high-ranking executive on the Director's staff.

I think one of the main reasons for the success of our unit was our basic and collective attitude of selfless service. During my 16 years at the FBI Academy, I observed this attitude in most of my peers and many of my supervisors. This mind-set was exemplified by the service of Jack Kirsch, Jim Cotter, Harold "Detroit Smitty" Smith, Con Hassel, and later, when I returned to the BSU, Roger Depue, also a former Marine.

With the passage of time, someone figured out that TRAMS was "smart" spelled backward. Not wanting to be the opposite of smart, our name was changed to Special Operations and Research Staff (SOARS). We said we soared with the eagles. I was told that then Director Judge Webster did not like acronyms, so the name was changed to Special Operations and Research

Unit, SOARU. It is now known as the Crisis Management Unit within the Critical Incident Response Group.

In addition to developing the hostage negotiations program for the FBI, the idea for a highly trained full-time special tactical team was another product of our unit. We did the research and ran the selection process for the FBI Hostage Rescue Team (HRT) that was created in 1982. The first leader of this truly amazing and proficient group of FBI agents was Danny Coulson. He has written about this organization in his book *No Heroes* (Coulson and Shannon, 1999). His title says it all about the HRT and the institution of the FBI, an organization of selfless civil servants.

Hostage Negotiations

One can rightfully credit the on-scene commander, U.S. Army Colonel Robert E. Lee, and his negotiator, U.S. Army Cavalry officer, Lt. Jeb Stewart, who operated with a USMC "SWAT" team from the Marine Barracks in Washington, DC, at Harpers Ferry, West Virginia, October 16 to 18, 1858, in one of the first instances of hostage negotiations in the United States. During this siege, the commander, Robert E. Lee, eventually elected to assault. However, to preserve human life, he ordered the Marines, commanded by Lt. Israel Green, to unload their muskets and affix their bayonets. The Marines, who lost one of their own, Private Quinn, successfully overpowered John Brown and his followers (Green, 1885; Shriver, 1859). The axiom of the preservation of human life was and remains the strategic and tactical goal of FBI crisis management.

Full credit for the development of the current concept and practice for hostage negotiations in law enforcement belongs to the New York City Police Department. The history of this program is well discussed by its two founders, Frank Bolz and Harvey Schlossberg. Bolz wrote *Hostage Cop*, and Schlossberg wrote *Psychologist with a Gun*, (Bolz, 1979; Schlossberg, 1974). Schlossberg, at the start, was a sergeant in the patrol division who had a doctoral degree in clinical psychology; he brought this expertise to bear on the problem. Bolz earned his bachelor's degree from John Jay, as he says "Magna Cum Regularis," a few years later. Both of these pioneers are so highly thought of in the law enforcement negotiations community that they have been awarded honorary life membership in the oldest and largest negotiator's association in the world, the California Association of Crisis Negotiators. They were so honored in spite of the fact that neither of them have ventured to the Golden State, except on business.

The involvement of the FBI in hostage negotiations is an excellent example of "The Pearl Harbor" syndrome. In brief, on the early morning of October 4, 1971, the FBI became involved in a domestic dispute on a private aircraft that was headed for the Bahamas via Jacksonville, Florida. George Giffe, Jr. and his associate, Bobby Wayne Wallace, dragged Giffe's estranged wife onboard an aircraft and then hijacked the plane. It landed in Jacksonville, where the pilot, Brent Quinton Downs, requested additional fuel to allow him to fly to the Bahamas. This request was refused. After approximately 15 minutes of negotiations, FBI agents fired at the aircraft to disable the plane. Upon hearing this shooting, Giffe shot and killed his estranged wife, the pilot, and then himself. The FBI became the defendant in a wrongful death suit that it initially won but lost on appeal (*Downs v. United States,* 382 F. 1973, Supp. at 752, 1975). It was during this litigation that then Director of the FBI Clarence Kelley ordered the BSU to develop a hostage negotiations program.

Director Kelley was a very special person. He was a retired FBI SAC who had also been a firearms instructor at Quantico and became the Chief of Police of Kansas City. He well understood the value of negotiations and fully supported its creation and development within the FBI. In this regard, I cannot begin to list the number of hostage situations where the local SAC was not allowing the process of negotiations to take effect, until he received a personal call from "The Director" who reminded him that his role in a crisis was that of the commander not the negotiator.

The BSU knew of the efforts of the NYPD. Therefore, Special Agent Supervisor (SAS) Pat Mullaney, a former Christian Brother, and SAS Howard Teten, a former USMC Sergeant, participated in the NYPD program in June 1973. They returned with such a glowing report on the NYPD program that the FBI sent other agents to the NYPD course. It was extremely rare in those days for the FBI to admit than anyone knew more about law enforcement tactics and techniques than we did. Nonetheless, agents from the New York Division of the FBI and two from Quantico, SAS James Siano (a former USMC Lieutenant) and SAS Bill Peters, attended the NYPD course.

To this day, my good friend Frank Bolz insists that the FBI sent agents to New York to steal his material. That just is not true ... and I have told Bolz this many, many times. The fact is, we were so impressed with Bolz's program that we invited him to Quantico to make a presentation to our staff. It was during his week at Quantico that we stole his material. Because of his firm grasp of and experience with field operations, Boltz had the nickname of "Nuts and Bolts" at Quantico. He has lectured at the FBI Academy more often and with greater acclaim than any other law enforcement officer.

The Federal Bureau of Investigation (FBI) Version of Hostage (Crisis) Negotiations

With Bolz's material in hand, I set about making some modifications to fit the typical hostage crisis faced by the FBI in 1974. I did this by interviewing police officers and FBI agents who had negotiated with hostage takers.

From them, I learned some tactics and techniques that tended to be effective. (When dealing with people, one cannot say "every time" or "always.")

The 1970s were the heyday of aircraft hijacking in the United States. Between 1968 and 1972 we suffered 147 aircraft hijackings that ranged from a high of 40 in 1969 to a low of 22 in 1972 (FAA, 1985). The people who hijacked our aircraft over the years have gone through a transition. In the beginning, we encountered criminals who hijacked for profit. They quickly learned that there were easier ways to steal money. We also had a few politically motivated types. However, the majority of the people who hijacked our commercial and private aircraft were suffering from Paranoid Schizophrenia. The other types of hostage-taking criminals most frequently encountered by the FBI were bank robbers. Typically, these subjects were people who had one of two personality disorders, Antisocial or Inadequate.

Armed with these observations, I drew on my background in mental health. (When I joined the FBI in 1968, I had a master's degree in social work that included one internship as a California Department of Corrections parole agent and another as a California Department of Mental Health psychiatric social worker at the California State Hospital for the Sexual Psychopath in Atascadero, California.) It was very clear to me that the tactics and techniques most successfully used by police and FBI negotiators approximated what I had learned and practiced as a therapist before entering the FBI. Therefore, I went back to the textbooks and back to my alma mater, Fresno State College (Fresno, California), to consult with my previous instructors. They helped me focus on the similarities between criminals and patients, both of whom were in crisis. I drew heavily from the therapy guidelines designed to "help cure" people with the types of mental disorders we were encountering among hostage takers, the Paranoid Schizophrenic and the two personality disorders, Antisocial and Inadequate. To verify the effectiveness of my work, I remain in constant contact with those who are negotiating. These basic guidelines that were developed some 40 years ago remain the foundation for crisis negotiations today.

We were assisted in this project by New Scotland Yard. In this regard, I cannot begin to stress the fantastic relationship the FBI generally, and the BSU specifically, has enjoyed with "The Yard." To this day, a reciprocal relationship exists between New Scotland Yard and the BSU. They regularly send their negotiators to the FBI Crisis Negotiations course, and the FBI sends agents and police officers to their course at Hendon, just outside London.

The initial FBI Hostage Negotiations program was fashioned into a 3-day instructional package. This program allowed travel on Monday, instruction during the week, and travel back to Quantico, or to another city, on Friday. It was 3 days of lecture, no role playing. Yet, when one is teaching a skill like shooting, swimming, or negotiating, one must practice.

In this case, engage in some structured and supervised role playing. It was decided to augment this program with 5 days of instruction at Quantico. For this endeavor, aspiring FBI negotiators were selected from those who (1) were volunteers, (2) had at least 5 years of law enforcement experience, (3) were good interviewers, (4) were recommended by their supervisors, and (5) had an appreciation for mental health matters. In this course, FBI agents were mixed with law enforcement officers from around the country and eventually around the world. After 1 year, and with the enthusiastic and very professional assistance of Inspector Roy Penrose and Deputy Assistant Commissioner Peter Walton of New Scotland Yard, the program was extended to 2 weeks. Walton and Penrose spent 6 weeks working with us at Quantico to include more role playing in our program. They provided us with the benefit of their experience in England and were both great people with whom to work and socialize.

More recently, and based on our experience in Sydney, New South Wales (NSW), Australia (a very professional police service with whom the FBI also enjoys an exchange program), the negotiations course now features many evening classes and other innovations pioneered by the NSW police.

I assisted the NSW police in the initial development of their first Hostage, now Crisis, Negotiators program. Later, Jim Siano, Fred Lanceley, and I made many trips "Down Under." We assisted our Australian friends in their program and brought back very effective negotiating techniques and training models that were implemented into the FBI program at Quantico.

Today, each Crisis Negotiators class taught at Quantico includes law enforcement officers from the United States and around the world, most of whom have some negotiations experience. During the course, they present their experiences during class or after hours in the classroom building or "The Board Room." The guidelines for crisis negotiations developed very early in the process are still used, with some modification, and have been reaffirmed over and over in the United States, Asia, Australia, across Europe, in Great Britain, and around the world. These guidelines form the basis of this text.

References

Anderson, W. C. (1983) *Bat 21*, Bantam, New York.

Bolz, F. (1979) *Hostage Cop*, Rawson and Wade, New York.

Campbell, J., and DeNevi, D. (2003) *Into the Minds of Madmen*, Prometheus Books, New York.

Clayton, M. (1975) *Union Station Massacre*, Bobbs-Merrill, Indianapolis.

Coulson, D., and Shannon, E. (1999) *No Heroes*, Pocket Books, New York.

Downs v. United States, 382 F. 2d, 990, Supp. 752 (1975).

Federal Aviation Administration (1985) Chronology of Hijacking of U.S. Registered Aircraft and Legal Status of Hijackers 1961–1984, U.S. Government Printing Office, Washington, DC.

Green, I. (1885) The Capture of John Brown, *North American Review*, December, pp. 565–569.

King James, Matthew 5:9.

Schlossberg, H. (1974) *Psychologist with a Gun*, Coward, McCann and Geogheagn, Inc., New York.

Shriver, E. (1859) Report to Brigadier General James M. Coale, 9th Brigade, Maryland Militia.

Strentz, T. (1997) Understanding Waco and Other Disasters, *Law and Order*, April, pp. 86–92.

Basic Concepts

1

The American Psychiatric Association (APA)

1

Introduction

The purpose of this chapter is to cover some very basic points that often cause confusion among law enforcement officers and to a lesser extent among correctional officers. Correctional staff members tend to have more regular contact with mental health professionals. Therefore, they tend to be less confused about who is who in the mental health bureaucracy and pecking order, as well as other matters that involve the mental health classification system.

Psychiatrists are medical doctors who, after 4 years of college, attend medical school for 3 years, then complete a 1-year internship, after which they perform a 3-year residency in psychiatry at a psychiatric hospital. Some may take additional training in several dozen specialties like addiction, adolescents, and anxiety issues. Another option is a specialization in the many types of depression. Like other medical specializations, this residency is usually conducted in a teaching hospital that is affiliated with a major university. As I recall, the psychiatric residents at Atascadero State Hospital, California, were students at Stanford University. Because they are medical doctors (M.D.), psychiatrists can prescribe medication. Other mental health professionals cannot. The others get around this problem by practicing in a psychiatric, psychological, or mental health group that includes a psychiatrist. When the non-M.D. thinks some medication might be appropriate, he or she discusses it with the M.D. who usually interviews the patient before writing the prescription. To monitor the effectiveness of the medication, the M.D. usually has monthly or more regular contact with the patient. The typical involvement of a crisis negotiator with a psychiatrist will usually involve the issue of a prescription or medication the subject has *not* been taking. The expression, "He is off his meds," is familiar to law enforcement and correctional staff. Most psychiatrists are members of the American Psychiatric Association (APA). They publish the *Diagnostic and Statistical Manual* (*DSM*) of the APA. This work, the mental health equivalent of the penal code, is now in its fourth iteration. I will discuss this book later in this chapter.

Psychologists are not medical doctors. Typically, they have finished a 4-year bachelor's degree program, a 1- or 2-year master's degree curriculum, and then 3 or 4 years of additional study leading to a doctor of philosophy (Ph.D.) degree. There are variations on this sequence. However, like the psychiatrist and the social worker, the training at all levels includes regular contact with patients and practical experience in the field. Like psychiatry, there are dozens of specializations. These include abnormal, adolescent, education, industrial, marriage counseling, testing, and others. A psychologist is the best contact for a negotiator seeking advice, or information on a suspect and his or her psychological problems. Psychologists are the only mental health professionals who are specifically trained to do psychological testing and assessments. Typically, they are most likely to be actively engaged in providing therapy or other interventions in the treatment of an individual. Some psychologists have only completed the master's degree level of training. Typically, one cannot call himself or herself a psychologist unless he or she has a doctorate. They also use the *DSM* to classify patients.

Social workers are different from psychologists because they tend to take a broader view of their patient as a member of a family or other social group. Like psychology, social work offers degrees at all three levels. The programs involve hands-on work with clients. They also use the *DSM* to classify patients.

Psychiatric nurses are usually registered nurses who have additional training in a psychiatric hospital. Some nurses who have had special and additional training can prescribe medication.

Mental health professionals are typically people with college degrees who work with patients in a mental health facility. They may have bachelor's, master's, or doctorate degrees. Typically, they have taken courses in psychology or social work; however, their degree is not in these fields. Within this classification are Marriage and Family Therapists (MFTs). MFTs may work in outpatient clinics and for health maintenance organizations (HMOs), and government-supported providers use them for therapy because they charge less.

The *Diagnostic and Statistical Manual* (*DSM*), in its current form, is a 943-page reference book, much like the penal code. By way of example, if a peace officer charges a person with burglary, the person must have committed an act that falls within the penal code description of burglary, versus theft, or grand larceny, and so forth. The penal code lists *elements of the crime*. Similarly, the *DSM* lists *symptoms of the disease*, like hallucinations, delusions, blunted affect, phobias, paranoid ideation, and panic attacks, to name a few. Like the elements of a crime, they are listed in the *DSM* under various classifications of mental illness such as bipolar disorder, paranoid schizophrenia, various depressions, and a dozen personality disorders.

The first *DSM* was an outline encompassing a hundred or so pages that was a polyglot of diagnostic labels with limited interpretations and descriptions, and it created considerable chaos. It was entitled *Standard Classified Nomenclature of Disease* and was first published in 1933. In 1952, with the cooperation of the Veterans Administration, the Army, the Navy, and the newly formed National Institute of Mental Health, some order was brought to the chaos with the printing of the 131-page *DSM-I*.

DSM-I served the mental health community for a short time. During the 1960s, a decision was made to base the American classification system on the current mental disorders section of the *International Classification of Diseases* manual. In 1968 the 134-page *DSM-II* appeared on the scene.

In 1974 the APA appointed a task force to begin work on *DSM-III*. This new manual would include a more realistic multiaxial approach to classifications. In brief, it recognized on paper what mental professionals had known for years. A person can have more than one mental disease or disorder as well as physical and social problems. Another reason for *DSM-III* is insurance companies. Because they were paying for treatment, they wanted a clear description of the diseases and disorders for which they were providing treatment reimbursement. Thus, the almost 600-page *DSM-III* was created and finally published in 1980. There were revisions; one known as *DSM-III-R* was published in 1987.

The current version, *DSM-IV*, is a much more comprehensive manual that encompasses 886 pages. It was published in 1994. Currently, there is an even more thorough manual known as *DSM-IV-TR* (TR stands for text revision) that has almost 950 pages.

Multiaxial Evaluation

The most pragmatic change that has occurred since *DSM-II* is the recognition of the fact that people can have more than one mental problem. In brief, the new APA system that uses the multiaxial model to classify people recognizes that just as a person may have more than one physical problem, like asthma, athlete's foot, and acne, people can have more than one psychological problem.

Simply stated, the multiaxial system is an assessment of several areas of human behavior.

Axis I lists clinical disorders, like Bipolar, Paranoid Schizophrenia, and other psychotic classifications as well as depression.

Axis II includes the dozen personality disorders (defined as a long-term pattern of maladaptive behavior, usually recognized in adolescence, like Antisocial, Obsessive Compulsive, and Narcissistic Personality Disorders). Not every Axis I diagnosis has an Axis II diagnosis.

Axis III requires a listing of general medical conditions.

Axis IV asks for a discussion of psycho/social and environmental problems. Many people have no such problems.

Axis V is a Global Assessment of Functioning. It is a score, on a scale from 0 to 100, that reflects a person's level of social, psychological, and physical functioning. On this scale, normal people are in the 90 to 100 range (*DSM-IV*, 2000, pp. 27–36).

To a crisis negotiator this means a person with an Axis I diagnosis of Paranoid Schizophrenia, Bipolar, or Depression with no Axis II diagnosis tends to be less dangerous than a hostage taker who, on Axis II has a diagnosis of Antisocial Personality Disorder. In my opinion, the most dangerous hostage takers are those who on Axis II have a designation of Antisocial Personality Disorder.

Mental Health Negotiators

It is not the job of the mental health professional to actually negotiate with the subject during a hostage barricade. Their job is to serve in a larger capacity by monitoring the overall situation, formulating opinions of the subjects' mental status, and offering suggestions about how to negotiate more effectively (DeBernardo, 2004). In addition, many mental health professionals provide stress-coping strategies to the tactical, command, and negotiating teams during a crisis as well as providing or making a critical incident stress debrief available to the staff.

A mental health professional can make the greatest contribution to the crisis management team by monitoring the mental status of the subject and victims, assessing personality characteristics of the subject, and helping assess the risk of suicide, self-injurious behavior, or violence (DeBernardo, 2004). The process of assessing the personality characteristics of the subject includes the development of negotiation strategies, tactics, and techniques.

In addition to the eight sources of professional conflict listed below, a major reason mental health professionals may not be effective as crisis negotiators is the issue of patient or client identification. In other words, who are they sworn to serve?

To better understand what a mental health professional can and cannot do, one must remember that today mental health is in the business of treating symptoms. With the exception of Bipolar Disorder, where a deficiency of the element lithium is suspected as the cause, the cause or causes of mental illness remain a mystery. As Dr. Anderson told me in September 1965 at Atascadero State Hospital for the Sexual Psychopath, we do not know the cause so we treat what we observe, the symptoms. An analogy would be for medical science to treat tuberculosis (TB) by giving the patient cough suppressant. One would not cure the patient of TB, but the patient would stop coughing. Thus it remains with mental disorders. Patients are provided with drugs to stop or mask their depression, hallucinations, delusions, and other symptoms with little knowledge of the root cause. Until science understands the root cause, or causes, of mental disorders, be they heredity, environment, or a combination of the two, and possible other factors like diet, they will continue to treat the symptoms and hope for the best.

Correctional staff and law enforcement officers serve society. In other words, when faced with a decision of what is best for a person versus what is best for society, we make decisions based on what is best for society. To the mental health professional, especially those in private practice, the client, the person they serve, is the individual. Therefore, they are more inclined to be at odds with law enforcement on the best course of action. The mental health professional, who is an employee of the state, has his or her feet in both camps and may, in the course of their service, face some ethical dilemmas.

The Declaration of Geneva to which psychiatrists abide states, among other points, that,

> The health of my patient will be my first consideration and I will respect the secrets that are confided in me. (World Medical Association, 1979)

Fortunately, for law enforcement, the issue of confidentiality has been addressed in the California case of Tarasoff. In this matter a University of California psychologist was told by a patient that he wanted to kill a professor at the university. The psychologist did not warn the intended victim nor advise the police. The rationale was patient–doctor privilege. After the homicide the victim's family successfully sued the university that employed the psychologist (Tarasoff, 1974).

According to Dr. Park Dietz, some common areas of ethical conflict for a mental health professional who negotiates include:

1. Personal versus professional relationship. They need a personal relationship with their client—during negotiations the negotiator–subject relationship, though close, is professional.
2. Use of deception. Negotiators try to be truthful. However, during a tactical maneuver, they may have to be deceptive.
3. A negotiator may have to withhold information from the subject.
4. When a negotiator is trying to talk the subject into surrender, the use of false assurances is common. We often minimize the seriousness of the situation.
5. False promise of help. This is a minor point because the negotiator may promise help is available without actually providing the assistance required or knowing who will do so.
6. Our most effective tactic is to tire the subject and stall for time. Mental health professionals try to provide the most expedient form of help.
7. Cater to the delusion. To assist in determining the dangerousness of the person, negotiators should ask the delusional person to talk about his or her false belief and/or hallucinations.
8. Informed consent means the hostage taker is told all of the consequences of each decision he or she is making (Dietz, 2001).

It is the opinion of Fuselier, a retired FBI negotiator who also has a doctorate in clinical psychology, that unless psychologists receive specific training in crisis negotiations, they best serve as consultants, not primary negotiators, during a siege (Fuselier, 1988, 2004).

Types of Disorders Typically Encountered by Crisis Negotiators

As crisis negotiators we generally face three classifications of mental diseases or disorders. It has been said that we negotiate with the *Mad*, the *Bad*, and the *Sad*.

1. The *Mad* are people who on Axis I have a classification of *psychotic* behavior. Psychosis is defined as a large group of major and very serious mental abnormalities observed in people who are out of touch with reality. Typically, they are experiencing delusions and hallucinations. They can justifiably plead not guilty by reason of insanity. Those typically encountered by crisis negotiators are people suffering from Paranoid Schizophrenia, Bipolar Disorder, depression, or paranoia. The psychosis known for years as paranoia is now called a delusional disorder. In legal parlance people suffering from a psychotic disorder are considered insane. In laymen's terms they are considered *Mad*.

2. The *Bad* hostage takers are those who on Axis II have a classification of a *personality disorder*. Typically, they are criminals and can be found among a dozen mental conditions characterized by long-term patterns of maladaptive behavior that are usually recognized by adolescence. Those typically encountered by crisis negotiators are people who are characterized as antisocial or inadequate.

3. The *Sad* are people we encounter as adults and adolescents in crisis as well as people who are under the influence of alcohol or other drugs who may not be included in the above listing. Typically, they are the largest classification we encounter. They are *Sad*. They are depressed and potentially suicidal people.

The above classifications are not designed to be trite or classifications. They are so named because the trilogy so stated is easy to remember. I am a firm believer in the axiom I learned in the U.S. Marine Corps (USMC) of "keep it simple stupid" (KISS).

The focus of this book is on mental diseases and disorders. That does not mean we immediately open the door to all mental health professionals to negotiate. I agree with the opinion of Dr. Fuselier, who said unless mental health professionals receive training in crisis negotiations, they best serve in a consultant role rather than as the primary negotiator during a siege (Fuselier,

1988, 2004). In addition, they must understand and share our priorities. The safety of police, hostages, and the community are the primary goals in our quest to preserve human life. Of course, we also seek to save the life of the hostage taker or person in crisis. However, we must set priorities as I have in the previous sentence. Very often the on-scene commander must make the crucial decision of continuing to negotiate or exercise a tactical option. It is not an easy call. However, that is why we set and abide by our priorities. One recent case where this difficult call was made occurred at The Discovery Channel building in Silver Spring, Maryland. The hostage taker (1) claimed to have a bomb, (2) had created a disturbance there before, (3) was making insane and escalating demands, and (4) was threatening the hostages. After prolonged negotiations these circumstances forced the on-scene commander to make the difficult decision to order his team to shoot the hostage taker to save the lives of the hostages.

The Axioms of the Negotiations Process

To understand the process of crisis negotiations one must have an understanding of the basic realities of this dynamic process that are listed below.

Listening

Contrary to popular belief and media representations, a good negotiator is a good listener, not necessarily a good talker. We learn when we listen. As negotiators we listen for the words, phrases, and subject's version of reality that tell us how to best extricate him or her from this self-created crisis that is their dilemma.

Remember, the good Lord gave us a mouth we can shut and two ears we cannot. Perhaps there is a message from the Almighty in this fact of anatomy. In this endeavor, we have our team and especially the secondary negotiator to help us listen.

Typically, the subjects we encounter during a hostage crisis have a story to tell. Effective negotiating teams pay close attention to this story. To help them tell their story, their version of reality, negotiators engage in the use of active listening skills (ALS). Typically, this story involves their version of events in which they portray themselves as, and believe they are, the victim.

Active Listening

Active listening has been around since the years immediately following World War II. As I recall it came from Carl Rogers' approach to treatment that he called patient-centered therapy. The point is this process has been around for many years because it is simple and it works. It is especially effective with emotionally upset people who have a story to tell.

My definition of ALS is doing something to encourage the other person to do most of the talking. That means we engage in activity to induce and produce more listening content. Remember, we learn when we listen.

Typically, emotionally driven people will tell you what they want to hear as they talk about their perception of the situation. In all honesty and candor I learned this from my wife. I knew that if I kept my mouth shut while she "vented," she would provide me with the answers she wanted to hear.

Typically, people in crisis want to talk about their stress and stressors. Remember, the good Lord gave us one mouth we can close and two ears we cannot. Perhaps there is a message in those facts of human anatomy.

The Mechanics of Active Listening Skills (ALS)

The process of active listening is multifaceted. But, you need not use all steps of the process:

1. *Tolerate silence*—When the other person finishes talking, say nothing. Wait for the other person to continue with his or her train of thought.
2. If you are uncomfortable and cannot sit and wait, *repeat* the last few words of what he or she said.
3. If you are more comfortable with *emotional labeling*, tell the person how he or she sounds—angry, depressed, and so forth.
4. *Summarize or paraphrase* what the person has said.
5. Ask *open-ended questions*—Do not solicit or encourage yes and no objective responses.
6. Use *minimal encouragers* like when? Really. Oh. Then what?
7. *"I" messages* like "I feel uneasy when you talk like that." This phrase can be used when the subject is very emotional and yelling.

I have difficulty using "I" messages. Further, I have yet to be involved in an interview, therapy session, or negotiation where I used all seven tactics. However, almost every session allowed for the use of silence, repeating the last word or words, summarizing, and asking open-ended questions.

By way of example, I was involved in a negotiation in Washington, DC, where a man took his young wife hostage. He was threatening to kill her because she was spending all of his retirement monies. His first wife had passed away and he recently married a younger woman. He earned many incentive awards for his work in the intelligence community during World War II and had accumulated many monetary awards and some royalties for his service and writings. He had just learned of her extravagance and self-indulgence at his expense and was very upset.

It was clear to me that the man was proud of his preretirement accomplishments, as well he should have been. I had read of his work and was very impressed. Now, he was in a crisis, and I was faced with helping negotiate the safety, if not the life, of one of my boyhood heroes.

I passed notes to the primary stressing some of the ALS listed above. Because of the stress level, silence worked well. The man had a tale to tell, so "we" encouraged him to tell us his story. This involved his work in the intelligence community during World War II. I am a history buff whose father and many uncles fought in that war. As an elementary school student I followed the war in both theaters because my dad and some uncles were in Europe and two of my uncles were Marines in the Pacific. All this is by way of saying that I was able to provide the primary with notes of minimal encouragers that bore on the discussions of various battles. By that I mean the negotiator was able to say something like, "wow, my uncle was with the First Marines on the Canal so I bet they used the stuff you developed," or "I had an uncle in the Navy at the Battle of Midway and I know they used what you created to figure out what the Japanese were trying to do." In addition, the subject discussed things he did that were still classified. I was able to pass notes to the primary suggesting he say things like, "I heard about that, but I think it is still classified." These are some examples of "expanded" minimal encouragers.

The primary also used silence very well. However, on more than one occasion we had to cover his mouth so he would remain quiet while the subject vented on his deeds and the spending spree of his young wife.

Eventually, the subject agreed to come out. Come out. Not surrender. His condition was that he be allowed to talk with the primary about World War II. The subject said, "I have given many lectures at universities on my work during the war. No one in any of those audiences understood what I did and how I did it as well as Officer Jones. He is brilliant." Well, "Jones" is a great guy and a good negotiator. I am not so sure about brilliant. As I recall, "Jones" was born in 1961. My job was to give him a quick synopsis of World War II so he could carry on an intelligent conversation with the hero. According to "Jones" the postincident discussion went well because he just used the same ALS he perfected during the negotiations.

The point of all this is quite simple. ALS work when we keep our mouth shut and let the emotionally driven subject do the talking. This is not a control issue. It is just a commonsense approach of letting the more emotional person talk about his or her stress and situation. In the course of his or her talking, we gather intelligence on the person's IQ, his or her perception of reality, his or her dedication, and many other clues that will help us ensure a peaceful conclusion.

Remember, we learn when we listen. Use ALS. Shut your mouth and open your ears. *Listen and learn.* This will take longer than telling the person what to do. However, we must use time to defuse the siege and bring everyone out alive. As negotiators we must operate as if we are getting paid by the hour, not by the job.

Victimization

As mentioned above, typically the hostage taker or suicidal subject has a story to tell. Typically, once this story has been told the subject is more likely to peacefully exit. A big part of this story is his or her perception that the subject is the real victim. It is the subject's perception that he or she was forced into this course of action by a person, persons, or circumstances beyond his or her control. Often this view involves the use of two psychological defense mechanisms: projection and rationalization. These mechanisms are discussed below.

To maintain the most effective mind-set, the negotiator must remember that as a law enforcement or correctional officer, we deal differently with subjects than with their victims. Here we have a situation where the subject believes he or she is the victim. Therefore, we as negotiators must make the necessary adjustments to our tone of voice, mind-set, and approach.

Tone of Voice

Since 1976, I have interviewed dozens of hostage takers. Typically, the interview occurred years after the siege in a state or federal prison. It is interesting to note that in most cases, years after the incident the subject did not remember if the negotiator was a male or a female. However, the subject always remembers the negotiator's calm and reassuring tone of voice. It has been said that your tone of voice is the body language of telephonic communications. The tone of the successful negotiator's voice reflected, in the mind of the subject, the negotiator's concern for his or her safety. It was this perceived concern, not the content of the communications, that usually led to a peaceful end.

Role Change

To achieve the above one must change roles. In this role, the effective and successful negotiator is not an interrogator or an investigator. One must put his or her badge in a pocket and switch roles from correctional officer or cop to counselor. This is not easy, but it is necessary. The communication of empathy is essential. It is not easy, but it too is essential. Mental health professionals know that the expression of empathy is a step toward a trusting relationship that will strengthen their influence upon their patient to change their behavior or perceptions. Similarly, negotiators can more easily convince subjects to come out, fold their tent, walk away, or live to fight another day if they have a trusting relationship with the subject.

Time

In most correctional and law enforcement situations the quicker we act the more likely we are to succeed. Therefore, this axiom is difficult for many to accept or believe.

It is difficult, if not impossible, to present in a paragraph or page the importance of the intelligent use of time to ensure the peaceful resolution of a hostage siege. Gary Noesner devoted his entire book to this topic (Noesner, 2010). In his reference to the importance of using time to the advantage of the negotiating team, Dr. Harvey Schlossberg coined the term "Dynamic Inactivity." In other words, it appears we are doing nothing while we are engaging the subject in protracted discussions and decisions that serve to provide us with intelligence, fatigue the subject, and typically lead to his or her eventual surrender.

Be patient. Let it play out. Encourage the subject to tell us his or her side of the story, his or her version of events. Use ALS to encourage the active participation of the subject in this protracted process.

Surgeons wait for the anesthetic to take effect before making an incision. Similarly, negotiators should delay until the subject is sufficiently fatigued, has had the opportunity to tell us his or her side of the story, and now feels vindicated and ready to exit. As negotiators we operate more effectively when we have the mind-set of one being paid by the hour not by the job. The longer we negotiate, the more money we earn.

No

Avoid the finality of saying "no." Replace it with "not now" or "not yet" or "in a little while." With some subjects the expression "The boss says not now" is effective. "Not now" does not necessarily mean "never" or "no." It can mean "later." Remember hope springs eternal. Keep the subject occupied with conversation. Negotiation means communication, not capitulation.

Defense Mechanisms

It is very important that negotiators understand two very common psychological defense mechanisms. The concept of ego defense was introduced by Freud. Simply stated, defense mechanisms are involuntary reactions that serve to protect or defend one's ego or self from hurt or harm. A quick example is that of denial. Denial is not a large river in Egypt. It is an involuntary psychological reaction to bad news or events that one cannot immediately accept. An example of denial is learning of the death of a friend and immediately responding with a statement or thought like, "I was just talking with him yesterday." You do not say to yourself this is bad news. It hurts. I cannot accept it. Therefore, I will react in a comfortable manner. You react automatically and eventually accept and deal with the bad news.

Defense mechanisms become pathological, maladaptive, or sick reactions to life when one uses them constantly and adheres to them in the face of strong evidence to the contrary. The two most frequently encountered defense mechanisms when negotiators interact with a personality disorder like antisocial or inadequate are rationalization and projection. I must digress and explain that unfortunately, the old classification of inadequate has been replaced with the description of the disorder dispersed among the atypical, or mixed, or dependent classifications. For law enforcement and correctional negotiators the term "loser" is an excellent synonym.

Two Defense Mechanisms

Rationalization   This is a more common and less pathological defense mechanism than projection. We all use the defense mechanism of rationalization on *occasion*. It helps us salvage our "bent ego" and progress past a failure. A healthy example is when one falls short of the cutoff score for a promotion and says to himself of herself, "I really did not want that job." However, we study more rigorously for the next test.

Pathology enters the picture when people excuse illegal acts by rationalizing. This is the case where people excuse their actions by saying, "Well everybody does it."

I worked a case where the subject said he needed the money more than his victim so that justified the robbery. A common version of this defense mechanism is "Sour Grapes."

Again, we all rationalize. Pathology enters the picture when we justify illegal activity or when we constantly use this defense mechanism in the face of evidence to the contrary.

Projection   The defense mechanism of projection, seen in most personality disorders and considered by many as the basis for paranoia, is an extremely powerful psychological ploy that serves to enhance one self-concept in the face of facts that negate this belief. Basically, those who use this defense mechanism to excess believe that nothing negative in their life is ever their fault. They place the blame/responsibility for their problems and predicaments on others. In this process they view the world and events in refraction.

Over the years, their practice of this ploy becomes more ingrained in their social interactions and therefore more effective. It works for them. They emerge as a victim. "They get damn good at blaming others for their faults." It is frequently so effective that they not only convince themselves that "others" are to blame for their problems, but they put these "others" on a "guilt trip" over their role. They are masters at this manipulation.

Others begin to believe they could have or should have done more to help. Others begin to believe that because of their role in this person's life, they are at least partially responsible for them not achieving their potential or experiencing some or a series of failures. They begin to believe it might be their fault, or at least they had more than a minor role in creating or contributing to the adversity. Thus, they fall into the trap the "projecting person" has set for them and try to rectify the problem that is not their fault but for which they feel somewhat responsible. This, of course, is exactly what the "projecting person" wants and all too often achieves. People who are kind, considerate, and compassionate are especially vulnerable to this manipulation, and subsequently attempt to rectify a problem that is not their fault. All this well-intended behavior only serves to enhance the pathological use of projection.

By way of criminal examples, I interviewed a man who had stabbed his victim 31 times. His explanation was, "It ain't my fault. The knife went out of control." Another example is the case on a military reservation when a civilian driver hit a civilian in a cross-walk. His lament was "She should have been watching where she was walking." He went on to complain of the damage she did to his car. The truth is he was busy sending a text message and was speeding.

There was the case where a subject robbed his victim of several hundred dollars. His excuse was, "That fool should have known better than to carry that much money around. I did him a favor. I'll bet he won't make that mistake again."

I was involved in a negotiation where a bank robber said it was not his fault that he took people hostage. It was the fault of the Washington, DC Police Department. His version of reality was that their quick response forced him to take customers hostage to protect himself and them from the police. The pathology here is that he really believed this. He finally agreed to come out when the negotiator promised to tell his version of the incident to the magistrate.

On the lighter side, the story is told of the famous New York Yankee catcher Yogi Berra who became their manager. He was watching a new player trying to field grounders at third base. He kept missing them. Yogi said, "Step back. I will show you how to do it." Well, Yogi also missed one ball after another. He finally threw the glove back at his new player saying, "Son, you have so messed up third base that now no one can play it properly."

You may decide to refer back to these two defense mechanisms when reading the chapters on the Inadequate and Antisocial Personality–disordered people in crisis.

Finally, as I said earlier, there remains a sad but true reality. The cause of mental illness remains in many, if not most cases, a mystery. Years ago, at the beginning of my fall-semester internship at the Atascadero State Hospital for the Sexual Psychopath on the Central Coast of California, I met with my mentor Dr. Anderson. What he said to me in September 1965 remains true today and is worth remembering. He said, "We do not know the cause of most mental illnesses; therefore, we treat the symptoms. Medically that is like prescribing a cough suppressant to a patient who has tuberculosis (TB). The cough suppressant stops the cough but does nothing to cure the TB. So, it is with our antipsychotic medications, our antidepressant medications and a host of others. The symptoms are remedied, the sickness remains." Remember, the symptoms are remedied but the sickness remains, because as negotiators we must deal with that sickness. It was sad then and remains true today. Therefore, law enforcement and correctional staff encounter with a very high degree of frequency those who are "off their meds" and back into their social sickness and require our response to protect and defend.

Two Typical Symptoms of Psychosis

Delusions

A delusion is a false belief. By that I mean a serious false belief like the ability to fly, walk on water, or be on a special mission from God, not a more common false belief like "I know she loves me." This strong belief is held in spite of strong persuasion or overwhelming evidence to the contrary. More simply said, it is out of touch with reality.

Hallucinations

This is a sense perception for which there are no appropriate external stimuli. Again, it is out of touch with reality. In other words one or more senses are malfunctioning like hearing voices that no one else can hear because no one else is talking. Although we have five senses, the most common hallucination is audio and is said to account for about 80 percent of hallucinations. Other malfunctioning senses like seeing things, smelling nonexistent odors, taste, or touch (tactile) are less common.

Excellent Idea

During the last several California Association of Hostage Negotiator Annual and Regional Training sessions, the Los Angeles Police Department and the Los Angeles Sheriff's Department have made presentations on their program of contacting hostage takers for a follow-up interview (CAHN, 2011). During these recorded interviews they learn what worked well and what did not. It is an excellent form of self-critique and reminiscent of what I did many years ago when I began interviewing negotiators and hostage takers to develop the FBI program.

Conclusion

Remembering or referring back to these axioms will provide the reader with a better understanding of the dynamics of a hostage or suicidal siege.

References

CAHN (2011) LAPD and LASD presentations at conferences.

DeBernardo, C. R. (2004) The Psychologist's Role in Hostage Negotiations, *International Journal of Emergency Mental Health*, Vol. 6, No. 1, pp. 39–42.

Dietz, P. (2001) Presentation to the California Association of Hostage Negotiators, San Diego, CA. May 31.

DSM-II (1952) *Diagnostic and Statistical Manual of Mental Disorders*–2nd Edition, American Psychiatric Association, Washington, DC.

DSM-III (1980) *Diagnostic and Statistical Manual of Mental Disorders*–3rd Edition, American Psychiatric Association, Washington, DC.

DSM-IV (2000) *Diagnostic and Statistical Manual of Mental Disorders*–4th Edition, American Psychiatric Association, Washington, DC.

Fuselier, G. D. (1988) Hostage Negotiation Consultant: Emerging Role for the Clinical Psychologist, *Professional Psychology: Research and Practice*, Vol. 19, No. 2, pp. 175–179.

Fuselier, G. D. (2004) Personal conversation, Baton Rouge, LA. March 8.

Noesner, G. (2010) *Stalling for Time*, Random House, New York.

Tarasoff v. the Regents of the University of California, S. F. No. 23042. State of California, Superior Court No. 405694, 529 P. 2nd 553 (1974) rehearing 551 P. 2nd. 334 (1976).

World Medical Association (1979) Declaration of Geneva, Quoted in Viedman, C. "I Swear by Apollo..." *World Health*, July, pp. 24–29.

Characteristics of Effective Hostage/ Crisis Negotiators

2

Introduction

Prior to and into the early 1970s, there were three common ways to deal with criminals and others holding hostages. Most frequently, the police surrounded the hostage holder, or subject, and ordered the subject's surrender. This was usually followed by the use of chemical agents. When these two options failed an assault on him or his position by the use of sniper fire or tactical teams usually ended the siege. Occasionally, these options were preceded by talking and trying to convince the subject to surrender. If the subject did not acquiesce quickly enough, the tactical options listed above were immediately initiated (Strentz, 1983).

To live is to change. When dealing with barricaded gunmen, suicidal subjects, and other people holding hostages, including suicidal people who are holding themselves hostage, one should remember that *preservation of human life is paramount.* In response to the recognition of this preeminence, police and corrections have, for the most part, made this their primary priority. We have learned that even those threatening the lives of innocent civilians must be provided with a reasonable opportunity to talk and surrender (*Downs v. United States*, 1975). The experiences of law enforcement agencies in the field, and in courts, have helped mold many of these changes.

It is important to recognize a basic difference in the mind-set and orientation of those responding to a hostage crisis situation. Commanders and the tactical team tend to respond and react as if they are getting paid by the job. Crisis negotiators are more effective if they maintain the mind-set and response of a team that is being *paid by the hour.* Properly used, time is the greatest and most effective weapon of the negotiations team (Noesner, 2010).

What Is Past Is Prologue

Hostage takings and barricaded gunmen crises have occurred in the United States and around the world at a seemingly ever escalating rate. These include the now infamous 1972 Munich Olympics. The July 4, 1976, Entebbe raid by Israel to rescue its citizens and others held hostage in Uganda by that depraved, degenerate, and draconian dictator, Edie Amin, is not to be forgotten. In October 1977 Lufthansa Flight 181 was hijacked as it left France. After hours of negotiations, the incident ended at Mogadishu in Somalia. There, the now famous German counterterrorist team, GSG-9, lead by Lt. Colonel Ulrich Wegner, successfully rescued *all* of the hostages on that ill-fated airplane. Since then most international hijackings of commercial aircraft have been resolved through negotiations. Of the 800 hijackings of commercial aircraft around the world, less than 10 have been resolved by armed intervention of police or military forces (Strentz, 1994). Clearly, the typical Russian response, as reflected in their tactics at the opera house in Moscow and, more recently, the school in Beslan, is to assault (Dolnik and Fitzgerald, 2008). Not all nations of the world, or incident commanders, share our concern for the sanctity and preservation of human life.

The Way We Were

During the early incidents, many forms of communications were attempted. In each case the discussions were in some small sense successful. They developed a dialogue with the terrorists and secured the release of some hostages. Typically, they delayed or prevented the shooting of additional victims.

In another way, they assisted the tactical team in completing their mission with a higher degree of success than would have been possible without their assistance. This assistance came in two forms. The negotiator delayed additional acts by the hostage holder and in so doing bought the time needed for the tactical team to prepare. Another, though not necessarily less important function of negotiations, was and remains the gathering of intelligence on and about the barricaded adversary.

An example of the use of these tactics is the rescue of those held hostage in the Iranian Embassy in London by Iraq-supported terrorists in spring 1980. A case can easily be made for the tactical use of negotiations as an adjunct to assault teams over the last 20 years. Negotiators buy time while the tactical teams prepare for the *best* assault option rather than an *emergency* assault option.

The Way It Should Be

The times and our tactics have changed. The practice of hostage negotiations has grown from an adjunct to the tactical team to the singular most effective and humane way of resolving hostage or barricaded gunmen or suicide crises situations.

Twenty years ago the primary job of the hostage negotiator was to assist the special weapons and tactics (SWAT) team. In those days the negotiator typically talked to the subject until the SWAT team was in a position to assault. Today, progressive police departments and correctional institutions use their SWAT teams to assist the negotiator. The process and practice of negotiations has progressed from the periphery to preferable.

The negotiator *must* speak from a position of strength. That power is provided by the fear of an armed intervention by SWAT. This prospect is an undesirable alternative that the typical hostage holder would like to avoid. Hostage holders know they cannot survive an armed confrontation with the authorities. Today, the vast majority of hostage situations are resolved without a shot being fired by the police (HOBAS, 2011; Strentz, 1983; University of Vermont–SOARU, 1991).

An example of the effectiveness of crisis negotiations is an American version of the previously stated international aircraft hijacking resolution statistic. Like those in other countries, the overwhelming majority of U.S. aircraft hijackings have been resolved by negotiations versus those in which a rescue of the hostages by a tactical team was necessary. To date over 400 hijackings of U.S. aircraft have occurred. A few, 2 percent, have been resolved by the use of force (FAA, 2011).

The purpose of this research and chapter is not to negate the necessity of a well-trained, properly equipped, and well-positioned SWAT team. This was clear during the 444-day drama at the American Embassy in Iran. Negotiations with the government of Iran, without a perceived SWAT alternative, were worthless. Our hostages were not freed until after the attempted rescue when the Ayatollah feared an air raid by the newly elected president. Hostage or crisis negotiators must speak from a position of strength.

Who Talks the Talk So SWAT Does Not Have to Shoot?

This chapter will focus on the social-psychological traits of successful negotiators. To do this I will identify the traits of those who have effectively resolved dangerous situations without the loss of human life by talking rather than taking lives. In this regard it is important to remember that when a crisis incident commander authorizes the use of deadly force by committing the SWAT team, he or she is jeopardizing lives. The lives placed on the line are those of the tactical team, other police officers, the hostages, and the subject.

Today, many if not most modern law enforcement agencies have a pool of trained crisis negotiators. They work as part of a crisis resolution team with command and other tactical units to bring about a peaceful solution to a potentially dangerous and deadly dispute.

Psychological selection criteria and the training of crisis negotiators have been discussed and researched (Allen, Fraser, and Inwald, 1991; Birge and Birge, 1994; Fuselier, 1988; Gelbart, 1979; Getty and Elan, 1988; Hibler, 1984;

San Jose, 1995, 2004). The study conducted by Allen et al. identified several characteristics of effective negotiators. They evaluated and reported on 12 veteran negotiators of a large, southeastern metropolitan police department. In spite of their limited number of subjects, a high level of agreement was achieved by using a different instrument in this study. They found that the competent negotiator is insightful, intelligent, rational, clear-thinking, logical, self-controlled, self-confident, decisive, able to make concessions, assertive, determined, and values success. The competent negotiator is persistent, trustful, tolerant of ambiguity, expresses frustration appropriately, and has the ability to empathize and use insight to either help or hurt others.

Birge and Birge (1994, 2011) report that the police employment history of the candidate is an excellent indicator of future crisis behavior. They state that if a candidate has resolved disputes in the past as a patrol officer or detective by listening and talking rather than getting involved in a physical confrontation, they are prone to do so in the future. Conversely, if this person is prone to use physical tactics rather than words, he or she may *not* be a good negotiator.

The research done by Gelbart in 1979 was also conducted in California. He used police officers who were selected to be negotiators by the Los Angeles County Sheriff's Department. The instruments used on 44 subjects were the California Psychological Inventory (CPI), the Taylor Manifest Anxiety Scale, and the Psychopathic Deviate scale of the Minnesota Multiphasic Personality Inventory (MMPI). Additional data were collected on a questionnaire. The study found that those who were identified as effective negotiators were characterized as having highly adequate social skills, communications ability, self-assurance, and social presence, and were intelligent and able manipulators. On the Cs, capacity for status, scale of the CPI they were rated as ambitious, active, forceful insightful, resourceful, and versatile. Their scores on this scale also indicated that they were effective communicators with wide interests.

These findings are consistent with the research done in Northern California years later. A major problem encountered by many researchers who seek to identify the personality characteristics of effective police hostage negotiators through the use of psychological tests is that most of these instruments were designed to identify pathology. Thus, they are of marginal value when used as identifiers of specific traits of normal people who may have characteristics that could contribute to the selection and training of an effective crisis negotiator.

The better selection programs today choose from volunteers with about 5 years of police experience who are interviewed by a board of experienced negotiators. Their personnel files are reviewed, and they have the opportunity to demonstrate their skills in a role-playing scenario supervised by current team members. The final decision may be made by the chief (San Jose, 1995, 2004).

Today, many effective training courses for crisis negotiators are conducted in the United States. Some are sponsored through state universities. The FBI runs an intense 2-week course at its academy on the Marine Base in Quantico, Virginia. There is an excellent program in Australia sponsored by the federal government and run by the New South Wales Police Department. In England, New Scotland Yard began the first 2-week negotiators course and assisted the FBI in its program. Canada conducts extensive and superb training (Ruming, 2004).

It is vital that those chosen to attend these schools be carefully and intelligently selected. The use of objective and uniform tests and procedures to identify those with characteristics and experience already present in successful negotiators seems like a logical place to start.

Method

The subjects were 100 sworn West Coast police officers. Most worked in California. They were students in one of three Hostage Negotiators Courses certified by Police Officers Standards and Training (POST) who were taught through the San Jose State University, Administration of Justice Bureau in October and December 1995 and again in 2004.

Fifty-one of these officers attended Hostage Negotiator Up-Date Courses. Thirty-three attended the Basic Course in October. Sixteen attended the October Command Course. Of the 16 in the Command Course, all but two were trained and experienced crisis negotiators who had been promoted to commander of a negotiations team. The data were collected during class time and tabulated in early 1996 and again in 2004.

All of the subjects were given a modified version of the 300-item Adjective Check List (ACL) and asked to identify all characteristics that described an effective negotiator. They were also asked to complete an ACL for a person whom they considered an ineffective negotiator and to note if the person they were describing was themselves. Ten subjects identified themselves on an ACL. All 10 considered themselves effective negotiators. The 100 subjects identified 21 ineffective and over 100 effective negotiators.

They also completed a form that asked them to describe effective and ineffective negotiators by sex, marital status, age, years in the department, type of assignments, and training. Finally, each was asked to list specific personal, social, educational, and professional characteristics they thought contributed to this person's success or failure as a crisis negotiator.

Results

The results were tabulated by hand and listed on a master ACL and demographic characteristics sheet for each group: Basic, Command, and Up-Date.

One list was for effective or good negotiators, and another was for poor or ineffective crisis negotiators.

When describing effective negotiators, there was a high level of agreement, 90 percent or better, on such characteristics as adaptable, alert, calm, capable, clear thinking, mature, patient, sociable, and tactful. There was less agreement, between 75 and 89 percent, on such items as clever, confident, conscientious, intelligent, interests wide, logical, persistent, practical, reasonable, reliable, and understanding. Similarly, the characteristics of ineffective crisis negotiators were well agreed upon. The highest level of agreement, 95 percent, was on the adjective "argumentative." In the 85 to 94 percent range, the characteristics of aloof, arrogant, bitter, bossy, deceitful, egotistical, prejudiced, rigid, and vindictive were identified. Only a few were found in the range between 75 and 84 percent. They were cold, stubborn, and unfriendly.

Commanders of hostage negotiations teams agreed with the characteristics listed above. Interestingly and understandably, they added characteristics they identified as attributes of people who were easy to supervise. These were patient and relaxed. When listing the traits of ineffective negotiators, they identified characteristics of people who did not work well with others or were difficult to supervise. The adjectives of arrogant, bossy, hardheaded, lazy, and quarrelsome received 100 percent agreement.

Not surprisingly, the person whom his or her peers and commanders consider to be an effective hostage/crisis negotiator has traits that are consistent with common sense. Unfortunately, the ACL does not include such traits as attentive listener, good interviewer, people person, streetwise, and team player. These were reported with a high degree of agreement, over 90 percent, on the separate list where the participants were asked to note other characteristics of a good negotiator.

On this separate sheet they listed male or female with an age of 35 to 50 with a variety of law enforcement assignments. They emphasized that the person should have at least 5 years of experience with an ability to relate to people, should have training in suicide prevention, and must be a good listener.

Conversely, those identified as ineffective negotiators were younger and had fewer years of police service. Traits included being hot headed, macho, conceited, a know-it-all, and a person with limited life experiences.

Both questionnaires, one in 1995 and the other in 2004, reflected almost identical results.

Conclusion

The preservation of human life must remain our primary objective for the successful resolution of hostage crises. The police practice of using hostage negotiations as the primary and preferred tactic to resolve hostage and barricaded gunman crises has come a long way during the last 20 years. We continue to learn from our past. Not to do so is to repeat our mistakes. Today, the majority of aircraft hijacking and other hostage situations are resolved without violence. We have learned that most, but not all, such situations can be resolved through negotiations. We know that one cannot negotiate a prison riot. We were reminded in August 1992 at Ruby Ridge, Idaho, and again in spring 1993 at Waco, Texas, that tactical teams and negotiators must work together more effectively to resolve these crises. The preservation of human life through teamwork in crisis resolution is paramount. To strengthen the performance of crisis negotiators they must be effectively, objectively, and systematically selected prior to their training. One cannot make a silk purse from a sow's ear. A good selection process helps weed out those who are ill-suited to the tasks of listening and reasoning to resolve crises by bringing the hostage taker to his or her senses, not necessarily to his or her knees.

The hostage crisis is coming. These incidents can be curtailed if we are prepared. Their effects can be muted if we carefully select our staff, train, and care enough. These crises may provide for personal and professional growth if we plan ahead and are fortunate enough. We can affect the character and results of these crises, but we cannot alter their inevitability (Kennedy, 1963).

References

Allen, S. W., Fraser, S. L., and Inwald, R. (1991) Assessment of Personality Characteristics Related to Successful Hostage Negotiators and Their Resistance to Post Traumatic Stress Disorder, *Critical Incidents in Policing*, FBI Academy, Quantico, pp. 1–5.

Birge, A. C., and Birge, R. (1994) Crisis Negotiators: Personnel Selection, *The U.S. Negotiator*, Winter, pp. 5–7.

Birge, A. C., and Birge, R. (2011) Personal interview, Yuciappa, California.

Dolnik, A., and Fitzgerald, K. M. (2008) *Negotiating Hostage Crisis with the New Terrorist*, Prager Security International, London.

Downs, Brent et al. v. United States of America (August 8, 1975) USC 6th Circuit, #74-1660.

Federal Aviation Administration (2011) Criminal Acts against Civil Aviation, Office of Civil Aviation Security, Washington, DC.

Fuselier, G. D. (1988) Hostage Negotiation Consultant: Emerging Role for the Clinical Psychologist, *Professional Psychology: Research and Practice*, Vol. 19, pp. 175–179.

Gelbart, M. (1979) Psychological, Personality and Biographical Variables Related to Success as a Negotiator, *Dissertation Abstracts International*, Vol. 39, p. 4558-B.

Getty, V. S., and Elan, J. D. (1988) Identifying Characteristics of Hostage Negotiators, and Using Personality Data to Develop a Selection Model. In J. Reese and J. Horn (Eds.) *Police Psychology: Operational Assistance*, pp. 159–171.

Hibler, N. S. (1984) *Hostage Situations: A Consultation Guide for Mental Health Professionals*, Office of Special Investigations, Washington, DC.

HOBAS (2011) FBI Hostage and Barricade Database System, Crisis Management Unit, Quantico, Virginia.

Kennedy, R. (1963) U.S. Senator, Speech before the Senate on terrorism.

Noesner, G. (2010) *Stalling for Time*, Random House, New York.

Ruming, D. (2004) Detective Sergeant, New South Wales Police Department, Sydney, Australia. Personal interview.

San Jose State University Administration of Justice Bureau (1995) Personal interviews. Members of Up-Date Hostage Negotiators Classes, San Jose, California.

San Jose State University Administration of Justice Bureau (2004) Personal interviews. Members of Up-Date II Hostage Negotiators Classes, San Jose, California.

Strentz, T. (1983) Statistical Analysis of American Hostage Situations, unpublished handout, FBI Academy, Quantico, Virginia.

Strentz, T. (1994) Where Have All the Hijackers Gone? *Proceedings, 11th Session of the Southern California Aircraft Cabin Safety Symposium*, Long Beach. February.

University of Vermont and Special Operations and Research Unit (1991) Hostage Negotiations Questionnaire, unpublished research project. FBI Academy, Quantico, Virginia.

Cross-Trained versus Cross-Qualified

3

"A little knowledge is a dangerous thing, drink deep or taste not of the Pierian spring."

Pope (1711)

Introduction

It was over a quarter century ago that the New York City Police Department in the persons of Frank Bolz and Harvey Schlossberg developed, practiced, and taught the innovative police crisis response process of crisis negotiations. We have learned a lot over this quarter of a century. Many, if not most, of their ideas are still in use around this country and throughout the free world. One modification to their original plan is the cross-training of crisis team members.

There is a growing, basically healthy, and well-intended trend in this country for agencies to train their special weapons and tactics (SWAT) team members in negotiations and provide negotiators with SWAT training. One of the goals of this cross-training is to help each person understand the role of other crisis response team members. Churchill said that we should not judge another until we "Walk a mile in his moccasins." In many ways cross-training enhances teamwork.

However, the major concept for team leaders and members to understand is after one has some training in hostage negotiations, he or she may not be qualified to negotiate any more than a person who has fired a rifle for familiarization is qualified to work as a sniper. It is important that we separate cross-training from cross-qualifying; a little knowledge is a dangerous thing.

Few people enjoy the tension created by diversity and different views. As social animals, people tend to want consensus. That is the basic problem that flaws a decision-making process and is called "Group Think" that is discussed in greater depth in Chapter 21. In most settings diversity of opinion and orientation, constructive competition, helps ensure success. A healthy difference of opinion is not, repeat *not,* what the Federal Bureau of Investigation (FBI) experienced at Waco, Texas, and Ruby Ridge, Idaho. During these crises, the differences were exacerbated by an unbalanced command structure that had no real appreciation for the process of crisis negotiations. The results were tragic (Strentz, 1997).

There are many examples of the need for diversity, competing opinions, within effective systems. Our democratic form of government is well served by the checks and balances ensured by the existence of the executive, legislative, and judicial systems. Within the judicial system we have opposing counsel. We have two major political parties that serve to keep each other honest. We have the media who view themselves as the fourth estate in a role that keeps politicians, and others in government and industry, honest. In other words, everyone, especially society and justice, benefits when checks and balances operate effectively.

As an undergraduate student in 1960 I recall a lecture by a Jesuit Priest who spoke about his role and that of the Roman Catholic Church in the history and development of the Americas. At the end of his insightful presentation he asked for questions. I am a Lutheran. I thought I would stump him. I asked, "What purpose do you see the Protestant church serving in the world today?" Without hesitation he answered, "Young man, they keep us honest." Thus, this prince of the Roman Catholic Church admitted that there were elements within his organization that might tend toward extreme views, were it not for a loyal opposition. Certainly, the Spanish Inquisition and the Salem Witch Trials tell us that even the Christian church needs a watchdog element.

It is with these examples in mind that I offer my views on the need for cross-training while I try to remain mindful of the dangers of cross-qualifying members of crisis teams. There are major law enforcement agencies in this country that pride themselves on the fact that SWAT team members are also qualified as negotiators, and in the mind of the crisis incident commander can function effectively in either role during a crisis. I will, however, admit that while there may be some "Renaissance Men" who can function effectively in these two basically and inherently divergent roles, we are in danger of mixing metaphors. We are in danger of thinking that because a few can function in these diverse assignments, everyone can. We are in danger of substituting exceptional personalities who can occasionally calm a crisis for a *system* that will help regularly and reliably ensure a successful solution.

It is like comparing a monarchy with democracy. A monarchy is more efficient. A good monarch can provide the best form of government. Yet we all know that power corrupts, and absolute power corrupts absolutely.

Most tactical team leaders to whom I have spoken recognize their team members earn their assignments by repeatedly practicing and demonstrating proficiency in their specific skills. They would not think of permanently assigning people as entry team or sniper team members based on their order of arrival at the scene. They recognize and employ their knowledge of the skills of each officer in making their decisions about assignments during a crisis deployment. The courts, in *Moon v. Winfield*, and again in *City of Winter Haven v. Allen*, have made it clear that this practice is appropriate.

Similarly, there are trained negotiators who work well gathering intelligence as the secondary negotiator or team leader, while lacking the disposition or prerequisite skills or experience to work effectively as the primary negotiator. Negotiation team commanders, who are administrators, regularly talk about the variety of skills required within their team. Most know well that the secondary negotiator or coach may not have the experience or grace under fire to function as the primary.

Yet, some well-intended but misinformed people tend to view the role of the crisis negotiator and the negotiation process as just talking to the subject until the tactical team can exercise its entry or shooting skills. They may have forgotten that the court in *Downs v. United States* said that as long as the subject is talking, not threatening to kill or injure hostages or others, the commander is hard pressed to justify an assault (Downs, 1975).

Effective crisis negotiation is the result of a conscious process. Like successful shooting, it requires the participant to follow certain basic concepts and procedures to help ensure success.

An example of this process and its shooting similarities might include:

Shooting	Negotiating
Stance	Containment
Breathing	Time
Grip	Communication
Sight picture	Listening
Trigger squeeze	Rapport
Target	Demands

Containment is crucial. A hostage holder who can move is thinking escape, not negotiate. The tactical team plays a vital role to help the negotiations process by guaranteeing immobility.

Time can work for or against the Crisis Resolution Team. The team must remain conscious of the positive and negative effects of this vital element upon us, our team members, and our adversary.

The two items that are really time sensitive are sunset and the behavioral consequences of a person who has not taken his or her medication. Most other issues like traffic buildup, overtime costs, and such are quite artificial, at least in the eyes of the court. Let it play out.

Communication is a two-way street. While we understand the importance of listening to the hostage taker, are we certain that he can hear and understand us? Is our equipment working?

Listen to the hostage taker ventilate. Separate facts from emotion. Identify and isolate instrumental from expressive demands. Remember that the hostage taker may be "drunk on his hormones." He or she probably sees himself or herself as the real victim and needs to tell his or her story before he or she is ready to come out. Tolerate the silence to draw him or her out to a full expression of needs. People who listen are those who care. Use your secondary and the think tank to assist in this vital function. Remember, a good negotiator is a good listener.

Rapport means trust not manipulation. The courts have said in *United States v. Crosby* and *State v. Sands* that negotiators are not legally bound to tell the truth (*State v. Sands*, 1985; *United States v. Crosby*, 1983). However, lying is not in our best interest. Unless it is necessary to save a life, lying is probably counterproductive. If the negotiator is caught in a lie, he or she loses credibility. Credibility to a negotiator is as important to the negotiations process as the sight picture is to the sniper.

Demands that are realistic usually mean that the hostage taker is not suicidal. However, a well-trained and qualified negotiator knows that he or she must resist the pressure from command to ask the hostage taker for demands. Continued pressure for demands often forces the hostage taker to make up some demands just to satisfy the negotiator. Then the department expends resources unnecessarily. From the beginning, the negotiator should say, "My name is…, I am with the…department, are you OK, or can you tell me what's going on." Not, "What do you want."

We live in a litigious society. One reason we have such an excellent Constitution is that when the United States was founded we had more literate people, college graduates, and attorneys per capita than any other nation in the world. It is often our concern with civil litigation that helps keep us honest. As law enforcement officers we can help limit litigation by keeping ourselves honest in the crisis negotiations process by ensuring that our negotiators are carefully selected and qualified, not just trained in this stressful, psychologically punishing, and very arduous process.

Remember our goal is *the preservation of human life*, not saving money, time, or looking good during an assault.

References

City of Winter Haven v. Allen (1989) 541 So. 2d. 128 (Fla App.).

Downs v. United States (1975) 382. F. Supp. 752.

Moon v. Winfield (1974) 383 F., Supp. 31 (N.D. Ill.).

Pope, A. (1711). *An Essay on Criticism,* London, Lewis.

State v. Sands (1985) 145 Ariz. 269 1369 (Ariz. App.).

Strentz, T. (1997) Understanding Waco and Other Disasters, *Law and Order*, April.

United States v. Crosby (1983) 713 F. 2nd 1066 (5th Circuit).

First Responder Guidelines

4

Life and Crime Scene Analogy to the Crisis Scene First Responder

The common expression, "You have only one chance to make a good first impression" certainly applies to crisis response as well as other law enforcement and correctional crisis situations. There is no substitute for getting off to a good start. In this regard, the use of good judgment is paramount. The purpose of these few pages is to provide some focus to good judgment used by first responders and remind them of common mistakes made with the best of intentions that later impeded the negotiations process.

As any investigator will attest, what those who first respond to a burglary crime scene do or do not do can make or break the case. If those who arrive before an investigator trample on evidence, bump into and break items, or pick up things and misplace them, they are setting the stage for yet another unsolved burglary. I speak from experience. I have arrived at too many crime scenes to find them not the way the subject left them but in a state of shambles from first responders who thought they were doing the right thing.

So it is with first responders to a hostage/barricade/suicide crisis call. If those who arrive early give the subject what he or she wants too quickly, fail to take time to listen, or order the subject around, among other common errors, they are creating unnecessary obstacles for the negotiating team who then must focus on undoing the damage rather than peacefully resolving the crisis.

Three Factors

This brings us to three very important factors that first responders and crisis negotiators must understand and implement to peacefully put an end to the pending pandemonium. Remember, our goal is "The preservation of human life." It is not to save property, money, or time and in so doing jeopardize our primary life-saving objective. Frankly, but in fact, if on-scene commanders understood this priority, then catastrophes, like Waco, Ruby Ridge, and the hijacking that ended in Jacksonville, Florida, known as *Downs v. United States* would not have occurred.

First

Negotiating is a process. It is not a synonym for capitulation. It is an effective form of communication and interaction designed to defuse a difficult and dangerous situation (Dolnik, 2008).

Second

Unlike many law enforcement or correctional encounters, in this case, time is not necessarily of the essence. Now, delay, slowing events, asking questions rather than telling people what to do, listening to what is said and perhaps not said, while recording events is paramount. Basically, but in fact, *listening* is more important than talking. That's right, shut your mouth and open your ears. The subject has a story to tell. Remember, the good Lord gave us one mouth we can close and two ears we cannot. Perhaps this is a not too subtle message from the Almighty about how to best communicate. We learn while and when we listen.

Many years ago, Dr. Harvey Schlosberg, New York Police Department (NYPD), coined the term "dynamic inactivity" (Schlossberg, 1974). In other words, it appears we are doing little when in fact we are listening and gradually taking control of the crisis by assessing the subject and the circumstances. More recently, Gary Noesner, Federal Bureau of Investigation (FBI), reinforced this axiom in his book *Stalling for Time* (Noesner, 2010).

Third

Third, is the mind-set of the subject who usually paints himself or herself as the real victim. This is their twisted sense of reality. In this twisted perception of events, it is not their fault. Psychologists call this projection. Remember, they have a story to tell. It is within this story that we as negotiators identify the factors that can lead to a peaceful resolution or may convince us that a peaceful end may not be an option. Their victim orientation, right or wrong, is their belief. It is the mind-set with which we must deal. This is part of the process known as negotiations. It is not an interrogation. Further, we deal differently with victims than we deal with subjects. In this situation we have a subject who is convinced that he or she is the victim. Therefore, to effectively communicate we must adjust our strategy and responses accordingly.

Our Past Is Our Prologue

Back in the 1980s, two FBI agents, John Dolan of the FBI San Diego Division and Dwayne Fuselier from Quantico, wrote an article entitled "A Guide for

First Responders to Hostage Situations" (Dolan and Fuselier, 1989). Most of what they wrote still applies. What they said then now deserves a review with a few modifications.

The findings of Bill Spaulding of the Prince Georges County Police, also some 20 years ago, remain true today. The first 15 to 45 minutes of a hostage crisis are the most dangerous (Spaulding, 1987). The next most dangerous time is at the 9- or 10-hour mark. Typically, that is when a suicide by cop (SbC) scenario occurs. All too often this SbC includes the injuring of a hostage to force a response from the authorities.

Some Good Guidelines

First responders must remain mindful of their own safety as they attempt to isolate, contain, and evaluate the crisis. Remember, the first responder knows very little and what you have been told may not be correct. Your primary job is to slow things down and obtain information from the subject, not fill him in on current events. "Play dumb." Just because you know some facts does not mean you must relay them to the subject. Take your time to do things well and right.

A *good opening* first responder statement is "My name is… I am with the…department. Is everything under control in there? Has anyone been hurt? In this sequence you are being personal by identifying yourself, professional and authoritative by identifying your department, and concerned with the welfare of everyone. Note I did not use the term "hostages." It is important to focus on the subject. When we ask about those held we should refer to them using humanizing terms like "people," "fellow employees," "customers," or other humanizing nouns like their names. However, just because you know something, like the names of those involved, you need not reveal this information. Good judgment must prevail. When in doubt, say nothing or tell the subject you will find out. In other words, and again, delay.

Legally, all you know is "hearsay." I am not demeaning dispatch. But, the bottom line is what you know you have heard from others. More often than not, what we think we know early in a siege is wrong. All that is typically true during the early minutes is that confusion and miscommunications own the opening.

The subject may ask you questions. You cannot know all the answers. Therefore, a good reply is something like "I don't know, I'll find out and get back to you." In this sequence you are laying the groundwork for delays to come. Another good response is "I was told that…." By using that phrase you are separating yourself from misinformation or a lie.

If someone was shot by the subject he or she may ask about that person's condition. If you know or suspect that person was transported to the hospital a good response is something like, "All I know is he or she is at the hospital and a lot of people are working on him or her." Basically, that is an answer that says nothing. Do not assume they did not want to kill someone or more commonly fired at random. Again, you cannot know everything. Saying you do not know something because you are occupied talking with the subject sets the stage for future questions and focuses on the subject. The subject wants this to be his or her show so we initially play along and then gradually take control.

Avoid telling a lie. When one is caught in a lie, credibility is lost. Credibility to a negotiator is as important as a sight picture to a sniper. Be vague in your response or admit you do not know but will try to find out.

Avoid saying no. Avoid this even if the subject asks for something you suspect will not be delivered. A good response is, "I understand what you are saying. I will check on that and get back to you." Be sure to get back to the person even if it is only to say no one has gotten back to you. Again, you are laying the foundation for stalling for time.

Soften stuff. If the subject asks for $50,000 in the next 15 minutes, a good response is "As I understand it, you want a lot of money fast. I will get back to you on that." Avoid beating an expression like, "we are working on that" or "I will get back to you on that" to death. Come up with similar delaying statements like "I asked someone to do that and was also wondering what was taking so long," or "That is a good question that I thought I asked them a long time ago. I will check on it for you."

Deadlines can be crucial. We used to say "Never set a deadline on yourself." We now understand that in some cases we can use self-imposed deadlines to build credibility. An example is "I will call you back in 10 minutes." Watch the clock and call back before 10 minutes are up. In the United States, we have had one hostage killed at a deadline back in June 1981.

Avoid using nonlaw enforcement or noncorrectional negotiators. They may have good intelligence on the scene or subject. However, when we allow them to contact the subject we lose control. Keep them around for the negotiating team to debrief and evaluate. Typically, pastors and priests share our goal of the preservation of human life; relatives, reporters, inmates, and politicians may have their own agendas and priorities.

Do not allow an exchange of hostages or weapons and do not exchange yourself for a hostage. In any setting and in the mind of most hostage takers, an officer is a more valuable hostage than a relative, fellow employee, inmate, or stranger. Further, unless you wanted to take revenge on the authorities, would you want to exchange a civilian for an officer? We have had situations where, with the best of intentions, a negotiator put down a weapon in exchange for the subject doing the same only to have the subject retrieve the officer's weapon leaving his empty pistol in its place.

On that point, we can *talk about anything.* If a subject says something outlandish we can respond saying, "I never thought of it that way before."

When it comes to demands remember talking about them does not obligate a delivery. As negotiators we can discuss anything. Decisions on delivery are above our pay grade. We can easily blame confusion or a misunderstanding for the delay or indecision.

If you suspect the person is *suicidal,* they probably are. Therefore ask the difficult question. "Are you thinking about killing yourself?" Mental health professionals have assured us that asking this question will not implant the idea or initiate the act. It does tell the subject that you are sensitive to his or her situation and understand his or her stress. Further, recent research has shown that hostage sieges account for less than 10 percent of negotiator calls while suicide calls are approaching 30 percent.

Finally, early and often you should make it clear to the subject that coming out is an option. Remember, you may not be dealing with a genius. I would avoid using the term "surrender." To complicate matters, *Roget's Thesaurus* has very few, if any, nice synonyms for "surrender." "Throwing in the towel" comes to mind or saying something neutral like "walking out" or "folding your tent" does not necessarily imply failure.

One statement that often works is "You know the longer this situation goes on the more likely it is that someone will be hurt and then the courts will blame you." This plays into their defense mechanism of projection and helps encourage an early exit.

It is not the intent of these few pages to turn every first responder into an accomplished crisis negotiator. However, by following these guidelines the first responder can help ensure a peaceful resolution to a potentially deadly encounter.

References

Dolan, J. T., and Fuselier, G. D. (1989) A Guide for First Responders to Hostage Situations, *FBI Law Enforcement Bulletin*, April.

Dolnik, A. (2008) *Negotiating Hostage Crisis with the New Terrorists*, Prager Security International, London.

Noesner, G. (2010) *Stalling for Time*, Random House, New York.

Schlossberg, H. (1974) *Psychologist with a Gun*, Coward, McCann, and Geoghean, New York.

Spalding, W. G. (1987) The Longest Hour: The First Response to Terrorist Incidents, *Law Enforcement Technology*, July–August.

Strentz, T. (2011) First Responder, *Crisis Negotiator*, Summer, Vol. 12, No. 3, pp. 6–9.

Non-Law Enforcement/
Correctional Crisis
Negotiators

5

The Role of Third-Party Intermediaries

The process of negotiating, that of listening, gathering intelligence, evaluating, planning, and talking rather than waiting and attacking, has proven very successful (HOBAS, 2011; Noesner, 2010) We have learned that the crisis intervention process is more successful if we wait and talk rather than react and retaliate (Noesner, 2010). In hostage and other crisis situations, success is defined as saving the greatest number of human lives as possible (Schlossberg, 1980).

Even in those situations when a dynamic entry and rescue are inevitable, the process of talking with the hostage holder ensures the gathering of intelligence and passage of time (Strentz, 1991). During this interim, the assault team can prepare. The commander can gather and use additional intelligence to help achieve a safe and successful solution while saving the lives of the entry team. Why more on-scene commanders do not understand this logic lies beyond my comprehension.

One way or another, through protracted negotiations or a rescue, the authorities must gain and maintain *control* of the crisis. To achieve control we diminish outside access to the hostage taker, limit his or her options and access to information, and lower the level of stress experienced by the authorities. As the stress level lowers, the commander and others can make more reasonable decisions that will help ensure the success of the operation. Remember the axiom that as emotion diminishes, reason and logic increase.

The crisis/hostage negotiator plays an integral role in this process. He or she is in the best position to measure the current emotional state of the hostage holder (subject) and determine his or her propensity for violence and report these indicators in a Negotiation Position Paper (Dalfonzo and Romano, 2003). One of the best ways to evaluate the subject is to *listen* to his or her rhetoric and tone of voice. We must remember that in some cultures high volume and animated speech may indicate anger while in others it may not (Fuselier, Van Zandt, and Lanceley, 1989).

We in law enforcement and corrections tend to rely too heavily on our sense of sight. We train and learn early to read body language (Strentz, 1977). This method of evaluating people serves us well on the street or cell block. When we are limited to listening, our other senses do not serve us as well because they are not as well trained and exercised. Therefore, we must practice and train to listen more carefully.

To Whom Are We Listening?

To negotiate effectively, every negotiator must carefully and attentively listen the subject and respond to his or her expressed, as well as implied, demands (Strentz, 1991, 1995). The negotiator must know, understand, and communicate via a position paper what the subject is *really* saying.

When one is negotiating through a third party, such as an interpreter, one must remember that he or she is *listening to the interpreter not the hostage taker*. Much may be, and has been, lost or misinterpreted in its translation. Even a well-trained, well-intentioned, and necessary intermediary can cause crisis counselors and hostage negotiators *serious* problems. Even in the very best of circumstances, some filtering of phrases, statements, and real intent takes place.

Legendary Linguistic Lapses

To illustrate this point, a few examples of historically embarrassing and catastrophic mistranslations are in order.

When Chevrolet introduced the Nova into Spanish-speaking countries, they learned that in Spanish *nova* means "no go." Their sales were adversely affected (Eisiminger, 1989).

Peugeot had to change the name of their "strangler knob" to *choke*. Many remember the humiliating error of President Carter's interpreter when in 1977 he translated "I want to know more about the Polish people" into "I desire the Polish people carnally." When the *Living Bible* was published in 1971, many claimed it was anti-Semitic. One example in the King James Version of Galatians 5:1 reads, "stand fast and do not submit again to a yoke of slavery." The *Living Bible* says, "Now make sure you stay free and don't get all tied up again in the chains of slavery to Jewish laws and their ceremonies" (Eisiminger, 1989). From my youth I recall mention of the sinful *Bible*. It was a 1600s translation that listed the sixth commandment as "Thou shalt commit adultery."

The most catastrophic example of a misinterpretation may have occurred in July 1945. That summer, after the fall of Nazi Germany, the Allies met in Potsdam, outside Berlin, to settle among themselves the terms for the surrender of the Japanese. Their conditions were transmitted to Japan. The Japanese cabinet did not like the terms of the agreement. They recognized that they were losing the war and the terms could have been much stiffer. They *did not vote* to reject the terms dictated by Truman, Churchill, and Stalin. The cabinet chose a middle ground and stated that it was holding an attitude of "mokusatsu." This meant that no decision had been made. They were deliberately cautious.

Tragically, the Domein News Agency, the voice of the government of Japan in 1945 as *Tass* was for the Soviet Union during the Cold War, translated "mokusatsu" as "ignore." The Allies listened and were disappointed at this rejection. Less than a month later, on August 6, 1945, President Truman announced the first atomic attack and cited the Japanese rejection of the "Potsdam terms" as his justification for the bombing (Eisiminger, 1989).

Actually, *mokusatsu* is an ambiguous word. It may mean "to withhold comment" or "to ignore." It seems that one badly chosen word and its interpretation may be responsible for the combined catastrophes for the Japanese at Hiroshima and Nagasaki (Eisiminger, 1989).

On the contrary, when the former astronaut, now Senator John Glenn of Ohio, visited Japan he spoke to a group of students. They asked him what he found on the moon. In an attempt at humor he said he "found no cheese." To translate the U.S. cultural fable of the moon being made of cheese, the interpreter, knowing the culture of Japan, said that "there were no rabbits on the moon." In Japan children are told that the moon is inhabited by rabbits as evidenced by the lop-eared rabbit outline formed by the moon's craters (Caplan, 1994).

Potential Problems

Within most languages there are many dialects and different meanings for the same word. To an Australian a *rubber* is an eraser, a *Sheila* is a female, and *tucker* is food. Further, no self-respecting Christian Australian female would root for the home team. By so doing she would be violating the sixth commandment. Similarly, within the Spanish language there are class, cultural, and national differences in certain meanings. The interpreter must know the culture as well as the language. If a Cuban uses the word *caballo*, he or she may intend a compliment, meaning the person is big as a horse, a super person. A Puerto Rican could believe he or she is being called a "horse's ass." Similarly, the term *bicho*, could be understood as talking about an insect in one culture or a penis in another. (I will leave you to speculate on the origin of the confusion between insect and penis.)

Those who do not learn from their history are condemned to repeat it (Santayana, 1905). Crisis negotiators must learn from these actual and potential misinterpretations and correct cross-cultural communications. We must double-check our interpretation before we make assumptions about the meaning and intent of our adversary in a crisis. The goal of all involved will be best served by a peaceful termination from which all of us can walk away and live to see another day.

Time Is on Our Side

Every trained negotiator understands that in most crisis situations, time, when we let it, works for us (Noesner, 2010). The use of interpreters will automatically increase the amount of time taken to communicate. One should remember the amount of time taken during a crisis to gain a successful solution will pale in comparison to the time required at hearings, inquests, and wakes when one moves too quickly. The saying, "A moment of passion may mean a lifetime of regret," comes to mind.

As valuable as it is to gain time, we must use time we earn by engaging in effective problem solving with the hostage holder or just listening to him or her talk. Remember, we learn when we listen. To do this we must be certain that we are communicating effectively and accurately. It is important to remember that the hostage taker may not hear all of our words. Therefore, the tone of our voices or the third-party's voice must convey our concern.

Typical Third-Party Problems

Usually, and most effectively, law enforcement and corrections use their own trained multilingual staff as negotiators. This helps maintain complete control of the crisis. Third-party, or nonpolice, negotiators can create more serious troubles than those they were selected to correct. When we pass the telephone to a nonpolice person like a parent, priest, peer, politician, or reporter, we lose some control. There may be times when a third party, like an interpreter, is necessary. We must recognize that the use of this person entails certain, and sometimes serious, risks. We must assess the situation and determine if the risk, this deviation from usual practice, is worth taking (Birge and Strentz, 1995). Will the use of a third party help ensure the preservation of human life? If so, what can we do to ensure that this third party can and will help us work toward our goal?

In the early 1970s, when the FBI began its hostage negotiator training programs, we recognized problems inherent in the use of translators and other third parties in this process.

These problems include:

1. There may be social class differences, dialects, and accents that create additional problems between the translator and the hostage holder. Not all Puerto Ricans like people who speak Spanish with a Cuban, Mexican, or Colombian accent, and vice versa. A very good interpreter can overcome this problem.

2. They may not be proficient in the language or dialect of the hostage taker. We must verify their proficiency prior to the crisis. Not everyone from South of the Border or Southeast Asia speaks the same language or shares the same cultural values. Certainly, one would not use a Croatian to negotiate with a Serbian just because they may speak the same Slavic language.

3. Under stress they may revert to comfortable behavior. A priest or psychiatrist, while translating for the negotiator, may focus on the soul or the psyche of the subject rather than the goal of the police.

4. The hostage holder's view of the person may be one of antagonism. He or she may not like priests or psychiatrists.

5. They may not be accustomed to violence. Unlike police and correctional staff, most people do not live or work in a violent world.

6. They may not be accustomed to talking with criminals. The majority of citizens are not victims of crime and never see the inside of a police station and certainly not a prison.

7. Their participation in a police tactical maneuver could jeopardize the entire operation. How much must they know to help? Will too much information scare them? What are the legal constraints and considerations?

8. If face-to-face negotiations are necessary, the presence of nonpolice personnel may endanger the lives of all involved. How will they react to the stress of a face-to-face meeting?

9. Control is jeopardized when we pass the phone to another.

10. Is their agenda the same as ours? Do they intend to save lives or are they more interested in revenge, ventilation, publicity, or some other political or personal goal?

Some Simple Solutions

In the early 1970s, our first solution was to train FBI interpreters, usually nonagent personnel, in a short course of hostage negotiations. As FBI interpreters they were identified with law enforcement. We added to this foundation the aims, tactics, and goals of crisis negotiations. It was our intent they fully understand the goals of the FBI at the macro level while they worked with the negotiators at the micro level. This was a stopgap measure. It was designed to fill a need while we searched for special agents who, in addition to having the qualities necessary to negotiate, possessed the language skills to communicate with the variety of ethnic and linguistic groups in our nation (Birge and Birge, 1994; Strentz, 1996). This goal was eventually achieved. Today, the FBI is much more effective in its negotiations endeavors for having multilingual crisis negotiators in its ranks.

An option is to force the subject to speak your language. This may not be immediately preferable to him or her. It was done at the Princes' Gate Iranian Embassy Siege in London during the spring of 1980. At this crisis the police initially used an interpreter. The interpreter was a female whom the subjects, Middle-Eastern men, did not respect (Brock et al., 1980).

As previously stated, the best option is to have sworn law enforcement officers and correctional staff who know the language and culture of the subject and who are also trained as negotiators. Perhaps the most compelling argument for the translator to be one of us is the potential need for their participation in face-to-face or other tactical maneuvers (Strentz, 1995a). Can a civilian be used effectively in this capacity? If so, what are the legal ramifications?

The fourth option is the most common. It is exemplified by the London siege. That is the use of an interpreter who knows the language but may not fully appreciate the culture or the social class of the subjects. He or she may be demeaned by the subjects and may not have been trained by the police in the process of negotiations.

Professional Models

For decades police have used professionals to assist in complex investigations. To help establish premeditation, archaeologists have assisted in the exhumation of bodies and have testified to the amount of time it would have taken the subject to dig a grave. Anthropologists have identified bodies from bones. Dentists have assisted in the processing of crime scenes that required plaster impressions of unusual and difficult markings. Physicians have assisted in many assault, homicide, and rape investigations.

One professional with whom most police and correctional staff have had the greatest amount of contact is their psychologist. Not long ago this psychologist was limited to family and personal counseling. Today, that role has expanded into teaching, selection, profiling, and assisting the crisis management team and the negotiator. Law enforcement and corrections gradually got to know their psychologist. One product of our familiarity was trust and their gradual movement from support into operational roles (Havassy, 1994; Reese, 1987).

A similar model can be applied to the interpreter. Just as police and correctional staff know and have worked with their psychologist they call to assist in a crisis, so should they have previous professional contact with an interpreter. Those used during negotiations should have worked with us during routine interviews, investigations, and interrogations. To help gather intelligence during a hostage crisis, interpreters can assist us in their interviews of friends and relatives of the subject or hostages.

Law enforcement and corrections should use two interpreters during a hostage or crisis siege. This will allow them to verify meanings among themselves and provide simultaneous translations. While one is carefully listening to what the subject is saying the other can give the negotiator, the commander, and others an ongoing thumbnail sketch of what is being communicated.

Prior to their use during a hostage crisis, interpreters and other third-party negotiators should have some training in the process of negotiations. They should be alert for the danger signals, how to avoid saying no, and how to understand the meaning of various psychological shifts that may occur and communicate this to the primary negotiator (Strentz, 1991, 1995).

Also, prior to beginning work in a crisis, the interpreter should have a complete briefing and be given updates as new information becomes available to the crisis management team. *The interpreter must work as an integral part of the negotiating team.* Tactics and strategies being considered by the team should be discussed with the interpreter to guarantee his or her understanding and assurance that the ploy will work cross-culturally.

Control of Non-Law Enforcement/Correctional Interpreters

Interpreting is not just talking in two languages. The interpreter's brain, like that of the negotiator, is engaged in more tasks than that of an individual involved in a normal conversation.

In addition to engaging in the complex process of crisis negotiations, the interpreter is constantly shifting back and forth between cultures and languages. *This process requires a very high degree of concentration that should not be interrupted.*

Questions of the interpreter who is negotiating should be directed to the secondary interpreter or other negotiator. It is very difficult for an interpreter to tune out background noise. Complete quiet is paramount.

During negotiations, interpreters must concentrate on concepts rather than words. Words by themselves in colloquial use may vary in meaning from country to country, culture to culture, and class to class. Crisis negotiators must remember that plays on words, jokes, rhymes, slang, and cultural sayings may not translate.

Finally, nonpolice and noncorrectional staff interpreters are not negotiators. Their job is to assist the negotiator in his or her effort to communicate. As soon as we pass the phone to another person, a degree of control is lost. The basic consideration in negotiations is to ensure the preservation of life by gaining and maintaining control of the crisis. We exchange items for promises or hostages to strengthen our control of the crisis. We restrict information given to or received by the subject because knowledge is power and power means control. We can more accurately predict what the subject will do when we as negotiators speak with and listen to the subject. We listen to the subject's breathing, silences, what is not said, and how the subject phrases his or her statements. When a third party is involved, we may not accurately hear; not hearing, we cannot evaluate these indicators. When a third party is used, an element of control is sacrificed to improve communications. Negotiators must weigh the value of closer control versus more correct communications.

The Interpreter Cannot Be Allowed to Improvise

The conversation, meaning, and tone of the exchange must be monitored and controlled by the primary negotiator, with the assistance of a second interpreter. Like a good negotiator, the interpreter should be guided into making small talk with the subject. It is during these conversations that we gain intelligence, develop rapport, psychologically disarm, and emotionally defuse the subject. Interpreters, like the rest of us, are subject to the Stockholm Syndrome. The second interpreter can help prevent or at least control this transformation.

Because of the issues mentioned above that can exacerbate a hostage crisis, the interpreter used by us should be known by us and should feel comfortable working with the negotiator and the negotiations team. In this capacity, the interpreter becomes familiar with our terms and can better translate them. In a Spanish version of a U.S. book on crime scene investigations that was translated by a person not familiar with law enforcement, the term "search and seizure" was translated as "watch out for convulsions." In the best of situations, the use of an interpreter will create additional difficulties in the hostage crisis. Because of the need to clarify and correctly translate words, phrases, meanings, and emotions, the process will take longer. This may take twice as long as regular conversation. How much time are we prepared to invest to save a human life?

Like other members of the crisis negotiating team, the translators should be included in the postcritical incident debrief process. In this process they can assist others in their cross-cultural understanding of what occurred as well as ensure their own continued and sound mental health.

Third-Party Intermediators Do Not Guarantee Success

The fall of 1995 experience of the Royal Canadian Mounted Police (RCMP) at Gustafson Lake in British Columbia and the FBI in Montana raises another issue. What about intermediators? Outside intermediators have been used with marginal success over the years in prisons and with terrorists. Generally their role is to convince the hostage holders that they can rely on the authorities to keep their word.

At the state prison in Huntsville, Texas, the third-party intermediary, Father O'Brien, was taken hostage by the inmates. During the Iranian Embassy siege, a local Mullah was brought in by Scotland Yard. He was ineffective. During the federal prison riot in Atlanta, a Roman Catholic Bishop, Augustine Roman, was very useful (Fuselier, Van Zandt, and Lanceley, 1989). Paul Harvey, via his radio broadcast, is credited by many with convincing Randy Weaver to trust the FBI and surrender at Ruby Ridge, Idaho, in August 1992. He succeeded where the Iowa relatives of Weaver and his wife failed (Walter, 1995). At Waco, Texas, the FBI used local defense attorneys to no avail.

Dr. Webster said that most of the third parties the RCMP used to convince the native American Indians and others to capitulate at Gustafson Lake were effective. Some had their own agendas and made matters worse. However, in the long run, the majority held sway and the Indians surrendered (Webster, 1996).

During the spring of 1996 in Montana the FBI relied heavily on third parties, mostly conservative politicians, to convince the "Freemen" to trust the government and capitulate. Many of these third parties left in disgust with the recommendation that the FBI assault. After 83 days reason prevailed and the fugitives surrendered without firing a shot.

One advantage to using third parties is that they consume additional time, fatigue the fugitives, and give credibility to our efforts. By their use, successful or not, we will at least have tried. We can claim in court to have made a reasonable effort to resolve the siege without the loss of life. That was the message from the court in *Downs v. United States*. We must make a reasonable effort to communicate or negotiate before initiating an assault.

The courts have made it clear that we must try, make a reasonable effort, to negotiate a peaceful settlement. They have not ordered us to succeed. The careful use of third-party intermediaries is another way of attempting to peacefully resolve a siege. Given the publicity and seeming success of this strategy in Montana, we can be certain that the courts will expect future crisis managers to consider this tactic.

Conclusion

The use of intermediators and third-party negotiators, like interpreters, during a hostage crisis may be necessary. However, it is a potentially dangerous tactic. Crisis management teams must maintain control and should plan ahead. We should think long and hard before we partake of this option. In the best of all worlds, police or correctional staff negotiators are trusted by hostage holders and are fluent in every language and comfortable in every culture in their community.

We must plan ahead for when our credibility is questioned or a language resource is not available, and we should identify appropriate third parties in advance of a crisis and include them in our training. Whenever possible those candidates with language skills should be used in more mundane assignments. Their personal and professional potential for use in a crisis should be evaluated during training scenarios and routine assignments. This type of preparation and screening will help us to achieve our goal of the preservation of human life, even when we must deviate from our established guidelines and procedures (Birge and Strentz, 1995). Properly identified, trained, briefed, and used, this intermediary will help us achieve our goal of the preservation of human life.

References

Birge, A. C., and Birge, R. (1994) Crisis Negotiators: Personnel Selection, *U.S. Negotiator,* Winter, pp. 5–7.

Birge, R., and Strentz, T. (1995) Procedures for Deviating from Established Crisis Negotiation Guidelines, *The U.S. Negotiator*, Summer.

Brock, G., Lustig, R., Marks, L., Parker, R., Seal, S., and McConville, M. (1980) *Siege: Six Days at the Iranian Embassy,* Macmillan, London.

Caplan, N. (1994) Personal communication, San Diego Police Department.

Coates, J. (1995) *Armed and Dangerous*, Hill and Wang, New York.

Dalfonzo, V. A., and Romano, S. J. (2003) Negotiation Position Papers: A Tool for Crisis Negotiators, *FBI Law Enforcement Bulletin*, October.

Eisiminger, S. (1989) The Consequences of Mistranslation, *Translation Review*, pp. 47–49.

Fuselier, D., Van Zandt, C. R., and Lanceley, F. J. (1989) Negotiating the Protracted Incident, *FBI Law Enforcement Bulletin*, July.

Havassy, V. (1994) The Psychologist as Part of the Negotiating Team, Unpublished, Psychological Resources, Los Angeles, California.

HOBAS (2011) Federal Bureau of Investigation, *Hostage Barricade Database System*, Quantico, Virginia.

Noesner, G. (2010) *Stalling for Time*, Random House, New York.

Reese, J. T. (1987) *A History of Police Psychological Services.* U.S. Government Printing Office, Washington, DC.

Santayana, G. (1905) John Bartlett, *Book of Familiar Quotations*. Little, Brown and Company, Boston, 1960, p. 703.

Schlossberg, H. (1980) Crisis Negotiation Teams, *Annals of the New York Academy of Sciences,* Vol. 347, pp. 113–116.

Strentz, T. (1977) Proxemics and the Interview, *The Police Chief,* Vol. 42, pp. 74–76.

Strentz, T. (1991) Thirteen Indicators of Volatile Negotiations, *Law and Order.* September, pp. 135–139.

Strentz, T. (1995) The Cyclic Crisis Negotiations Time Line, *Law and Order.* March, pp .

Strentz, T. (1995a) To Face or Not to Face, *The U.S. Negotiator*, 1994 The Year in Review Special Edition.

Strentz, T., and Barzelatto, V. (1996) Negotiating with Extremists, *Law & Order,* October, pp. 169–178.

Walter, J. (1995) *Every Knee Shall Bow*, Regan Books, New York.

Webster, M. (1996) Gustafson Lake Siege, California Association of Hostage Negotiators Annual Training Center, San Diego, California, June 2.

The Crisis Negotiation Team

6

Introduction

Over a quarter of a century ago, in September 1971, the riots, hostage siege, and assault that claimed many lives of inmates and staff at the Attica Prison in New York occurred. The next September, the "Massacre at Munich" resonated around the Western world as it "proclaimed the 'disenfranchised'" of the Arab community and yet undeveloped world. Correctional institutions and police departments across Europe and from the United States to Australia responded by developing an array of crisis response philosophies and team structures.

At that time, I was a member of the Federal Bureau of Investigation's (FBI) Special Operations Unit at our academy. We ran a symposium at which Dr. Manfried Schreiber, the German Police Commander at Munich during the siege, gave a presentation featuring the incident. His official title was President of Police, Munich, Republic of West Germany. In this capacity he was the incident commander, the special weapons and tactics (SWAT) commander, and the negotiator. This situation, or more accurately the conglomeration of conflicting roles, he was in was identical to that played a year before in Jacksonville, Florida, by the Assistant Special Agent in Charge (ASAC) of that FBI response. By his admission, he was wearing too many hats and had not been trained for an event of this magnitude, and there was no one else to call on for advice or assistance. Within a few years, in the fall of 1977, the German three-tiered approach was outstanding as was proven by their response to the hijacking of Lufthansa Flight 181, a passenger plane in Mogadishu, Somalia. During that protracted incident, one team negotiated with the terrorists while the tactical element practiced and prepared. The efforts of both teams were coordinated and directed by a well-trained on-scene commander. The result was the rescue of all passengers and crew, the terrorists killed or captured, and no injury to GSG-9 operators. This success was not replicated until the Scotland Yard and Special Air Service (SAS) siege some 3 years later in London. This was another example of the tactical use of the invaluable information gathered by negotiators that enabled the tactical team to more effectively complete its mission. As a negotiator, I still wonder when our tactical brothers will get the message that we can help them in the safe and successful completion of our mission.

Figure 6.1 Negotiators always work as a team.

Figure 6.2 The team consists of many roles, including intelligence and primary and secondary negotiators.

Figure 6.3 It is the team leader's responsibility to control the number of people on site.

The Team Concept

The State of New York and the Republic of West Germany faced crises from which we all learned. Like the police in Munich, we in the rest of the civilized world share the goal of the *preservation of human life*. To further this goal, the idea of using a team concept and response to professionally and effectively respond to and manage a hostage crisis occurred to many departments. But not everyone listening to Dr. Schreiber's message came to the same conclusion about how many and what types of teams were necessary. All too many departments still give one person too many jobs or field a response with too few or poorly trained teams or untrained crisis incident commanders.

Most departments saw the need for a SWAT team and trained accordingly. In 1974, the FBI initiated an Anti-Sniper Survival Training (ASST) program that trained agencies from around the country in SWAT procedures. The SWAT team concept was so popular that many departments that individually lacked the manpower to field a finely tuned team, entered into mutual aid pacts with neighboring departments. Regional SWAT teams began to emerge and became the model. This concept, though it looked good

Figure 6.4 The team member called the chronographer keeps a current chart of activities.

on paper, was a disaster waiting to happen. Officers from many departments left our academy at Quantico as a finely tuned team. However, the fact is they had time-sensitive and perishable skills. Once back home, they were not afforded the opportunity to train as a team. Thus their collective expertise existed only on paper. The lack of follow-up training in each community caused the FBI to discontinue this program. Common sense, the FBI Office of Legal Counsel, The Range, and The Crisis Negotiations Unit agreed that these were very perishable skills.

Many institutions and police departments also engaged in hostage crisis management training. They soon learned that with some slight modifications, the management skills needed to coordinate the response to a major incident, such as the closing down of a major thoroughfare during rush hour, were similar to those required to manage a hostage crisis. In spite of this similarity, uniformity of training of on-scene commanders remains the major weakness in crisis response.

Unfortunately, the training of on-scene crisis commanders remains the weak link in crisis response. Too many commanders are chosen by geography or shift assignment rather than their crisis management training or skills. This was one of the problems in the FBI response at Ruby Ridge, Idaho, and Waco, Texas.

The third major component of law enforcement crisis response, the Crisis Incident Negotiations Team (CINT), was either overlooked or was considered unnecessary in many departments. Most department "teams" consisted of one person who was designated the negotiator.

The problem was then, and remains today, that all too many departments have not recognized that a crisis negotiator, like the tactical response and command staff, must work as a member of a team. One negotiator versus one hostage holder, barricaded gunman, suicidal subject, or otherwise deranged person, is a setup that stacks the deck against success and courts death and disaster, along with a civil lawsuit. The FBI learned this lesson in Jacksonville, Florida, in 1971—how many times must local law enforcement and corrections learn this locally?

The court, in *Downs v. United States* in 1975, and at Ruby Ridge where Randy Weaver settled out of court for over $3 million in 1993, has made it clear to law enforcement that to ensure the preservation of human life, a reasonable attempt at negotiations must be made prior to a tactical intervention (*Downs v. United States*, 1975; Ostrow, 1995). Note the court said a "reasonable attempt." They did not order negotiators to succeed only to make a reasonable attempt. In the *Downs* case, a few minutes of negotiations was not considered a reasonable attempt. How many times must we learn this lesson?

Downs v. United States

For those unfamiliar with this case and for others who think they know what happened let me digress. The facts set forth below were learned from Andrew Downs, the son of the pilot who was murdered by George Giffe during a hijacking. Andy Downs, after some 40 years of trying, was able to gain access to sealed documents and audiotapes of the 1971 incident. Thanks to Downs, Southwest Texas State University is now the repository for these documents and tapes (Downs, 2011).

The *Downs v. United States* decision remains the foundation case for crisis negotiations in the United States. It involved the hijacking of a private aircraft. On October 3, 1971, George Giffe arranged for a charter flight from Nashville, Tennessee, to Atlanta, Georgia. He said he wanted to depart at 0100 on October 4. Prior to departure he came to the airport with luggage and paid for the flight. At approximately 0130 he arrived with his wife, Susan Giffe, and Bobby Wayne Wallace. As the three of them approached the aircraft Susan Giffe began screaming. George Giffe told bystanders she was a mental patient and he was her doctor taking her to Atlanta for treatment. The pilot, Brent Q. Downs, asked for verification of the story. Giffe produced a pistol, claimed he had a bomb, and forced the pilot to take off. Ground crew notified the tower of the hijacking and thus the FBI.

En route Giffe changed his destination to Freeport, Bahamas. The pilot told Giffe he would refuel in Jacksonville, Florida. The pilot called ahead to Jacksonville to advise them of the situation and told them he needed charts, fuel, and flotation gear. He expected to arrive at 0500.

The Jacksonville FBI was notified. Based on a prearranged FBI/Federal Aviation Administration (FAA) plan in place at all airports, FBI agents and FAA personnel were dispatched and on scene well before the aircraft arrived. By this time, FBI agents in Nashville learned and passed on to agents in Jacksonville, that George Giffe and Bobby Wayne Wallace had kidnapped Mrs. Giffe as she left work the previous evening. It was also learned they were estranged and had a history of marital discord.

The aircraft landed at approximately 0508 and was directed to an area of the field near the Air Kaman hangar. At approximately 0513, it stopped there. FBI agents were positioned around the aircraft. The pilot advised the tower that Giffe and his friend Bobby Wayne Wallace were armed with handguns. In addition, Giffe claimed to have over 12 pounds of plastic explosive in his luggage. The pilot advised the tower, and thus the FBI, of the weapons and said he needed charts, fuel, and flotation gear. He also advised that he was down to about 30 minutes of fuel.

To clarify the FBI actions, it was then and remains our policy to keep a hijacked aircraft on the ground. From the very beginning, the FBI and FAA feared what eventually happened on September 11, 2001. The policy is strategic, not tactical. It does not specify how this should be accomplished because such actions are situation specific.

J. J. O'Connor the Assistant Special Agent in Charge of the Jacksonville Division of the FBI was the on-scene commander, the face-to-face negotiator, and the director of the tactical response. He ordered the pilot to turn off both engines. At 0521, O'Connor told his agents they would play a waiting game. The pilot shut down the left engine so copilot Ronald Crump could exit the aircraft to press for fuel. Crump advised the FBI that the hijacker was drinking and in his inebriated state might shoot the pilot. He verified the earlier statement of the pilot that now the aircraft had about 20 minutes of fuel. He was not further debriefed. His statement that Giffe had explosives was considered by O'Connor as "A bunch of malarkey." A few minutes later, Wallace exited the aircraft to bargain for fuel. He was disarmed and taken into custody. He was not debriefed.

Basically, the sum and substance of approximately 6 minutes of the waiting game that included "negotiations" was "I want fuel" versus "you ain't getting any."

At this point, 0527, when the fuel level was down to about 16 minutes, the 6-minute waiting game of O'Connor ended by his ordering agents to shoot at and deflate the tires of the plane. I think most people know that flat tires will not prevent an aircraft from taking off. However, flat tires will make landing a challenge for the most experienced pilot.

Additional rounds were fired at the still running right engine. Shots then were heard from inside the plane. O'Connor, who had been negotiating face-to-face approached and opened the door of the aircraft. He found the pilot Downs dead in his seat, Mrs. Giffe dead on the floor, and George Giffe fatally wounded.

The total number of rounds that hit, versus those fired at, the aircraft is unknown. However, the over-wing two-engine Turbo Hawk Commander 681 was deemed beyond repair and today sits in the hanger of a local technical school that teaches avionics.

Mrs. Downs sued the FBI and won on appeal. It was the first successful civil suit ever won against the FBI. The second and last one to date involved Randy Weaver in Idaho. Both cases involved limited negotiations and a very aggressive, some say an overly aggressive, tactical response.

The court said the initial waiting game in Jacksonville resulted in *two people* exiting the aircraft. *After* the FBI began shooting *three people died*. The court said the better alternative to protect human lives was disregarded. The more reasonable attempt was too quickly abandoned.

Obviously, there are many ways to prevent an aircraft from taking off, especially one with less than 16 minutes of remaining fuel, than shooting at the aircraft, its engines, and its tires.

The Process of Crisis Negotiations

According to the court, a reasonable attempt includes the negotiating team *taking the time* to help the hostage taker past the present psychological crisis and into a less emotional mind-set that includes walking away from the scene rather than causing unnecessary injury, death, and destruction. To help achieve the goal of the preservation of human life, the negotiating team will be more effective if they work as if they are being *paid by the hour not by the job.*

I designed, developed, and directed the FBI Crisis Negotiations program at our Academy from the mid-1970s until the late 1980s. For the last quarter of a century, the FBI (along with friends at the New York, San Francisco, and many other police departments) recognized and taught the need for a crisis incident negotiations team. I take small comfort in the fact that I am not alone in my frustration over the reluctance of many departments and correctional institutions to consider fielding a CINT. Even though luminaries like Frank Bolz, Harvey Schlossberg, and others have stressed the need for a team response by negotiators, our message still falls on too many deaf ears. I regularly talk with Bolz, who, like me, continues to teach crisis negotiations around the country. Both of us conduct all too many classes to which departments send a one-person negotiation team.

I question the motives, mind-set, and thought processes that create and follow a one-person response model. These departments have multiperson

SWAT teams, and many have a set SWAT team command structure, yet have only one negotiator. Have they made the assumption that the job of the negotiator is only to talk while the tactical team takes up position to assault, or shoot? Do they believe it costs less to select, train, and equip a SWAT team than to field a negotiation team? I am at a loss to explain their rationale, because they are *wrong*, sometimes *dead wrong*, in their assumptions. Like the tactical response, the negotiation response requires a team.

The negotiations team must work closely with the tactical element of the department's response to ensure a well-orchestrated delivery of items, release of hostages, surrender of the subject, or safe entry for the tactical team.

Despite our slow start, the CINT concept has been implemented in several variations by a growing number of departments. Some agencies have arrangements with neighboring jurisdictions to provide special skills to their team, such as psychologists, and many share intelligence functions. Further, the California Association of Hostage Negotiators (CAHN), other similar associations in Louisiana, Arkansas, Texas, the Pacific Northwest, and others around the country provide regular training for their members. Negotiators *can and must* sharpen their team and individual skills on a regular basis. Unlike a tactical team, negotiators can practice some of their individual skills on a daily basis each time they interview a person, or deal with their kids, spouse, or boss. However, team training is necessary to keep honed this very perishable skill.

Team Structure

Ideally, an agency's CINT should consist of about 11 positions or jobs, with several variations on the actual number of people per team. This means there may be 11 jobs. However, some of the responsibilities listed below overlap. In some cases one person can perform more than one job. Other responsibilities can be carried out by several persons. There are over 150 tasks that must be completed by a negotiations team during a siege (Birge, 2002). Logically, these 150 tasks require more than one person.

I wish I could identify the date when the FBI and other agencies made the move from individual negotiators to a team structure. Unfortunately, I cannot. Each negotiator I question and every agency I contact comes up with the same answer. The team concept developed out of experience and the recognition that the job of negotiating a crisis was not a one-person show. My guess is the transition began in the 1970s, as we learned that we needed a team to effectively handle this chore.

A properly structured team should have a commander, a primary negotiator, a secondary negotiator or negotiators, an intelligence officer or officers, a think tank, messengers, guards, chronographers, a technician (radio operator), a tactical liaison, and a behavioral science expert or two. Some of these functions overlap, some require one person, and others require more. Together they form the nucleus of an effective CINT.

The practices of identifying and using third-party negotiators and interpreters are outside the scope of this chapter. However, when these issues arise and the need is identified, the appropriate resources should be known to or through the team commander or the behavioral science resource person.

1. The CINT *commander* should be of equal rank with the SWAT commander. Like the SWAT team commander, who is not a member of the entry or sniper observer team, the negotiations commander manages the team. He or she does not negotiate with the subject anymore than the SWAT commander functions as a member of the entry team.

   The negotiations team commander has many responsibilities. These include, but are not limited to, selecting new members, organizing training sessions, structuring and restructuring the team, and running an operation in the field. During an operation, the negotiations commander consults regularly with the SWAT commander and the on-scene commander to ensure a coordinated, informed, uniform, and professional response to the incident (Birge, 2002). The commander remains current on the progress, or lack of negotiations progress, via regular meetings with the team and the use of position papers developed by the CINT to appraise the on-scene commander of their ideas, plans, and assessment of the crisis. A one-page example of this document is shown in Appendix A. These criteria are being developed by the Crisis Negotiations Unit I started at Quantico some 45 years ago and reflect a work in progress.

2. A *primary negotiator* is essential. Like the commander, there is *only one person* in this position. His or her primary responsibility is to communicate with the perpetrator, or in FBI parlance, subject, of the crisis.

3. The *secondary negotiator* position may be filled by *more than one* person. Typically, the secondary serves as the assistant to the primary; monitors the primary; screens and passes on intelligence; provides help as necessary; provides backup, support, and suggestions; and does the many jobs required to keep the focus of the primary negotiator on the subject. Trying to delineate the role of the secondary negotiator is like trying to specify the responsibilities of a partner on patrol.

4. Current, accurate, and appropriate *intelligence* is vital to any operation. This is a job for many people during a crisis, *not all of whom* need be trained negotiators. Because each aspect of an operation

requires different information, some agencies specify intelligence as a totally separate function in their crisis response command structure. It must be stressed, the CINT needs intelligence gathered, or at least evaluated, by a person trained in negotiations so the appropriate information can be sent to the secondary negotiator and think tank for evaluation and use during the crisis.

SWAT teams need intelligence on the structure of the building; the negotiating team needs intelligence on the structure of the personality of the subject and the hostages. The criminal, psychiatric, and medical records of the subject and hostages are vital to the CINT. Also of great use is information about the hostages, especially if there are medical, psychological, or other issues, such as a volatile relationship with the hostage taker.

5. The *think tank,* all of whose members need not be negotiators, is the practical filter of the information gathered by the intelligence unit and serves as the brains of the negotiator. These operatives draw from their experience as medical or psychiatric professionals, negotiators, and law enforcement/correctional officers, who apply common sense in their analysis of the available intelligence. They typically take the information gathered from various sources and come up with ideas to assist the negotiator in developing strategy and a logical approach that will lead to a peaceful surrender. We have all heard the expression "He's the brains of the outfit." That expression is especially appropriate for the think tank—they are the brains of the negotiating team.

6. The *messenger,* or messengers, need not be trained negotiators. They are vital because the flow of intelligence is frequently the weak link in an operation. Often the SWAT team has information needed by the negotiations team and vice versa. The messenger(s) must keep the flow of information current. (Current information can also be transmitted by regular meetings during the crisis to ensure that everyone is up to date on tactics, problems, strategies, intelligence, and other issues as they arise.) During training sessions it is interesting to note the amount of time required for intelligence interjected by controllers to reach the appropriate crisis response element.

7. There must be a person or persons at the door(s) to curtail the flow of folks into the negotiations site. This site, though linked to the on-scene commander, should be isolated from the raucous atmosphere that is generally found in and around the command post. Thus the *guard(s)* at the door(s) of the negotiations room can be another member of the team (this need not be a trained negotiator). Regardless of his or her training or rank, this person serves as the on-site

representative of the on-scene commander and keeps curiosity seek-ers and other nonessential people out of the negotiations room. This includes everyone who does not have an immediate need to interrupt the negotiator. This includes the incident commander. The negotia-tions site tends to act as a magnet that attracts everyone who is just curious, or for the moment has nothing else to do, and wants to add his or her opinion to the process. This curiosity can be satisfied by using a speaker to broadcast the negotiations to another site.

8. The *chronographer* maintains the negotiations time line and situa-tion board. This is an intelligence position that can be filled by more than one officer (who does not have to be a trained negotiator). The chronographer puts items on the board that are color coded to ease the reading process for those interested in specific categories. As an example, all demands might appear in green, deadlines in red, hos-tage information in black, subject information in blue, and so forth. This board provides people coming on duty the opportunity to learn, at one location, what is happening. Those who might otherwise want to talk to the negotiator can read this board to bring themselves up to date on the status of the negotiations process.

9. The *radio operator,* or technical resource person, is typically a tech-nician and need not be a trained negotiator. He or she keeps the negotiations equipment in working order and corrects problems in advance or as they occur. During the operation, this person is ready to remedy technical trouble and has the job of regularly checking and maintaining the equipment when it is not in use. He or she must also keep abreast of new developments in the field and arrange for the training of team members in the operation of the equipment. Additionally, he or she may train team members in troubleshooting and quick-fix procedures.

10. The *tactical liaison* function is generally performed by a member of the tactical team who sits with the negotiators to ensure immediate and accurate intelligence flow between the two units. The FBI HOBAS report has shown that over 80 percent of hostage/barricade situa-tions are resolved through negotiations (HOBAS, 2011). However, the negotiator must negotiate from the position of strength; this is provided by a well-trained, properly positioned, and well-informed tactical team.

11. The *behavioral science resource* person, or mental health professional, is generally the departmental psychologist, who is available to assist the team in dealing with a wide variety of stress issues. He or she can also provide a quick diagnosis of any psychological problems mani-fested by the perpetrator, suggest an appropriate approach to deal

with the malady, and assist in any liaison with mental health and community psychological and social service resources. Additionally, this person should be skilled in hearing and understanding layered messages in the hostage taker's monologue and should be sensitive to issues of medication effects and prescription withdrawal or overdose symptoms. Finally, and most important, the mental health professional is generally more adept and more experienced in successfully dealing with depressed and suicidal individuals than most law enforcement officers. This person usually works as a member of the think tank.

The Successful Approach—Teamwork

When a department responds to a crisis with one negotiator, or just a few folks who perform unclear roles to assist the negotiator, it is courting disaster. Just as a full SWAT team responds, and just as each sniper must have an observer, each negotiator must have the support of a team whose staff performs the roles outlined above. Small departments should have mutual aid pacts and agreements with neighboring jurisdictions for their negotiation teams. Negotiators should belong to, and participate in, statewide or regional associations to maintain their skill level. These associations also provide contacts that are invaluable when the necessary elements of a properly staffed CINT must be obtained from outside the department.

Hopefully, modern crisis incident commanders will hear and learn the lessons of Attica, Munich, Jacksonville, Ruby Ridge, and Waco. People died at these locations because officers with no hostage negotiations training were the first to respond to a hostage crisis. A crisis command team, a SWAT team, and a negotiations team working as one unit were a necessity but were not available at Ruby Ridge and Waco and did not work together. It takes teams— a command team, a SWAT team, and a negotiations team—to properly and professionally respond to a hostage crisis. One person cannot and should not negotiate a crisis.

Santayana (1905) said, "Those who do not study and learn from their history are condemned to repeat it" (p. 703). Within law enforcement and corrections, if we do not learn from our history, people die unnecessarily, and we pay millions of dollars in civil damages that could have been spent more effectively in training and preparing our officers.

To paraphrase a statement by Senator Robert Kennedy, the hostage crisis is coming, and it will bring changes. These changes can be positive if we are prepared. We can alter the character and effect of this crisis; we cannot alter its inevitability (Kennedy, 1963).

Crisis Negotiations Team

1. Negotiations team commander (same rank as the SWAT commander)
   a. Monitors team
   b. Liaison with on-scene and SWAT commander
   c. Training and selection
2. Primary negotiator
   a. Listens
   b. Talks to subject
   c. Develops intelligence
3. Secondary negotiator
   a. Monitors negotiations and the negotiator
   b. Listens
   c. Provides the primary with potential topics for discussion
   d. Controls access to and relieves the primary
4. Intelligence
   a. Gathers and disseminates information to the team
5. Think tank
   a. The brains behind the negotiator
   b. The filter of intelligence
6. Messengers
   a. Assures communication with tactical and command
7. Guards
   a. Controls access to the negotiations site
8. Chronographers
   a. Maintains the negotiations log and the critical incident board
   b. Intelligence resource person
9. Technical resources
   a. Maintains and monitors all technical equipment
10. Tactical liaison
    a. Channels information between tactical and negotiation functions
11. Behavioral science experts
    a. Monitors stress level of team and recommends negotiations techniques and approaches
    b. Interpreters and third-party intermediaries

References

Birge, R. (2002) The Vital Balance, *Law and Order*, March.

Downs, A. (2011) Personal interview at the Annual Crisis Negotiation Competition, Southwest Texas State University, San Marcos, Texas, January 11.

Downs v. United States 382 F. 522F 2nd 990 (6th Cir. 1975).

HOBAS (2011) Federal Bureau of Investigation, Hostage Barricade Database System, FBI Academy, Quantico, Virginia.

Kennedy, R. (1963) U.S. Senator, Speech before the Senate on terrorism.

Ostrow, R. J. (1995) U.S. to Pay $3.1 Million for '92 Idaho Shootout, *Los Angeles Times*, Part A, p. 1.

Santayana, G. (1905) *John Bartlett, Book of Familiar Quotations*, Little, Brown and Company, Boston, 1960, p. 703.

Voss, C. (2004) FBI Crisis Negotiations Unit Crisis Negotiations Site Assessment, Presentation to the Louisiana Association of Crisis Negotiators Annual Training Conference, Gonzales, Louisiana, March 6.

Appendix A

FBI Crisis Negotiations Unit Crisis Site Assessment II

Type of Incident
Hostage
Nonhostage
Barricade
Barricade with victims

Threats
Unconditional
Offensive
Defensive
None

Person Held
Selected
Romantic relationship
Family member
Stranger

Hostage/Victims Out
Yes   No

Initiation of Incident
By subject
By hostage/victim
911 call
Other

Preparation
Planned
Prepared for
Spontaneous

Demands
Unrealistic
Changing
Nonsubstantive
Substantive
None

Crisis Site
Subject's residence
Subject's employment

Timing of Violence
After contact
Relative to demand
History of violence
Initially
Type

Degree of Violence
Death
Injury
Random

Bomb
Real
Fake
Alleged
Unknown
N/A

Weapons
Shoulder
Handgun
Knife
Other

Weapon Tied to Subject
Yes   No

Subject's Demeanor
Angry/aggressive
Yes   No

Deadlines
Specific
Uncertain
None

Passed
With incident
Without incident

Psychiatric History
Yes   No   Unknown

Criminal History
Yes   No   Unknown

Degree of Communication
Noncommunicative
Brief exchanges
Lengthy exchanges
Willing to talk

Escape
Desire to escape
Not mentioned

Calm/Controlled
Sad/depressed
Confused/incoherent
Other

Suicide
Suicide by cop
Stated
Desire to live

Loss
Health, job, relationship
Status/self-esteem
Money
Freedom

Drugs and/or Alcohol
During
Prior
History
Type
Quantity

Has Your Assessment Changed?
Yes   No
Why, how, when, suggesting what?

Source: Adapted from Voss, C. (2004) FBI Crisis Negotiations Unit Crisis Negotiations Site Assessment, Presentation to the Louisiana Association of Crisis Negotiators Annual Training Conference, March 6, Gonzales, Louisiana.

Crisis Negotiator Stress 7

Introduction

According to Gilbert and Sullivan, the policeman's lot is not a happy one (*HMS Pintefore*). This was a fact during 19th-century England. It remains valid today in the United States and around the world. It is especially true for the typical law enforcement hostage/crisis negotiator. Like many aspects of police work, negotiation for the release of hostages is very stressful. I doubt that negotiations will be less of a strain in the future. However, we can mitigate the effect of debilitating stress by recognizing its symptoms and learning to more effectively deal with this reality.

Stress is part of life. To live is to change, and change brings the stress of adjustment. Those without stress have already gone on to their reward. A hostage crisis includes change. Some changes are beyond the control of the response team, thus the negotiator and others will experience stress. We cannot eliminate stress. However, we can learn to deal with it in a practical and productive manner.

Tough times do not last, tough people do.

Dr. Nancy Bohl published an article, "Hostage Negotiator Stress," in the *FBI Law Enforcement Bulletin* (Bohl, 1992). Her material was so accurate that it was reprinted in the *U.S. Negotiator* (Bohl, 1995). I have drawn from her ideas.

We Have Met the Enemy and He Is Us

The first step in successfully dealing with a problem is to recognize its existence. Denial of negotiator stress will only make matters worse. Accepting and dealing with this tension in appropriate ways will assist in effective short- and long-term coping and eventual recovery. Every hostage, potential suicide, or barricade situation has multiple built-in stressors. Many of these originate within the crisis management team and its hierarchy.

This includes the fact that the goals and practices of some participants may be at odds with those of others who claim to be on the same team. Some participants may think that the fastest solution is the best. Others may want to stall for time (Noesner, 2010). Some give "lip service" to the goal of the *preservation of human life* while pressing for an unnecessarily perilous but quick solution. Some have been well trained and have practiced and gained experience in their crisis resolution roles, while others have been pressed into service. Some are team players while others seem intent on making a name for themselves. Some have practical or professional goals while the aims of others may be personal or political, and then there is the minor issue of the hostage holder and his victims. A negotiator's lot is not a happy one.

In addition to these considerations, there are several questions that should be answered. Has the negotiator accurately assessed the situation? Is this crisis negotiable? Are the correct negotiation tactics being used? Does the approach of the negotiator match the personality of the subject? In addition to these considerations, law enforcement and correctional officers, perhaps more than anyone, fear failure. Lack of success in negotiations may result in the use of force that may mean death to a police officer, staff member, or hostage.

Therefore, the call to activate the negotiating team may result in the common psychological responses of anxiety or denial. This concern with mission success is not limited to crisis response teams. When an anxious astronaut, Alan Shepherd, was on the launch pad, the prayer that he uttered aloud was, "Dear God, please don't let me _____ up."

Denial occurs but is less common among those who are well trained. It frequently affects folks faced with unexpected and severe stress. It takes the form of verbal utterances that mirror the mental state. When Patricia Campbell Hearst was abducted she was heard to yell, "No, not me. No, not me" (Hearst, 1982, 1986). When hearing bad news, many people automatically say, "Oh no." I have interviewed many hostages who successfully coped with the stress of the early hours of confinement by believing that their captivity was a bad dream from which they would soon awaken.

A final indicator that the enemy lies within is reflected by the chart below that sets forth, according to Mitchell, the personality traits of emergency service personnel. Note the need to be in control ranks very high. As a negotiator this need may remain elusive during the crisis and could dramatically increase your sense of stress (Mitchell and Bray, 1990). In addition to the stress of a hostage or barricade situation, we have the personality of the responder. Mitchell believes that, as a group, emergency service personnel hold themselves to a high standard. We are more self-critical and more likely to condemn ourselves for missing 5 questions on a 100-item test than congratulate ourselves for getting 95 questions correct. Does that mind-set sound familiar?

General Personality Traits of Emergency Personnel

Need to be in control
Easily bored
Obsessive (desire to do a perfect job)
Risk taker

Strong need to be needed
Rescue personality
Highly motivated by internal factors
Highly dedicated
Need for immediate gratification
Compulsive
High need for stimulation
Action oriented (Mitchell and Bray, 1990)

Negotiating and Negotiators' Stress

One effective way to deal with the stress of negotiating is to *compartmentalize the problem*. There are several issues in each of three phases that can mitigate stress. They are common problem areas that the negotiator should remember.

Preincident Precautions and Preparation

1. The proper selection of personnel is probably the best way to mitigate the effects of stress on staff and the responding team during any traumatic event.
2. Training is an excellent form of stress reduction. This activity provides well-founded self-confidence and serves to identify areas a team should address to ensure effective functioning during a crisis.
3. Additional preparation includes active membership in professional organizations and reading of appropriate literature to remain current in the field. One should be an active participant in team, department, association, and other training programs. Attendance at professional conferences and related training seminars is also very helpful. All of these also impress the court that more and more are holding negotiators to the same standards usually applied to *expert witnesses*.
4. Good nutritional practices also contribute to effective stress management. This includes limiting alcohol intake and not smoking.
5. Prior to an incident, it is a good idea to identify logical resources. These include, but are not limited to, interpreters, psychologists, other mental health professionals, poison center contacts, other medical resources, suicide prevention professionals, telephone and utility company contacts, and contacts with other agencies and negotiators for consultation and backup.
6. Take time to complete a video mapping of logical targets in your jurisdiction.

Incident

1. Violence during a hostage crisis is not in anyone's best interest. Should a situation become tumultuous, the hostage taker is most likely to be the ultimate victim of his or her own aggression. The hostage taker knows this. He or she knows that law enforcement has more weapons, personnel, and resources. *Unless suicidal*, the hostage taker may talk about killing, but in the final analysis the hostage taker recognizes that his or her best interests are served by tranquil negotiations and a peaceful solution. However the hostage taker usually needs time to tell you that he or she is the victim, and it really is not his or her fault. Remember the discussion of projection and rationalization from Chapter 1.

2. This is the hostage taker's problem, not yours. Your job as a negotiator is to assist him or her in recognizing the futility of hurting anyone and the logic of eventually coming out. Help the hostage taker to avoid making a bad situation worse; play down what has occurred. Put your badge in your pocket and listen.

3. Your job is to get the hostage taker through this present crisis, not solve all of his or her problems. Many juvenile delinquents have multiple social-psychological, and perhaps medical, problems that you recognize when you arrest them, but are not called upon to solve. Similarly, hostage takers are usually problem people. Do not make the job more difficult than it is. Focus your efforts on the immediate and presenting issue—get everyone out alive. They have spent years making a mess out of their lives. You cannot straighten things out in one negotiation. Later, other professionals will deal with their problems.

4. Initially and for most of the time, the negotiator should listen to the subject. We gather intelligence and allow the hostage taker to ventilate when we listen. Many times, in this process of talking, the hostage taker solves his or her own problems, or we identify the "hook" to bring the hostage taker out.

5. While listening, evaluate. Try to identify the real issues and eventually speak to them. Remember that one talks differently to and with an Antisocial person versus a person who is suffering from Paranoid Schizophrenia or Depression. Make your technique and tactics fit the hostage taker's personality.

   Further, you may have a subject who considers himself or herself the victim. We deal differently with victims, so make the appropriate change in your delivery and demeanor.

6. Your commander and others on the department who are on your crisis response team may not understand the practice of negotiations. Because of their ignorance, they may be threatened by what you are

doing and become hostile or obstinate. Someone on your team, probably the team leader who is of the appropriate rank, should be prepared to educate others on the rationale for this process and logic of your procedures. I have debriefed negotiators who have told me they were getting along better with the hostage holder than with some key members of their own team. Basically, effective negotiators work as if they are getting paid by the hour. Most commanders and tactical team members work as if they are being paid by the job.

7. Do not try to do more than your job. Allow others to do theirs. Concentrate on listening, evaluating, gathering intelligence, planning, and communicating.

8. Remember your responsibility to provide intelligence to others on the team. Regardless of the records that may be available on the subject, you have the hostage taker on the line now. Thus, you have the most up-to-date information about his or her potential for violence versus the likelihood that he or she will acquiesce. Use the material in Chapters 19 and 20 to assist in this evaluation.

9. Use your team members. Consult with your secondary. Hold periodic conferences with the rest of the team to ensure their input into the problem-solving process. This tends to guarantee that everyone is working toward the same goal.

10. If your shift ends before the incident is over, consider the use of defusing or demobilization debriefings discussed later in this chapter (Mitchell and Everly, 1994).

Postincident

1. After the incident, be sure that a tactical, as well as a psychological, debrief is conducted by and with competent staff. In addition to the defusing or demobilization debriefings held prior to the end of an incident, the better-known practice of Post Critical Incident Stress Debriefings (CISD) should be conducted (Mitchell and Everly, 1994).

2. Do not dwell on or take full responsibility for an unsuccessful end to the negotiations process. You are not solely responsible for the outcome of the incident. Certainly, the subject is more to blame for placing himself or herself and many others in harm's way.

3. Limit your intake of alcohol. Alcohol interrupts rapid eye movement sleep. A good night's sleep helps us process the day's events physically and psychologically. Excessive alcohol inhibits this processing. Your time would be better spent in a debriefing, getting some exercise, and eating a light nutritious meal rather than drinking.

4. Use appropriate portions of your negotiations and lessons learned for training sessions.

5. Long-term problems occur when negotiators and others fail to deal effectively with their feelings of guilt. These feelings can be dealt with by using the CISD process (Bohl, 1992).

Critical Incident Stress Debriefings

We have discussed what a negotiator can do to prevent or ameliorate the negative effects of excessive stress. Now we will focus on dealing with the negative effects of excessive stress after the incident. Stress is an equal opportunity malady.

The most effective work in this field has been done by Jeffrey Mitchell, a former Baltimore, Maryland, fireman who developed very effective debriefing processes. He has earned his doctorate and teaches his techniques around the world. The phone number and address for more information about the international critical incident stress foundation can be found in Appendix A.

Eighty percent of the people who die of nontraumatic causes actually expire from diseases related to stress (Mitchell and Bray, 1990). From an evolutionary perspective, stress is not intended to end but to enhance life. It is designed to prepare the body for fight-or-flight to survive or evade danger. When the subsequent physical and needed psychological actions do not occur, chemicals designed to enhance survival turn inward and we pay a price. In other words, if after a crisis, we just sit there rather than talk about the incident and get some physical exercise, we are more likely to experience the adverse effects of stress.

Stress consists of a well-known combination of neurological, neuroendocrine, and endocrine arousal response mechanisms that can and do affect and alter every organ and function of the human body (Mitchell and Everly, 1994). In many cases, it is not the stress that kills. It is the way people cope with this physical and psychological reaction to trauma that results in death rather than development.

The word *stress* is derived from ancient Latin. It means "force," "pressure," or "strain." For the purpose of this chapter *stress* will be defined as a response to something in the environment that requires change in behavior. Thus, there is positive as well as negative stress. This is demonstrated by the Holmes–Rahe stress scale presented in Appendix B (Holmes and Rahe, 1967).

The *Diagnostic and Statistical Manual of Mental Disorders* (*DSM*) defines *stress* in terms of a person who is suffering from its negative effects. They identify the patient as an individual who has experienced an event that is outside the range of usual human experience. This event would be markedly distressing to almost anyone. They go on to list the most common physical and psychological symptoms. The symptoms should have lasted for at least a month but are less severe than a generalized anxiety disorder that is similar but shorter and less intense. Today, this mental malady is called posttraumatic stress disorder (PTSD). In World War II, the term *combat fatigue* was used. During World War I, it was called *shell shock* (American Psychiatric Association, 2007).

The three types of traumatic incident debriefs discussed here are designed to prevent PTSD or identify those who need additional counseling. The processes are called debriefings, defusing, and demobilizations.

Debriefings

This process is best known by its longer name, a Critical Incident Stress Debriefing (CISD). This psychological process requires a group meeting with a discussion about a traumatic event in which the participants were involved or affected. The discussion is designed to mitigate the psychological impact of a traumatic event, prevent the development of a posttraumatic syndrome, and serve to identify individuals who may require professional mental health follow-up (Mitchell and Everly, 1994).

The CISD process requires a team approach. The team is professionally led and peer driven. The mental health professionals who serve on the team should have a master's degree in psychology, social work, psychiatric nursing, or counseling. They should have specialized basic and advanced training in CISD as well as experience participating in the CISD process before they lead a team.

Peer support staff should be drawn from emergency service organizations. Ideally, they are people who have had experiences similar to those they are debriefing and should, like the professional leader, have been trained in the basic and advanced CISD process. The mental health professional and the peer support staff form a pool of critical incident team members from which a response team is selected (Conroy, 1990).

The administration, boss, chief, or supervisor should order all participants in the traumatic event to attend the CISD. Each one may not participate, and some will talk more than others. However, everyone should be present.

The CISD process achieves its best effects when it is offered after 24 hours but before 72 hours following a critical incident. A mental health professional, assisted by two or three peers, should be able to conduct a CISD for 12 to 15 participants who are seated in a circle. The mental health professional and peer counselors should be spread among the attendees. The meeting usually lasts a few hours. It is not a substitute for psychotherapy. After the session a brief social with refreshments is scheduled to allow for immediate follow-up and the formation of friendships.

The process is a peer-driven, professionally supported limited seven-phase support service designed to keep staff functioning (Mitchell, 1993). The peers share their experiences and take responsibility for anyone who leaves the group. The CISD is a seven-step process. A brief overview of the session is as follows:

1. Introduction of peer and professional staff with a guarantee of confidentiality. The process is explained and expectations are set.
2. Participants are asked to explain the *facts* of the traumatic event from each participant's perspective on a factual level.
3. Participants are asked to discuss their *thoughts* about the facts they just described.
4. This phase focuses on the *emotional impact* of the event. Each person is asked to identify the most traumatic aspect for them and their emotional reaction to this trauma.
5. After the discussions of emotions the participants are asked to identify the physical and psychological *symptoms* they are having.
6. This phase focuses on *teaching* and focusing on the positive aspects of the event. This includes a discussion of stress management and provides the participants with the opportunity to learn that others are having similar psychological and physical reactions.
7. The final phase serves to *clarify* ambiguities and prepare the participants for the end of the session. If individual follow-up is required, it is done privately with a peer or a professional consultation or referral.

The CISD process has psychological and educational elements. It is not psychotherapy. It is a structured group meeting designed to help normal people who have been subjected to an abnormal amount of stress deal with their emotional and physical reactions to this trauma. As noted above, the CISD is carefully structured with seven major phases that allow the participants to move from facts into normal physical and psychological reactions and symptoms, to emotionally charged reactions, and gradually back to topics and issues that are less emotional. It ends with a positive discussion about the incident with a view toward training and returning to duty a stronger person who may be able to assist others.

Defusing

A defusing is usually a three-stage meeting. It is shorter than the CISD and has a different format. It is typically implemented immediately or shortly after a traumatic event. It lasts about an hour, is more flexible, and is used to eliminate or enhance a subsequent CISD (Mitchell and Everly, 1994). An advantage to the defusing is that its immediate implementation allows for a more open discussion of emotions before defense mechanisms set in and begin to close down expressions of feelings. It occurs when the participant's psychological guards are down and his or her needs are elevated. This process is aimed at the core group that was most seriously affected by the event. Examples include the negotiating and/or SWAT team that was directly involved in the incident. Although this process is very effective and saves time and money, it requires that a team be on site to implement this process very quickly. This process provides an opportunity to observe the symptoms of distress and allows the peers and professionals to make some decisions about other treatment or the use of a CISD later. Because of the 48- to 72-hour delay, a CISD team can be assembled for the longer debrief later.

1. Like the CISD there is an introductory phase that serves the same purpose.
2. Phase 2 is a combination of CISD phases 2, 3, 4, and 5. It includes facts, mental and emotional reactions, as well as any symptoms.
3. Phase 3 attempts to normalize reactions and educate the participants about stress and stress management and trauma. Follow-up contacts and services are always necessary after a defusing to assure that the personnel are managing their stress effectively (Mitchell and Everly, 1994).

Demobilizations

The third type of structured processing of the trauma of an emotionally charged incident is called demobilization. Like the defusing, it occurs immediately. Thus it requires that CISD staff be on site. It is an informational and rest session that is used when operational units have been released from service at a major incident and before they return to normal duties. Unlike the other processes, this one does not feature discussions from the participants. It involves the giving of information from a CISD-trained person and some rest and food for the participants. These sessions should be reserved for major incidents, like disasters, that involve over 100 participants.

The function of all these sessions, CISD, defuse, and demobilization, is to help *normal* people cope with the effects of an incident in which they were exposed to an abnormal amount of stress that they need to process to continue functioning at home and at work. It is said of the CISD and similar debriefs: "Our team keeps your team on the job."

Often the job exposes us to severe trauma. Stress is a common problem in law enforcement and corrections officers. The three types of debriefings are often very useful to eliminate many symptoms of trauma. Should additional help be needed, some very effective treatment programs are available (Davis and Marcey, 1995). One reason these treatments are so effective is that the officer is a mentally healthy person who is experiencing a powerful reaction to a stressful experience.

Conclusion

In conclusion, it should be remembered that stress is part of life. Through study and training, we learn how to limit the amount of stress inherent in hostage incidents. The deployments of our resources raise the normal level of stress by introducing the element of time compression, threats against human lives, lack of solid intelligence, and many other factors that disrupt our sense of control. These unknowns jeopardize our sense of order and threaten our sense of control. The lessons learned from a hostage crisis can act as constructive guidelines for future responses.

Effective stress management programs benefit negotiators and their departments. Staff who learn to manage stress successfully can return to their jobs with renewed confidence and commitment. Departments that institute stress management programs reap the benefits of employees who can handle crisis incidents in a healthy and professional manner (Bohl, 1992).

With proper preparation, conduct, and postincident care, the department is less likely to lose a lawsuit and its staff through disability retirements. Preparation and good postincident care enable us to view the incident as a test that was passed with a grade less than 100%, rather than a crisis that left us helpless. We can grow stronger from an incident that otherwise may be disabling.

References

American Psychiatric Association (2007) Post-Traumatic Stress Disorder, *Diagnostic and Statistical Manual of Mental Disorders*–4th Edition, (*DSM-IV*). APA, Washington, DC, p. 424.

Bohl, N. K. (1992) Hostage Negotiator Stress, *FBI Law Enforcement Bulletin*, August, 23–26.

Bohl, N. K. (1995) Hostage Negotiator Stress, *U.S. Negotiator*, pp. 1–4.

Conroy, R. J. (1990) Critical Incident Stress Debriefing, *FBI Law Enforcement Bulletin*, February, pp. 20–22.

Davis, N., and Marcey, M. (1995) Treatment of Symptoms of Post Traumatic Stress Disorder in Law Enforcement Officers with Brief, Intense, Image-Based Techniques, *Organizational Issues in Law Enforcement*, 237–256.

Eliot, R. S., and Breo, D. (1984) *Is It Worth Dying For?* Bantam Books, New York.

Hearst, P. (1982) *Every Secret Thing*, Doubleday, New York.

Hearst, P. (1986) Personal interview, FBI Academy, Quantico, Virginia, September 6.

Holmes, T., and Rahe, R. (1967) The Social Readjustment Rating Scale, *Journal of Psychosomatic Research*, Vol. 11, pp. 213–218.

Mitchell, J. T. (1993) Lecture during Basic CISD Course, University of Maryland, Baltimore Campus, January 12.

Mitchell, J. T., and Bray, G. P. (1990) *Emergency Services Stress: Guidelines for Preserving the Health and Careers of Emergency Services Personnel*. Prentice Hall, Englewood Cliffs, New Jersey, p. 3 (Chart p. 21).

Mitchell, J. T., and Everly, G. S. (1994) *Critical Incident Stress Debriefing: The Basic Course Workbook*, International Critical Incident Stress Foundation, Ellicott City, Maryland.

Noesner, G. (2010) *Stalling for Time*, Random House, New York.

Appendix A

The International Critical Incident Stress Foundation, Inc. is located at 3290 Pine Orchard Lane, Suite 106, Ellicott City, Maryland, 20142. The telephone number is 410-750-9600; Web site: www.icisf.org.

Appendix B

Holmes–Rahe Stress Scale

Rank Event	Value Score
1. Death of spouse	100
2. Divorce	73
3. Marital separation	65
4. Jail term	63
5. Death of close family member	63
6. Personal injury or illness	53
7. Marriage	50
8. Fired from work	47
9. Marital reconciliation	45
10. Retirement	45
11. Change in family member's health	44
12. Pregnancy	40
13. Sex difficulties	39
14. Addition to family	39
15. Business readjustment	39
16. Change in financial status	38
17. Death of close friend	37
18. Change in number of marital arguments	35
19. Mortgage or loan over $10,000	31
20. Foreclosure of mortgage loan	30
21. Change in work responsibilities	29
22. Son or daughter leaving home	29
23. Trouble with in-laws	29
24. Outstanding personal achievement	28
25. Spouse begins or quits work	26
26. Starting or finishing school	26
27. Change in living conditions	25
28. Revision of personal habits	24
29. Trouble with boss	23
30. Change in work hours or conditions	20
31. Change in residence	20
32. Change in schools	20
33. Change in recreational habits	19
34. Change in church activities	19
35. Change in social activities	18
36. Mortgage or loan under $10,000	18
37. Change in sleeping habits	16
38. Change in number of family gatherings	15
39. Change in eating habits	15
40. Vacation	13
41. Christmas season	12
42. Minor violation of the law	11

Total

Appendix C

Life Change Indicators and Disease Risk Patrol—School Version

1. Death of a spouse 100
2. Divorce 73
3. Marital separation 65
4. Killing someone in the line of duty 63
5. Death of a close family member 63
6. Personal injury or illness 53
7. Marriage 50
8. Assigned to high-stress or boring work for more than 2 years 47
9. Marital reconciliation 45
10. Retirement 45
11. Change in health of family member 40
12. Pregnancy or gain of family member 40
13. Sexual difficulties 39
14. Having an affair 39
15. Promotion, transfer, or demotion* 39
16. Change in financial state* 39
17. Death of a close friend 37
18. Under investigation for a major infraction 36
19. Change in number of arguments 35
20. Mortgage over $100,000 31
21. Foreclosure of mortgage or loan 30
22. Son or daughter leaving home 29
23. Trouble with in-laws 29
24. Outstanding personal achievement, commendation, or award 28
25. Spouse began or stopped work 26
26. Began or finished school* 26
27. Identified as part of "in" or "out" group 25
28. Change in personal habits, smoking alcohol, eating* 24
29. Trouble with supervisor 23
30. Change in work hours or conditions* 20
31. Change in residence 20
32. Working a second job 20
33. Change in recreation* 19
34. Change in church activities 19
35. Change in close friends/work group* 18
36. Mortgage or loan less than $20,000 17
37. Change in amount/habit of sleep 16
38. Change in number of family events 15
39. Change in eating habits/type of food* 15
40. Major vacation with spouse 13
41. Working holidays* 12
42. Under investigation for minor infraction 11

Notes: Pay particular attention to the items marked with an asterisk because those almost automatically happen when a person goes to patrol training.

What your total score means:

If you score below 150 points, chances are about one in three that a serious stress-related health problem will happen to you in the next 2 years. If your total score is between 150 and 300, your chances of a stress-related health problem rise to about 50 percent. If your score is over 300 points, you are operating at maximum tolerance and your chances of a major stress-related illness in the next 2 years increase to 90 percent.

The average patrol trainee starts out with a stress score of approximately 268, just because of the major life changes that a transfer to patrol involves. No matter what your score, you still have some control over whether you fall into the percentage group that develops a major stress-related illness. Practicing good stress management can make the difference in your stress level and in your life.

There are many sources of assistance. One of the better texts available is entitled, *Is It Worth Dying For?* (1984) by Dr. Robert S. Eliot and Dennis L. Breo. It has been reprinted several times.

Source: Adapted from, and used with the permission of Los Angeles Sheriffs Office Employee Support Services Bureau (Telephone: 213-738-3500). The major work was done by Jack Seitzinger, Ph.D. LASD.

Dealing with the Other Victim

2

Negotiating with Normal People

8

Mission Statement

Crisis negotiations is a process designed to *preserve human life*—that of police, hostages, civilians, and hostage takers. We take time to listen so the crisis can be resolved by bringing the subject to his or her senses, not necessarily to his or her knees. By definition, the call for crisis negotiators means there is a stressful, if not life-endangering, set of circumstances that we have been called upon to resolve as peacefully as possible. Again, as peacefully, not as quickly, as possible (Noesner, 2010).

Stress Is Personally Defined

More than any other professional or public servant, law enforcement and correctional officers, on a daily basis, repeatedly deal with people in stressful situations. Most calls for service involve a citizen or inmate who is in crisis. *Stress and crisis are self-defined.* For proof of this, review the Holmes–Rahe stress scale in Appendix A (Holmes and Rahe, 1967). A quick reading will reveal that what is stressful for some people may be no problem for others.

One example for law enforcement and correctional officers is the last item—is there such a thing as a minor violation of the law for an officer of the law? I think not. Even the most minor violation could result in suspension, a transfer, severe disciplinary action, or the loss of a job.

I recall an Internal Revenue Service (IRS) audit of items I listed on my Form 1040 that I deducted and I should have depreciated. As a result, I owed our government a few thousand dollars. For the average citizen, this would be a minor financial problem. As a Federal Bureau of Investigation (FBI) agent I had to prove to our equivalent of Internal Affairs that it was an error of misinterpretation with no intent to defraud the federal government. Consider the problem of proving a negative. My stress level was extremely high as I wrote more than one memo trying to explain my ignorance of what I considered some finer points in the tax code, which I had not read.

Every Call for Service Means Stress for Someone

When people need help, they call the police. The mere presence of a law enforcement officer at the scene usually means there is a crisis, or at least some stress for those involved. From a traffic stop to a domestic dispute, or when dealing with a victim or a witness to a crime, most law enforcement encounters with the public are with people who under normal conditions would probably be quite rational. However, given the present set of circumstances the citizen is upset. The citizen is in crisis and is experiencing stress.

A similar set of circumstances exists within institutions. Correctional staff interacts and deals with inmates on a daily basis. When an inmate has a crisis, the dealings become very stressful. Further, when a visitor to an institution has a problem, this can upset the entire population of the visiting area as well as the inmates.

While I do not intend to demean the hostage crisis that involves "normal" people, I think this type of encounter is quite common. Therefore, to effectively deal with a normal person in a hostage crisis involves the transfer of skills from one setting to another. Every police and correctional academy teaches some form of crisis intervention. These skills, learned long ago and practiced on a daily basis, are typically most appropriate for dealing with an inmate or citizen in a hostage crisis. This applies to the citizen who has taken hostages as well as those who are being held. For more information on how to best deal with hostages, see Chapter 25.

Other chapters will deal with hostage takers who are experiencing mental problems. Many of the tactics and techniques listed in this chapter also apply to people who are abnormal. However, when dealing with abnormal people, one must make certain adjustments to the tactics listed here.

Initially, and of paramount importance, is the need for the negotiator to "put your badge in your pocket" (Anderson, 2010). In other words, you must change roles from correctional officer or cop to that of a counselor. This is the negotiations process. Negotiators empathetically listen, not enthusiastically interrogate.

The proper mind-set for negotiations with persons in crisis, whether they are "normal or not" is to remember that they usually consider themselves to be the *victims*. By some slight or serious alteration or aberration in their thinking process, they have developed the idea that they had no other logical choice but this course of action. They see themselves as having been victimized by the hostage or society and forced into this course of action. In their mind, it is not their fault.

As a law enforcement officer, one deals differently with victims than one does with suspects in, or subjects of, an investigation. Correctional staff deals differently with families and victims of inmates than with denizens of their institution. In a crisis setting, it is very effective to deal with the hostage taker, the subject, as if he or she is the *victim*. Remember, we want to "get inside the head of the hostage taker." If the hostage taker sees himself or herself as the victim, the most effective negotiations tactic to deal with him or her is to take this approach. It is not the job of the negotiator to challenge or change this mind-set. That is the responsibility of the psychotherapist. It is the negotiator's job to *listen and offer hope.*

In my experience, the best way to deal with people in crisis is to listen to them tell their story as many times and with as much passion as they feel comfortable expressing to effectively ventilate their feelings and fears to communicate their emotions. Typically, each telling tends to lessen the stress level and allows them to become more rational and, therefore, more amenable to a reasonable discussion of their dilemma. I do not mean to suggest that the role of the negotiator is to solve the problems of each person in crisis. It is our job to listen and aid people in crisis in their quest for a resolution and return to normalcy. Normal hostage takers know, at some level, they cannot remain at the site and in their emotional state forever. However, they must have the opportunity to tell their side of the story to a person who is willing to actively listen.

I have interviewed many hostage takers. A common theme I have noticed is they are typically unaware of what the negotiator said during the crisis. However, they remember his or her *tone of voice*. In the tone they perceived an expression of concern for them as a victim in need of help. Again, to be an effective crisis negotiator, one must put his or her badge in his or her pocket.

Active Listening

Over half a century ago, an American psychologist, Carl Rogers, developed a simple, yet very effective method of psychotherapy called active listening (Rogers, 1951). There is another longer version of his material available to corrections and law enforcement (Noesner and Webster, 1997). I believe in KISS (keep it simple stupid) and have reduced his material to four stages. The basic idea is to draw the other person into a discussion of what is basically bothering him or her. When dealing with a hostage taker one must get the hostage taker talking about his or her version of the crisis.

A great feature of the long or short version of active listening is it can be practiced during routine interviews, while interacting with peers, or at home with your spouse. I found it best to practice on my children. As a general rule, they were not as smart or sophisticated as I, at least until they became teenagers, and thus provided the perfect setting to hone this technique. I am comfortable with the sequence listed below. However, to the best of my knowledge, there is no correct sequence to the active listening process.

1. *Say nothing.* This is the very simple act of keeping one's mouth shut—sometimes easier said than done. I have heard it said that the average American can tolerate 10 seconds of silence. So, practice silence for 11, 12, 13 seconds and gradually develop this skill until you can outwait all others. Some cheat by coughing or clearing their throat. As I said in Chapter 1, God gave us a mouth we can close and two ears we cannot. Perhaps therein lies a message from our creator.

2. If one cannot tolerate the silence, an effective psychological break is to *repeat* the last few words the other has said and then remain silent. Very often this gets them talking again. It certainly shows you are paying attention.

3. *Reflecting on their emotional level* also works well. This is simple enough. The negotiator may say, "You sound angry, or you sound upset," or whatever their emotional level might be. Again, this is easy and effectively demonstrates you are attentive and responsive.

4. *Summarize.* Finally, one may periodically review what the other has said. This is a very effective way of building rapport and using time. It also clarifies the issues for all participants. Summarizing also provides the negotiator with the opportunity to soften the threats, demands, and deadlines.

All threats and deadlines must be forwarded to command and tactical as soon as possible. In addition, the negotiating team must provide them with some insight into the seriousness of the situation.

An example of softening: When the hostage taker says something like "I am going to start shooting hostages if you don't get me $100,000 in 10 minutes," the negotiator could come back with, "As I understand it, you want some money or things could get violent." If the hostage taker says "yes," you have softened the amount of money, the threat, and may have turned the corner toward a peaceful resolution. If he says "No," "I said $100,000 in 10 minutes or I am going to start killing these people," we may have a nonnegotiable situation. For more information on this issue see Chapters 19 and 20.

Negotiating Guidelines*

Properly introduce yourself. *Personal*: My name is... (no rank or title). *Authority*: I am with the ... Department. *Concern*: Are you OK? The use of the noun *Negotiator* should be avoided. For many people, *negotiate* means "capitulate." We want to avoid giving that impression.

---

* For a more complete listing of negotiating guidelines see Lanceley, F. J. (1999) *On Scene Guide for Crisis Negotiators*, CRC Press, Boca Raton, Florida; McMains, J. J., and Mullins, W. C. (2011) *Crisis Negotiations*, 4th Edition, Anderson Press, Cincinnati, Ohio.

Do not lie. More realistically, do not get caught telling or having told a lie. Be vague. The truth is as important and necessary to a crisis negotiator as a good sight picture is to a sniper. Sooner or later the hostage taker is going to walk out because the negotiator promised that no one will shoot. He or she is more likely to believe the negotiator at this crucial juncture who has not lied to him or her during the siege. As negotiators we must have credibility. Lies cause us to lose credibility. Be vague. When the hostage taker asks a question you are not prepared to answer, get back to him or her. Check with your team and think tank. If you must stretch the truth, write it down. We remember the truth; lies require reminders. In addition, should your secondary pick up the phone in your absence, he or she knows the truth—misstatements are another matter.

Play down and minimize recent events. Try to downplay what has happened so far. If someone has been shot by the hostage taker, remember the negotiator cannot know everything. Delay your response to find the facts and call him or her back. If the person the hostage taker shot is dead, one might say in response to a question about this individual, "As I understand it, or I have been told, he/she is in the hospital and a lot of people are looking at him/her." By qualifying your comments with phrases like, "as I understand it" or "they told me," you have some defense against his or her claim that you lied. I recall a statement from the movie *Cadillac Man* after the hostage taker had shot a police officer in the foot. He was told that he had not shot a cop, he shot a shoe.

Let the hostage taker do most of the talking. Use *active listening* tactics. The Louisiana State Police negotiating team focuses on an 80/20 ratio. The subject should talk 80 percent of the time and the negotiator only 20 percent. This is an excellent ratio—it works for them and they are one of the very best negotiating teams in the country. I know that because I have worked with and trained them. In addition, they have successfully negotiated situations the FBI thought were hopeless. They are good because they practice and follow the 80/20 ratio.

Stall for *time* to fatigue the hostage taker (Noesner, 2010). While we are wearing the hostage taker down, remain fresh by taking breaks, using multiple negotiators, and eating a proper diet. Operate as if you are being paid by the hour, not by the job.

Do not say *no*. Substitute "The boss says not now." This strongly suggests that it could happen a little later. Use other phrases that offer hope and not a negative finalizing statement. "Sounds good to me, let me run it past the powers that be" is another example. The negotiator must remain the "good cop" while blaming others for bad news and negative responses.

Offer *hope* and broaden the hostage taker's horizon. Stress the bright side. Use your think tank to full advantage. One on one, the negotiator may not be as smart or cunning as the hostage taker. That is one reason why we use a negotiating team.

Clarify the situation to, and with, the subject. Does the hostage taker fully understand the law? Is the hostage taker making a mountain out of a molehill?

As crisis negotiators, do we ever talk to normal people? The answer is, yes, on occasion. More often, as crisis negotiators we deal with people who are suffering from a high level of stress or mental disorders. These problems may be classified as psychotic behaviors or personality disorders and are the focus of this book.

References

Anderson, D. (2010) Lecture to Basic Crisis Negotiators Course, Pacific Grove, California, February 3.

Holmes, T. H., and Rahe, R. H. (1967) The Social Readjustment Rating Scale, *Journal of Psychosomatic Research*, Vol. 11, pp. 213–218.

Lanceley, F. J. (1999) *On Scene Guide for Crisis Negotiators*, CRC Press, Boca Raton, Florida.

McMains, J. J., and Mullins, W. C. (2001) *Crisis Negotiations*, 4th Edition, Anderson Press, Cincinnati, Ohio.

Noesner, G. (2010) *Stalling for Time*, Random House, New York.

Noesner, G., and Webster, M. (1997) Using Active Listening Skills in Crisis Negotiations, *FBI Law Enforcement Bulletin*, August, pp. 13–19.

Rogers, C. R. (1951) *Client Centered Therapy*, Houghton Mufflin, Boston.

Appendix A

Holmes–Rahe Stress Scale

Rank Event   Value Score

1. Death of spouse.. 100
2. Divorce... 73
3. Marital separation.. 65
4. Jail term 63
5. Death of close family member.. 63
6. Personal injury or illness 53
7. Marriage.. 50
8. Fired from work 47
9. Marital reconciliation.. 45
10. Retirement.. 45
11. Change in family member's health 44
12. Pregnancy... 40
13. Sex difficulties 39
14. Addition to family.. 39
15. Business readjustment 39
16. Change in financial status 38
17. Death of close friend... 37
18. Change in number of marital arguments................................. 35
19. Mortgage or loan over $10,000 31
20. Foreclosure of mortgage loan 30
21. Change in work responsibilities 29
22. Son or daughter leaving home.. 29
23. Trouble with in-laws.. 29
24. Outstanding personal achievement 28
25. Spouse begins or quits work 26
26. Starting or finishing school 26
27. Change in living conditions... 25
28. Revision of personal habits 24
29. Trouble with boss 23
30. Change in work hours or conditions 20
31. Change in residence 20
32. Change in schools... 20
33. Change in recreational habits 19
34. Change in church activities 19
35. Change in social activities 18
36. Mortgage or loan under $10,000.. 18
37. Change in sleeping habits... 16
38. Change in number of family gatherings 15
39. Change in eating habits 15
40. Vacation 13
41. Christmas season 12
42. Minor violation of the law 11

Total

Negotiating with the Adolescent Hostage Taker

9

Introduction

Most adults who reflect upon their teenage years are amazed that they are alive today or did not end up in jail. As adolescents, we all made some very poor decisions and by some miracle lived to remember and talk about our near disasters. Recent research has demonstrated what most of us have known for years: because of the physical developmental process of the brain, adolescents tend to make poor decisions. Clearly, adolescents are in a state of transition that contributes to their overrepresentation in criminal statistics and auto accidents. Increasingly, wild adolescent behavior that was once blamed on raging hormones is seen as the logical by-product of surfeit hormones and the paucity of cognitive controls necessary for mature decision making and behavior (Park, 2004). Thus humans typically have a child's brain in an almost adult body.

Recent research has shown that the adolescent brain has not yet fully developed the circuitry that balances risks and rewards that lead the adult brain to make level-headed decisions (Morse, 2006). More simply said, the prefrontal cortex, known as the executive part of the brain, has not yet fully developed in the average adolescent and I suspect never develops in the person with an Antisocial Personality Disorder.

As an example, consider the following scenario. On a quiet April evening in San Diego, the police department received a call reporting that a young man was holding an employee of the Travelodge® at gunpoint in a corner room on the ninth floor. A rapid police response succeeded in securing the crime scene and verifying that there was a hostage situation on the otherwise deserted top floor of the motel. Investigation determined that the hostage holder was a 19-year-old white male who had just escaped from prison in Colorado. He burglarized a home, stole a shotgun and a vehicle, then drove to California. Further investigation revealed that he had escaped the day before he would have completed his sentence. His parole plan required that he return to the home of his mother. She was reluctant to accept him. Since early childhood, his mother, a self-styled sorceress, had told him that he would die a violent death before his 20th birthday. During negotiations, he revealed that his initial plan had been to drive from Colorado to San Diego so he could commit suicide by jumping off the Coronado Bridge. Upon arrival he became lost and could not find the bridge.

This example may be extreme. However, and most typically, teenagers who take hostages are frequently distressed or depressed dependents of dysfunctional families. The process of negotiating with an adolescent falls into the category of low probability but high risk (McMains, 2005). This risk can be managed effectively by using proper techniques.

The Role of the Negotiator

As a hostage or crisis negotiator, a police officer must remember that his or her job is not to solve all the problems, real or imagined, that may face a troubled youth. Other professionals, social workers, psychologists, psychiatrists, and the like, have the responsibility of helping troubled people find short- and long-term solutions. Your job is different. However unreal, illogical, minimal, or fictional the problem may seem to you, the trauma is very real to the troubled teenager. *Remember that your job is to get him or her past this immediate crisis.* If you work with the mind-set that you are getting paid by the hour, not the job, the negotiations process will be less stressful.

On the street, police regularly arrest people with problems. The job there is to make the arrest and help when or if you can. The primary responsibility of the police on the street is to achieve a short-term or quick fix. The primary responsibility of the crisis negotiator is similar—get the subject past this crisis into custody.

Defining Adolescence

There is limited agreement on what constitutes adolescence. When does it begin and end? Are there stages within this period? Some studies rely on x-rays of the development of cartilage in the wrist to mark the onset of adolescence. Others suggest social criteria like beginning high school. However, some high schools start at the ninth grade while others begin in the tenth. The end is even less clear. Does high school graduation end adolescence or must one be working, married, in the military, or simply over age 21? Recent research suggests that in our society age 25 is a more realistic end to this transition period (Park, 2004).

Adolescence—Phase 1

During the early years, ages 12 to 14, the young person usually experiences a rising level of very active hormones and a growing interest in sexual matters. Yet, most children in this age range are still strongly tied to the same-sex peer group. During this period the self is defined more by the group to which one belongs than by one's individual interests. Groups are, and peer pressure can be, a very powerful force in the life of the developing adolescent. He or she would rather die than be different. He or she can demonstrate tremendous loyalty to his or her peers. Individually, the child can be obnoxious. He or she knows all the answers, has an opinion, and is certain it is correct on every subject from abortion to zoology. This is the age that spawned the expression, "Hire a teenager now while they still know everything." This period is also marked by dramatic growth spurts. Some adolescent problems may simply be the result of sudden physical growth (Webber, 1991).

Adolescence—Phase 2

Mid-adolescence, ages 13 to 17, features a growing need to conform to the peer group. Collectively and individually this age group revolts from social norms by testing adult limits. Typically, this brings the youth into conflict with authority figures. These figures may be parents, priests, pastors, principals, or police. Peer pressure pervades every decision made; in fact, these adolescents seem desperate to prove themselves to their peers. Their still-developing self-concept is weak. They see themselves not as individuals but as members of a group. A commonly used psychological defense mechanism of weak egos, and therefore of adolescence, is projection. When bad things happen, regardless of what the adolescent may have done to precipitate the incident or event, it is someone else's fault. Someone made them do it. If they injure someone they blame the victim. Statements like "They could see I was driving fast, they should have gotten out of the cross-walk more quickly," are typical.

Adolescence—Phase 3

Late adolescence, ages 16 to (who knows when?), is the beginning of maturity with some continued dependence on others. In normal adolescents, these years involve decisions about what kind of a person to become. They move toward decisions on a lifelong mate, vocations, professions, lifestyles, associates, and begin to see themselves as individuals with an identity apart from their peers. The teenage hostage taker may be in this age range physically but emotionally be much younger. Research shows that between the ages of 17 and 25, the brain's frontal lobes finish maturing. If this process is not complete, the individual has less than optimal ability to think in the abstract, plan for the future, or foresee the consequences of his or her actions. Therefore, it is important to listen to what the hostage taker is saying and what he or she is not saying. We gather intelligence by listening patiently, assessing, clarifying, rewording, and asking open-ended questions (Webber, 1991). Determining the hostage taker's emotional age will be crucial in deciding what negotiating techniques are necessary.

Normal Adolescents

Most adolescents live in very turbulent times. They are forced to make life-style decisions that they may not be equipped to handle. They are trying to become adults in a complex society that continues to redefine the qualifications for adult membership. While they may be adults physically, many if not most adolescents are far from able to function independently in our complex industrial society. They are trying to make decisions about separation and individualization with little, no, or incorrect advice.

Most school systems have problems with normal adolescents in the classroom, but these typically do not provoke a hostage crisis. Adolescents have problems with themselves. Does anyone get along well with a teenager? I do not think so. They are unhappy with each other and especially unhappy with themselves. Their noses are too big or they have too many pimples. They are not strong enough or they are too thin or too obese. No one likes them at school and as a group they like themselves even less. They are a mass and a mess of uncontrolled hormones in a growing body. They move around in a society that treats them as children 1 minute and as adults the next. They are allowed to die for their country and vote at age 18, but they are not allowed to drink alcohol until age 21. However, they can obtain a license to kill themselves in an automobile at age 16.

These are troubled times for normal adolescents—if there is such an animal. How much more troublesome are these times for those who are burdened by membership in a dysfunctional family and by real physical, psychological, or social problems?

Elizabeth Sowell, a neuroscientist from the University of California, Los Angeles (UCLA), says that scientists and the general public have attributed the bad decisions teens typically make to hormonal changes. However, recent research has shown that the part of the brain that makes people responsible does not complete the maturation process until after adolescence (Park, 2004). On a day-to-day basis, teenagers are typically ill-equipped to make good decisions. Therefore, in a hostage crisis, the negotiator must be patient and more directive than in most negotiations.

The Crisis Mind-Set

Typically, people in crisis have a very narrow focus. Police officers involved in shootings tend to see only the immediate threat. Their peripheral vision diminishes. There is a similar psychological phenomenon. People in crisis have difficulty identifying alternative courses of action that may be obvious to a person who is not emotionally involved in the situation.

Each of us has experienced an incident where our ability to think and solve problems was negated by our emotional involvement; we were so personally committed that we were psychologically restricted from identifying logical and reasonable alternatives. As the old saying goes, we could not see the forest for the trees. This is a problem faced by many hostage takers. Like others in crisis, they are so blinded by emotion that options that seem logical to more reasonable people escape their attention.

Adolescent Crisis Resolution Skills

That heading may be redundant or ridiculous. To be an adolescent is to live in a constant state of problem solving and crisis. Yet they typically lack the skills required to make serious decisions. When dealing with adolescents one must be aware of their abilities and their inadequacies.

The typical troubled teenager has limited crisis resolution skills, partly because he or she has less experience with the problem-solving process than most adults. Also, adolescent egos are not fully developed and they fear failure more than most people. To make matters worse, their adult role models may be faulty. Be it nature or nurture, genetic problems or poor role models, our troubled teenage hostage taker may not have inherited the ability or have learned how to solve serious real or imagined difficulties. This may be one of the reasons he or she became a hostage taker.

Recent research has shown that the area of the brain that is the last to mature is the area capable of making decisions (Park, 2004).

Common Clinical Conditions

Adolescents are victims of the same types of psychological maladies that we see in adults. To conduct an effective negotiation, we must listen to the adolescent hostage taker and make an assessment of his or her mental state based on his or her demands, the setting, and the identity of the hostages. When this has been accomplished we can refer to sources referenced below for techniques to negotiate with various types of hostage takers.

Depression

Adolescent depression can be triggered by anxiety over abandonment. This may come about by the fear of parental divorce or failure to be included in a desired peer group. The fear of not being selected as a cheerleader may seem trivial to some, but to one teenager in Texas it was so important that her mother felt compelled to kill the mother of her rival. Her rationale was that her daughter's rival would be too depressed over the death of her mother to compete. This would, in the mind of the murderess, assure her own daughter that coveted place on the squad.

Depression can result from real or feared rejection, and it can stem from something as subtle as being stood up for a date or not being accepted into a sorority pledge class. Whatever the rejection, remember that the reaction to it will be aggravated if the subject also suffers from low self-esteem. The subject is driven by a hopeless and helpless dependent feeling. Even though the real or perceived rejection may seem trivial to the negotiator, it is crucial to the hostage taker. In three separate incidents, teenage hostage takers in Tennessee, Alabama, and California had each experienced a recent rejection. Divasto, Lanceley, and Gruys (1992) deal with these issues in their article entitled "Critical Issues in Suicide Intervention."

Anxiety/Inadequacy

When Eric Houston took 60 hostages at his former high school in Northern California he was anxious about, and projected blame for, his failure to graduate 2 years before the incident. He shot over a dozen faculty and students, killing four, before he was negotiated out of his dilemma by the police. In his mind, he did not fail Social Studies, the teacher failed him and caused him not to get his diploma. He had the opportunity to take Social Studies again during the summer or later in night class. He chose not to avail himself of that opportunity. A year later when Houston's employer learned that he had not graduated from high school, which was a requirement for employment, he was fired. Because of his weak ego, Houston could not accept responsibility for his termination. In his mind it was the fault of the school and his teacher. Therefore, he returned to Linhurst High School seeking revenge. And, as with most adolescent hostage takers, the original plan did not include taking hostages. He intended to shoot his former Social Studies teacher, run to his car, and drive away. But during the shooting, panic developed. As he ran, he turned the wrong way in a hallway he had walked for 3 years and ended up in a study hall, not in the parking lot. His dilemma sounds similar to those created by the inadequate personality. Negotiating with this type of person is the focus of a separate article and Chapter 9 (Strentz, 1983).

The Adolescent Criminal—Antisocial Personality

A hostage taker with an antisocial personality may be young or old, of either sex, and any race, color, or creed. If during negotiations you get the impression that the hostage taker is a cold and calculating criminal who is not suffering from any other malady, consider talking to him or her as you would talk to an adult Antisocial Personality. In this regard Lanceley (2003) has developed some guidelines for this type of negotiating, and other suggestions appear in Chapter 11.

The Psychotic

To suffer from a psychosis is a terrible and frightening ordeal. The onset of the disease can be traumatic and terrifying. This is especially true for the adolescent who has not experienced hallucinations or delusions. In addition to the usual guidelines for negotiating with this type of person, you must reassure this very frightened young person that there is medication and professional assistance that can help him deal with these scary symptoms (Strentz, 1986). Material on two psychotic types of hostage takers can be found in Chapters 12 and 13.

Negotiating Guidelines

As in adult hostage crises, you must make an initial assessment of the motivation of the adolescent hostage taker. Because this subject is an adolescent, is this crisis complicated by other issues? If so, you should consider using a blend of common sense, experience, and appropriate negotiating techniques listed or referred to in this chapter to help the troubled teenager resolve his or her crisis. Common and effective negotiation tactics include the use of rationalizations, projections, and minimizing. The use of projection is especially common in normal adolescents.

There are two types of demands, expressive and instrumental (Turk, 1982). Expressive demands are the need for attention, recognition, and satisfaction that created the crisis. Instrumental demands for a car, money, and other worldly goods address the physical and practical desires of the subject and situation. Turk's categorization is especially true with the adolescent. You must establish what is really wanted and avoid getting caught up in what the subject demands.

Remember that 80 to 90 percent of communication is nonverbal. Carefully monitor your volume and tone and the rate of your speech. We learn when we listen. Use the Carl Rogers techniques of dynamic silence—listening, repeating, restating, reflecting, and reviewing. This technique is the most effective to defuse an adolescent (McMains, 2005).

Remember the phrase, "He is not playing with a full deck?" Well, the adolescent may or may not have a full deck. However full his or her deck may be, we now know that all the usual parts of the deck are not yet fully connected. So, you are dealing with a person who is disabled. As adults we would do well to remember this when negotiating and when dealing with our kids.

As I said earlier, being 16 is as close as most people ever come to being mentally ill.

Guidelines for Negotiating
with an Adolescent Hostage Taker

1. Remember your role is to *resolve the immediate problem* and help the adolescent get past this present crisis. Long-term solutions are available and can continue after the hostage crisis has ended. *Work as if you were being paid by the hour, not the job.*

2. Clarify the adolescent's statements. *Actively listen* to understand what is really being expressed. Identify and separate the *expressive from the instrumental* demands. Do not assume you know what the adolescent means. (How well do you know teenage slang?)

3. Be conscious of typical teenage *authority issues and conflicts.*

4. Make the adolescent part of the *process.* Ask for his or her help in a cooperative search for realistic alternatives. Teenagers are frequently frustrated by their powerless status in an industrial society that extends their dependence beyond that of agrarian or agricultural societies.

5. Let and *encourage the adolescent to talk* while you and your secondary listen.

6. Are you having problems with an adolescent in your life? Can you be *objective*? There may be transference problems because the hostage taker probably has problems with authority. Do not double the trouble—find another negotiator.

7. *Acknowledge the adolescent's power.* Say things like "Yes you can do that." Generate a dialogue as you both search for alternatives.

8. Expect the adolescent to *project* blame for this and other problems onto others. Projection is a defense mechanism that is very common among all adolescents. When they err, it is usually the fault of others. The adolescent probably believes that it was not his or her fault. In his or her mind the police or someone forced him or her to take hostages.

9. Encourage the adolescent's use of projection to help *minimize* the gravity of his or her actions and the situation. Discuss his or her actions with him or her as "accidents." Determine if the adolescent has a grasp of the implications of his or her actions. As a group, adolescents do not assess risks very well. This is especially true when they are in a group of or are appealing to their peers.

10. Discuss any shooting as an accident. Help the adolescent *rationalize* his or her behavior. Remind the adolescent that other people have taken hostages. Stress what he or she has to gain by letting everyone go.

11. Avoid using the word *surrender.* Use synonyms like "come out," "leave the building," "meet me out here," and so forth. Help the adolescent save face.

12. Stay *calm* and objective. Do not become agitated. Do not respond emotionally to his or her words, threats, or deeds. The adolescent may be trying to manipulate you into an angry response. An angry response from the negotiator may provide him or her with an excuse to injure hostages. Then he or she will project the blame for his or her actions onto the negotiator. Remember and tactfully remind the adolescent that each choice has its consequences.

13. Take your *time* and do it right. Let the adolescent talk and have a sense of control as you gently steer him or her into an honorable surrender scenario.

14. Remember the power of *peer pressure* on this age group and the importance of saving face. A younger adolescent may be more concerned with status in a peer group than he or she is with staying alive.

15. Get intelligence from, but do not use, parents or other *third parties*, except as a last resort. Once the negotiator gives the phone to a third party, the negotiator has lost control.

References

Divasto, P., Lanceley, F. J., and Gruys, A. (1992) Critical Issues in Suicide Intervention, *FBI Law Enforcement Bulletin*, August, pp. 13–16.

Lanceley, F. (1981) The Antisocial Personality as a Hostage Taker, *Journal of Police Science and Administration*, Vol. 9, No. 1, pp. 28–34.

Lanceley, F. (2003) *On Scene Guide for Crisis Negotiators*, 2nd Edition, CRC Press, Boca Raton, Florida.

McMains, M. (2005) Negotiating with Special Groups, 15th Annual Crisis Negotiators Competition, Southwest Texas State University, San Marcos, Texas, January 13.

Morse, G. (2006) Decisions and Desire, *Harvard Business Review*, January.

Park, A. (2004) What Makes Teens Tick, *Time Magazine*, Vol. 163, No. 19, pp. 56–63.

Strentz, T. (1983) The Inadequate Personality as a Hostage Taker, *Journal of Police Science and Administration*, Vol. 11, No. 3, pp. 363–368.

Strentz, T. (1986) Negotiating with the Hostage-Taker Exhibiting Paranoid Schizophrenic Symptoms, *Journal of Police Science and Administration*, Vol. 14, No. 1, pp. 12–16, Vol. 11, No. 3, pp. 363–368.

Turk, A. (1982) Social Dynamics of Terrorism, *Annals of the American Academy of Science*, Vol. 463, pp. 119–128.

Webber, N. (1991) Negotiating with the Troubled Adolescent, Third Annual California Association of Hostage Negotiators Training Conference, San Diego, California, May 31.

Negotiating with the Inadequate Personality

10

Introduction

Judging from perceptions and conversations while teaching and reviewing hostage cases with experienced crisis negotiators, the person formerly labeled as having an Inadequate Personality Disorder is an individual very frequently encountered as a hostage taker (Birge, 2004). This person may be a male or female. Because most hostage takers are male, the pronoun *he* will be used throughout this chapter. Like so many other hostage takers, his actions are irrational, inappropriate, and represent an inaccurate and often counterproductive response to the problem he is seeking to solve. These types of hostage takers have a penchant for making a bad situation worse.

Incidence in Society

It is difficult, if not impossible, to state with any degree of statistical accuracy just how many people in our society could be classified as having an Inadequate Personality Disorder. It is equally difficult to point to a cause for this behavior pattern. As discussed in Chapters 1 and 11, there is evidence to suggest that some personality disorders may be congenital. No such evidence is available to identify the cause of the Inadequate Personality Disorder. Some speak of a person with this disorder as the product of a poorly functioning family. There are many anecdotal examples of heredity as well as environmental causes. When I served my internship at the Atascadero State Hospital for the Sexual Psychopath in California, I encountered many patients who were labeled as having an Inadequate Personality Disorder. Many were exhibitionist or had engaged in arson. During many interviews with their families, I encountered pathology in some and none in others.

It is not uncommon to find a patient with an Inadequate Personality Disorder who comes from a family of "overachievers." Typically, others in the patient's family had a history of dealing with obstacles by trying harder. Conversely, when faced with an obstacle, the patient gave up. I recall one patient whose father, mother, and siblings were all well educated, wealthy, and successful. His identical twin brother was the youngest Ph.D. to graduate from the Colorado School of Mines. He was working for an oil company and was quite successful. The patient gave the impression that while his siblings sought challenges as a measure of their ability, he avoided them because he believed he would fail. His I.Q. measured about 135. Yet, because of failing grades, he quit school at age 16. Whatever the cause, the person with an Inadequate Personality Disorder has a history of losing. He has been beaten by life, his employment record is poor, and his sexual relationships are marginal. If he is married, his spouse clearly and overtly dominates the relationship. He is a follower who works well under close adult supervision.

The jury is still out on the issue of heredity versus environment, nature versus nurture. Many may have come to expect authority figures in their life to be both critical and nurturing in such a way as to send the message that these people are incapable or unable to do things for themselves. They get the message from their parents that though they are not capable, they are loved enough that authority figures, their parents, will do things for them (McMains and Mullins, 2010).

The American Psychiatric Association Version

Basically, individuals with personality disorders are not psychotic or legally insane. They are *not* out of touch with reality. They have a long-term pattern of maladaptive behavior that is usually recognized by their teenage years. An observant teacher can spot this disorder in elementary school.

In the most recent edition of the American Psychiatric Association's reference text, entitled *Diagnostic and Statistical Manual of Mental Disorders,* 4th edition (*DSM-IV*, 2000), the traits of the Inadequate Personality Disorder from *DSM-II* are scattered among those with the current diagnosis of an Avoidant Personality Disorder as well as the person with a Dependent Personality Disorder.

Prior to the publishing of *DSM-III* in May 1987, this person was labeled the "inadequate personality."* However, discussions with experienced negotiators made it clear that there is a subset of hostage takers who frequently function inadequately (McMains and Mullins, 2010; Shelton, 2004). He or she was described in *DSM-II* as follows:

> An individual whose behavior is characterized by inadequate responses to intellectual, emotional, social, and physical demands. They are neither physically nor mentally grossly deficient on examination, but they do show in-adaptability, ineptness, poor judgment, lack of physical and emotional stamina, and social incompatibility. (*DSM-II*, 1952)

---

* For a more complete description of the *Diagnostic and Statistical Manual of Mental Disorders*, see Chapter 1.

Because this description of their behavior is so commonly seen by law enforcement, the term *Inadequate Personality Disorder*, found in this older *DSM* definition, will be used in this chapter to characterize this type of hostage taker.

Regardless of the current psychological label, avoidant, dependent, or inadequate, he or she is a loser. They may have a normal I.Q., but whatever the task, it is just "too much" for them. It is often said that this type of person "cannot walk and chew gum." Many make it through life by inducing others to do things for them. In an early phase of development, normal children engage in this type of manipulative behavior. Normal children mature, grow, and learn to fend for themselves. For reasons still unclear, the person who develops an Inadequate Personality Disorder does not make the transition from such dependent and manipulative behavior into adult self-sufficiency.

The Military Version

Those with military experience will remember this person as the 10 percent who never made it through basic training or boot camp. I recall an individual in my platoon at the Marine Corps Recruit Depot (MCRD) who could not make his bed, polish his shoes, or effectively clean his rifle, and so forth.

Eventually, he was discharged from MCRD as a Section 8. He was unable to adjust to military service. However, before his departure, and after we were convinced that we would all graduate or none of us would complete our training at MCRD, we were well into the Marine Corps tradition of teamwork and tried to help him make the grade.

As a manipulative, passive–aggressive person with the label of Inadequate Personality Disorder, he was most appreciative of our assistance. Yet, time and time again, when on his own, he made his rack, shined his shoes, polished his brass, cleaned his rifle, and so forth, but he could not do it right. Deeply imbued with the concept of teamwork, we literally carried him through the early weeks of boot camp. On alternating days, some of us would make his rack, others would shine his shoes, others would clean his rifle, and so forth.

One example of his inept and manipulative behavior occurred at our Sunday shoe-shining seminar. A group of us invited him to join us as we prepared our shoes for the following week. We sat on our foot lockers with our shoes, shine rags, and shoe polish as we alternately applied shoe polish and saliva to achieve a lustrous shoe shine.

With the benefit of hindsight, we should have taken more notice of the orange he was eating as he watched us spit shine our shoes. When he tried to follow our example, he could not. His shoes would not cooperate. Instead of developing a deep lustrous shine, his shoes were turning yellow. After switching brands of shoe polish and changing shine rags, both with negative results, we finally concluded that the citric acid in his saliva was the culprit. I was dumbfounded. If I wanted to malinger and induce others to shine my shoes, I would not be so inventive as to think of using his citric acid technique. He achieved his purpose. As he so gratefully watched, we shined his shoes. There are many other examples of his aberrant behavior. Suffice it to say, one day when we returned from our training he was gone. His wall locker was empty, his foot locker and mattress were missing. The rest of us achieved our goal and graduated from MCRD as a trained group of professional killers, without him.

The Movie Version

An excellent Hollywood representation of this personality disorder was played by Tim Robbins as the hostage taker named Chuck, in *Cadillac Man* (Metro Goldwyn Mayer, 1989). Even though there are over a dozen misrepresentations of how a crisis negotiating team operates in this movie, Tim Robbins portrays a character who is a classic example of someone with an Inadequate Personality Disorder. In his role, he plays the part of an unemployed husband who believes his wife is cheating on him. To solve his problem he confronts her at her place of employment where he suspects her lover is also employed. Chuck arrives with a loaded AK47 and crashes his explosive-laden motorcycle through a large window and into the car dealership. He takes about a dozen customers and employees hostage. He is surprised, confounded, and confused when the police arrive. When the police call, he does not answer the phone. A hostage, Robin Williams, does this for him and throughout the siege serves as his negotiator. As negotiations between the hostage and the police drag on, Chuck comes to the conclusion that this was not a good idea. It certainly did not solve his problem. He realizes he has made a bad personal situation into a much worse media event that is now a public circus. He makes the typical transition from an aggressive and disorganized hostage taker to a suicidal subject. It ends with his surrender. This process, like everything else in his life, he messes up, and he is justifiably shot by the police.

Another good Hollywood depiction is that of John Travolta who plays the role of a terminated museum security guard who takes his former boss, several children, their teachers, and a newsman, played by Dustin Hoffman, hostage in *Mad City* (Warner Brothers, 1998). As in *Cadillac Man* (Metro Goldwyn Mayer, 1989), there are many misrepresentations of how a negotiation should be and typically is conducted. All this aside, John Travolta plays the role of a man who is dominated by his wife, cannot hold a job, does not know how to deal with life, and now creates an untenable situation that, if anything, makes his life more difficult. Like the typical inadequate, he sees suicide as the only logical option.

The Law Enforcement Version

Dr. Harvey Schlossberg, New York Police Department (NYPD) (Retired), suggests that any criminal who becomes a hostage taker is an inadequate person because hostage taking is not an appropriate response to his dilemma (Schlossberg, 1982).

In many ways the person with an Inadequate Personality Disorder is his own worst enemy (Strentz, 1983). This person has a very poor self-concept. He is the exact opposite of the person with an Antisocial Personality Disorder who believes that he is OK and the rest of the world is not OK. This individual believes that everyone else is OK and capable, but they are not OK. Many tend to engage in a lifestyle of a self-fulfilling prophecy. They seem to make it a point to fail in life to prove they are not OK. Therefore, they are very comfortable as they enable and allow people to do things for them. Police may encounter this person as a prostitute who always forgives her pimp for assaulting her, typically saying, "I should have given him all of the money." Again, in her mind, the pimp is OK, and she is not.

Further, this personality disorder, like every other mental malady, is not unique to any country or culture. I was recently engaged in a crisis negotiation and tactical training program in Eastern Europe. One afternoon I was scheduled to talk to the tactical team about the role of negotiators in resolving a crisis. When I arrived at the tactical team classroom I saw Jay, one of their three interpreters, outside smoking a cigarette. I recognized him as a new interpreter who was quite intelligent. He was an electrical engineer. He was fluent in several languages. He had been assigned to the tactical class as an observer to learn tactical technical terms. I entered the classroom and stood at the rear where I saw Dave, one of the tactical instructors. I asked him why Jay was not in the room. Dave said Jay was having a nicotine fit and had to step out for a smoke. When I gave my lecture Jay sat in the room for a few minutes and then went out for another smoke or to stare at the sky.

During our joint exercise, the lead tactical instructor, John, sent Jay to me to be used as a suicidal role player. I carefully briefed Jay on his role as a person who was depressed over recent events to include his loss of a job and family health problems. I told him to force the negotiators to convince him to surrender rather than kill himself. I also told him that we needed to test the negotiators' and tactical team's patience and the ability to work together to iron out the mechanics of a surrender plan. I tried to impress upon him the importance of creating obstacles and problems for the negotiator. I gave him several examples that included hanging up the phone, crying, sighing, asking for repeated reassurances to force the negotiator to convince him that life was worth living, and so forth. This briefing took about 15 minutes. In closing I said, "We have to stretch this surrender scenario out for about an hour, call me with questions and ideas to cause realistic problems for the negotiator and the tactical team." Jay said he understood the role so I left. It took me about 2 minutes to walk from the crisis site to the negotiators' location.

When I arrived, I learned that Jay had surrendered and had walked out behind me. Before I could ask him what he was thinking or why he surrendered so soon, he was on his bicycle riding home from the Field Training Exercise (FTX). I went over to John, the lead tactical instructor, to express my dismay.

John said, "That's not the half of it." Earlier in the week, Jay had been assigned to guard the MP5s on the range while he and Dave took the tactical team on a live-fire, practical pistol exercise where they engaged targets in and around the range with their 9-mm Glocks. While guarding the submachine guns Jay took a blank 9-mm round from a Glock clip, placed it in the MP5, and fired it. The MP5 did not extract the shell casing. Jay could not dislodge it. So, he placed the MP5 back in the tactical bag. When the tactical team returned, Jay said he had to go home and peddled off on his bicycle. Fortunately, John engaged the tactical team in the proper safety procedures before firing the MP5. The unextracted shell casing was discovered before the weapon was fired and anyone was injured.

After the FTX, John and I spoke with and counseled Jay. We stressed the importance of learning from experience and moving on to new challenges. Jay said he understood and was looking forward to a fresh start the following day. The next evening I asked John how Jay's fresh start went. I learned that Jay called in sick.

Jay is not stupid. He has a degree in electrical engineering from one of Europe's finest technical universities. His language ability is outstanding. However, his judgment is poor, he is impulsive, he has trouble making decisions, he engages in submissive and clinging behavior, he needs others to assume responsibility for most major areas of his life, he consistently makes the wrong decisions, and he is always looking for someone to take care of him. Other common symptoms are available in *DSM-IV*.

Many members of cults fit this classification. Typically, they are faithful followers in these organizations (Strentz, 1980, 1988). A law enforcement example of their role as followers can be seen in the behavior of two people, Kate and Keith Haigler. They belonged to an Arkansas cult called "The Foundation of Ubiquity" and followed the teachings of Father Fou. For starters, who among us would follow anyone who called himself Father Fou? To make matters worse, Father Fou convinced the Haiglers they were the two prophets spoken of in the book of Revelations in the *Bible*. Their destiny was to spread the word of God for a specific period of time and then be put to death. To complete this prophesy, 3 days later they would rise from the dead. As part of their divine mission, after they completed the required number of days spreading the word, they hijacked a bus, took about a dozen people hostage, and then forced the Arkansas State Police to shoot them.

To no avail law enforcement negotiators and several local preachers tried to convince them that their leader, Henry Mayo Lamb, had misinterpreted the *Bible*. They finally exited the bus, knelt down, kissed each other, and pointed their loaded weapons at the Arkansas State Police. When the police fired and wounded them, they shot and killed each other.

Another siege that involved a person with an Inadequate Personality Disorder as a hostage taker occurred in Portland, Oregon. A young man attempted to obtain money for an operation needed by his son. Rather than contact social services, he decided to rob The Red Lion Motel where he had worked as a gardener. He lost that job because he irreparably damaged expensive grass cutters and edgers. En route to the motel, his car ran out of gas. When he arrived at the motel he entered the wrong office, confronted five bookkeepers, and demanded money. They told him they only had receipts. They said the money was at the front desk. He dispatched one of them to bring the money to him. When she failed to return, he sent another. The second met the first at the front desk where she was speaking with the manager and a police officer.

After negotiations were initiated an attempt was made to calm the hostage taker. An arrangement was made to place a small amount of the money he was demanding outside one of two doors to the siege site. The hostage taker sent a third hostage out the wrong door to get the money. He was now down to two hostages and still had no money. Negotiations proceeded for another 2 hours during which time the hostages did most of the negotiating with the police. Just when negotiations appeared to have reached an impasse the hostage taker announced, "I quit." As he exited the room the hostages protested to the police that they need not be so rough with him (Simpson, 1979). This type of hostage taker, because he seems so troubled and inept, typically provokes a strong Stockholm syndrome response from his hostages.

The subsequent incident interview of him by Detective Lt. David Simpson of the Portland Police Bureau is typical of how this person interacts with others. The underlying dynamics are that he does not want to talk. Simpson wanted a statement. After providing him with his Miranda Warning, Simpson tried to get the subject talking by saying something like, "As I understand it, you needed money for your son's operation so you decided to rob the motel." Simpson waited for a response, and finally the subject said "yeah." Simpson tried a minimal encourager by saying, "And then?" The subject said nothing. So, Simpson said, "You went to the bookkeepers' office to get money." Simpson waited and waited, and finally the subject said "yeah." This went on and on. Simpson ended *his* 45-minute confession with an intermittent and occasional "Yeah" from the subject (Simpson, 1979).

A final example is a young man named Donald Dunn whose family nicknamed him Lennie. You may recall that is the name of the oaf in Steinbeck's book *Of Mice and Men*. The final encounter Dunn had with the King County

Sheriff's Department occurred when he was caught in a stolen car with his girl-friend. They had decided, according to the suicide notes left behind, to move from Seattle to Idaho or commit suicide. Dunn's car had been impounded by the police when he left it at a mall from which he fled after his girlfriend attempted to use a stolen credit card. The evening of the hostage siege, as they tried to make their way to Idaho, they stole a Volkswagen van. It ran out of gas. They had other problems with a second stolen vehicle. At around 0200 they were in the third stolen vehicle, with gas for the first one, which was just a few yards away, when they were stopped by the sheriff. They abandoned the third vehicle and fled to the first. Using their K-9 unit, the sheriff's office traced them to the van and negotiations began. Dunn held a gun to his girlfriend as he spoke with the negotiator. He demanded cigarettes; they were delivered but never retrieved. He then demanded a pencil and paper; they were delivered but never retrieved. He then demanded a cell phone. This request was denied. He gave the deputies less than a minute to deliver the phone or he would kill his hostage. He knew from the previous deliveries that they took time. So he forced the officers to fail to justify shooting and killing his girlfriend. He then attempted suicide but missed and ended up in the Walla Walla, Washington, state prison for over 20 years (Strentz, 2007).

Conclusion

The characteristics of the person with an Inadequate Personality Disorder are such that his history of and penchant for failure in life may result in a bungled criminal act. In this failed criminal act, his history of poor decision making typically takes over, and he takes hostages to solve his problem. Once again, he has succeeded in making a bad situation worse. His penchant for getting into difficult situations and his practice of getting others to help him out of trouble suggest that the most effective negotiation tactic is to be firm and understanding.

This requires a negotiator who has police experience and certainly one who can provide a sense of parental acceptance while maintaining control. The negotiator must try to convince this individual that the best way to resolve this dilemma is to work together. Because this person has a history of failure, the negotiator must remember that another failure could be fatal for him and his hostage. Therefore, he must engage in ego support and enable the hostage taker to honorably withdraw from this dilemma, *not surrender*. He does not need another failure in his life. In his negotiation, Dave Simpson used the phrase "fold your tent" rather than the term "surrender." It worked well in Portland and is certainly worth considering. Frankly, I have searched dictionaries and the thesaurus for acceptable synonyms to "surrender." I found very few. "Fold your tent" or "live to fight another day" are among the few good ones I found.

Negotiating Guidelines and Their Rationales

As a crisis negotiator, we frequently encounter the person with an Inadequate Personality Disorder at a poorly planned robbery, as a member of a cult, or in a domestic dispute. His demands are outrageous. He typically starts by telling law enforcement to go away. He may want a million dollars in gold or several hundred thousand dollars in $5 bills.

Initially, to effectively deal with this type of hostage taker, the crisis negotiating process requires that the negotiator be very open, accepting, and nondirective. Be patient. When I deal with this type of person, the mind-set that usually works is for me to play the role of a very understanding and patient parent who has caught his child in a lie. As a parent, I want my child to benefit and learn from this experience, and become a stronger person. As a crisis negotiator it is recommended that one remember this mind-set, proceed very slowly, and be tolerant. *Put your badge in your pocket.*

1. Remember this person was previously labeled an inadequate personality.
   a. Try to build the person's fragile ego. "You sound like a big man to me."
   b. Build this person's self-esteem. "Certainly, a person as intelligent as you realizes..."
   c. Law enforcement negotiators of the opposite sex should be considered.
2. Because of this person's weak ego, penchant for failure, and previous problems with authority figures, he may prefer that a hostage negotiate for him.
   a. This person may have a history of manipulating others into doing unpleasant tasks for him.
3. As a reaction to the stress of the crisis, we frequently encounter a strong Stockholm syndrome reaction. The hostages tend to feel pity for this person. If there are female hostages who have strong motherly instincts they will tend to be very protective of the subject and will attempt to protect him from the police and gladly negotiate for him.
4. Show understanding and uncritical acceptance.
   a. Have you been in sticky situations before? Tell me about it.
   b. Help this person *rationalize* his situation, *project blame,* and *minimize* problems.
5. After rapport has been established, the negotiator may become more directive.
6. Because of the attention this person is getting, he may not want the situation to end.

7. Because this person is impulsive and tends to fatigue easily, he may suddenly decide to come out.

8. This person probably does not realize the gravity of his predicament.

9. Do not introduce nonpolice negotiators to observe their failure. This includes police officers who may have known the subject since childhood. While these resources may provide good intelligence, do not put them on the telephone.

10. Suicide is a real possibility. Be aware of verbal will and a suicide-by-cop scenario.

11. Avoid any mention of the tactical team as such. Remember, this person is in well over his head. He does not need any additional stress. On the other hand, if he is suicidal, remember he typically sees himself as a victim. With this mind-set he may engage in suicide by cop.

12. Strive to convince this person of the honorable, brave, and logical withdrawal, *not surrender*, from this situation that you have proposed.

References

American Psychiatric Association (1952) *Diagnostic and Statistical Manual of Mental Disorders*–2nd Edition, American Psychiatric Association, Washington, DC.

American Psychiatric Association (2001) *Diagnostic and Statistical Manual of Mental Disorders*–4th Edition, American Psychiatric Association, Washington, DC.

Bible, Revelations 12:3–13.

Birge, R. (2004) Personal interview during Basic Hostage Negotiations Course, Pacific Grove, California, February 12.

McMains, M. J., and Mullins, W. C. (2010) *Crisis Negotiations*, 4th Edition, Anderson Publications, Cincinnati, Ohio.

Metro Goldwyn Mayer (1989) *Cadillac Man*, Hollywood, California.

Schlossberg, H. (1982) Personal interview with Dr. Schlossberg, Traverse City, Michigan, April 6.

Shelton, L. (2004) Personal interview, Baton Rouge Police Department, May 9; Kosovo Police Service School, Vushirru, Kosovo, May 26.

Simpson, D. (1979) Personal interview, Portland Police Bureau, Portland, Oregon, August.

Strentz, T. (1980) Terrorist Organizational Profile, An Act to Combat International Terrorism U.S. Congress, Senate, Committee on Governmental Affairs. Washington, DC, U.S. Government Printing Office: 1980, Y 4. G 74/9:96-831.

Strentz, T. (1983) The Inadequate Personality as a Hostage Taker, *Journal of Police Science and Administration*, Vol. II, No. 3, pp. 363–368.

Strentz, T. (1988) A Terrorist Psycho-Social Profile: Past and Present, *FBI Law Enforcement Bulletin*, Vol. 61, No. 11–18, April.

Strentz, T. (2007) Personal interview with Donald Dunn in Walla Walla State Prison, Washington.

The Antisocial Personality Disorder (It's All about Me!) Hostage Taker

11

Introduction

A few years ago, police in New England cornered a young man, who, after a long hot pursuit from an aborted bank robbery in Vermont entered a residence in Massachusetts and took a deputy sheriff and his children hostage in their home. This individual, who said he had to rob the bank because his parole agent was demanding he repay the car loan that he lost gambling, met his father for the first time when they were in the same state prison. During protracted negotiations, he rationalized his situation and blamed others for his troubles. The siege ended when the deputy assaulted the subject and escaped out the window as the police entered the home. Typically, and due to his large ego, this hostage taker acted as his own attorney. He was found guilty on all counts and sentenced to 40 years in state prison (Special Agent Liane McCarthy, 2000).

It is easy to recognize an Antisocial Personality Disorder (ASP*) hostage taker† by his glibness, his narcissism, his seemingly stress-free voice and attitude, his high verbal skills, and his constant use of rationalization and projection to justify his situation. His demands will be for money, escape, and other self-serving needs. Remember, "It's all about me!" His demeanor will remind you of criminal informants with whom you have been involved. When one compares his chronological to his emotional age, he appears to many to be an adult adolescent. During the siege, he will challenge the negotiator as if the life and death hostage siege is a game.

Over the years, the person now labeled as having an antisocial personality by the American Psychiatric Association has had several other labels and has wreaked havoc on humanity for centuries. In colonial times, he was called "Morally Insane," then the "Constitutional Psychopathic Inferior," the "Psychopath," the "Sociopath," and most recently, the "Antisocial Personality."

---

* The acronym ASP, a snake, rather than APD will be used because ASP more accurately describes the behavior of the person with an Antisocial Personality Disorder. He is a snake.

† Hostage takers and people with the Antisocial Personality Disorder come in both sexes. Because most hostage takers are males, the pronoun he will be used in this chapter.

There may be other professional or more generic names, but these five come to mind and will pass the censors. The changing labels reflect a professional attempt to more accurately describe the typical behavioral pattern and perhaps explain this social pariah.

This disorder has been around for a long time. If you are familiar with the New Testament in the *Bible* you will recall that Judas Iscariot, in addition to being an informant, was stealing money the disciples had collected for the poor (John 12:6).

The best description of this disorder is in the excellent and well-titled text *Without Conscience*, by Dr. Robert D. Hare:

> The Antisocial Personality, Psychopath, is a social predator who charms, manipulates, and ruthlessly plows his way through life, leaving a broad trail of broken hearts, shattered expectations, and empty wallets. Completely lacking in conscience and feeling for others, he selfishly takes what he wants and does as he pleases, violating social norms and expectations without the slightest sense of guilt or regret. (Hare, 1993)

It's All about Me

If one were to create a continuum and move from normal to greedy, to self-centered, to self-indulgent, to a sense of entitlement, to dangerously narcissistic, then well beyond this beginning, one would find the antisocial person who, according to Dr. Joyceln Roland, the lead psychologist for the Los Angeles Sheriff's Office, views life as "It's all about me!" They are your friend, as long as there is something in it for them. They are takers, not givers. All they ever give their associates and family are heartaches and hard times (Roland, 2003).

Civilized society is based on trust. It is this trust that the ASP manipulates, ignores, and violates to suit his immediate wants. When he sees something he wants, he takes it. In a word, he is impulsive. His attitude is that rules, regulations, tenets, commandments, and laws apply to others. Be it speeding in a car or boat or serial killing, he does not believe the laws apply to him. He is not crazy, but he knows that by some civil or criminal code, certainly not his, what he is doing is wrong, he just does not care. He does what suits him when it suits him, because "It's all about me." By any name, he is a social predator on the society law enforcement and corrections officers are sworn to serve and protect (Ochberg et al., 2003). The only good thing one can say about the ASP is that for law enforcement and corrections personnel, he represents job security.

The Antisocial Personality Disorder

By way of introduction, the official label *Antisocial Personality Disorder*, though very descriptive, is on the surface quite misleading because most typically, the ASP can be very socially adept, quite engaging, and a very pleasant and charming individual. However, this thin veneer covers the monster that dwells within. An example is the handsome, charming, and gregarious serial killer, Ted Bundy, who killed dozens of young women from Tacoma, Washington, to Tallahassee, Florida, during the 1970s and 1980s.

The cause of this disorder remains a mystery. There is ample and yet inconclusive evidence of genetic influences as well as environmental factors. Perhaps it is an interplay of these two diverse influences that is the root cause (Deitz, 2001). Some have suggested demonic possession.

In many cases, the ASP begins to exhibit this disorder at a very early age, usually by age 6 or 7. There is anecdotal evidence of this disorder evidencing itself in children who are just learning to speak, when according to their parents, "They engage in constant lying about everything." The term *psychopathic liar* is also used to describe the ASP. "The youthful triad" of behaviors has been seen in male subjects since the Spanish Inquisition. These three behaviors—enuresis, arson, and cruelty to animals—are discussed in some detail under the classification of Conduct Disorder in the *Diagnostic and Statistical Manual, IV-2000*, of the American Psychiatric Association (*DSM-IV*, 2000, pp. 85–91).

Many young boys wet the bed. Although most respond to therapy, the budding ASP does not. As a group, normal children play with matches more than normal adults. However, the child who starts a fire under his parents' bed or sprays lighter fluid onto another and then ignites his victim is another matter. Children, as a group, are not as kind to animals as are adults. However, the youthful ASP is more than unkind to pets; he tortures and often kills them. Some say he really wants to torture and kill people, but he is not yet big enough, so he is taking his wrath out on pets that most children love and cherish.

The Movie Version

By way of example, this personality type has been the subject of many movies. He was well portrayed by Robert Mitchum in the 1940s and more recently by Robert DeNiro, as the charming and chilling killer in *Cape Fear* (MCA Universal, 1991). The serial killer and seductive character portrayed by Sharon Stone in *Basic Instinct* (LE Studio, 1992) and the seductive and manipulative character portrayed by Kathleen Turner in *Body Heat* (Warner Brothers, 1981) were entertaining, as was the lethal con-artist portrayed by Matt Damon in *The Talented Mr. Ripley* (Paramount, 1999). More recently, there is the less-than-lethal con-artist played by Leonardo DiCaprio in *Catch Me If You Can* (Dream Works, 2002). A more humorous example was the character portrayed by Jack Nicholson in *One Flew Over the Cuckoo's Nest* (Republic Pictures, 1975).

The Law Enforcement Version

Each of these characters portrayed a person who engaged in a variety of crimes. Perhaps the best example of this criminal behavior is seen in the quote from an interview conducted by Supervisor Special Agent, Robert K. Ressler, of the FBI Behavioral Science Unit. During a prison interview he spoke with one ASP, G. Daniel Walker:

Ressler: "How long is your rap sheet?"
Walker: "I would think the current one would probably be about 29 or 30 pages."
Ressler: "Twenty-nine or thirty pages! Charlie Manson's is only five."
Walker: "But, he was only a killer" (Hare, 1993).

What Walker meant was that while Manson may have specialized in murder, he, Walker, was a criminal of enormous versatility, a fact of which he was quite proud. He boasted of having committed more than 300 crimes for which he had not been caught (Hare, 1993).

Infamous examples, like those of serial killers Ted Bundy, Angelo Bono, and Kenneth Bianchi, may be extreme, yet they depict people whom every law enforcement and corrections officer has dealt with time and time again. Each of us has been "conned" by this person who can and has turned many a professional into a very cynical person.

American Psychiatric Association (APA)

The APA publishes a reference book entitled, *The Diagnostic and Statistical Manual*, that is now in its fourth edition. This text lists and describes the many mental diseases and disorders the APA recognizes, much like state penal codes list and describe violations of the law. It lists about 100 disorders. Among them are 11 specific personality disorders that are generally described as enduring patterns of behavior that deviate markedly from the expectations of one's culture, are pervasive and inflexible, have onset in adolescence, are stable over time, and lead to distress or impairment. Of the 11, this was the first one identified by the APA (Ochberg et al., 2003). Briefly, it is a pattern of disregard for, and violation of, the rights of others (*DSM-IV*, 2000, pp. 649).

The specific diagnostic criteria for the ASP listed in *DSM-IV* (2000, pp. 649–650) (Note that italicized emphasis is that of the author and is not found in *DSM-IV*):

> A. There is a pervasive pattern of disregard for and violation of the rights of others occurring since age 15, as indicated by three (or more) of the following:

(1) failure to conform to social norms with respect to lawful behaviors as indicated by *repeatedly* performing acts that are grounds for arrest

(2) deceitfulness, as indicated by *repeated* lying, use of aliases, or conning others for personal profit or pleasure

(3) impulsivity or failure to plan ahead

(4) irritability and aggressiveness, as indicated by *repeated* physical fights or assaults

(5) *reckless* disregard for the safety of self or others

(6) *consistent* irresponsibility, as indicated by repeated failure to sustain consistent work behavior or honor financial obligations

(7) lack of remorse, as indicated by being indifferent to or rationalizing having hurt, mistreated or stolen from another

B. The individual is at least 18 years old.

C. There is evidence of Conduct Disorder with onset before age 15 years. (This includes, but is not limited to arson, cruelty to animals/adults, the use of a deadly weapon, and sexual assault.)

D. The occurrence of antisocial behavior is not exclusively during the course of Schizophrenia or a Manic Episode.

Note the use of the adjectives "repeated, reckless, and consistent." Many normal people engage in some of this behavior from time to time. It is the consistent pattern that generally triggers this diagnosis. In addition, most adult ASPs with whom I have dealt, had a Conduct Disorder, or more commonly, were juvenile delinquents, in their younger days (*DSM-IV*, 2000, pp. 85–91).

Their involvement in criminal activity is well documented and discussed by Dr. Marvin Wolfgang, in his famous "Philadelphia Cohort Studies," which showed a small percentage of the criminal population was responsible for most of the crime. In other words, some people commit one or two crimes. The ASP commits dozens. Briefly, Wolfgang followed 9,945 boys born in the same year for 20 years. He found that 6.3 percent of these boys, about 596 of them, committed *well over* half of the crimes for which this age group was arrested (Wolfgang, Figlio, and Sellin, 1972).

Like most mental disorders, the ASP is found in every race, color, creed, and civilization. According to Hare (1993) they represent about 2 to 3 percent of our population. Thus, in the United States, with a current population of over 350 million, their numbers are around 6 to 8 million—certainly enough to keep law enforcement busy and our correctional institutions full for decades to come.

Typically the ASP is impulsive. Immediate gratification is his norm. When he sees something or someone he wants, he takes it or them. He makes *excessive* use of two common psychological defense mechanisms: *projection* and *rationalization*. An example of projection is that of blaming others for his situation. I interviewed a person, diagnosed as being an ASP, who had stabbed his victim three dozen times. But, it was not his fault, "the knife went out of control." An arsonist may claim that he did not burn down the building, "the fire did." The rapist may claim that he did not sexually assault his victim, "she wanted rough sex." A killer may say that the victim "should have done what he was told or should not have looked at him that way." Another common projection is that "If he did not want to be assaulted and robbed, why did he carry that much money in this neighborhood?" The key here is that he really believes what he is saying. In his mind, it really is not his fault. He is always OK. "It's always about me!"

Rationalization is a defense mechanism many people use on a daily basis. However, the ASP rationalizes almost hourly to excuse criminal behavior. A drug dealer will excuse his crime by saying, "If I don't sell them drugs, someone else will." I interviewed one serial killer who said, "People are born to die, all I did was speed up the process."

In 1965, as a student earning my master's degree in social work, I did an internship at Atascadero State Hospital for the Sexual Psychopath, located on the Central Coastal of California, where I met and attempted therapy with many young men who had a diagnosis of Antisocial Personality Disorder. One young man had been incarcerated for shooting and killing his grandparents because he said, "I always wondered what it would feel like to kill a person." (Remember, "It's all about me.") He provides an example of the truly dangerous ASP.

He was a member of my adolescent group that met with me on Tuesdays and Fridays. In an attempt to ingratiate himself to me, he placed himself in the role of "junior therapist" and gathered the group on Monday and Thursday. Each morning, as I entered the hospital, he would meet me at the front door and walk with me to my office. During this stroll, he would tell me of the progress he was making with the group and with himself, "thanks to your brilliant insight, Dr. Strentz." Each time I corrected him on my title, he would respond with a statement to the effect that I should be a "doctor," because I was so insightful and effective with the patients.

During this time, he was exhibiting, more accurately "faking," some "success" in his treatment. He had stopped fighting, was making his bed, began to take responsibility for his crime, and worked well in various assignments around the hospital. Eventually he had his own office with a coffeepot, a "perk" and certainly a real status symbol within the hospital, especially for a patient. As an intern, I shared my office with three other interns, and we had no coffeepot.

Just before the end of my internship, he stopped meeting me at the door and ceased playing "junior therapist." I made some inquiries and determined he learned I would be leaving in February, months before his annual status hearing. Since I would not be at his hearing and thus could not do him any good, he dropped me like a bad habit. Because I could not help him, he moved on to someone he thought could and would. Again, "It's all about me!"

As an epilogue, after about 10 years, he was released from the California Department of Mental Health and remanded to the custody of the California Department of Corrections. Contrary to the recommendation of the staff at Atascadero, they decided to place him on parole in the care and custody of his mother. He is now back in prison. Within a year of his release, he began killing and sexually assaulting young girls he picked up along the highway. He eventually killed his mother and her friend. In his mind, according to one of the videos he made, these homicides were not his fault. His victims were the cause of the crimes. The young girls should not have been hitchhiking, and his mother should not have tormented and harassed him. As for her friend, well, "that was too bad." He killed her because she was the one person most likely to miss his mother and he needed time to get away. "It's all about me!"

Hostage Takers

In my opinion, the two most difficult types of hostage takers encountered by law enforcement are subjects with Antisocial Personality Disorder and those who are suicidal. The suicidal person is dangerous because he wants to die. He may want the police to kill him, he may try to force their hand, and he may not care how many people he takes with him. This person is discussed further in Chapters 14 and 15.

Similarly, the ASP may take chances, make threats, and issue demands that sound suicidal. He may challenge the police. It may appear that he wants to die, but unlike the suicidal person, he does not. Typically, he is convinced that he is smarter, stronger, and has other virtues that will allow him to escape from the scene, regardless of how unrealistic his plan may be.

Negotiating Guidelines and Their Rationales

This person is most likely to be encountered as a hostage taker in a robbery that has gone bad, a workplace incident, or as a perpetrator in a domestic dispute who is holding his "significant other(s)" hostage. To the ASP, the snake, they are "insignificant others."

The following are recommended guidelines for negotiating with the ASP:

1. Do not share sensitive or personal information. This tactic can be effective with the person who is considering suicide. The ASP will try to learn about you so he can use this information against you. The negotiation process is a game to him. He does not believe he will ever die.

2. Keep him busy. He needs psychological stimulation and challenges. They have a powerful need to be in control. Further, when occupied with decisions and discussions, they are less likely to injure hostages.

3. Keep him involved in the negotiation process. Use expressions like "Certainly, a person as intelligent as you understands that..." or "I know you are smart enough to realize that..."

4. He must be convinced that the safe return/release of the hostages, as well as anything else he does, is to his personal advantage. While doing this, be careful not to place social or personal value on the hostages. He certainly enjoys the suffering of his victims. Do not let him know you are concerned about them. He will use this against you.

5. Do not attempt to put the ASP on a "guilt trip." The snake has no conscience. An attempt at a guilt trip strategy will tell him what you value. That is information about you that he can, and certainly will, use against you in his game of manipulation and intimidation.

6. Negotiations must be "reality oriented." Remember, the ASP enjoys taking risks and is stimulated, not frightened, by the danger of this situation. He is not suicidal. He is very egocentric and wants to survive. Typically, he loves himself too much to die.

7. It is unlikely that good rapport will develop between the ASP and the negotiator or any of the hostages. They do not experience the Stockholm Syndrome. However, because of their charm and manipulative nature, their hostages may experience "identification with the aggressor." They trust and may adore him. The ASP does not reciprocate these feelings.

8. Like other personality disorders, the ASP is impulsive.

9. His stress level is very low. What frightens others delights him.

10. He makes excessive use of projection and rationalization.

11. He probably has a criminal record. Do not lie to him about the criminal justice system or process. He knows the system and the process. He may try to trick you into telling him something that is not true so he can mock you and play his game of "Gotcha."

12. Nonpolice negotiators will be of marginal value because they are more easily conned by this person or have experience on a personal level with him that prevents them from being objective.

13. Play the rationalization game with him. Taking hostages is no big deal, it is not even listed in the penal code. Others have done it. What choice did he have?

14. Understand and play into his use of projection. Remember, in his mind he is OK, others are the cause of his troubles. He just intended to rob the store. The police responded too quickly and forced him to take hostages as an act of self-defense. Similarly, any shooting he did was also in self-defense.

15. Minimize what has happened. As Robin Williams says in the movie *Cadillac Man*, "You did not shoot a police officer, you shot a foot."

Psychologically, there is no known cure for this malady. The aging process tends to slow them down physically. But, until we learn the cause, the cure will continue to elude us. In the meantime, they remain a menace to the society we are sworn to serve and protect. Perhaps the best single explanation for this disorder was given to us by a University of California Psychologist, Margaret Singer, who said, "They may simply be evil" (Singer, 1999).

Remember, for the person with Antisocial Personality Disorder, "It's all about me!"

References

American Psychiatric Association (2000) *Diagnostic and Statistical Manual of Mental Disorders*–4th Edition (*DSM-IV*), APA, Washington, DC.

Deitz, P. (2001) Mad or Bad, presentation to the California Association of Hostage Negotiators, Annual Training Conference, June 1, 2001, San Diego, California.

Hare, R. D. (1993) *Without Conscience: The Disturbing World of the Psychopaths among Us*, Guilford Press, London.

McCarthy, L. (2000) FBI Special Agent, Salem, MA Corrections Officer Hostage Incident, presentation to the California Association of Hostage Negotiators, Annual Training Conference, June 2, Monterey, California.

Ochberg, F. M., Brantley, A. C., Hare, R. D., Houk, P. D., Ianni, R., James, E., O'Toole, M. E., and Saathoff, G. (2003) Lethal Predators: Psychopathic, Sadistic, and Sane, *Emergency Mental Health*, Vol. 5, No. 3, Summer, pp. 121–136.

Roland, J. (2003) Assessing the Hostage Taker from a Mental Health Professional's Perspective, presentation to the California Association of Hostage Negotiators, Annual Training Conference, May 28, Long Beach, California.

Singer, M. (1999) The Antisocial Personality, presentation at the CAHN Northern Regional Training, April 22, Alameda, California.

Wolfgang, M. E., Figlio, R., and Sellin, T. (1972) *Delinquency in a Birth Cohort*, University of Chicago Press, Chicago, Illinois.

Negotiating with the Paranoid Schizophrenic Hostage Taker

12

Introduction

At 5:00 P.M. on Friday a tall, white male, Joseph Billie Gwin, age 28, entered the KOOL Television Station in Phoenix, Arizona. He was armed with a .38 caliber revolver, carried his own portable TV set, and had a lengthy statement written on legal-size paper folded up in his pocket. He fired a shot, assaulted two employees, held another around the neck, and demanded that he be given air time to read his long statement. The Phoenix Police Department (PPD) that shared a parking lot with KOOL TV was called and responded immediately.

In spite of their speedy response, Gwin took hostage an announcer, the floor manager, a technician, a production assistant, a cameraman, and two others. Gwin arranged his arrival to air his views during prime time on the daily 6:00 P.M. news broadcast. Much to his dismay, the PPD successfully delayed this reading and fatigued Gwin until 10:00 P.M. They secured the release of all but one hostage before granting Gwin his request. They convinced him that a trained announcer (his last hostage) who had credibility with the TV audience should read his demands (Hawkins, 1982). In spite of the fact that his primary hostage, under the influence of the Stockholm syndrome (Strentz, 1979), was extremely upset with the police during the incident, this hostage crisis was successfully resolved without further violence by well-trained negotiators who worked in close conjunction with the special weapons and tactics (SWAT) team. The key to success was proper analysis and handling of the hostage taker. They let him tell his story and thereby complete his mission. Mission completed, he surrendered. Gwin pleaded not guilty by reason of insanity. Thirty years later, to make certain that Gwin takes his medication, the PPD maintains regular contact with him. On occasion they take him to the local pharmacy to refill his prescriptions.

In April 2004, at about 0300 hours, the Baton Rouge Police Department, Louisiana, responded to a call that a man had climbed about 200 feet up a government radio transmitting tower. The tower is used by the city to dispatch fire equipment and is shared with the federal government. While the tactical team and negotiators were responding to the tower, calls were made, and arrangements finalized, for the affected agencies to use alternate transmitting towers. This capability is part of the East Baton Rouge Parish

117

hurricane response plan. Once the switch was made, electrical power to the tower was cut. This allowed the police to move in and around the structure safely. It also eliminated the danger to and possibility of the subject accidentally electrocuting himself.

By observing the subject through binoculars and after interviews with his relatives, who had made the initial 911 call, it was determined that he was unarmed, was living in a mental health facility, and was suffering from Paranoid Schizophrenia. His relatives suspected that he had stopped taking his medication.

Having accomplished these preliminary tasks, the negotiating team used a fire department hoist to elevate the negotiator to a position where he could safely converse with the subject. The subject, John Jones, age 31, was concerned with the current direction of U.S. foreign policy and wanted to communicate with the president. The negotiator encouraged Jones to tell him about his concern with our foreign policy as well as his instructions from God to communicate his ideas to the president. It is still not clear why he chose this tower for his mission. There is no sign saying that the federal government uses this facility—logic dictates that it was near his residence and convenient. Persons unknown had cut a hole in the protective fence. Jones was quite athletic and had the upper body strength to shimmy about 40 feet up a leg of the tower that gave him access to the internal ladder. Fortunately for the negotiator, and for Jones, it was not a windy night. The role of the tactical team was focused on observing Jones to make sure he did not have a weapon. As Jones told his story he waved his arms and gestured violently. April in Baton Rouge is warm. Jones was wearing shorts and a t-shirt. He was very unhappy with our president and wanted the world to know his concerns and understand his story. Because of the real possibility that he might fall, his relatives were moved from the scene as were some local denizens who were challenging Jones to jump.

The negotiator listened, asked questions, and communicated a genuine interest in Jones's plight and frustration with the government. When Jones was finished telling his story, he descended the tower and was taken into custody.

Today, in Baton Rouge, as over a quarter of a century ago in Phoenix, the successful tactic was to take time to allow and *encourage the subject to ventilate*, let him tell his important story. Once the story is told, and the subject is sufficiently fatigued, the Paranoid Schizophrenic subject typically considers his mission complete and is prepared to surrender.

Does this tactic always work? No. One can never predict with 100 percent reliability what tactic will work when dealing with people. However, it works in well over 90 percent of the cases. The negotiator must ask the right questions to learn the cause of the crisis and the nature of the subject's hallucinations and delusional system. Is there a message and mission from God? What is the mission? Is it harmless, such as broadcasting a belief, or is it harmful, like killing hostages?

There was an incident in Memphis, Tennessee, called the Shannon Street Siege that occurred in mid-January 1983 where the mission/delusion of the hostage taker was dangerous but was not treated as such. In this case a Paranoid Schizophrenic hostage taker, Lindberg Sanders, age 49, who considered himself the "Black Jesus," was the leader of a cult that lured two Memphis police officers into their residence. His delusion was that police officers were agents of Satan and, as such, were logical and legitimate foes for him and his followers. Other beliefs of the cult included not eating pork or drinking water. One officer escaped with a gunshot wound to his face. His partner, Officer R. S. Hester, was hit on the head and trapped in the house. The police negotiated for 30 hours, during which Sanders told the negotiator of his belief system. By the time the tactical team was allowed to enter the residence, Officer Hester had been killed by members of the cult, all of whom died in the assault (United Press International, 1983).

This is why we ask the hostage taker questions, listen to, and evaluate his answers. Certainly, a delusion that police officers are agents of the Devil professed by a person holding a police officer hostage who considers himself the "Black Jesus" is a very dangerous delusion. Remember, a good negotiator is not necessarily a good talker. However, and without any doubt, he or she must be a good listener, especially when dealing with a Paranoid Schizophrenic who has a story to tell and within that story are the "hooks" and the "hot buttons."

Unlike the antisocial or inadequate personality (Lanceley, 1981; Strentz, 1983) or the political assassin (Hassel, 1974), the Paranoid Schizophrenic hostage taker defies generalization. Joseph Billie Gwin and John Jones suffered from Paranoid Schizophrenia (Hawkins, 1982; Shelton, 2004). They were successfully apprehended because negotiators, in conjunction with the tactical team, used specialized techniques effective with this type of person.

The purpose of this chapter is to discuss this type of hostage taker. Paranoid Schizophrenia will be examined in terms of etiology, incidence, and symptoms. Then specific negotiation techniques will be suggested to deal with a person suffering from this type of disorder.

Etiology

Despite extensive research on this disorder, its causes remain unclear. Underlying causes are multifactorial; they include hereditary, biological, psychological, environmental, faulty learning, and sociocultural factors. The mainstream theory postulates a genetic predisposition in combination with a severely disturbed mother/child relationship, particularly in the first years of life (American Psychiatric Association, 2000). Coleman, Butcher, and Carson (1984) state that none of these causes are mutually exclusive, and current research indicates they are all involved (Wesselius, 1984).

The cause of this disease remains a mystery. Therefore, the current treatment for this illness focuses on dealing with, or masking, the symptoms—not attacking the disease. To use a medical analogy, the psychiatric treatment for Paranoid Schizophrenia by providing medication like thorazine, zyprexa, mellaril, and clozaril is the equivalent of a medical doctor treating a person with tuberculosis by prescribing a cough suppressant. The cough suppressant stops the symptom of coughing, but the disease is left to run its course. Paranoid Schizophrenia is not fatal. So the medication seems to provide a cure, because the symptoms are gone. However, most psychotropic medications have side effects like nausea, impotence, and headaches. Therefore, many patients with Paranoid Schizophrenia grow weary of these side effects and believe they are cured so they stop taking their medication.

The Movie Version

A good example of this illness, and the patient's reluctance to remain on medication, was portrayed by Russell Crowe in the movie about the Nobel Laureate Dr. Nash entitled *A Beautiful Mind* (Universal Studios, 2002). You may recall his visual hallucination of having a roommate and seeing the little girl were very real to Dr. Nash. As a member of the audience, I also believed they were real. Once treatment began, Dr. Nash returned to normal. However, he was experiencing impotence and so he stopped taking his medication. His impotence ended but his hallucinations, his roommate and the little girl returned. Like Dr. Nash, most Paranoid Schizophrenics are not violent nor of his caliber. But, he shared and demonstrated the common reluctance to take the prescribed medication, and he, like they, suffered the consequences.

Definition

In the American Psychiatric Association *Diagnostic and Statistical Manual* (*DSM-IV*) Diagnostic Code, *Paranoid Schizophrenia* describes this schizophrenic syndrome as manifesting delusions, hallucinations, unfocused anxiety, anger, argumentativeness, paranoia, and violence (2000, p. 287).

A symptom frequently seen in the schizophrenic hostage taker is labeled "ideas of reference," where the subject believes that public media broadcasts address him personally and convey special coded messages. Gwin wanted to use the media to send his own message about the imminent end of the world that he claimed came to him from God. In schizophrenia, internal mental events are confused with external world happenings, resulting in faulty perceptions and disturbed logic. One of the best discussions of this illness in the literature appears in the book *A Mind That Found Itself* (Beers, 1907). In this classic, Clifford Whittingham Beers tells of his journey from and back to madness. His well-written first-hand account of delusions, hallucinations, secret messages, and mistrust is a moving presentation of the power of this illness over the human spirit.

Incidence in Society

It is difficult to determine with any degree of statistical accuracy how many persons in our society are afflicted with schizophrenia. Coleman, Butcher, and Carson state that they are about 1 percent of the world's population (1994, p. 7). Because the disease often coexists with good physical health, cannot be readily cured, and is one of progressive mental deterioration, they constitute the majority of patents in mental hospitals.

Law Enforcement Exposure

Contact between the person suffering from Paranoid Schizophrenia and law enforcement is frequent. In fact, some argue that mentally ill people, especially the Paranoid Schizophrenic, can be more dangerous than a normal person (Swanson et al., 1990). Some state that mentally ill people are more prone to violence if they have *violent* delusions or hallucinations (McFarland et al., 1986). Therefore when we negotiate with this type of person we should ask him or her to tell us about his or her beliefs, fears, and thoughts. When, on Axis II, this person has a diagnosis of an Antisocial personality, one can expect a violent reaction to his or her hallucinations and delusional system (Rice, Harris, and Quinsey, 2002). The Phoenix and Baton Rouge police departments did this very effectively with Gwin and Jones as they kept them talking for several hours. When Gwin's demands were finally met and when Jones finished expressing his foreign policy concerns, they were fatigued and satisfied that their missions had been completed to the best of their ability and surrendered without incident (Hawkins, 1982; Shelton, 2004).

A historical example of contact between law enforcement and the Paranoid Schizophrenic resulted in the first insanity plea entered in 1843, by McNaughten in London, after the attempted to kill Sir Robert Peel, then Prime Minister of Great Britain. He believed Peel was collaborating with the pope to take over England. Many assassins, like McNaughten, are suffering from Paranoid Schizophrenia and are responding to delusions and hallucinations that command them to kill (Hassel, 1974). Schizophrenics frequently visit police stations and commonly call the police to report their delusions and hallucinations. Therefore, police officers often meet the person with Paranoid Schizophrenic symptoms early and often in their careers.

My first law enforcement contact with a person suffering from Paranoid Schizophrenia occurred when I pulled complaint duty while assigned to the Federal Bureau of Investigation (FBI) Washington, DC Field Office (WFO). My first visitor was a female "referral" from the Washington, DC Police Department, whom they sent to the FBI because her complaint involved a violation of federal statutes that we investigated. After she verified she was in the Washington, DC Field Office of the FBI and that we investigated violations of the Federal Communication Statute, she told me she was appearing nude on the radio. As a child we had a large RCA radio in our living room. I had a quick flash of her sitting on top of our radio, and in my visualization, she was rather attractive. However, no matter how attractive she was, she did not like the idea of appearing nude on the air waves for all to see. She may have been mentally ill but she was modest. So, I listened, took copious notes, and let her talk, and talk, and talk. To speed her departure I told her I would get right on the case just as soon as she left. So, she decided she was finished telling her story, she thanked me for listening, and she left.

During her monologue, I learned she was from Philadelphia. After she left, I called the FBI Philadelphia Field Office and learned that she had been in Baltimore the previous day. Because it was late fall, they told me that she would probably visit our Richmond Field Office the next day, and then on to Charlotte, North Carolina, Charleston, South Carolina, Atlanta, Georgia, and Savannah, Georgia, as she journeyed to Florida for the winter. It was my judgment that she was harmless. She was seeking a legal remedy to her dilemma. After all, this was the mid-1970s and no self-respecting person wanted to appear nude on any radio station. Her delusion, her false belief, was very broad, no pun intended, and harmless. She was not focusing on one person or one organization that was responsible for her exposure.

This is one criterion to accurately and effectively evaluate their potential for violence. As long as their concern is with *they* or *them*, the chances are that no violence will occur. To the contrary, if and when their focus narrows to a *specific person* or *organization* responsible for their problems, then there is cause for concern. Remember the example of Sanders in Memphis. Once he identified the Memphis Police Department as the enemy, the earthly representatives of the Devil, he took an officer from that department hostage.

Major Symptoms

Two primary symptoms characterize the Paranoid Schizophrenic Disorder: *hallucinations* and *delusions*. Verbal examples of these symptoms can take the form of incoherent statements that express or describe the subject's hallucinations or delusional thinking. Most hostage takers who express disordered and distorted delusions are mentally ill, but they may not be as sick as those who are experiencing and responding to hallucinations. Hallucinations, in particular, pose a serious problem when violence is involved because the person may respond to these violent images and act them out (Wesselius, 1984).

A *delusion* is a distortion of reality, a false belief, and usually takes the expression of grandeur. Many, if not most, Paranoid Schizophrenics believe they have an important role to play in the course of world events, and that God has entrusted them with a special skill, talent, or knowledge to complete this mission. Another form of the delusion of grandeur is a belief of persecution in which internal ideas are projected onto the environment. The individual's feelings of hate and rage are seen as external. The use of projection is common and is mirrored in the practice of projecting self-hatred onto others—that is, I do not hate me, you hate me and are causing me to suffer.

On the other hand, a *hallucination* is an incorrect perception of one's senses. The most common hallucination is auditory. That is, the individual hears voices and perceives them as coming from the external world, such as from God. The "voices" often issue commands that he feels compelled to carry out. Less common are visual hallucinations, tasting, feeling, smelling, and a body sense dysfunction. These symptoms may make the individual unpredictable and increase his excitation level. In the case of a hostage taker, such unpredictability and increased excitation decreases his ability to respond to a negotiator's tranquil demeanor or to his appeals based on logic.

Another way to diagnose the Paranoid Schizophrenic hostage taker is to ask him or her what type of medication he or she is or, more accurately, was taking. Typical prescriptions to treat the symptoms of Paranoid Schizophrenia are the drugs Haldol; Haloperidol: Respirdol; Respiridone and Thorazine; and Chlorpromazine. As soon as any hostage taker mentions medication, the logical course of action is a quick call to a pharmacy or an Internet search, your department's mental health professional or the *Physicians Desk Reference*, or a quick call to the FBI Crisis Negotiations Response Unit at Quantico, which will help you determine what type of malady the drug is designed to treat (Arey, 2003). Once the malady is identified one can customize his negotiation techniques to fit the disorder. When in doubt, and as a good general practice, listen. Let the subject do the talking. We learn when we listen. This takes time. Remember to operate as if you are being paid by the hour. Typically, the negotiator must rely on the passage of time and on the subject's sheer fatigue to reduce the level of agitated behavior.

Law enforcement usually encounters the Paranoid Schizophrenic hostage taker or barricaded person when he or she is "off meds." Remember, the Paranoid Schizophrenic's medication is designed to mask symptoms from him or her and society, not cure the person of this malady. Until medical science learns the cause of Paranoid Schizophrenia, they will continue to treat the symptoms. They have no other choice.

Negotiating Guidelines and Rationale

1. *Stall for time.* Most importantly, allow and encourage the mentally ill subject to talk, ventilate, and relieve his or her frustrations on the negotiator so he or she does not act out his or her hostility on the hostage(s). The most effective negotiation technique by far is to allow and encourage the subject to exhaust himself or herself by talking, yelling, and telling you and the world about his or her dilemmas and delusional system. This will probably include the instructions and guidance God has provided him or her to share with you and the world. By doing this the negotiator is meeting the hostage taker's important expressive demand for attention, understanding, and his or her sense of self-worth. Although sitting and listening sounds easy, it becomes very difficult when commanders are demanding action. When working with the mentally ill, one has to learn to be a good listener. No one listens to crazy people. The negotiator must be the exception to this rule. Listening is the most effective way to develop rapport. Convincing the subject of your interest in what he or she has to say also buys time and drains off his anxious energy. The person with schizophrenic symptoms is powerfully motivated to talk about his or her mission. The negotiator can elicit conversation about these important matters by simply being curious. Engaging in conversation will enable the negotiator to gauge the hostage taker's dedication, intelligence, threat level, and ability to act upon his or her threats. Gary Noesner, the recently retired Unit Chief of the Crisis Negotiations Response Unit at Quantico, devoted an entire book to this topic (Noesner, 2010).

   A good mind-set to assume that will assist the negotiator in this stalling tactic is to conduct negotiations as if you are being paid by the hour. Of course, this mind-set will be at odds with the boss and tactical team who consider themselves paid by the job.

2. *Do not expect a relationship or trust to develop.* As a general rule, the person suffering from Paranoid Schizophrenia does not trust people. The more you say "trust me," the more the person "knows" he or she cannot. However, by following the suggestions listed above, one can gain some rapport.

3. *Listen.* The active listening techniques discussed in Chapter 8 work very well with the person suffering from Paranoid Schizophrenia. That person has a story to tell the world.

4. *Good negotiators may not last too long.* Because of the problem people suffering from Paranoid Schizophrenia have in and with relationships, they tend to become suspicious, distrustful, and uncommunicative

when a person "gets too close." Even in the tranquility of a psychiatric hospital, mental health professionals have great difficulty getting emotionally close to the person suffering from Paranoid Schizophrenia. Given the stress of a hostage siege, the possibility to develop a close relationship is even more remote. However, if the negotiator can communicate sincerity, this obstacle may be diminished.

5. *Sincerity.* The negotiator can, verbally and psychologically, draw the subject out by being sincerely interested in what the subject has to say. Do not attempt to persuade him or her to give up on his or her belief system or delusion. The delusion and the hallucinations are very real to this person. One approach might include the statement that though you do not hear the voices, you understand that he or she does. Tell the subject you understand these voices are very real and important to him or her and you want to learn more about the belief system. It is suggested that the negotiator practice saying this to his or her secondary to make certain the statement sounds sincere.

6. *Never* as a negotiator enter the hallucinations or delusional systems of the person with Paranoid Schizophrenia. Do not say you also hear the voices. A person with Paranoid Schizophrenia does not want to talk to another nut. At some level the person knows the voices are not heard by others so such a statement from the negotiator will feed into a failure of the negotiations process. A good answer to the question about the voices or other hallucinations is "No I do not hear those voices, tell me about them. Have you heard them before? How long did they last? What did you do in response to them?" Remember the axiom that the best indicator of future behavior is past behavior.

7. *Ask questions about the subject's view of the world—that is, his or her delusion(s).* One way to move toward a sincere frame of mind is to ask intelligent questions about the subject's delusional system. Probe. Listen and record the answers to your questions so others, such as your departmental psychologist, can assist in evaluating the subject's threat level and develop an effective negotiations strategy.

8. *Confrontation.* Do not argue with the subject about the validity of his or her delusions or hallucinations. They are as real to him or her as everyday sounds and your identity is to you. Listen, learn, and record, do not validate or challenge.

9. *Is he or she taking medication?* This is a straightforward question. "Are you taking any medication?" A truthful answer will be of great assistance in determining the nature and severity of the hostage taker's mental problems. In most cases, he or she will admit that he or she was taking medicine. However, the side effects of the prescription caused him or her to stop. This is a serious and common problem with psychotropic medication. The side effects, impotence, loose

bowels, nausea, headaches, mild convulsions, and many others, can be more severe than the illness.

10. *Be sensitive to sexual concerns and projection.* Because the male Paranoid Schizophrenic typically has problems with his sexual identification and tends to misinterpret acts of friendship as homosexual advances, female negotiators may be more successful. A female Paranoid Schizophrenic may also have problems with sexual identity and may be sensitive to suggestions that she is a prostitute (Wesseluis, 1984).

11. *Publicity may be of value.* Exposure to the media may meet the expressive needs of a person with Paranoid Schizophrenia. This may be of interest to the subject and provide one topic for discussion. The details of such exposure can take hours to work out. Also access to the media may be offered to the subject in exchange for the release of a hostage or some other gesture of good faith. This was done with great effectiveness by the Phoenix and Baton Rouge police departments.

12. *Avoid using family members.* Family members, or other third parties, can be excellent sources of intelligence. However, allowing direct contact with the hostage taker is another matter. Once the negotiator passes the phone to another person, the negotiator has lost control. This is especially true when family relationships consist of intense and unresolved hate in the context of marked dependency. Although exceptions might be found to this rule, most police departments have found that the relative of the Paranoid Schizophrenic who volunteers to help the police is often the person who drove the subject to this act of desperation to prove he or she has power (Bolz, 2004).

13. *No Stockholm Syndrome.* This phenomenon, discussed in Chapter 24, requires a reciprocal relationship of trust. Typically, the person suffering from Paranoid Schizophrenia trusts no one. Identification with the aggressor may occur and interfere with the intelligence-gathering process. However, people suffering from Paranoid Schizophrenia tend to intimidate others, not initiate or cultivate an affectionate relationship.

14. *Indicators.* The key indicator of danger, in addition to the material discussed in Chapter 20 is the content of the delusion and the intensity of the hallucinations. What are the voices telling him or her to do? One might ask if the subject has heard these voices in the past and if so how did he or she respond?

Conclusion

Negotiators dealing with a hostage taker who is suffering from Paranoid Schizophrenia should remember that they have dealt with this personality type before. From their first months as officers they have spoken on the phone, interviewed, or encountered people on the street claiming a God-given mission and expressing delusions or hallucinations. Almost automatically, experienced officers will mollify this type of person by listening, sounding interested, and asking probing questions to elicit more information on the "important subject." Despite the stress of a siege situation, these same techniques will help the negotiator meet the expressive needs of the hostage taker and pave the way for a peaceful resolution.

Throughout the siege, the negotiator must listen, sympathize, stall, and understand the subject. He must at the same time continually reassess the dangerousness of the hostage taker. Generally, after talking to and telling the negotiator of his or her belief system, the subject will tire and seek an honorable solution to this dilemma. The successful negotiator must be prepared to provide such a solution by understanding and meeting the needs of the hostage taker while safely resolving the situation for the hostages, law enforcement officers, and hostage taker.

References

American Psychiatric Association (2000) *Diagnostic and Statistical Manual of Mental Disorders*–4th Edition, APA, Washington, DC.

Arey, J. B. (2003) Dealing with the Mentally Ill, Louisiana Association of Crisis Negotiators Annual Training Conference, Gonzales, Louisiana, March 10.

Beers, C. W. (1907) *A Mind That Found Itself*, University of Pittsburgh Press, Pittsburgh.

Bolz, F. (2004) Personal E-mail communication, April 20.

Hassel, C. V. (1974) The Political Assassin, *Journal of Police Science and Administration*, Vol. 2, No. 4, pp. 399–403.

Hawkins, E. C. "Rusty" (1982) Personal communication during hostage negotiations in-service course, FBI Academy, Quantico, Virginia, October 19.

Lanceley, F. (1981) The Antisocial Personality as a Hostage Taker, *Journal of Police Science and Administration*, Vol. 9, No. 1, pp. 28–34.

McFarland, B. H., Faulkner, L. R., Bloom, J. L., Hallaux, R., and Bray, J. D. (1986) Chronic Mental Illness and the Criminal Justice System, *Hospital and Community Psychiatry*, Vol. 40, pp. 718–723.

Noesner, G. (2010) *Stalling for Time*, Random House, New York.

Rice, M. E., Harris, G. T., and Quinsey, V. L. (2002) The Appraisal of Violence Risk, *Current Opinions in Psychiatry*, Vol. 15, No. 6, pp. 589–593.

Shelton, L. (2004) Personal interview, Baton Rouge, Louisiana, May 6.

Strentz, T. (1979) The Stockholm Syndrome: Law Enforcement Policy and Ego Defenses of the Hostage, *FBI Law Enforcement Bulletin*, April, Vol. 48, No. 4, pp. 1–11.

Strentz, T. (1983) The Inadequate Personality as a Hostage Taker, *Journal of Police Science and Administration*, Vol. 11, No. 3, pp. 363–368.

Strentz, T. (1984) Preparing the Person with High Potential for Victimization as a Hostage, *Violence in the Medical Care Setting: A Survival Guide*, edited by James T. Turner, pp. 184–196, Aspen Press, Rockville, Maryland.

Swanson, J., Holzer, C., Ganju, V., and Jono, R. (1990) Violence and Psychiatric Disorder in the Community: Evidence from the Epidemiologic Catchment Area Surveys, *Hospital and Community Psychiatry,* Vol. 41, pp. 761–770.

United Press International (1983) Officer Killed, *New York Times,* Section A, p. 1, January 14.

The Bipolar (I Am Focused and Flying High!) Hostage Taker

13

Law Enforcement Encounters with Bipolar Hostage Takers

On the 242nd birthday of George Washington, 44-year-old Sam Byke of Philadelphia, Pennsylvania, attempted to hijack an Atlanta-bound DC-9, Delta 523, that was in the boarding process at the Baltimore Washington Airport (BWI). With his .22 caliber pistol, he shot and killed the BWI police officer at the magnetometer, ran to the nearest boarding aircraft, and then ran down the Jetway and into the cockpit. He shot and killed the copilot and wounded the pilot. He grabbed a frightened female passenger, dragged her into the cockpit, and ordered her to fly to Washington, DC. Like most airports, the aircraft was at the gate with its nose facing the terminal. A tow would be required to pull it back and onto the tarmac for taxi and eventual takeoff. Byke did not take these facts into account. During this initial confusion, the Delta flight attendants responded by opening the emergency doors that activated the slides and evacuated the aircraft.

The BWI police and others from the Anne Arundel County Police Department responded. They engaged Byke in a firefight. Byke killed himself.

From his car parked at the airport, the police and the Federal Bureau of Investigation (FBI) retrieved hours of audiotapes on which Byke had recorded his plan. Byke had mailed copies of these tapes to then American Federation of Labor (AFL)/Congress of Industrial Organizations (CIO) President George Romney, the popular conductor and pianist Leonard Bernstein of the New York Philharmonic Orchestra, and Jack Anderson, a columnist for the *Washington Post*.

In some insane way, Byke envisioned these three diverse, national personalities were people who would understand and possibly further his cause. According to the hours of audiotapes he recorded, he intended to crash the plane into the White House, killing then President Nixon to publicize and attract followers to his quest for world peace. This story was aired on The History Channel under the title of "The Plot to Kill Nixon" (The History Channel, 2004).

According to the mailed audiotapes, Byke recognized he would kill many people, but in his deranged and delusional mind, this act made so much sense that he was prepared to sacrifice himself to further his "noble cause"—his search for world peace.

To this day Byke's reasoning remains inconceivable, illogical, insane, and preposterous. But to Byke and others with a Bipolar Disorder, who may also have an Antisocial Personality Disorder, it is necessary and logical.

More recently and also in the State of Maryland, there were the irrational and illegal actions of Joseph C. Palczynski, Jr. (Joby). He, like Sam Byke, was bipolar and antisocial. He went on a murderous rampage searching for his girlfriend who left him. He drove to an apartment where he believed she was living. He found her and killed the friends with whom she was living. Upon hearing the shots, a neighbor inquired. Palczynski shot and killed him also.

He fled with her. She escaped from him the next day when she saw a police car near them. She ran to them while Palczynski ran away. She was placed in protective custody at the police department. Her parents were warned of the danger and offered police protection. They declined the offer.

As the manhunt intensified, Palczynski fled to Southern Maryland and eventually to Northern Virginia. However, he was obsessed by the escape of his girlfriend. In his mind she was his property. In an attempt to get her back, he returned to Maryland and took her family hostage.

During the next 5 days of intense negotiations, Palczynski slept very little and repeatedly threatened to kill the family if they did not order their daughter to join them. On one occasion he began a "countdown." He told police negotiators he would kill their young son if they did not deliver their daughter to him. Because of excellent intelligence the police knew he was bluffing. On the fifth day, his hostages slipped him some powerful drugs and escaped. Palczynski heard them depart, and was killed by the arrest team as he reached for his weapons.

These incidents are extreme and Maryland does not have a disproportionate number of violent psychotic people who are bipolar and antisocial. Byke and Palczynski represent a minority of the people who suffer from the psychosis known as a Bipolar Disorder. The vast majority of people who have this disorder are *not* a danger to society. Because of the depth of depression they often suffer, they are more prone to commit suicide.

History is filled with examples of outstanding people who suffered from Bipolar Disorder but were not antisocial. Famous American comedians like Red Skelton and Jackie Gleason come to mind as does the inventor Thomas Alva Edison and the Austrian composer, Wolfgang Amadeus Mozart. Military and political luminaries include, Alexander the Great, Napoleon Bonaparte, Lord Nelson, Oliver Cromwell, Alexander Hamilton, and Winston Churchill (Fawcett, Bolden, and Rosenfeld, 2001). More recently, Jane Pauley of NBC announced she suffered from Bipolar Disorder. When, as these people evidence, the bipolar person turns his or her efforts and energy toward worthwhile endeavors, he or she can be an excellent example of just how productive a person with this disorder can be.

A friend of mine, who is a "work-a-holic," told me of a former boss who was bipolar. When he was depressed his boss would often sit at his desk and stare into space. Upon entering his office he would ask my friend what was wrong with the world in such an intelligent and convincing way that he also became depressed.

When he was up, he was a bundle of energy and enthusiasm. Their work hours were 0800 to 1630. When my friend would arrive at 0630 his boss would greet him asking why he was late. When he was leaving at 1800, his boss questioned his dedication. Because of his dynamic leadership, their accomplishments were legendary. They received a large 1-year grant to research terrorism and train domestic civilian law enforcement. Through several intergovernmental alliances he initiated, and very effective cost-cutting methods the boss developed, their program was significantly enhanced. They researched domestic and international terrorist activity. They trained domestic and international civilian and military law enforcement. To top it off, the money lasted many years. Eventually, they returned a sizable amount of the grant to the government.

The American Psychiatric Association (APA) Multiaxial Evaluation

To help explain the difference between productive people like my friend's boss, Mozart, Edison, and Churchill versus destructive criminals like Sam Byke and Joseph Palczynski, remember or review the APA classification system from Chapter 1. In brief, the new APA system uses the multiaxial model to classify people and recognizes that just as a person may have more than one physical problem, like asthma, athlete's foot, and acne, men and women can suffer from more than one psychological disorder. Although no gender is immune from any disorder, the few gender differences that exist reflect the age of onset, not the disease or disorder. Simply stated, the multiaxial system is a simultaneous assessment of several areas of human behavior (APA, 2000, pp. 27–36).

According to the APA, about 1.5 percent of the U.S. population suffers from a Bipolar Disorder. This translates to about 3 million people, the great majority of whom are law-abiding citizens.

As previously stated, the law enforcement problem with people who suffer from a Bipolar Disorder is most frequently found among those who, on Axis II, have a personality disorder known as "Antisocial."* It is easy to rec-

---

* Hostage takers and people with a Bipolar Disorder and Antisocial Disorder come in both sexes. Because most hostage takers are male, the pronoun he will be used in this chapter.

ognize an Antisocial Personality Disorder (ASP*) by glibness, narcissism, seemingly stress-free voice and attitude, high verbal skills, and constant use of rationalization and projection to justify the situation. The person's demands will be for money, escape, and other self-serving needs. Remember, to the ASP, "It's all about me!" This disorder is discussed in Chapter 11. His demeanor will remind you of many criminal informants with whom you have been involved. When one compares his chronological to his emotional age, he appears to many to be an "adult adolescent."

The best description of this disorder I have read is in the text *Without Conscience*, by Dr. Robert D. Hare:

> The Antisocial Personality, Psychopath, is a social predator who charms, manipulates, and ruthlessly plows his way through life, leaving a broad trail of broken hearts, shattered expectations, and empty wallets. Completely lacking in conscience and feeling for others, the ASP selfishly takes what he wants and does as he pleases, violating social norms and expectations, without the slightest sense of guilt or regret. (Hare, 1993)

If one were to create a continuum and move from normal to greedy, to self-centered, to self-indulgent, to a sense of entitlement, to dangerously narcissistic, then well beyond this beginning, one would find the ASP who, according to Dr. Joyceln Roland, the lead psychologist for the Los Angeles Sheriff's Office, views life as "It's all about me!" This person is your friend, as long as there is something in it for him or her. These people are takers, not givers. All they ever give their associates and family are heartaches and hard times (Roland, 2003). For more information on the Antisocial Personality Disorder, see Chapter 11.

Because of their penchant for criminal behavior, including the taking of hostages, the focus of this chapter will be on the bipolar person who, on Axis II, is also antisocial.

The Bipolar Disorder and the American Psychiatric Association

Prior to 1987, this psychotic disorder was called Manic-Depressive Psychosis. This name referred to the extreme mood swings that are its primary symptoms. In other words, this person might be manic and full of energy, depressed and really down in the dumps, or might swing between the two

---

* The acronym ASP, the snake that allegedly killed Cleopatra, rather than APD will be used because ASP more accurately describes the behavior of the person with an Antisocial Personality Disorder—he or she is a snake.

extremes. With the publishing of *DSM-III* in 1987, the name was changed to Bipolar. The symptoms are similar, as discussed briefly below and at length on over 15 pages of *DSM-IV* (APA, 2000, pp. 382–397).*

For reasons as yet unclear, this malady is more prevalent in Scandinavians than any other ethnic group. Because many of those who suffer from a Bipolar Disorder also have a form of color blindness and tend to have an inability to extract the mood-controlling element Lithium from their food, a genetic predisposition is suspected (Fawcett et al., 2001; Torrey et al., 1994).

Normal people often have mood changes. However, there are two fundamental differences between the mood swings of the bipolar and those of normal people. These are the *degree* and *reason* for the change. A person with Bipolar Disorder has *excessive mood swings* that are internally or *chemically* driven. Their swings, on a scale of one to ten, with a norm of five, could range from depression at one or two, up to a manic nine or ten: deep depression to hyperactive, or manic behavior. A normal person's change in mood on this scale would range between a "sad" four and "happy" six. In a person with Bipolar Disorder, these changes in mood are *not reality oriented*. They are not sad because they have just heard bad news or happy because of good news. Their mood swings are internally controlled and are driven by *chemical changes* in the brain that do not necessarily reflect reality or recent events.

The Bipolar Disorder and Hollywood

A motion picture depiction of this manic behavior is portrayed in the role played by Harrison Ford in *Mosquito Coast* (Warner Brothers, 1986). In this role, Harrison Ford plays a brilliant but undisciplined inventor who moves his family from the agricultural Salinas Valley in Coastal California to the tropical north coast of Venezuela. From scratch, he and his family plant gardens, construct a large air-conditioned residence as well as an enormous ice machine. He then decides that they must deliver a large block of ice that weighs several hundred pounds to natives who live on the other side of a mountain range because the natives have never seen ice. He engages his entire family in this very arduous tropical trek that involves pulling, pushing, and dragging a home-made, ice-laden, wooden sled through a thick jungle that extends up and over the mountains to the natives' village. By the time they

---

* DSM stands for the *Diagnostic and Statistical Manual* of the APA. It is the mental health equivalent of a penal code. Law enforcement officers consult a penal code to determine if the elements of a crime warrant a specific charge. Similarly, mental health practitioners consult the *DSM* to determine the proper diagnosis for the symptoms they observe.

complete the journey the several hundred pound cake of ice is about the size of a snowball, and the natives are not very impressed.

In my experience, his dedication and ability to recruit and convince others of the necessity of this task is very typical of people who are in the manic phase of their Bipolar Disorder.

A second movie that comes to mind is *Amadeus* (Warner Brothers, 1984). Wolfgang Amadeus Mozart, as portrayed by Tom Hulce, had a Bipolar Disorder. When he was down, he could not get out of bed. In the movie his high energy level, sexual excesses, and brilliance portrayed a very gifted bipolar in the manic phase. A clue to Mozart's mania is that he did not write lullabies.

As portrayed in these two movies, when this same person is at the upper extreme, he or she often remains awake for days working, partying, and encouraging others to follow his or her lead. They typically work on a project as if they are possessed. Bipolar symptoms, when the person is in the manic state, are frequently and easily confused for the delusions of grandeur frequently seen in those suffering from Paranoid Schizophrenia. The high of a Bipolar Disorder can be very pleasurable. At this end of the spectrum, the person feels grandiose and omnipotent. Some are willing to risk death, by not taking their medication, to experience this high or manic state.

At the other extreme, when this person is depressed he or she is not only suicidal but considers the world such a terrible place that the best thing he or she can do for loved ones, "to remove them from this veil of tears," is to kill them and then commit suicide. This type of crime scene might feature children dressed in their church clothes, lying in their beds having been suffocated or killed in a "humane way."

A Hollywood example of the mania and depression is portrayed by Richard Gere in the movie entitled *Mr. Jones*. Gere portrays a person with Bipolar Disorder who thinks he can fly, lead an orchestra, defend himself in court, and does not need his medication. The movie includes the common misdiagnosis of bipolar people as suffering from Paranoid Schizophrenia (TriStar, 1993).

A third type of bipolar is the person who swings between the two extremes of mania and depression. The *most dangerous* time for the person with a Bipolar Disorder is when they are changing levels. The time required for a level change can range from a few days to just an hour or less. This can be determined by talking with associates to evaluate their mood over the last few hours or days or asking the bipolar person about how they feel now versus how they felt a few hours ago. One theory that helps explain the danger of the change is when they are up and headed down, they fear the deep depression they know is coming, so they avoid it by killing themselves. Once they are down, they may lack the energy to commit suicide, so they suffer. As they turn back up, they gradually regain physical energy, while they retain the pain of depression. It is then that suicide is a possibility. I recall one person with

Bipolar Disorder who said that what really scares her is she does not fear death. Instead, she sees death as a challenge, making suicide a logical alternative.

One effective treatment is the prescription of the element Lithium. However, stabilizing a patient on the correct dosage of Lithium usually requires hospitalization. Lithium and other drugs work best when used in conjunction with individual or group therapy monitored by the regular drawing of blood to ensure the correct maintenance level. For normal people, Lithium is a very powerful depressant. For the person with a Bipolar Disorder, Lithium levels the mood swings at both ends of the spectrum and keeps them within a normal emotional range.

Side effects of Lithium include kidney damage, convulsions, tremors, and because of the low prescription to lethal dose ratio, accidental death (Arey, 2003).

Hostage Takers

The two most challenging and difficult types of hostage takers encountered by law enforcement are the ASP and suicidal subjects. When one is dealing with a person who is bipolar and on Axis II has a diagnosis of an Antisocial Personality Disorder, one can expect a monumental challenge that will test the entire negotiating and crisis management team. On the one hand, he may be exhibiting very high levels of energy and be *grandiose, if not confrontational*, in his thinking and actions. At the opposite end, as a *suicidal* person, he is dangerous because he wants to die. He may want the police to kill him, so he may try to force their hand. As an ASP he may not care how many people he "takes" with him.

Similarly, the person with Bipolar Disorder, like the ASP, may take chances, make threats, issue demands that sound suicidal, and may challenge the police. Typically, he is convinced that he is smarter, stronger, and has other virtues that will allow him to escape from the scene, regardless of how unrealistic his plan may sound.

Negotiating Guidelines and Their Rationale

These guidelines are similar to those used with the Paranoid Schizophrenic who is exhibiting delusions of grandeur or those of the depressed person as well as those commonly used with the Antisocial Personality Disorder. As negotiators, we focus on the presenting symptom, not the psychiatric diagnosis. In other words, what type of behavior is he currently exhibiting? Is he grandiose, confrontational, or suicidal?

This person may be encountered as a hostage taker in a variety of settings—a robbery that has gone bad, a workplace incident, or a perpetrator in a domestic dispute who is holding his significant other(s) hostage. To the person with bipolar, who is also antisocial (the ASP), his hostages are always "insignificant others." As a very depressed individual he may want to end it all for himself and those he loves.

In addition to his grandiose, or extremely depressed ideation, another way to identify the person who is bipolar is to ask what type of medication he is or was taking. The more common prescriptions for Bipolar Disorder are Lithium, Carbolith or Escalith, Depakote, Valborate or Depakane, Topomax, and Zyprexa. No matter what the medication, a quick call to a pharmacy to learn what malady the hostage taker's medication is designed to treat is a commonsense solution and a shortcut to a diagnosis and negotiation strategy (Arey, 2003).

Recommending guidelines for negotiating with a person with Bipolar Disorder is difficult because they depend upon the subject's mental state. One must determine if the person is manic or depressed and if the person has an Axis II diagnosis of Antisocial Personality Disorder. When dealing with this disorder it is imperative that the team approach be used. The intelligence and energy level of the typical person with Bipolar Disorder will exceed that of any single negotiator.

The following are recommended guidelines for negotiating with a person with Bipolar Disorder:

1. If he is depressed and potentially suicidal, consider sharing sensitive or personal information. However, his depression may be chemically driven and be very illogical. The depth of the depression exceeds any sadness a normal person has ever experienced.

   (For more information on this tactic, see the guidelines and suggestions offered in the following chapters on negotiating with depressed people.)

2. If he is manic, keep him busy. He needs psychological stimulation and challenges. Persons with this disorder have a powerful need to be in control. The negotiator may want to say things like, "Yes, you can do that, if you really want to. However, there are always consequences."

   Like the adolescent's developing brain, the connection between the frontal lobes and the rest of the brain may be impaired. Further, when occupied with decisions and discussions, they are less likely to injure themselves, their hostages, or do something dangerous.

3. Keep him involved in the process. Use expressions like, "Certainly, a person as intelligent as you understands that..." or "I know you are smart enough to realize that..."

4. Negotiations must be "reality oriented." The person with Bipolar Disorder who is feeling grandiose enjoys taking risks. He is stimulated, not frightened, by the danger of this situation. You might

consider acknowledging his intelligence by saying something like, "I am sure that you have 10 points on my I.Q." I suspect he will answer by saying something like, "For a cop you are pretty smart, I think the difference is more like 20" (Arey, 2003).

5. Nonpolice negotiators will be of marginal value because they are more easily "conned" by the antisocial side of this person, influenced by the manic side, or have experience on a personal level with him that may prevent them from being objective. For more information on how to negotiate with the antisocial person see Chapter 11 entitled "The Antisocial Personality Disorder (It's All about Me!) Hostage Taker."

6. If, like the Paranoid Schizophrenic hostage taker, the person is on a mission, publicity may be of value. However, weigh this alternative carefully and be mindful of how the FBI was outmanipulated by the ASP David Koresch during the 1993 siege in Waco, Texas. For additional information, see Chapter 21 entitled "Group Think."

7. Do not challenge the ASP or the person with Bipolar Disorder in the manic stage unless you are engaged in tactical negotiations. This means that one *does not argue* with the hostage taker with the expectation of convincing him to surrender. One argues to divert his attention from the hostages and force him to focus on the negotiator while the tactical team is engaged in maneuvers. Go along with his view of the world and reality, unless tactical considerations dictate otherwise.

8. "Active listening" skills are *invaluable*. This person needs to be in charge and wants to talk and tell you about his view of the world. For more information on active listening see Chapter 8, "Negotiating with Normal People" (Noesner and Webster, 1997).

9. In all probability, they are in this predicament because they have gone "off their meds." Their medication may have had uncomfortable, unwanted, or painful side effects. Further, in the manic stage, they probably feel superior to the doctor who prescribed the medication and physically strong enough to live without the use of "artificial aids or controls." The negotiator should exercise care when discussing medications, as reference to them may result in a violent response. If this is the case, consult with their doctor to determine what course of action is most appropriate. All too often, just going back on the usual dosage of medication will not be enough to stabilize them. Once off, they may require hospitalization to be restabilized.

10. After this subject has been taken into custody and hopefully hospitalized, it is recommended that someone from the negotiating team follow up with a contact when they are normal. In this regard, the Los Angeles Police Department has an excellent program that has provided a great deal of intelligence on how to better negotiate (CAHN, 2011).

Quick Summary of Negotiation Strategies

Symptoms	Strategies
Depressed person	Ego support
	Sympathy, empathy, and patience
	Listen
	Active listening techniques
Manic	Questions
	Humble role
	Reality considerations
	What is in it for him?
Antisocial	Remember, it's all about me

The energy level, guile, and intelligence exhibited by the typical person with Bipolar Disorder who is manic, and on Axis II and antisocial, will try the patience, ability, and professionalism of any Crisis Negotiating Team. His actions are irrational and inappropriate and represent an inaccurate and often counterproductive response to the problem he states he is seeking to solve. The stress created for the on-scene commander by the manic phase, bipolar, antisocial hostage taker will cause the on-scene negotiator to consider early retirement and challenge the Crisis Management Team as no other hostage taker ever has.

References

American Psychiatric Association (2000) *Diagnostic and Statistical Manual of Mental Disorders*–4th Edition, APA, Washington, DC.

Arey, J. B. (2003) Dealing with the Mentally Ill, Louisiana Association of Crisis Negotiators, Annual Training Conference, March 10, Gonzales, Louisiana.

CAHN (2011) LAPD presentation at the San Diego Annual Training Conference, June.

Fawcett, J., Bolden, B., and Rosenfeld, N. (2001) *New Hope for People with Bipolar Disorder*, Three Rivers Press, New York.

Hare, R. D. (1993) *Without Conscience: The Disturbing World of the Psychopaths among Us*, Guilford Press, London.

Noesner, G., and Webster, M. (1997) Crisis Intervention Using Active Listening Skills in Negotiations, *FBI Law Enforcement Bulletin*, August, pp. 13–19.

Roland, Joyceln. (2003) Assessing the Hostage Taker from a Mental Health Professional's Perspective, presentation to the California Association of Hostage Negotiators, Annual Training Conference, May 28, Long Beach, California.

The History Channel (2004) *The Plot to Kill Nixon*, A&E Television Networks.

Torrey, E. F., Bowler, A. E., Taylor, E. H., and Gottesman, I. I. (1994) *Schizophrenia and Manic-Depressive Disorder: The Biological Roots of Mental Illness as Revealed by the Landmark Study of Identical Twins*, Basic Books, New York.

The Suicidal Hostage Holder (Also Known as the Solo Suicidal Subject)   14

Introduction

There are many aspects of suicide that affect police. The disproportionate percentage of law enforcement officer suicide is one. However, this chapter will concentrate on hostage and crisis situations that include the threat of suicide by the subject who may or may not hold hostages.

> The mind is its own place, and in itself can make a heaven of hell, and a hell of heaven. (Milton, 1667)

The date of that quote is not a misprint. Human depression all too often leads to suicide. It has been a personal/social phenomenon and tragedy for centuries. Even the *Bible*, in the Old and New Testaments, speaks of suicide:

> And there was Saul leaning upon his spear; and lo, the chariots and horse men were close upon him...and he said to me "Stand beside me and slay me; for anguish has seized me, and yet my life still lingers." (RSV, II Samuel 1:6–9)

In the New Testament there is a correctional institution situation when a jailer was considering suicide because he thinks his prisoners have run away:

> When the jailer woke and saw that the prison doors were open, he drew his sword and was about to kill himself, supposing that the prisoners had escaped. But Paul cried with a loud voice, "Do not harm yourself for we are all still here." (RSV, Acts, 16:27–28)

Over the centuries, civil and religious strategies have been enlisted to understand, cope with, and try to prevent this behavior. As hard as we as a civilization have tried, we remain as ignorant and ineffective today as we were in the Middle Ages in our efforts to understand and prevent suicide. In Medieval Europe, long before insurance company accounts and actuaries calculated life expectancy rates, the local lords devised a method they expected would prevent suicide. It included a tariff upon the family of the departed that was equivalent to the amount of money the deceased would have paid in taxes to the crown had he or she lived. When this did not work the Roman Catholic Church got into the act. They made it clear that suicide was a violation of the second commandment, "Thou shalt not commit murder." To punish the deceased sinner, he or she could not be buried on church property (ASIST, 2003).

Neither of these approaches did much to prevent suicide. If anything, one could argue that one result of the stand of the church on this problem is the phenomenon of suicide by cop. Overall, the *act* of suicide is as common, perplexing, and difficult to understand and prevent today as it was in biblical times.

In contrast, a great deal of progress has been made in the search for biological causes of depression and suicide. One indication of the progress and the problem of melancholia is the large number of prescriptions written annually to combat depression in the United States. According to a recent NBC news program, 157 million prescriptions for antidepression drugs are written each year in the United States. Because the population of the United States is around 300 million, a large portion of which is children, the 157 million figure is significant (NBC, 2004). These drugs are quite effective in masking the symptoms of depression. In many cases, the cause or causes remain a mystery and often go unresolved.

Law enforcement will not have a problem recognizing the solo suicidal subject. His despondent tone of voice, slow responses, and a general sense of hopelessness will pervade his demeanor. When the negotiator senses that the person is suicidal, that is the time to ask the difficult question.

Asking the Difficult Question

When dealing with a depressed person, who in the mind of the negotiator is considering suicide, the negotiator should always ask the difficult question, "Are you thinking about killing yourself?" If an experienced law enforcement or correctional officer thinks an individual is considering suicide, they probably are. Yet, this is a difficult question to ask. Most people are not comfortable making such an inquiry. Perhaps we fear the answer. Responses of either yes or no are difficult to deal with.

Believe me, no one will respond, "No I was not, but hearing you say it makes it sound like a good idea."

Briefly, an answer of yes, though difficult to hear, is good news. Our suspicions are confirmed. It usually means the solo suicidal subject trusts the negotiator enough with his or her emotions to be honest. This is the single best indicator of successful negotiations (Strentz, 1995).

On the other hand, an answer of no, though personally more comfortable, is professionally unacceptable. Certainly, one must follow up by saying something like, "I understand what you are saying. However, the tone of your voice concerns me. Over the years, when I have spoken with people who sounded as depressed, down in the dumps, disheartened, demoralized, or discouraged as you, they admitted they were considering suicide."

Most authors suggest that one ask "Are you going to commit suicide?" (Divasto, Lanceley, and Gruys, 1992). There is no single "best way" to ask this question. However, it is imperative that the question be asked and the issue be aired.

The Golden Gate Bridge, Doubt, Alcohol, and Judgment

The material included in this segment is designed to delay the act of the solo suicidal subject. As crisis negotiators, we are not trying to change the subject's mind (let the psychologist concentrate on that); we are buying time. Our intent here is to very diplomatically instill doubt in their judgment, logic, and the timing of their plan. They can always die another day.

It has been reported that of the approximate 2,000 people who have leaped to their death from the Golden Gate Bridge in San Francisco, by some miracle, about two dozen have survived. When each of the survivors was interviewed, they stated that immediately after they jumped, they had second thoughts; they changed their minds. Suddenly it became very clear to them that jumping to their death was a bad idea. They reported that they had not really thought through and considered all the alternatives (ASIST, 2003; Ritter, 2005). Fact or fiction, one might consider using this story to buy time and instill *doubt* in the mind of the suicidal person. Remind the person that he or she can always die another day. If that person dies today, he or she will not have that option.

You may also recount the tragedy in Glendale, California, on January 25, 2005. Juan Alverez attempted suicide by parking his SUV on the train tracks. He changed his mind at the last minute and caused the most serious train accident in the recent history of California (Kasindorf, 2005).

The point, again, is many suicidal people change their minds. One can only speculate on the number who changed their minds but were unable to alter the course of events and died when they did not want to.

Well over 50 percent of people who consider or commit suicide are under the influence of alcohol or some other judgment-affecting drug (ASIST, 2003). It is commonly known that alcohol impairs human judgment, reactions, and responses. Talking and stalling for time with a person who has taken drugs allows the person's body to process the drugs and creates tactical opportunities for law enforcement.

Judgment is especially and effectively impaired by alcohol and drugs. In Freudian terms, alcohol has been called a "solvent for the superego." Some call it "the great enabler." In other words, people do things when they are drunk that their conscience, or common sense, would not consider or allow when they are sober. As an analogy, one would not want the pilot of a commercial aircraft to be drunk while on duty, nor would one want an intoxicated surgeon operating on a loved one.

These are a few ways in which a negotiator can instill doubt when dealing with an inebriated and suicidal subject. One can use these logical arguments to at least delay if not dissuade them from their stated and intended course of action. Remember, our goal is to delay their action. Let us not make the job of crisis negotiations more difficult than it is. As crisis negotiators our job is to buy time to let reason replace emotion, or some sense of sobriety replace inebriation. It is the job of others in mental health to treat people and help them find a cure for their ills.

I guarantee you that sooner or later you will negotiate with a suicidal person whose life is a disaster. After listening to that person tell you about all of their problems, you will probably say to yourself, "My God, if I were you, I would kill myself." Law enforcement officers deal with problem people. In this case our goal is to buy time and delay their action. Do not think that it is your job to resolve the troubles of everyone with whom you negotiate. Further, and in fact, the courts have not ordered crisis negotiators to succeed. They have insisted that crisis negotiators make a reasonable effort (Downs, 1995).

The Less Than Lethal Alternative

In recent years, many jails, correctional institutions, and police departments have purchased and practiced with a multitude of less than lethal weapons. Agencies tend to have a great deal of confidence in the effectiveness of these weapons because they work so well against staff during practice sessions. However, their use in the field has had mixed results. Most people against whom these weapons are used seem to have, for a variety of reasons, some immunity to their potency.

Therefore, it is recommended that a backup plan be in place when these weapons are employed. It is strongly suggested by the Los Angeles Sheriff's Department that police agencies use less than lethal weapons as a diversion, not as an end in themselves. When a quick follow-up response is not used, all too often these devices only succeed in escalating the incident. Departments should have a clear and practiced plan on how the subject will be apprehended during the vital few seconds of distraction achieved by the use of less than lethal weapons (Honig, 2001).

It is strongly recommended that law enforcement officers, who are crisis negotiators, attend local training provided by community "hotline services" and participate in this service by working the phones to hone and polish their skills. Obviously, community hotline services deal almost exclusively with their clients over the telephone. Conversely, law enforcement officers deal almost exclusively with their clients and the public in face-to-face settings. Law enforcement officers become very good at reading body language. However, this is often at the expense of listening skills. There are many very different listening and speaking skills that each setting requires. One good way to develop listening skills is to attend hotline training sessions.

Community hotline training is one resource. Another is the International Critical Incident Stress Foundation (ICISF). ICISF provides excellent hands-on training around the country, at a nominal cost, in a variety of skills. Among them is suicide intervention. Their schedule is available on their Web site, www.icisf.org.

Police and Solo Suicidal Subjects

Typically, law enforcement will encounter the solo suicidal subject in his or her home and will have been called by friends, relatives, mental health specialists, or neighbors. The other common encounter is with the trapped armed robber and hostage taker who may initially be quite arrogant. However, as time takes its toll on his energy level and he begins to recognize the gravity of his situation, he may become despondent over his plight and slip into a suicidal mode. This transition is well depicted by Tim Robbins who played the hostage taker in *Cadillac Man* (Metro Goldwyn Mayer, 1989). In this role he portrays an irate and unemployed husband who takes hostages at the job site of his wife because he believes she is having an affair with a fellow employee. After some initial bravado, shooting, and threatening, he realizes that by taking people hostage he has made a bad situation worse and sinks into solo suicidal behavior.

Depression in the *DSM-IV*

The *Diagnostic and Statistical Manual*, 4th edition (*DSM-IV*) of the American Psychiatric Association, lists mental diseases and disorders on two axes. Axis I lists clinical disorders, like Paranoid Schizophrenia, Bipolar and other psychotic classifications as well as Depression. In spite of their listing on this axis, not all depressions are a form of psychotic behavior. Axis II lists 11 less severe forms of aberrant behavior called personality disorders. These include antisocial, narcissistic, and nine other disorders. One way to gauge the gravity of depression, a frequent precursor to suicide, is that of the 943 pages in *DSM-IV*, there are some 84 pages that deal with various types of depression (American Psychiatric Association, 2000).

In addition there are a dozen different pages that set out the need for further research into five additional types of depression that include Minor Depressive Disorder, Recurrent Brief Depressive Disorder, Mixed Anxiety-Depressive Disorder, Postpsychotic Depressive Disorder of Schizophrenia, and certain aspects of the Dependent Personality Disorder. Thus, 10 percent

Figure 14.1 Negotiating face to face with a jumper requires a team effort. Note the weapon and the protective hold of the secondary on the primary negotiator to prevent the jumper from taking her down.

of the pages in this manual deal with some form of depression. Needless, to say, this is a serious mental problem.

There are many types and causes of depression. Some people suffer from a psychotic depression, like a Bipolar Disorder, while others may have a less severe depression that may not be as long lasting or extreme.

Because bipolar hostage takers are discussed in Chapter 13, they will not be included here. However, when one is dealing with a depressed and suicidal person who cannot clearly articulate why he or she is depressed, the negotiator should consider the possibility of a chemical imbalance, like a bipolar disorder, as the cause. This is an important and necessary distinction. Trying to counsel a person who is chemically depressed will be as effective as ordering a drunk to sober-up. The person with a chemical imbalance needs medication. Talking may help, but medication is the answer.

One way to differentiate between the two is typically, the "normally depressed person" has suffered a personal crisis, loss, or serious stressor in the last 24 hours. Remember, as set out in Appendix B, stress and crisis are personal matters, what is a crisis or stressful for some may not affect another. On the other hand, when the negotiator probes to learn the cause of the depression, the "chemically depressed person," will probably say things like, "Everything in the whole world is shit. Shit, shit, shit." When asked about recent life events, crisis, or a loss that may have caused the current depression and subsequent suicidal behavior, this person is typically unable to point to an event like losing a job, a relationship gone bad, being passed over for or missing a promotion, or a recently diagnosed personal or family member illness.

Suicide by Police

This topic is addressed at length in the next chapter. However, some issues, as they apply to and can be compared and contrasted with solo suicides are discussed in this chapter on solo suicidal subjects.

This phenomenon is commonly called "suicide by cop" and has many causes. Certainly, the closing of many mental hospitals without the implementation and development of the promised alternative care has made a substantial contribution. Once again, law enforcement must pick up the pieces and deal with the consequences of poor public planning by our local, state, and federal legislators.

Snakes with and without Venom

It is very important to separate solo suicidal subjects from those who are engaged in suicide by cop. Although each of these individuals is engaged in suicide, their methods are quite different. That is why two separate and distinct chapters are used to discuss this behavior. To help understand the difference, consider the analogy of encountering and trying to capture two snakes. One snake is venomless. The other is poisonous.

The solo suicidal subject is the venomless snake. (See Figure 14.1.) The bite of this snake will require some medical attention and perhaps a tetanus shot. The police officer who negotiates with a solo suicidal subject and is unable to prevent him or her from taking his or her own life may require some counseling and may suffer from Posttraumatic Stress Disorder, a very treatable malady.

The suicide-by-cop subject is the poisonous snake. The police officer who negotiates with the suicidal subject who is intent on suicide by cop is dealing with a deadly snake. This snake is intent on biting the officer to insure he, she or their peers, will kill it. Thus, in addition to the above treatment, some, many, or most of the officers involved in this scenario may require surgery or the services of the county coroner, not a pleasant picture. This is a very deadly business.

The good news is that we are making progress identifying and more effectively dealing with the suicide-by-cop subject, the poisonous snake. Some suggest that the number of law enforcement encounters with this person has always been very high. Today, we are better at identifying this individual and counting more accurately than in the past. This may well be the case. Whatever the cause, better counting or more encounters, it is a problem well worth addressing.

The most radical and law enforcement–related change in the phenomenon of human suicide in the United States is the recent and dramatic increase in the involvement of police in the suicide scenario. This is documented in a recent Los Angeles County Sheriff's Department (LASD) survey. It verifies what many law enforcement officers have suspected for years. Law enforcement contact with suicidal subjects is much more common today than it was years ago. The LASD has chronicled officer-involved shootings for many years. Between 1987 and 1997, they recorded a 100 percent increase in suicides in Los Angeles County. This includes a 27 percent increase in all officer-involved fatal shootings from 1987 to 1997 (Hutson et al., 1998).

Civilian Suicide

One indicator of our concern with, and confusion over, this phenomenon is the vast number of books on this subject. One need only visit a bookstore or public or university library to see the large number of books devoted, in whole or in part, to the many aspects of this phenomenon. There are books on depression and its symptoms and causes as well as how to cope and get help. As strange as it may seem, there is a unique book that was on the *New York Times* best-seller list for months which was written to help people commit suicide (Humphry, 1991).

This 206-page paperback has 26 chapters with titles like: "Shopping for the Right Doctor," "Beware of the Law," "The Cyanide Enigma," "Death Hollywood Style," "Bizarre Ways to Die," "Life Insurance," "Going Together," "Where Do I Get the Magic Pills," "Death in the Family Car," "Self-Deliverance Using a Plastic Bag," and so on. In his bibliography, Humphry (1991) lists two dozen related books. The fact that this book was on the best-seller list for months points out that many, many people, for a variety of reasons, are interested in and have researched this topic. To help establish the commitment level of the solo suicidal subject, a crisis negotiator should ask the suicidal subject if he or she has read *Final Exit* or any related text. In other words, have they done their homework and carefully planned this scenario, or is this an impulsive act? One must establish the potential effectiveness of their plan.

Dr. Kavorkian's name is known in most American homes. There are dozens of Web sites providing data including statistics, help in almost every aspect of this process, and attempts to ease the pain of those affected by this behavior. The Behavioral Science Unit of the FBI has an excellent CD available to law enforcement entitled "Suicide and Law Enforcement." It, more than any text I have read, provides a police perspective into this social problem (Sheehan and Warren, 2001).

Mental Health Professionals

To help the negotiator in this situation, it is strongly recommended that when dealing with a depressed person, the negotiating team consult with and enlist the services of the departmental psychologists or mental health professionals. Mental health professionals deal with depressed people on such a frequent basis that many of them must talk with a peer to help them deal with the subsequent depression they feel. The point is, they encounter depression regularly and learn very quickly how to assess the depth of and deal with depression.

I can assure you that during the civil deposition and again at the trial, the counsel for the family of the successful solo suicidal subject with whom you have negotiated will ask the negotiator about resources that were contacted. Usually, the mental health professional will be of great help. Even if not, one will have covered this very vital base in the negotiations process.

Negotiating Guidelines and Rationale

As crisis negotiators, our role is to delay, instill doubt in their plan, offer options, and listen. We are not there to solve their problems. Problem solving is the job of other community resources.

Evaluate Preincident Behavior

Is there a history of domestic or criminal violence?

Is there recent violence or threats of violence? (crucial when a deadly weapon is involved)

Has there been a recent breakup or a threat of dissolution of a significant relationship?

Has a life-threatening illness been recently diagnosed? (especially if diagnosed in the last 24 hours)

Has the solo suicidal subject been giving away money or personal possessions?

Have there been prior suicide attempts? (same method may mean they
   want attention, different methods usually mean they are determined)
Drastic mood swings may signify a bipolar disorder. Is the subject on
   or off medication?
Did the subject deliberately commit a criminal act to elicit a police
   response? If so, consider suicide by police as a motive. See the following chapter.
Has the subject set a deadline for his or her own death?

Incident Behavior: Use the CPR Acronym

Evaluate the subject's *current plan*—How realistic is the plan? Will it work?
Prior behavior—What has he or she done to implement the plan?
Resources—Does the subject have the means at hand to kill himself
   or herself?
Is the subject engaging in behaviors that escalate the tension, such as:
   Demanding that police kill him or her
   Noncompliance with police orders and directions
   Advancing toward or taunting the police
   Forcing a confrontation, exiting the building with a hostage, or bran-
      dishing a weapon
   Weapon tied to the subject

   See the data sheet in Appendix I and suicide-by-cop material in the next
chapter.

Suggested Officer (Negotiating Team Activities) Behavior and Strategies

See also Birge (2002), Honig (2001), Hutson et al. (1998), Monahan (1992),
and Strentz (1991, 1995).

Contact your mental health resource immediately.
Put your badge in your pocket as you change roles from cop to counselor.
Ensure containment and isolate the individual.
Identify any and all weapons involved.
Obtain as much preincident intelligence on behavior, as identified
   above, as possible.
Consider the use of less than lethal weapons as a diversion. Have a clear
   plan to apprehend after the diversion.
Assess the violence and suicide potential. Is there a history of this
   behavior, are there previous attempts, how were previous encounters
   resolved, and what resources are available?

Negotiating Techniques

To be effective the crisis negotiator must communicate care and concern.
Slow down the situation by using active listening techniques.
Attempt to establish and maintain rapport.
Do not lie, unless you absolutely must to preserve human life.
Listen and be sympathetic. (See Appendices C and D.)
Ask them if they are thinking about killing themselves.
Convey that you are trying to help.
Evaluate their plan: Is it likely to be effective?
How much time and planning have they done?
Is there a history of suicide, by this person or within their family?
Does this person or the community have resources available to assist? Have any been used?
Concentrate on offering hope, not a solution.
Buy time, "Why now? You can kill yourself tomorrow. If you die today, you eliminate any and all other options."
Instill doubt. Use the "Golden Gate Bridge" story.

Postincident Considerations

Expect local and federal investigations in cases where someone is injured or killed.
Recognize the need for a critical incident stress debrief.

References

American Psychiatric Association (2000) *Diagnostic and Statistical Manual of Mental Disorders*–4th Edition, APA, Washington, DC.

ASIST (2003) Applied Suicide Intervention Skills Training, a workshop conducted by the Baton Rouge Crisis Intervention Center, Baton Rouge, Louisiana, March 26–27.

Birge, R. (2002) Personal interview during Update II Hostage Negotiations Course, Pacific Grove, California, September 12.

Divasto, P., Lanceley, F. J., and Gruys, A. (1992) Critical Issues in Suicide Intervention, *FBI Law Enforcement Bulletin*, August, pp. 13–16.

Downs v. U.S., U.S.C. 6th Circuit, #74-1660 (1975).

Herbert, Lt. Brenda (2005) Hand Out and Lecture to Update II Crisis Negotiations Course, Los Gatos, California, March 3.

Holmes, T. C., and Rahe, R. (1967) The Social Readjustment Rating Scale, *Journal of Psychosomatic Research*, Vol. 11, pp. 213–218.

Honig, A. L. (2001) Police-Assisted Suicide: Identification, Intervention, and Investigation, *The Police Chief*, October.

Humphry, D. (1991) *Final Exit: The Practicalities of Self-Deliverance and Assisted Suicide for the Dying*, Dell, New York.

Hutson, H. R., Anglin, D., Yarbrough, J., Hardaway, K., Russell, M., Strote, J., Canter, M., and Blum, B. (1998) Suicide by Cop, *Annals of Emergency Medicine*, December.

Kakesako, G. K., and Barayuga, D. (1996) Hostage Drama Grips City, *Honolulu Star Bulletin*, February 8, p. A-1.

Lanceley, F. J. (2003) *On Scene Guide for Crisis Negotiators*, CRC Press, Boca Raton, Florida.

Levitt, G. A. (2000) Practical Suicide Prevention, *Corrections Today*, December, pp. 110–116.

Milton, John (1667) *Paradise Lost*, London.

Monahan, J. (1992) Mental Disorders and Violent Behavior: Perceptions and Evidence, *American Psychologist*, Vol. 47, pp. 551–521.

NBC (2004) *Evening News*, Story on Anti-Depression Drugs on the U.S. Market, March 22.

Ohira, R., and Morse, H. (1996) I'll Take a Bullet, *Honolulu Star-Bulletin*, February 7, p. A-1.

Ritter, J. (2005) Suicides Tarnish the Golden Gate, *USA Today*, January 31, p. A3.

Sheehan, D. C., and Warren, J. I., Eds. (2001) Suicide and Law Enforcement. A compilation of papers submitted to the Suicide and Law Enforcement conference, FBI Academy, Quantico, Virginia, September 1999, U.S. Government Printing Office, Washington, DC.

Strentz, T. (1993) Thirteen Indicators of Volatile Negotiations, *Law and Order*, Vol. 39, No. 9, September, pp. 135–139.

Strentz, T. (1995) Cyclic Time Line of Crisis Negotiations, *Law and Order*, Vol. 41, No. 3, March, pp. 73–76.

Appendix A: Some Web Resources

American Association of Suicidology: www.suicidology.org

American Foundation for Suicide Prevention: www.afsp.org

Suicide Awareness Voices of Education (SA/VE): www.save.org

Yellow Ribbon Program for the Prevention of Teen Suicide: www.yellowribbon.org

The Suicide Information and Education Centre, Calgary, Alberta, Canada: www.suicideinfo.ca

San Francisco Suicide Prevention: www.sfsuicide.org

National Alliance for the Mentally Ill: www.nami.org

Surgeon General of the United States: www.surgeongeneral.gov

Appendix B

Holmes–Rahe Stress Scale

Rank Event	Value Score
1. Death of spouse	100
2. Divorce	73
3. Marital separation	65
4. Jail term	63
5. Death of close family member	63
6. Personal injury or illness	53
7. Marriage	50
8. Fired from work	47
9. Marital reconciliation	45
10. Retirement	45
11. Change in family member's health	44
12. Pregnancy	40
13. Sex difficulties	39
14. Addition to family	39
15. Business readjustment	39
16. Change in financial status	38
17. Death of close friend	37
18. Change in number of marital arguments	35
19. Mortgage or loan over $10,000	31
20. Foreclosure of mortgage loan	30
21. Change in work responsibilities	29
22. Son or daughter leaving home	29
23. Trouble with in-laws	29
24. Outstanding personal achievement	28
25. Spouse begins or quits work	26
26. Starting or finishing school	26
27. Change in living conditions	25
28. Revision of personal habits	24
29. Trouble with boss	23
30. Change in work hours or conditions	20
31. Change in residence	20
32. Change in schools	20
33. Change in recreational habits	19
34. Change in church activities	19
35. Change in social activities	18
36. Mortgage or loan under $10,000	18
37. Change in sleeping habits	16
38. Change in number of family gatherings	15
39. Change in eating habits	15
40. Vacation	13
41. Christmas season	12
42. Minor violation of the law	11

Note: More than 300 points in a year usually signifies that the prospect of a serious health problem is very likely within the next few months.

Source: Adapted from Holmes, T. C., and Rahe, R. (1967) The Social Readjustment Rating Scale, *Journal of Psychosomatic Research*, Vol. 11, pp. 213–218. With permission.

Appendix C: Phrases That Work

To do this effectively, the crisis negotiator must communicate care and concern. Typically, the spoken words are not as important as the tone used and attitude communicated.

How can I help?
Are there any other people in there with you?
My name is…, can we talk?
We want to do what is best for everyone.
Let's see if we can work this out.
Let me see what I can do for you.
I am not here to tell you what is right. I am only trying to help.
What do you think really caused this?
I'll stay here with you.
No matter how bad it looks, we can work it out.
We can talk as long as you like.
Do you need anything?
Sometimes it works out that way.
I'll find out and let you know.
Could you tell me about it?
I guess that's pretty important to you.
I would like to hear your side. (Herbert, 2005)

Appendix D: Some Effective Answers

"I just can't take it anymore." What can't you take anymore?
"There's nothing left to live for." Tell me what happened.
"I just want to die." Why?
"My life is a mess." Why do you think so?
"It hurts so bad." What hurts?
"I want the police to shoot me." Why do you want the police to do it?
"What's the use of living?" Why do you want to die?
"No one understands." Whom have you spoken to?
"How can you possibly know what I'm going through?" I would like to try.
"You tell me what I should do." First tell me what you have tried.
    (Herbert, 2005)

Appendix E: Suicide Intervention Flowchart (Lanceley, 2003)

The key is ambivalence. If they were not undecided they would be dead. Is there enough indecision for us to manipulate, delay, or change their mind? If you think they are suicidal, they probably are. *Immediately contact* your mental health consultant or contractor. They deal daily with suicidal people.

Who is their doctor and has he or she been advised and asked for help?

Are they on medication? If so what kind? Who prescribed it for what and when?

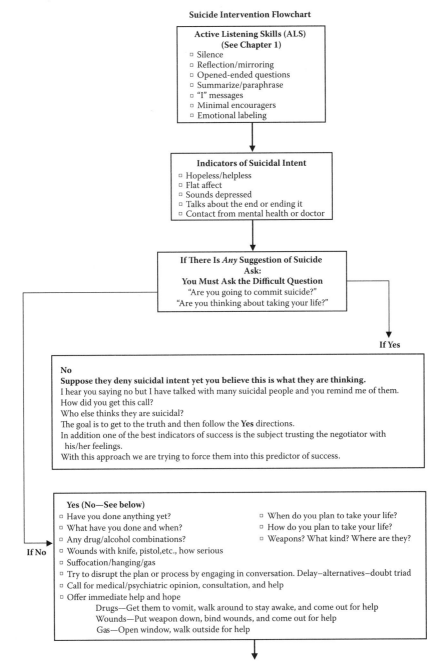

Suicide Intervention Flowchart

Active Listening Skills (ALS)
(See Chapter 1)
▫ Silence
▫ Reflection/mirroring
▫ Opened-ended questions
▫ Summarize/paraphrase
▫ "I" messages
▫ Minimal encouragers
▫ Emotional labeling

Indicators of Suicidal Intent
▫ Hopeless/helpless
▫ Flat affect
▫ Sounds depressed
▫ Talks about the end or ending it
▫ Contact from mental health or doctor

If There Is *Any* Suggestion of Suicide Ask:
You Must Ask the Difficult Question
"Are you going to commit suicide?"
"Are you thinking about taking your life?"

If Yes

No
Suppose they deny suicidal intent yet you believe this is what they are thinking.
I hear you saying no but I have talked with many suicidal people and you remind me of them.
How did you get this call?
Who else thinks they are suicidal?
The goal is to get to the truth and then follow the **Yes** directions.
In addition one of the best indicators of success is the subject trusting the negotiator with
 his/her feelings.
With this approach we are trying to force them into this predictor of success.

Yes (No—See below)
▫ Have you done anything yet?
▫ What have you done and when?
▫ Any drug/alcohol combinations?
▫ Wounds with knife, pistol,etc., how serious

▫ When do you plan to take your life?
▫ How do you plan to take your life?
▫ Weapons? What kind? Where are they?

If No

▫ Suffocation/hanging/gas
▫ Try to disrupt the plan or process by engaging in conversation. Delay–alternatives–doubt triad
▫ Call for medical/psychiatric opinion, consultation, and help
▫ Offer immediate help and hope
      Drugs—Get them to vomit, walk around to stay awake, and come out for help
      Wounds—Put weapon down, bind wounds, and come out for help
      Gas—Open window, walk outside for help

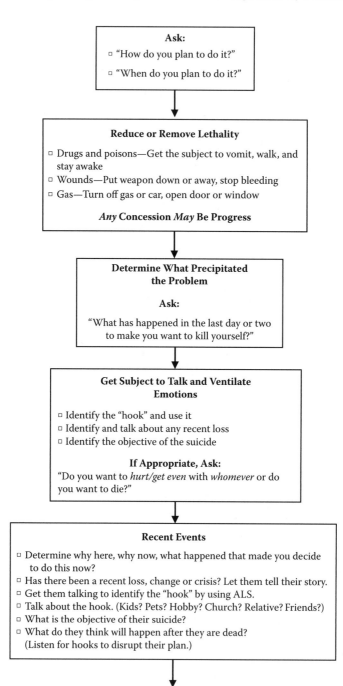

Ask:

- "How do you plan to do it?"
- "When do you plan to do it?"

Reduce or Remove Lethality

- Drugs and poisons—Get the subject to vomit, walk, and stay awake
- Wounds—Put weapon down or away, stop bleeding
- Gas—Turn off gas or car, open door or window

Any Concession *May* Be Progress

Determine What Precipitated the Problem

Ask:

"What has happened in the last day or two to make you want to kill yourself?"

Get Subject to Talk and Ventilate Emotions

- Identify the "hook" and use it
- Identify and talk about any recent loss
- Identify the objective of the suicide

If Appropriate, Ask:
"Do you want to *hurt/get even* with *whomever* or do you want to die?"

Recent Events

- Determine why here, why now, what happened that made you decide to do this now?
- Has there been a recent loss, change or crisis? Let them tell their story.
- Get them talking to identify the "hook" by using ALS.
- Talk about the hook. (Kids? Pets? Hobby? Church? Relative? Friends?)
- What is the objective of their suicide?
- What do they think will happen after they are dead?
  (Listen for hooks to disrupt their plan.)

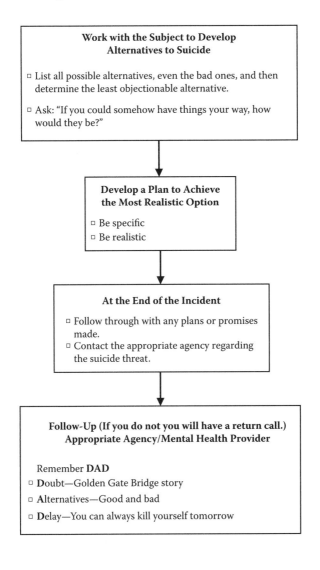

**Work with the Subject to Develop
Alternatives to Suicide**

▢ List all possible alternatives, even the bad ones, and then
   determine the least objectionable alternative.

▢ Ask: "If you could somehow have things your way, how
   would they be?"

**Develop a Plan to Achieve
the Most Realistic Option**

▢ Be specific
▢ Be realistic

At the End of the Incident

▢ Follow through with any plans or promises
   made.
▢ Contact the appropriate agency regarding
   the suicide threat.

**Follow-Up (If you do not you will have a return call.)
Appropriate Agency/Mental Health Provider**

Remember **DAD**
▢ **D**oubt—Golden Gate Bridge story
▢ **A**lternatives—Good and bad
▢ **D**elay—You can always kill yourself tomorrow

Police-Assisted Suicide 15

Introduction

There are several similarities between material presented in this chapter and in Chapter 14, "The Suicidal Hostage Holder (Also Known as the Solo Suicidal Subject)." The reason is that in both cases we are dealing with suicidal subjects. Their goal is the same, but their pathway is quite different. The reading of both chapters is encouraged because the value of the material will be enhanced by the repetition.*

Police-assisted suicide, or as it is more commonly and correctly called, "suicide by cop," seems to be a growing problem in this country. According to a 10-year study that is the largest and most thorough examination of this phenomenon done by the Los Angeles Sheriff's Department (LASD), there was a significant increase in officer-assisted suicides, aka suicide by cop. The data suggest that about 25 percent of all officer-involved shootings in 1997 could be classified as suicide by cop. This is almost double the rate of 1987 (Honig, 2001; Hutson et al., 1998). Unfortunately, but in fact, Los Angeles County is not alone. Other studies found similar statistics (Keram and Farrell, 2001).

One of the problems encountered when dealing with any law enforcement or corrections action is the definition. Dr. Honing admits that her definition of suicide by cop (SbC) used in the LASD study was narrow. Two quick examples will suffice.

I recently worked a case for the Portland, Oregon, Police Department to defend them in a wrongful death suit. Five of their officers confronted a knife-wielding subject who was holding a female with a knife pressed against her throat. The officers could not see the knife that witnesses reported and called to each other to determine if one of them could see the weapon. The subject, who was about 15 feet from the officers, heard their calls and responded, "Yes I have a f_____ knife and I am going to kill this bitch" as he waved it in the air for all to see. They ordered him to drop the knife. Instead he placed it back against her throat. He was shot and killed. The plaintiff claimed the police department should have played a waiting game and called for negotiators. The judge agreed that time was not on the side of law enforcement, the hostage was in immediate danger, and the shooting was justified. This incident would not have been counted as SbC in the LASD study. Not all situations are negotiable.

---

* Prior to reading this chapter, it is suggested that one read Chapter 14 on suicide. That chapter will provide the background and foundation necessary to understand this more aggressive and vicious form of suicide.

A more dramatic example occurred on December 9, 1982, when Norman D. Mayer took the Washington Monument hostage. He drove his rental vehicle, which he claimed was filled with explosives, across the lawn up to the monument. He allowed tourists to leave and demanded to speak to the media. He was protesting nuclear weapons. The U.S. Park Police, Washington, DC Metropolitan Police, and the Federal Bureau of Investigation (FBI) responded. He walked around the vehicle wearing a jumpsuit and claimed the device he held would activate his bomb. He was identified as a resident of Miami Beach, Florida. During the negotiations process, about 10 hours, the FBI in Miami conducted a thorough investigation. They learned that Mayer had recently engaged in presuicide behavior. No evidence of bomb-making material was located. However, the on-scene commander had to err on the side of safety and assume the large van contained a bomb. Further, it was thought that he had an accomplice in the van. He was warned not to leave the monument grounds else he would be shot. Obviously, law enforcement could not allow a truck loaded with explosives to drive around Washington, DC. After some 10 hours of negotiations Mayer drove the van toward the White House. He was shot and killed by a police sniper. There was no bomb in the van. Again, this case would not have been counted in the LASD study. The point is that we really do not know what percentage of police shootings are SbC. Everyone agrees it is a growing problem, but the exact percentage remains elusive. (See Figures 15.1 through 15.7.)

In this chapter, a suicide-by-cop incident refers to an event in which an individual engages in behaviors that pose an apparent risk of serious injury or death to themselves and others, with the intent to necessitate the use of deadly force by law enforcement personnel.

In fact, suicide by cop has been known for centuries. The *Bible* speaks of it: "and there was Saul leaning upon his spear; and lo, the chariots and horse men were close upon him...and he said to me 'Stand beside me and slay me; for anguish has seized me, and yet my life still lingers'" (RSV, II Samuel 1:6–9).

American Indians knew of it and called this behavior, "Crazy dog wishing to die." On the other side of the world the Koran addressed this behavior by noting suicide is forbidden. However, being killed by someone else is not (Andriolo, 1998).

Just as the American Indians said "Crazy dog wishing to die," so we see the modern equivalent in the subject who will consciously and subconsciously work against the negotiating team. We want that person to live. Their friends and relatives want him or her to live. However, the subject really wants to die and will do all he or she can to achieve this end. Thus, they engage in provocative behavior, and they refuse to obey police commands or converse with negotiators. They may have "painted themselves into a corner" so that the "logical" solution to their dilemma is death. This is why it is recommended that the crisis negotiating team identify and document subject behaviors prior to and during the crisis. Concurrent notes are good evidence

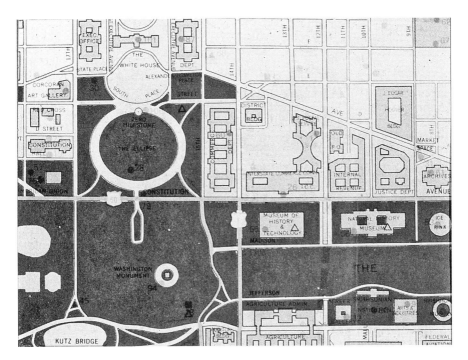

Figure 15.1 Diagram of grounds.

Figure 15.2 The subject on the grounds.

Figure 15.3 The subject on the grounds.

of the efforts made by police and the resistance encountered by law enforcement in our efforts to save the life of a person who wants to die. The deck is stacked against us. A win for law enforcement in a suicide by police negotiation may be that only the subject is shot (Birge, 2002).

Law Enforcement as Mental Health Professionals

Law enforcement has always had some involvement with people who have mental problems. However, this involvement has seen a dramatic increase since the 1960s. It was during these turbulent times that a national trend to close large mental hospitals in favor of small community-based, residential treatment centers was in vogue. The accusation leveled at mental health was, "You are just warehousing these sick people who need effective treatment, help, and care that cannot be provided in such large institutions." The intent

Figure 15.4 The subject on the grounds.

Figure 15.5 The subject on the grounds.

Figure 15.6 The grounds from the command post (CP) before it was moved, showing the subject's truck between the monument and us.

Figure 15.7 Tourists leaving the monument with the subject off to the right.

was to provide better treatment and save money. Therefore, a national two-phase plan was developed in each state that called for the phasing out of large hospitals in favor of smaller community treatment centers.

In California, the new clinics were to be called "Short Doyle Clinics," after the politicians who formulated the idea and shepherded it into law. Phase 1 was completed rather quickly. The large hospitals were closed. However, only a few of the required and envisioned thousands of replacement community treatment centers were ever completed. Mentally ill patients who were to be moved from large hospitals to community treatment centers were moved from large hospitals to the street.

In addition, we know little more today about how to treat and cure people who have a mental disease or disorder than we did half a century ago. With the notable exception of the bipolar disorders and some depressions, mental health today treats symptoms, not the causes of mental illness. A medical analogy would be to treat people suffering from tuberculosis by using a cough suppressant. Until the cause, or causes, of mental disorders are discovered, our mental health professionals will have no alternative but to treat the symptoms. In the meantime, mentally ill people are not cured and their aberrant behavior is chemically controlled, as long as they take their medication, and law enforcement has inherited a problem that seems to get worse.

One result of the closing of large hospitals, without the availability of alternative community-based treatment, and the current ineffective treatment of mental patients, is that thousands of mentally ill people roam the streets of our nation. Typically, as they wander about the city, their treatment consists of a prescription for medication to mask their symptoms. This prescription may or may not be current or filled, and the medication may or may not be ingested when taken. Thousands of these people are victimized daily by predatory criminals. When these people become victims of crime or "act out" because they are "off their meds," law enforcement steps in to deal with and attempts to treat the untreatable. Some of these former and "should be" patients are homicidal, suicidal, or a combination of both. Too many become subjects or victims in suicide-by-cop scenarios.

In addition to our mentally ill population, there are those in our society who are depressed, overstressed, physically ill, or suffered a recent dissolution of a significant relationship and cannot actively take their own lives. In some twisted form of logic, they think that although self-inflicted suicide is a sin, manipulating another person into doing the job for you is OK.

Snakes with and without Venom

It is very important to separate suicidal people from those who are engaged in suicide by cop. Although each of these individuals is engaged in suicide, their methods are quite different. That is why two separate and distinct chapters are used to discuss this behavior. To help understand the difference, consider the analogy of encountering two snakes. One snake is venomless. The other is poisonous.

The suicidal person is the venomless snake. The bite of this snake will require some medical attention and perhaps a tetanus shot. The police officer who negotiates with a suicidal person and is unable to prevent him or her from taking his or her own life may require some counseling and may suffer from Postraumatic Stress Disorder, a very treatable malady.

The suicide-by-cop person is the poisonous snake. The police officer who negotiates with the suicidal person who is intent on "suicide by cop," is dealing with a deadly snake. This snake is intent on biting the officer to ensure he, she, or their peers, will kill it. Thus, in addition to the above treatment, some, many, or most of the officers involved in this scenario may require surgery or the services of the county coroner—not a pleasant picture. This is a very deadly business.

One of many examples of how this phenomenon affects law enforcement is the increase in the behavior known as suicide by police. A graphic example of this occurred a few years ago in the Sand Island industrial area between the City of Honolulu and the airport. At 0750, a former and very disgruntled employee, 28-year-old, 6 foot 5, 250 pound, John Miranda, returned to his place of employment and took five employees hostage. The Honolulu Police Department (HPD) special weapons and tactics (SWAT) and Crisis Negotiations team responded, cordoned off the area, and attempted to negotiate with Miranda. Early in the siege, Miranda fired out the window at police and then shot one hostage in the leg. Throughout the seven and one-half hour siege, Miranda repeatedly told his hostages that he would rather take a bullet than go back to jail (Kakesako and Barayuga, 1996).

When he took his four other hostages with him to use the bathroom, the badly wounded hostage who was left lying in a pool of blood on the floor escaped out a window and lived. In a defiant and dramatic gesture designed to provoke suicide by police, Miranda exited the building with three remaining hostages. He had the butt of his sawed-off shotgun taped to his hand. The barrel was taped to the neck and was firmly against the head of one hostage who was of average build. For over 5 hours he paraded his hostages around the parking lot. During this defiant demonstration Miranda noticed that the shotgun was no longer tightly taped to the neck and against the head of his primary hostage. He sent one hostage back into the building to get more duct tape. When he entered the building, police took him into their custody. Shortly thereafter, another hostage ran off leaving Miranda and one hostage, with a loosely secured shotgun tied to his neck, walking around the parking lot.

At 1432, Miranda began a countdown at 60. He told police that the countdown would end with the shooting of his hostage. When the count reached 13, his hostage grabbed the weapon. He noticed, as Miranda had earlier, that the shotgun was no longer pressing against his head. Instead, it was bouncing off his neck and trapezius. He correctly assumed there was enough distance between his neck and the muzzle of the shotgun for him to grab the weapon, pull the muzzle away from his head, and, in a *David versus Goliath* battle, wrestle it far enough away to prevent Miranda from killing him. So, at the count of 13 he made his move. As they wrestled and spun around, Miranda twice fired the shotgun. In response, the HPD tactical team opened fire. During the spinning scuffle, Miranda was hit by a dozen police bullets. His hostage escaped, probably with some loss of hearing, but otherwise not seriously injured.

This is a very dramatic example of suicide by police. Fortunately, not every such encounter ends in death. One evening in March 2000, a young man in Southern California attempted to end his life in a police confrontation. He was on drugs, drunk, and distraught. His girlfriend had broken up with him. In an attempt to contact her, he inadvertently dialed 911. The dispatcher determined the dangerousness of this situation and police units were dispatched to his home. During a brief conversation with the police dispatcher it was learned that the subject had prior involvement with the police that included threats against his mother and sister, who were in the house at the time of the 911 call. Fearing that he would injure them, the dispatcher convinced him to exit his home. He was told to leave his weapon in the house and exit with his cell phone. He exited with both. He was told to drop the weapon he was holding at his side. Instead, he raised and pointed it at the police. He was shot and wounded. Four years later the U.S. District Court rejected his claim for compensation from the police with prejudice.

We are making progress identifying and more effectively dealing with the suicide-by-cop subject, the poisonous snake that some say is on the increase. Others suggest that the number of law enforcement encounters with this person has always been high. Today, we are better at identifying this individual and counting more accurately than in the past. This may be the case. Whatever the cause, better counting or more encounters, it is a problem well worth addressing.

The Golden Gate Bridge, Alcohol, Judgment, and Doubt

The material included in this paragraph is designed to delay the act of the suicidal subject. We are not trying to change the subject's mind—let the psychologist concentrate on that—we are buying time.

Figure 15.8 Preservation of life is important, but negotiator safety is crucial.

Our intent here is to very diplomatically instill doubt in the subject's judgment, logic, and the timing of the plan. The subject can always die another day. The problem is that developing a dialogue with a suicide-by-cop subject is very difficult. He does not want a dialogue, he wants to die. Even with this obstacle in mind, consider the following strategies (Figure 15.8).

1. It has been reported that of the hundreds of people who have leaped to their death from the Golden Gate Bridge in San Francisco, by some miracle, a few survived. When each of the survivors was interviewed, they stated that immediately after they jumped, they had second thoughts—they changed their minds. Suddenly it became very clear to them that jumping to their death was a bad idea. They reported that they had not really thought through and considered all the alternatives (ASIST, 2003). Fact or fiction, one might consider using this story to buy time and instill doubt in the mind of the suicidal person. Remind the person that he or she can always die another day. If the person dies today, he or she will not have that option.

2. Well over 50 percent of people who consider or commit suicide are under the influence of alcohol or some other judgment-affecting drug (ASIST, 2003). It is commonly known that alcohol impairs human judgment, reactions, and responses. Talking and stalling for time with a person who has taken drugs allows the person's body to process the drugs and creates tactical opportunities for law enforcement.

3. Judgment is especially and effectively impaired by alcohol and drugs. In Freudian terms, alcohol has been called "solvent for the superego." Some call it "the great enabler." In other words, people do things when they are drunk that their conscience, or common sense, would not consider or allow when they are sober. As an analogy, one would not want the pilot of a commercial aircraft to be drunk while on duty, nor would one want an intoxicated surgeon operating on a loved one.

4. These are a few ways in which a negotiator can instill doubt when dealing with an inebriated and suicidal subject. One can use these logical arguments to at least delay if not dissuade the subject from his or her stated and intended course of action. Remember, our goal is to delay the subject's action. Let us not make the job of crisis negotiations more difficult than it is. As crisis negotiators our job is to buy time to let reason replace emotion, or some sense of sobriety replace inebriation. It is the job of others in mental health to treat people and help them find a cure for their ills.

I guarantee you that sooner or later you will negotiate with a suicidal person whose life is a disaster. After listening to that person tell you about all of his or her problems you will probably say to yourself, "My God, if I were you, I would kill myself." Law enforcement officers deal with problem people. In this case, our goal is to buy time and delay their action. Do not think that it is your job to resolve the troubles of everyone with whom you negotiate. Further, and in fact, the courts have not ordered crisis negotiators to succeed. They have insisted that crisis negotiators make a reasonable effort (Downs, 1975).

Identification

The identification of behavior that is known to be associated with suicide by cop has been well researched, accurate, and looks good on paper. Its application during a fast-moving crisis is another matter. However, the opportunity for its application is enhanced as one slows down the crisis negotiation process to provide the intelligence function of the crisis negotiating team an opportunity to do its job. As noted below, some of the preincident behavioral indicators are obvious. Others require that knowledge of the subject's background be obtained through the interviewing of friends, relatives, and neighbors, and the reviewing of police and mental health files. Obviously, there is a marked similarity between the preincident suicide-by-cop behavior and that of the solo suicide. They share the same goal; it is their path that differs.

The Less Than Lethal Alternative

In recent years many, if not most, police departments have purchased and practiced with a multitude of less than lethal weapons. Law enforcement tends to have a great deal of confidence in the effectiveness of these weapons because they work so well against police officers during practice sessions. However, their use in the field has had mixed results. Most people against whom these weapons are used seem to have, for a variety of reasons, some immunity to their potency.

Therefore, it is recommended that a backup plan be in place when these weapons are employed. It is strongly suggested by the Los Angeles Sheriff's Department that police agencies use less than lethal weapons as a diversion, not as an end in themselves. All too often these devices succeed only in escalating the incident. Departments should have a clear and practiced plan on how the subject will be apprehended during the vital few seconds of distraction achieved by the use of less than lethal weapons (Honig, 2001).

It is strongly recommended that law enforcement officers, who are crisis negotiators, attend local training that is provided by community "hotline services" and participate in this service by working the phones to hone and polish their skills. Obviously, community hotline services deal almost exclusively with their clients over the telephone. Conversely, law enforcement officers deal almost exclusively with their clients and the public in face-to-face settings. Law enforcement officers become very good at reading body language. However, this is often at the expense of listening skills. There are many very different listening and speaking skills that each setting requires. One good way to develop listening skills is to attend training sessions.

Community hotline training is one resource. Another is the International Critical Incident Stress Foundation (ICISF). ICISF provides excellent hands-on training around the country, at a nominal cost, in a variety of skills. Among them is suicide intervention. Their schedule is available on their Web site: www.icisf.org.

The following listing of behaviors and recommendations comes from several sources (Honig, 2001; Lindsay, 1999; Lord, 1999; Monahan, 1992; Strentz, 1991, 1995).

Preincident Behavior

History of domestic or criminal violence

Recent breakup or a threat of dissolution of a significant relationship

Recent violence, history or threats of violence (especially when a deadly weapon is involved)

A life-threatening illness (especially if diagnosed in the last 24 hours)

Giving away money and personal possessions

Prior suicide attempts

Same method means they want attention

Different methods mean very serious

Drastic mood swings may signify a bipolar disorder; determine if they are on or off medication

Did the subject deliberately commit a criminal act to elicit a police response?

Did the subject set a deadline for his or her own death?

Incident Behavior: Use the CPR Acronym

Current plan

Prior behavior

Resources

Is the subject engaging in behaviors that escalate the tension, such as

Demanding that police kill him or her

Noncompliance with police orders and directions

Advancing on or taunting the officer

Forcing a confrontation, exiting the building with a hostage, or brandishing a weapon

Weapon tied to the subject

See the data sheet in Appendix D

Suggested Officer (Negotiating Team Activities) Behavior and Strategies (Birge, 2002; Honig, 2001; Hutson et al., 1998; Monahan, 1992; Strentz, 1991, 1995)

Put your badge in your pocket as you change roles from cop to counselor.

Ensure containment and isolate the individual.

Identify any weapons involved.

Obtain as much preincident intelligence on behavior, as identified above, as possible.

Consider the initial use of less than lethal weapons as a diversion; have a clear plan to apprehend after diversion.

Assess the violence and suicide potential.

Negotiating Techniques

Slow down the situation.

Attempt to establish and maintain rapport.

Do not lie, unless you absolutely must to preserve human life.

Listen and be sympathetic.

Ask them if they are thinking about hurting or killing themselves.

Convey that you are trying to help.

Use active listening.

Evaluate their plan; is it likely to be effective?

How much time and planning have they done?

Is there a history of suicide, by this person or within their family?

Does this person or the community have resources available to assist? Have any been used?

Concentrate on offering hope, not a solution.

Buy time, "Why now? You can kill yourself tomorrow. If you die today, you eliminate any and all other options."

Use the "Golden Gate Bridge" story.

Postincident Considerations

Expect local and federal investigations in cases where someone is injured or killed.

Recognize the need for a critical incident stress debrief.

References

Andriolo, K. R. (1998) Gender and the Cultural Construction of Good and Bad Suicide, *Suicide and Life-Threatening Behavior*, Vol. 28, No. 1, pp. 37–49.

ASIST (2003) Applied Suicide Intervention Skills Training, a workshop conducted by the Baton Rouge Crisis Intervention Center, Baton Rouge, Louisiana, March 26–27.

Bible, II Samuel 1:1–16, RSV.

Birge, R. (2002) Balance Is the Key, *Law and Order*, Vol. 50, No. 3, March, pp. 102–106.

Downs v. United States 382 F. Supp. 752, (1975).

Honig, A. L. (2001) Police-Assisted Suicide: Identification, Intervention, and Investigation, *The Police Chief*, October, pp. 89–93.

Hutson, H. R., Anglin, D., Yarbrough, J., Hardaway, K., Russell, M., Strote, J., Canter, M., and Blum, B. (1998) Suicide by Cop, *Annals of Emergency Medicine*, December.

Kakesako, G. K., and Barayuga, D. (1996) Hostage Drama Grips City, *Honolulu Star Bulletin*, February 8, p. A-1.

Keram, E., and Farrell, B. (2001) Suicide by Cop: Issues in Outcome and Analysis, *Suicide and Law Enforcement*, pp. 587–599.

Lindsay, M. S. (1999) Identifying the Dynamics of Suicide by Cop, In D. C.Sheehan and J. I. Warren (Eds.), *Suicide and Law Enforcement*, A compilation of papers submitted to the Suicide and Law Enforcement Conference, FBI Academy, Quantico, Virginia, September, pp. 599–606 [CD version of the document], U.S. Government Printing Office, Washington, DC.

Lord, J. I. (1999) Law Enforcement-Assisted Suicide: Characteristics of Subjects and Law Enforcement Intervention Techniques. In D. C. Sheehan and J. I. Warren (Eds.), *Suicide and Law Enforcement*, A compilation of papers submitted to the Suicide and Law Enforcement Conference, FBI Academy, Quantico, Virginia, September, pp. 607–626 [CD version of the document], U.S. Government Printing Office, Washington, DC.

Monahan, J. (1992) Mental Disorder and Violent Behavior: Perceptions and Evidence, *American Psychologist*, Vol. 47, pp. 511–521.

Strentz, T. (1991) Thirteen Indicators of Volatile Negotiations, *Law and Order*, Vol. 39, No. 9, September, pp. 135–139.

Strentz, T. (1995) The Cyclic Crisis Negotiations Time Line, *Law and Order*, Vol. 43, No. 3, March, pp. 73–76.

Appendix A: Some Web Resources

American Association of Suicidology: www.suicidology.org
American Foundation for Suicide Prevention: www.afsp.org
Suicide Awareness Voices of Education (SA/VE): www.save.org
Yellow Ribbon Program for the Prevention of Teen Suicide: www.yellowribbon.org
The Suicide Information and Education Centre, Calgary, Alberta, Canada: www.suicideinfo.ca
San Francisco Suicide Prevention: www.sfsuicide.org
National Alliance for the Mentally Ill: www.nami.org
Surgeon General of the United States: www.surgeongeneral.gov

Appendix B

Diagnostic Criteria for Suicide by Cop

History (3 of the 5 Required)

Mental or chronic physical illness	The subject may have a diagnosed or undiagnosed condition. Some may not be identified until the physical or psychological autopsy.
Drug or alcohol abuse	May be legal or illegal substances.
Low socioeconomic background	When individuals commit suicide they use the means with which they are most familiar. Within this category these people have had exposure to law enforcement.
Suicide attempts	Most suicidal people have a history of attempts.
Criminal history	The subject will have a history of some type of criminal background, most often of an impulsive nature.

Events (8 of 12 required)

Incident initiation	The subject or a third party approached the police or caused an action that led others to call police.
Event to ensure police response	The subject who wishes to die at the hands of the police: he or she will create an incident that is designed to bring police to the scene.
Subject forces confrontation	Instead of surrendering or appropriately responding to police orders, he or she will initiate actions that will escalate the incident.
Initiates aggressive action	The subject will become aggressive to heighten the officer's level of stress and fear that will result in escalating the incident.
Threatens officer with a weapon	Because the subject is motivated by suicide, he or she provokes the officer into shooting in self-defense or in defense of others.
Advances toward the officers	The subject will make some attempt to approach or appear to advance toward the officer. This is designed to reinforce the confrontation and the belief in aggressiveness on the part of the subject to the officer. Again, there is a subject-initiated escalation of the incident.
Refuses to drop weapon	The subject will not heed commands from anyone to drop the weapon. To do so would cause an immediate deescalation of the incident and interrupt their suicidal process.
Threatens citizen(s) with harm	The subject needs to be killed by the officers and will use citizens (hostages) to maintain pressure on the police.
Presence of deadly weapon	The subject possesses or displays a deadly weapon and refuses to put it down or out of reach.
Recent stressor	As with all suicides, there has typically been a crisis in the last 24 hours of the subject's life.
Injured officer or citizen	Normally, if there is only one officer present, that officer will not be harmed because he or she is the intended instrument of death. If there are citizens or additional officers present, the subject may attempt to harm them to escalate the incident.
Retreat by officer	The officer retreats out of fear of his or her life. Unlike most police shootings the retreat is intended to achieve cover or concealment. Officers have stated that they knew someone was going to die.

Appendix B *(Continued)*

Diagnostic Criteria for Suicide by Cop

Source: Lindsay, M. S. (1999) Identifying the Dynamics of Suicide by Cop, In D. C. Sheehan and J. I. Warren (Eds.) *Suicide and Law Enforcement,* A compilation of papers submitted to the Suicide and Law Enforcement Conference, FBI Academy, Quantico, Virginia. September, pp. 599–606 [CD version of the document]. U.S. Government Printing Office, Washington, DC.

Appendix C

Suicide-by-Cop Scale

History (Three)	Present	Not Present	Unknown
Mental or chronic physical pain			
Drug or alcohol abuse			
Low social-economic status			
Suicide attempts			
Criminal history			
Events (eight)			
Incident initiated by subject or third party, not police			
Precipitating event to ensure police response			
Subject forces confrontation			
Subject initiated aggressive action			
Threatens officers with weapon			
Advancement of subject toward officer			
Refuses to drop the weapon			
Threatens citizen (officer) with harm			
Presence of deadly weapon			
Recent stressors (loss/change)			
Injury to officer or citizen			
Repeat offender			
Retreat by officer			

Source: Lindsay, M. S. (1999) Identifying the Dynamics of Suicide by Cop, In D. C. Sheehan and J. I. Warren (Eds.) *Suicide and Law Enforcement,* A compilation of papers submitted to the Suicide and Law Enforcement Conference, FBI Academy, Quantico, Virginia. September, pp. 599–606 [CD version of the document]. U.S. Government Printing Office, Washington, DC.

Appendix D

LASD Study: 1987–1997

- Suicide by Police Scenario
- In 1997, a 100% increase over 1987
- 25% of All Fatal and Nonfatal Officer-Involved Shootings in 1997
- Narrow Definition

Source: Honig, A. L. (2001) Police Assisted Suicide: Identification, Intervention, and Investigation, *The Police Chief,* October, pp. 89–93.

Appendix E

You may be dealing with a suicide-by-cop or subject-precipitated homicide if (addition to contraindicators of negotiator progress)

1. The subject ignores police demands to drop their weapon, put their hands up, halt, and other common demands with which most people immediately comply.
2. The subject sets a deadline for his or her death.
3. The subject has an elaborate plan for his or her own death or has previous suicidal attempts.
4. The subject requests additional weapons or current weapons are secured to the subject.
5. He or she has just killed, or thought he or she killed, a significant other.
6. He or she provides you with a verbal will.
7. He or she sounds depressed to you but denies thoughts of suicide.
8. He or she shoots at police during the siege.
9. He or she refuses to negotiate with the police.
10. There are no clear demands.
11. There is an escalation of threats or increase in tone of voice over time.
12. The subject insists on nose-to-nose negotiations or otherwise presents himself or herself as a clear target.
13. Subject demands that the police shoot him or her.

Source: Honig, A. L. (2001) Police-Assisted Suicide: Identification, Intervention, and Investigation, *The Police Chief,* October, pp. 89–93.

Crisis Negotiations in the Correctional Setting 16

Introduction

The wake-up call identifying the need for prison crisis negotiation teams was the September 1971 disaster at Attica, New York. Interestingly enough, the Munich Olympics in September 1972, served as the wake-up call for law enforcement. In each incident, hostages died who, given what we know now, should not have been killed. In each incident, experience and good intelligence were lacking. In addition, command decisions were wrong, tactical maneuvers inappropriate, and effective crisis negotiations tactics and techniques nonexistent.

Given our limited knowledge and experience back then, what went wrong was predictable. The errors at Munich and Attica could, just as easily, have occurred in Miami and federal correctional institution (FCI) Atlanta. What is more important, is the progress we have made since these disasters. There is an old saying, "Those who do not study and learn from their history are condemned to repeat it" (Santayana, 1905). In our litigious society, if we do not follow his advice, we will be sued and we will lose. When the Attica suits were finally settled in 2000, the State of New York paid $12 million to inmates and their attorneys. In addition there were the hidden and incalculable costs of time, frustration, anxiety, and money paid by the State of New York to defend itself.

The Street versus the Institution

Over the years, it has become clear that there are some distinct differences between crisis negotiations as practiced on "the street" or by law enforcement versus how this process is implemented in prisons. In fact there are more similarities than differences. A similar observation has been made by Needham (1977) and Fuselier (1988). I have observed only six differences between the two settings. How this will play out as more and more prisons become privatized remains to be seen.

1. Since the mid-1970s, I have taught crisis negotiation courses for departments of corrections from Virginia to Louisiana, Minnesota, Michigan, in California, and Washington State. In each of these states I was impressed with their *immediate response plans and capabilities*. It is this capability that underlies a basic difference in approach. In street situations the average response time for a crisis team to arrive and set up is about an hour (Birge, 2004). This allows the hostage taker ample

opportunity to discuss his predicament with his hostages or a first responding officer. He also has time to fortify his position. Institutions usually eliminate this potential advantage by instituting a tactical response as quickly as possible with any and all available on-site staff. This may account for the relatively low number of hostage sieges that occur in jails and prisons. Given their volatile collection of denizens and plethora of potential hostages, one would expect that institutions would have far more hostage incidents than they experience.

2. A second basic difference is the *knowledge prison staff has of the location of the incident.* Each staff person who works in an institution knows the basic layout. A major problem is that prisons are designed to keep people locked in. This same design works in reverse when a tactical team is trying to force an entry into a location where they are locked out. The use of surreptitious listening and video devices may also be hampered by the construction of most institutions.

3. The negotiators know *the personalities of the players.* As noted in Terhune-Bickler (2004), Dr. Terhune-Bickler identifies positive and negative aspects of a preincident relationship. In her article, "Too Close for Comfort," she lists a dozen factors that can harm or enhance the negotiations process when dealing with a subject or hostage who is known to the negotiator. Although her focus is on law enforcement officers negotiating with peers, most of her findings can be generalized to any crisis negotiations setting where there is a prior negotiator–subject or negotiator–hostage relationship. A slightly modified version of her table appears below.

Negotiating with Fellow Officers

Dynamics Supporting Negotiations	Dynamics Harming Negotiations
Rapport may already be established: In-crisis officers are known and know the negotiator.	In-crisis officers may see the department as the source of the problem.
Information about in-crisis officers is easy to obtain.	In-crisis officers perceive the negotiator as "one of them."
Negotiator may be able to relate common problems/themes with in-crisis officers.	In-crisis officers are too embarrassed to talk to someone they know.
Third-party intermediaries are known and more easily controlled.	Negotiator may be too emotionally attached to be objective/effective.
Keeping the problem in-house may give in-crisis officers the illusion that it is "not a big deal."	In-crisis officers know what the department will deliver.
	Suicide is a high possibility.
	The negotiator is a secondary victim if the resolution ends in death.

4. In addition, there is the issue of prison subcultures. A factor more commonly encountered in any correctional setting than in most street sieges are the gang affiliations of the population. Knowledge of these groups, their values, hierarchy, culture, and influence within the facility is vital. McMains and Mullins (2010) and Turner and Miller (1991) identify some of these characteristics among several groups to include Jamaican, Haitian, and military veterans. One must remember that just because two groups speak the same language, do not assume they get along. Sometimes this common language breeds contempt between the groups. While working in Puerto Rico as a Federal Bureau of Investigation (FBI) agent, I learned that there are some very powerful prejudices within the Caribbean community of nations.

Also, there are diverse radical and racial groups, such as the Mexican Mafia, Aryan Nation, and Moslem extremists, each with its own value system, hierarchy, culture, and values, about which the intelligence section of any institution must and usually does possess current information. I do not have the expertise, and this text does not have the space, to adequately address all of these groups.

5. The fourth difference is the institutional tendency for decisions to be made at a *higher level* in the chain of command than is typically seen on the street (McMains and Mullins, 2010). This can work to the advantage of a crisis management team that has actively included the decision makers in their on-site training sessions. These sessions not only provide the leadership an opportunity to meet their staff but to understand their tactics, rationales, strengths, and weaknesses. On the contrary, most police and sheriff department's tactical and nego-tiation teams frequently train off site. This creates the problem of proximity and participation for their leadership. Frequently people in leadership positions find it very difficult to "get away from the office." Training on-site tends to overcome this problem or excuse.

The lack of crisis training for potential on-scene or incident com-manders (ICs) remains a serious problem for law enforcement and institutions. All too often crisis response teams have an on-scene commander who is "appointed" by geography or shift assignment, not by his or her crisis command training or ability. I have discussed this problem with many authors and experts in the field who share my view. All too often the IC is too busy to train but always there to take charge.

6. The final difference I have observed is the *staffing of institutional negotiating teams*. Typically, institutional teams have more people trained and available on site to cope with a crisis. It has been my experience that most law enforcement teams average two to four

people who perform over a dozen tasks. During the 1993 siege at Waco, Texas, the FBI team numbered over 20. This is an exceptionally large number, even for the FBI. Institutional teams usually enjoy the luxury of having a larger cadre of trained negotiators, support staff, and law enforcement available at any given time. This was obvious in the 2002 incident at the Lewis Prison just west of Phoenix, Arizona. In addition, medical and psychiatric records plus professional staff are immediately available. Unlike the average law enforcement team that must move heaven and earth to obtain relevant medical and psychiatric records of the hostage taker and the victims, these records are on site in a prison. Of course a very serious problem occurs when the crisis site is the records office. It is a good idea to store such records off site or at two or more locations. The FBI learned this lesson the hard way when our office in Atlanta, where all of the tactical teams gear was stored, became the site of a siege. Thank God for the Atlanta Police Department.

Daily Experience

More negotiations go on, day in and day out, between correctional staff and inmates than could ever be captured statistically. On the positive side, this interaction alerts staff to potential problems and provides first-hand intelligence and experience for everyone. However, just as staff learns from interaction with inmates, inmates also learn from their interaction with staff. Inmates learn who they can manipulate.

I have never worked in a prison. During my first year in graduate school, I had a field placement as a parole agent with the California Department of Corrections in their Fresno Field Office. I was in class 3 days and spent 2 days a week during two semesters, for a total of 9 months, as a parole agent with a caseload of about a dozen parolees. Many of our counseling sessions included discussions of their life and times in prison.

During September to January, the fall semester of the following year, I had a very intensive 5-month full-time field placement at the Atascadero State Hospital for the Sexual Psychopath. This institution, though a secure site and very much like a prison with guard towers, sally ports, and scores of security measures and procedures, was run by the California Department of Mental Health. I lived in an apartment on the hospital grounds about 100 miles from home.

This was a very interesting and intense experience. By that time I was 29, married, had satisfied my military obligation by service in the U.S. Marine Corps where I earned the rank of sergeant, E-4, had completed my undergraduate education plus the first year of a 2-year Master's of Social Work degree program, and had worked in the welfare department for about 4 years. My apartment at the hospital was on the top floor of a World War II barracks building on a hill that provided me with a grand view of the institution. When I looked out my windows I had a choice of views, the parking lot or the hospital. I had a frequent and reoccurring nightmare, at least one night each week, for most of those 5 months at Atascadero. I think it reflected my basic anxiety of working each day in a very secure institution with about 2,000 patients, some of whom were dangerous, all of whom had serious psychological and sexual problems. I still recall walking down a long, two-story, brick and tile corridor from the sally port to the ward. During this walk, on almost a daily basis, I was entertained by a patient with a magnificent voice who was singing his version of a then popular Perry Como song, "Wake the town and tell the people." His version that echoed and resonated throughout the tile corridor and in my brain was, "Wake the town and kill the people." What a way to start the day.

In my dream, I had finished my daily workout in the hospital gym and returned to my locker to find my clothing and identification gone. In the place of my suit was a patient's khaki uniform. I would dress in the patient garb and then try, always to no avail, to convince the staff that I was an intern not a patient. I discussed this dream with one of the staff psychiatrists who told me I was normal. That was very reassuring. However, the bad dreams continued until I left the hospital.

In many conversations with parolees and patients, several revealed just how very manipulative they were. As I recall, they always used the past tense. I was told they knew I was concerned with issues like being manipulated or escape while I was at work. They thought about, practiced, and perfected manipulation constantly. Escape, or manipulating the system for an "early out" was ever on their minds. They have the time to think about such issues and must, in their minds, be manipulative to survive in the institution.

In that regard, I think that an absolutely necessary reading for every institutional staff member is the book written by Dr. Hare, a Staff Psychologist from the British Columbia prison system. The first chapter in *Without Conscience* is entitled "Experiencing the Psychopath." Dr. Hare discusses the manipulative and cunning nature of many inmates (Hare, 1999). Although his focus is on the Antisocial Personality Disorder, his observations can be easily generalized to the entire population of the institution.

Hostage Survival

Institutional staff are always mindful of the potential for being taken hostage. It was certainly on my mind at Atascadero. One of the social workers on the staff had a black belt in karate or judo or some form of hand-to-hand combat.

He offered training to staff on a regular basis. Somehow, a social worker with a black belt seems something of an oxymoron. However, life at Atascadero was also something of an oddity.

The topic of my dissertation was hostage survival. I have included most of my findings in Chapter 26.

The Prison Population

I would venture a guess that most inmates in a county jail or state prison, by definition, have an Antisocial Personality Disorder (ASP). Negotiating guidelines for dealing with the ASP are identified in Chapter 11.

Certainly, a county jail has a disproportionate number of psychotic prisoners. This is probably due to the fact that the county jail is more "user friendly" to the average law enforcement officer than most mental hospitals or psychiatric wards in local hospitals. More simply stated, law enforcement officers know how to book a person into the county jail. The bureaucracy of a hospital and their admitting procedure is another matter. This incorrect incarceration may be one factor contributing to the disproportionate number of suicides in county jails versus any other location.

Encounters with a person who is psychotic or an inmate who is Paranoid Schizophrenic (Chapter 12), Bipolar (Chapter 13), or suicidal (Chapters 14 and 15) are common among hostage takers and are discussed further in the chapters identified above.

Some Sieges

Attica, New York; Oakdale, Louisiana; Atlanta, Georgia; Talladega, Alabama; Lucasville, Ohio; and Buckeye, Arizona: A Review of Some Lessons Learned and Implemented

Attica, New York, is named after a region in ancient Greece. Buckeye, Arizona, is named after a nut. That is an interesting contrast that sets the stage for the contrast in the responses to prison sieges. Federal institutions tend to have less exotic names. When one compares the two state prison sieges some 2,000 miles and 33 years apart the contrast is commendable. This comparison clearly reflects lessons learned and implemented to save lives in correctional institutions and in many ways changes in law enforcement as well.

When one compares the 1971 FBI response to the airport in Jacksonville, Florida, that resulted in *Downs v. United States* to the 1996 Freeman Siege in Montana and the 1997 Republic of Texas standoff, it is clear that even the FBI learns from its history.

It is not the purpose of this write-up to castigate the officials in New York for actions some 30 years ago. It is an attempt to show how much we have learned and the changes we have implemented at the state and federal levels.

One can argue that Attica was a riot that involved hundreds of inmates and Buckeye was an attempted escape that directly involved two inmates and the rest of the institution in a lockdown mode. That is true. However, both involved the negotiations process and as such will be discussed and compared to include recommendations from these incidents.

Attica

According to the New York State Special Commission on Attica, the siege was the result of tensions that had been building for several months. At 0845 on Thursday September 9, 1971, inmates broke through a defective door that separated their cell block from the master control area and unlocked all of the cells. In minutes, over a thousand inmates had control of the prison. They took 42 staff as their hostages. The inmate leaders had a list of 32 demands that included the replacement of the warden, religious freedom, minimum wages, the placement of the prison under federal jurisdiction, amnesty, and an airline flight for any inmate who wanted to leave. Obviously, their plan had been in the works for weeks. Over the next 3 days, state officials negotiated with the inmates. However, little progress was made and on Monday September 13, they ordered the New York State Police to regain control of the institution.

At approximately 1000, correctional officers and State Police firing shotguns and pistols retook the institution in about 15 minutes. In the process, they killed 39 people and wounded over 80. Of those killed, 11 were correctional staff. Thirty-three of the wounded were correctional staff. Some of the wounded staff were members of the assault team. One correctional officer and three inmates had been killed by the prisoners during the siege. After the siege many changes were made in the crisis response plan for New York prisons. The implementation of these plans received impetus from the $8 million lawsuit plus another $4 million for attorney fees. Some of the reasons listed by the Commission for the large settlement were the facts that the assault plan was just that, an assault not a rescue plan. Their choice of weapons was limited to those immediately available. No arrangements were made in advance to provide medical care to those wounded during the fracas (New York, 1972).

The bottom line is that some of the errors like a rescue plan, the use of proper weapons, and medical resources on site were obvious errors. Twelve million dollars later, new plans are in place.

Moving on, the November 1987 sieges in Louisiana and Georgia provide excellent examples of how much the federal government learned from the Attica siege. The federal sieges, like Attica, involved inmates who were rioting over specific grievances. I am certain that had another siege in New York State occurred 16 years later, their response in 1987 would have modeled that of the federal government.

Oakdale Correctional Facility (OCF) in Oakdale, Louisiana

The situation at OCF involved 987 Cuban inmates who were in the U.S. illegally, had committed crimes, and now had served their sentence. Yet, because they were in the United States illegally and Cuba refused to take them back, the federal government tried in vane to locate a country that would accept the former federal felons. So in federal custody they remained. They immediately took 54 hostages of whom 26 escaped and one wounded hostage was released. This siege lasted 9 days from November 21 to 29, 1987. OCF did not have a lockdown capability.

The Federal Correctional Facility in Atlanta (USPA)

The siege in Atlanta, an old prison, involved 1,370 Cuban inmates, most of whom, like those at OCF, had served their sentences. Like those at OCF, there was no place to send them. It began 2 days after OCF and ran for 12 days, November 23 through December 5, 1987. They took 75 hostages and trapped 41 in their offices. This siege was more volatile. It included arson and escape attempts.

The Federal Correctional Institution in Talladega, Alabama (FCIT)

In mid-August 1991 there was an attempted escape from FCIT in rural northeast Alabama on IH 20 about 100 miles west of Atlanta. From the beginning, it was anticipated that it would be more difficult to negotiate than the 1987 sieges because most of the inmates involved had participated in the USPA and OCF sieges. The inmates had gone so far as to cut a hole in the fence before local law enforcement and prison staff forced them back into Alpha Unit where they held 11 staff hostage. FBI and Bureau of Prison (BoP) negotiators and tactical elements soon arrived and the siege began.

Because of the opening in the fence, local nocturnal fauna from the surrounding 75-mile-long Talladega National Forest were entering the grounds each night to feast on the luscious grass. This fact became crucial. Also of great significance was the relationship the negotiators had with the inmates. The negotiators were not caught in a lie and came across as sympathetic to the inmates and their immigration status. However, there were those within the inmate population who were determined to injure staff to make their point. Therefore, after a week of negotiations it was determined that a rescue would be initiated. As the rescue team approached, some movement on the grounds was seen by the inmate on watch. He immediately called the negotiators to report his concerns. The negotiators reminded him of the nightly fauna feeding. He believed them and did not alert his associates. Moments later, the 11 hostages were rescued with no injuries to them or the federal teams (McGee, 2009).

I had retired by then. However, I was called by the U.S. Attorney as an expert witness to explain the Stockholm syndrome to the jury. This was crucial because one of the most vicious inmates from the USPA siege had seen and used the Stockholm Syndrome to control some of the staff. Therefore, one staff member was sympathetic to the inmate and saw him as his protector. Fortunately, this story did not carry much weight with the court. As I recall there were more defense attorneys than defendants at the trial.

Lucasville, Ohio State Prison

The early April 1993 incident at the state prison in Lucasville, Ohio, was precipitated by an institutional medical program that required inoculations that were objected to by the Black Moslem inmates. It soon involved 407 inmates in three sieges at three sites, the gym, the cafeteria, and a classroom. Although the 3-week-long incident was initiated by some members of the Black Moslem population, the Aryan Brotherhood and a Black Gang took over other sites with hostages and had their own demands. As in any situation of this sort, the "cause" is usually a minor matter that under most conditions would go unnoticed (Noesner, 2010). However, when there is a good deal of basic unrest or animosity, any incident can trigger a disturbance. Remember the 1965 Watts Riots in Los Angeles, California, began over a traffic ticket.

In Lucasville, one guard was killed by an inmate who bore a grudge against him. This killing was not part of the siege plan anymore than the attempted escape of some inmates from the USPA in Atlanta was part of the Cuban concern. As in other incidents, the inmates needed the time and opportunity to vent their anger and frustration over a variety, 21 in this case, of issues.

Lewis Penitentiary in Buckeye, Arizona

Eleven years later on January 18, 2004, two inmates at the Lewis State Prison in Buckeye, Arizona, took correctional officers hostage in a thwarted escape attempt. The two had three correctional officers as their hostages in a tower by the main gate where they had access to and used one of the AR-15 rifles to ensure their safety. They were locked in the tower but that was as far as they would get. Almost three dozen negotiators from local, state, and the Phoenix FBI responded. The majority of the Arizona negotiators at all three levels knew each other from training sessions or conferences. In addition, some FBI negotiators came from Quantico, Virginia, and other field offices. Ultimately, this somewhat diverse group worked well together in 12-hour shifts for just over 2 weeks.

I do not know how many tactical officers were on site. I do know the FBI at Quantico spent a few thousand dollars to buy glass the thickness of that in the tower from the same manufacturer who installed those tower windows. Dozens of rounds were fired to see if such a shot was practical. It was determined that the thickness and angle of the glass were such that the use of that tactic posed too many unknowns. Certainly, assault tactics were also planned and practiced. As I recall, the tower had quite an arsenal with ample ammunition. It was well fortified with a 360° view for hundreds of yards in every direction. Given the risks of a sniper shot at the subjects simultaneously, the weapons available to the inmates, and the fortress-like construction of the tower, it was decided that barring threats or attempts to kill the hostages, the ball would stay in the negotiator's court.

Additional information on these sieges can be found on the Internet. Also listed are the dozens of related publications. Of course, that means inmates may also have direct access or access through friends and relatives. Along those lines, the sister of Ricky K. Wassenaar, one of the inmates in Buckeye, Arizona, established and ran a Web site for her poor, misunderstood brother who is now serving 400 years for his many crimes (Rapp and Davis, 2006).

Lessons Learned

1. In most locations it took time to *identify leaders*. Because of their culture and perception of punishment, leaders called themselves spokespersons. This took time that was used well by the authorities.
2. *Time* was used effectively. Because the demands of release exceeded the authority of even the warden, the federal bureaucracy, being what bureaucracies are, took time to make decisions. This fact of bureaucracy was known by the inmates. In addition, the basic psychological need of the inmates to tell the world of their plight was satisfied. Further, the negotiators agreed with the inmates that it was taking a long time to get a decision and said it was as frustrating to them as it was to the inmates. In his book *Getting Past No*, Dr. Ury discusses this tactic under the heading of "Going to Their Side" (Ury, 1991). It is also discussed in McMains and Mullins, chapter 5, entitled "Communications in Crisis Negotiations" (McMains and Mullins, 2010).
3. The use of active listening skills, and the axioms and defense mechanisms identified in Chapter 1 became relevant in all of the situations discussed, except at Attica, from which we all learned valuable lessons.
4. *Twelve-hour shifts* were a must. This meant each person worked about 14 hours. He or she arrived an hour early to be briefed and stayed an extra hour to brief. Working two shifts a day was hard but much less confusing than working three shifts when one considers the mechanics of parking, going through security, on-scene briefing, and so on.

5. The negotiating team was composed of officers from *local and federal agencies* including law enforcement and the Bureau of Prisons. It became apparent that although the local officers knew each other and some of the FBI negotiators, the Bureau of Prisons (BoP) negotiators were new to them. It was decided that training together in the future would be a good idea.

6. The negotiators made every effort to be *truthful*. They did not lie to the inmates. This is always an excellent tactic. The credibility of the negotiator is as important to the success of negotiations as is the sight picture to the sniper. When the negotiator is caught in a lie, he or she suffers the loss of credibility. Therefore, being vague to avoid a possible negative truth is a good tactic. As I tell my students, "When you are asked about wounded people who have been removed from the scene, tell the subject that it is your understanding he or she is in the hospital and a lot of people are working on him or her." In so saying you have told them nothing and blamed this nothing on someone else. Remember that you cannot have an immediate answer to every question. Set the stage early by delaying answers. When you do answer be sure you are correct or say something like "I was told…"

7. The decision was made to negotiate mostly in *English*. However, this changed from time to time. In some cases it was necessary to remind non-Spanish-speaking police, FBI, and BoP staff that the loud and at times emotional rhetoric of the inmates was a cultural nuance and did not mean impending violence.

8. The importance of *recording* all negotiations became paramount and was a common practice. This helped when reviewing statements and in helping to brief the next shift.

9. The issue of a *third-party intermediary* (TPI) surfaced and was resolved by using a Roman Catholic Bishop and an Atlanta Cuban-speaking radio commentator known and trusted by everyone. In Lucasville an attorney who was the former head of the Ohio American Civil Liberties Union (ACLU) served as the neutral intermediary. It is important to identify potential TPIs in advance of a siege. Better to have their names on a list and not need them than to suddenly have to locate an acceptable TPI during the stress of a siege.

10. Interestingly enough, the *indicators of violence and surrender* discussed in Chapters 19 and 20 were equally predictive in the institution.

11. Face-to-face negotiations at a site that was out of view of the majority of inmates so "their spokespersons" were not under peer pressure to perform was crucial in Atlanta.

12. Finally, as a face-saving tactic, a rather elaborate *surrender ritual* was worked out. Frankly, I have tried to find a soft surrender synonym.

"Acquiesce" sounds nice but is probably not in the vocabulary of most subjects. "Fold your tent" has meaning in the United States but not necessarily with Cuban inmates. How about "Just come out?" Or "Come out and tell your story so the world knows your side of this argument or issue." The verbs "evacuate" and "leave" also come to mind.

Institutional Crisis Negotiations

See Figures 16.1 through 16.7.

1. Telling the *truth* is crucial in any negotiating process. The credibility of the negotiator is as crucial as a sight picture is to a sniper. Eventually the subjects will surrender because the negotiator promised them a fair hearing, airing of their demands, or whatever. In their minds, they are putting their lives on the line because they trust the negotiator. If the negotiator is caught in a lie, he has lost his foundation for effective crisis negotiations. This was especially crucial at FCI Talladega.

2. *Time* is always a factor that can be manipulated by the authorities to work in our favor. During the siege at Waco, Texas, the FBI failed to use time as effectively as we could have. In fact, the FBI used time against itself in Waco. For the most part, the FBI crisis response staff stayed in local motels, did not return home, and worked 14 hours a day, 7 days a week for 53 days. While the FBI was exhausting itself, the Branch Davidians were at home, rotating their people and remaining in a comfortable routing. Fortunately, as discussed in Chapter 21, the FBI corrected this problem when they responded to the 1996 Freeman Siege in Montana (Strentz, 1997).

3. Typically, inmates, like most hostage takers, have *a story to tell* about their victimization by the system. This takes time but helps to defuse the situation. Until they are satisfied with their telling, and the understanding of the authorities, they are not likely to surrender. It is interesting to note that during the FCI Atlanta siege, the inmates were offered on day 2 the exact terms they agreed to on day 12. However, first they had to tell their story (Fuselier, Van Zant, and Lanceley, 1989).

4. One can *measure negotiator progress* using criteria similar to that used on the street and discussed in Chapter 19. Some of these indicators may be unique to each institution and inmate population. Therefore, the institutional crisis response team should review the criteria in training sessions to determine how many indicators are appropriate for their setting.

Figure 16.1 The Louisiana State Penitentiary relies heavily on the Louisiana State Police and the Federal Bureau of Investigation (FBI) to provide assistance during a crisis.

5. In addition, criteria similar to the street indicators of *violence*, as discussed in Chapter 20, can also be applied to the institutional setting. It is again suggested that these criteria be reviewed in training sessions to determine which of them are appropriate for the institution.

6. Unlike the street, a *formal face-saving surrender ritual* may be required. In some situations, hostage takers want to leave with their heads covered. When dealing with inmates and cult members, a face-saving surrender ritual is crucial.

7. *Threats* are frequently factors that create a great deal of concern for negotiating and tactical teams as well as the incident commander and certainly the hostages. To more effectively evaluate a threat, it is important to differentiate between unconditional versus conditional offensive or defensive threats and statements. It is crucial that the incident commander be educated on types of threats. Although this can be done on site, it is more effective when dealt with during a training session with the incident commander and then reinforced on site.

   a. *Unconditional*: An unconditional threat is the most dangerous. It is a direct statement of harm. There is no action or inaction required on the part of the authorities or a hostage for the subject

Figure 16.2 One method to ensure accuracy includes the scribe wearing headphones to avoid distraction.

Figure 16.3 It is necessary to plan strategy while offline, between negotiation contacts.

Figure 16.4 The information recorded by the scribe must remain current so everyone can benefit from the intelligence.

to implement his threat. An example of an unconditional threat is, "I am going to kill this SOB!"

b. *Conditional Offensive*: An example is a statement like, "If the money is not delivered in 15 minutes, someone is going to die!" Though action is intended, the logical question is who is going to die? Does the subject intend on killing a hostage or himself? Further, we can manipulate this threat by using logic to delay the threat pending the delivery that is about to occur.

c. *Conditional Defensive*: The more common conditional defensive threat is quite different and might be a statement like, "If you come in here I will kill a hostage." This threat, contingent upon action on the part of authorities, though a threat, is quite different from the first two.

As delineated above, we have three threats. However, they are as different as day and night. When assessing the potential for a subject to surrender, the most predictive type of threat heard is defensive. This usually means he is buying time to tell the world how he has been victimized. During this time his adrenaline flow is gradually subsiding as he searches for an honorable or face-saving solution. It is important that the negotiating team clarify threats to the IC who may not understand the differences.

Figure 16.5 Louisiana State Police practicing face-to-face negotiations with inmates within a cell block.

Figure 16.6 Existing files can provide critical information during a siege.

Figure 16.7 Recommended way to set up the situation board.

Systems Approach to Crisis Management

The institutional crisis negotiations team is just one part of the crisis response system. This system is modeled after the Navy "man your battle stations" prototype. That is, each person on a vessel has a regular assignment and a combat responsibility. Just as the military practices its combat response, corrections must practice its crisis response. Atherton identifies seven areas of concern in his "systems approach" to crisis management, all of which must be tested, when necessary modified, on a regular basis. No plan is cast in stone. It must be flexible and have several versions (Atherton, 2004). Anyone familiar with World War I knows that one of the reasons for that conflict was the lack of a partial military activation plan. Every European power had one military activation plan: it was for total war. Once a single nation activated its military, every other nation followed suit, the war was on, and millions died.

1. Staff and inmate *accountability* should be tested regularly and completed within 30 minutes in an institution of 1,000 to 1,500 inmates.
2. An emergency *communication* system of dedicated frequencies and lines is necessary. A paging setup is better than calling. In addition, "dead areas" within every institution must be identified.
3. The *first response* always has an element of chaos and too many responders. Each shift should have a first responder arrangement that is briefed and equipped each day.
4. Staff *staging areas* must be identified and perimeter shutting down along with access and egress channels identified. In addition, out-of-area and off-duty staff must have a call-up plan and number.

5. *Checklist* information format is necessary, if not mandatory. In this instance, the acronym KISS (keep it simple stupid) comes to mind. Atherton recommends the Federal Emergency Management Agency (FEMA) Incident Command System that must be tested, modified, and trained for in every institution.

6. A *call-back* system for staff at home or outside the institution is essential. Clearly this system must be prioritized and practiced.

7. *Mutual aid* and memos of understanding are paramount. These agreements with local, state, and federal law enforcement and other crisis management resources are crucial. Logically, mutual aid agreements should be practiced. Given the remote location of most prisons, it seems logical that the institution would call upon available local resources for long-term or stop-gap assistance.

Conclusion

It is the intent of this chapter to provide institutional negotiators with a listing of some dynamics that have been associated with prison and jail hostage sieges. If correctional staff does not study the past and strive to learn from experiences, then we may be condemned to repeat our errors. If we do not learn from what has been, then we will have forsaken our primary objective, *the preservation of human life.*

References

Atherton, G. (2004) Corrections Emergency Management, *Corrections Today*, July, pp. 60–64.

Birge, R. (2004) Personal interview, San Jose State University, Crisis Negotiations Course, June 8, Pacific Grove, California.

Fuselier, G. D. (1988) Hostage Negotiation Consultant: The Emerging Role for the Clinical Psychologist, *Professional Psychology*, Vol. 19, pp. 175–179.

Fuselier, G. D., Van Zant, C. R., and Lanceley, F. (1989) Negotiating the Protracted Prison Incident, *FBI Law Enforcement Bulletin*, July.

Hare, R. D. (1999) *Without Conscience*, Guilford Press, New York.

McGee, J. A. (2009) *Phase Line Green*, Cold Tree Press, Brentwood, Tennessee.

McMains, M. J., and Mullins, W. C. (2010) *Crisis Negotiations*, Anderson Publications, Cincinnati, Ohio.

Needham, J. (1977) Neutralization of a Prison Hostage Situation, *Criminal Justice Monographs,* Vol. 8, pp. 1–48.

New York State Special Commission on Attica (1972) Bantam Books, New York.

Noesner, G. (2010) *Stalling for Time*, Random House, New York.

Rapp, K., and Davis, R. (2006) *Hostage*, Print Media Books, New York.

Santayana, G. (1905) In John Bartlett, *Book of Familiar Quotations*, Little, Brown, and Co., Boston, 1980.

Strentz, T. (1997) Understanding Waco and Other Disasters, *Law and Order*, April, pp. 86–92.

Terhune-Bickler, S. D. (2004) Too Close for Comfort: Negotiating with Fellow Officers, *FBI Law Enforcement Bulletin*, April, pp. 1–5.

Turner, L., and Miller, J. H. (1991) Cultural Implications for Behavior, a preliminary report from the Federal Detention Center, Oakdale, Louisiana, Federal Bureau of Prisons, Washington, DC.

Ury, W. (1981) *Getting Past No: Negotiating with Difficult People,* New York, Bantam Books.

Negotiating with the Extremist

17

Introduction

The recent radical right-wing activity at Ruby Ridge, Idaho; Waco, Texas; Oklahoma City; and Jordan, Montana, are indicators of what is coming. It is interesting to note, and I do not yet understand the reasons, that a similar rise in clerical fascism, religious fundamentalism, and radical political right-wing groups is evident across Europe, the Middle East, and in Africa. Perhaps the trend toward international concerns, our shrinking planet, a united rather than our present fragmented world, and other global issues are a serious threat to those of limited vision. This concern is certainly seen in their frequent references to the mark of the beast, one world government, and various conspiracies to rob us of our national identity. One should remember that the single greatest cause of World War I was this type of chauvinistic, xenophobic thinking across Europe.

It is interesting to note that as the former Union of Soviet Socialist Republics (USSR) breaks into smaller republics, ethnic groups not yet separated seek their independence. They too want a smaller world. They seek self-rule by people who are ethnically similar to themselves rather than those in Moscow. Certainly, the hostage-taking activity of Chechnyan terrorists in the Moscow theater in 2002 and the 2004 taking of almost 400 schoolchildren and their parents in the southern city of Beslan, reflect the use of terrorism and hostage taking by radicals. Unfortunately for all involved, the Soviets tend not to negotiate. They talk until they can go tactical. I think they mistake the negotiations process for a downhill process of capitulating to the demands of the hostage takers.

On a lighter note, there is a humorous look at the bizarre thinking of the radical right in the United States. I suggest one read *Rush Limbaugh Is a Big Fat Idiot: And Other Observations* (Franken, 1996). I do not suggest, nor does this book, that Mr. Limbaugh holds bizarre political thoughts. However, Franken has included other observations from Pat Robertson, the Montana Militia, Pat Buchanan, and others who decry and proclaim the great one world government conspiracy that will, in their mind, soon engulf and enslave us all (Franken, 1996). A more serious view can be obtained by reading the *Turner Diaries* (Macdonald, 1978), or *Fascism, Past Present and Future* (Laqueur, 1996).

In an attempt to understand the mind of the radical or terrorist with whom we must negotiate, it is recommended that the reader become familiar with two other articles. In a paper published in the *FBI Law Enforcement Bulletin* (*LEB*) a few years ago, I discussed the emerging radical right-wing terrorist groups (Strentz, 1988). Two years later, Noesner and Fuselier wrote an article entitled, "Confronting the Terrorist Hostage Taker." It also appeared in the *LEB* (Fuselier and Noesner, 1990).

What we said in these articles about domestic and terrorist hostage crisis situations still applies today. The political orientation of our adversaries may have changed. Our time-proven stabilizing and effective negotiating tactics have not.

If past is prologue, most local law enforcement officers, more than the Federal Bureau of Investigation (FBI), are acquainted with local right-wing radicals. It was my experience as an FBI agent in Texas and again at the FBI academy that federal officers tended to know about left-wing and international groups (Farley, 1994). Because of the local nature of most right-wing radicals, local officers are better informed about "home-grown extremists." Further, many of them consider the local police and sheriff more of an ally than law enforcement officers from the state or federal levels. They were more likely to talk freely with local police and actively recruit them and others around their localities. Therefore, local law enforcement would learn of their activities long before their peers at the federal level. To compound this are the current guidelines under which the FBI and other federal law enforcement agencies must work when investigating suspected subversive organizations.

Types of Hostage Holders

For decades the FBI has grouped hostage holders in broad categories. These include those who are mentally ill and others who are common criminals. Within each category there are subgroups. The same basic tactics work with each group. However, some subtle differences exist. Narratives of these types and their differences are the subject of several articles authored by the FBI academy staff over the years (Fuselier and Noesner, 1990; Fuselier, Van Zandt, and Lanceley, 1989; Lanceley, 1981; Lanceley, Divasto, and Gruys, 1992; Strentz, 1981, 1983, 1986, 1988, 1990).

With slight modifications, one can negotiate with an extremist as effectively as one can with a criminal. In fact terrorist and related extremist groups tend to be composed of three types of personalities. These include the possibly paranoid leader, the absolutely antisocial element, and the inherently inadequate follower (Strentz, 1981, 1988). The first task for the negotiator is to determine the orientation of the hostage holder. We do this by listening. It does not matter if the hostage holder is politically, psychologically, religiously, socially, or criminally motivated. The same tried and true tactics apply. Listen, evaluate, gather intelligence, identify the wants and needs of this person, and then respond.

The Extremist

Perhaps the most unique aspect of the extremist hostage taker is his or her interest in favorable media coverage. Although other types also have an interest in the media, the extremist and the paranoid schizophrenic are especially excited over good coverage. In both cases, media exposure for their cause may be their primary concern, if not the sole intent of the operation. Many years ago, Brian Jenkins said that, "Today, terrorism is the theater of the absurd" (Jenkins, 1976). Simply stated, while other hostage holders may want the press present to guarantee their safety, most extremists want good press for their cause. The French used this to their advantage as they negotiated with and neutralized the hijackers of Air France 8969 in December of 1994. Remember, whatever a hostage holder really wants we can and should use to help ensure our goal of the preservation of human life.

For years, we in law enforcement faced and defeated left-wing political extremists. They and their cause have subsided. A new threat is emerging. The accompanying chart in Appendix A compares some characteristics of these very different radical groups and may be of help to crisis negotiators when formulating their tactics.

Those on the radical right tend to talk at length about their First [freedom of religion, speech, and assembly] and Second [keep and bare arms] Amendment rights. They are also concerned about the Fourteenth Amendment [equal protection under the law that guarantees the rights of females and foreigners to be on par with those of white males] and its effect upon their view of "The American Way of Life" (Coates, 1995). In 1988 I characterized the radical right as a minimal but growing threat. I captioned my comments, "Thunder on the Right: or is it a Firecracker?" At that time it was a firecracker. With the pictures of Oklahoma City so fresh in our minds, it is clear the threat has changed.

The historical precedent of the present right-wing radicals, to include their youth group known as Skin Heads, today are Adolph Hitler's Brown Shirts. A reading of the history of the growth and development in the 1930s of the Nazi Party in Germany will reflect many similarities (Becker, 1977; Shirer, 1960). In fact the present extremists actively emulate the Nazi movement as they collect and adorn themselves with Nazi insignias and ranks. One can also see similarities in the Identity Church and its relationship with the Skin Heads and conventional churches and their relationship with their youth groups. We as negotiators should study history so we will not have to relearn the lessons of our predecessors. We must not seek "Peace in our time," only to learn that it is but a brief respite for our adversary before he initiates an attack on his terms.

The Terrorist Mystique

Terrorists or other extremists are not supermen, nor are they suicidal (Fuselier and Noesner, 1990; Strentz, 1981, 1988). Although one should strive to avoid underestimating an adversary, neither should one make them into supermen. They are a force to be reckoned with but must be viewed within the perspective of reality. By listening to our adversary we can more accurately gauge his or her dedication, education, intelligence, and a host of other factors and characteristics that will give us the necessary intelligence to achieve a peaceful solution. In one situation after another, the authorities in country after country have learned that terrorist hostage takers tend to be less sophisticated than many criminals. They may have planned to take hostages but do not have a clue about negotiating tactics or techniques.

Brief Case Studies from 1980

In Bogota, Colombia, during February 1980 at the Dominican Republic Embassy, a sophisticated takeover by terrorists disguised as soccer players rapidly deteriorated. The terrorists, who had planned the takeover well enough to warn Communist diplomats to discretely depart, had no idea what to do with their hostages or how to negotiate for their demands. Ultimately, the hostages, many of whom were diplomats, successfully negotiated for their own freedom (Asencio and Asencio, 1983).

Those who held hostages in London at the Iranian Embassy for almost a week in the spring of 1980 were characterized by Scotland Yard as country bumpkins. They were trained for only a few hours in the use of firearms by their Iraq sponsors. They were Iranian busboys who had fled their country and wanted to get even with the Ayatollah. They died during the successful rescue of their hostages by the British Special Air Service.

In August 1980 in Chicago, two Croatians took over the German Consulate. They demanded that an associate be released from a German jail. After prolonged discussions with the terrorists, contact was made, through the U.S. Department of State, with their associate who said he did not want to leave jail. So, they surrendered. During this siege, their associate acted as an intermediary to induce them to surrender.

More recently we have seen the successful use of non-law enforcement intermediaries (Fuselier, Van Zandt, and Lanceley, 1989). The key is the term *intermediaries*. They are not negotiators or substitute negotiators. They are mediators who help promote a settlement between parties who are at variance. Their primary role is to assure our adversaries that we are negotiating in good faith with an objective of the preservation of human life. In most hostage crises, the police negotiator plays the role of mediator between the subject and the establishment. Politically, socially, and other radically motivated hostage takers tend to see everyone in government as their enemy. Thus, the law enforcement negotiator may have to reach out to this resource to help achieve our goal of the preservation of human life.

The Role of Third-Party Intermediaries

The process of negotiating, that of listening, gathering intelligence, evaluating, planning, and talking rather than waiting and attacking, has proven very successful. We have learned that law enforcement can be more successful if we wait and talk rather than act and assault. In these crisis situations, success is defined as saving the greatest number of human lives as possible (Schlossberg, 1980).

Even in those situations when a dynamic entry and rescue is inevitable, the process of talking with the hostage holder allows us to gain time (Noesner, 2010; Strentz, 1991). During this interim, the assault team can prepare. The commander can gather and use additional intelligence to help achieve a safe and successful solution. The role of intermediaries is more fully discussed in Chapter 5.

Those who do not learn from their history are condemned to repeat it (Santayana, 1905). Crisis negotiators must learn from these actual and potential misinterpretations and correct our cross-cultural communications. We should double-check our interpretation before we make assumptions about the meaning and intent of our adversary in a crisis. Remember that the goal of all involved will be best served by a peaceful termination from which all of us can walk away and live to see another day.

Time Is on Our Side

Every trained negotiator understands that in most crisis situations time, when we let it, works for us. The use of interpreters will automatically increase the amount of time taken to communicate. One should remember that the amount of time taken during a crisis to gain a successful solution will pale in comparison to the time required at hearings, inquests, and wakes when one moves too quickly. The saying, "A moment of passion may mean a lifetime of regret," comes to mind. As valuable as it is to gain time, we must use the time we earn by engaging in effective problem solving with the hostage holder. To do this we must be certain that we are communicating effectively and accurately.

It is important to remember that the hostage taker may not hear all of our words. Therefore, the tone of our, or the third party's voice, must convey our concern (Webster, 1996).

Conclusion

It is important to identify the type of person with whom we are dealing. Is he or she the leader or just the spokesperson? What type of personality does this person seem to have? Are the guidelines for negotiating with various aberrant people applicable?

The use of intermediators and third-party negotiators, like interpreters, during a hostage crisis may be necessary. However, it is a potentially dangerous tactic. Law enforcement must maintain control and should plan ahead. We should think long and hard before we partake of this option. When our credibility is questioned or this language resource is not available, law enforcement should identify appropriate third parties in advance of a crisis. Whenever possible those candidates with language skills should be used in more mundane assignments. They should be provided with some training. Their personal and professional potential for use in a crisis should be evaluated during training scenarios and routine assignments. This type of preparation and screening will allow law enforcement to achieve our goal of the preservation of human life, even when we must deviate from our established guidelines and procedures (Birge and Strentz, 1995).

Negotiating with Extremists

1. Stabilize and contain the situation.
2. Identify yourself as a law enforcement officer.
3. Avoid asking for demands.
4. It is more important to *listen* than to talk.
5. Ask questions about their welfare, demands, and cause.
6. If you do not understand, ask, clarify, paraphrase, and summarize. Be sure you understand them and they understand you.
7. Divert attention away from the hostages and onto yourself. You may become the symbolic hostage.
8. Play down recent events.
9. Do not offer anything except reassurance.
10. Consider using an interpreter to better understand their language and culture.
11. Call for assistance from experts.
12. Soften their demands by general restatements.
13. Avoid saying no.
14. Avoid face-to-face negotiations.
15. Do not set a deadline and try to avoid theirs.
16. Stress that good publicity for the cause can be gained by their demonstration of humanity.
17. Stress that a powerful person can demonstrate strength by showing patience and restraint.
18. Consider using nongovernment mediators as intermediaries to help convince the hostage taker that you are negotiating in good faith.

References

Asencio, D., and Asencio, N. (1983). *Our Man Is Inside*, Little, Brown and Co., Boston.

Becker, J. (1977) *Hitler's Children*, J.B. Lippincott, New York.

Birge, R., and Strentz, T. (1995) Procedures for Deviating from Established Crisis Negotiation Guidelines, *The U.S. Negotiator*, Summer.

Coates, J. (1995) *Armed and Dangerous*, Hill and Wang, New York.

Farley, C. J. (1994) Patriot Games, *Time*, December 19.

Franken, A. (1996) *Rush Limbaugh Is a Big Fat Idiot: And Other Observations*, Delacorte Press, New York.

Fuselier, D., and Noesner, G. (1990) Confronting the Terrorist Hostage Taker, *FBI Law Enforcement Bulletin*, July.

Fuselier, D., Van Zandt, C. R., and Lanceley, F. J. (1989) Negotiating the Protracted Incident, *FBI Law Enforcement Bulletin*, July.

Jenkins, B. (1976) Personal interview, FBI Academy, Quantico, Virginia, October.

Lanceley, F. J. (1981) The Antisocial Personality as a Hostage-Taker, *Journal of Police Science and Administration*, Vol. 9, No. 1, pp. 28–34.

Lanceley, F. J., Divasto, P., and Gruys, A. (1992) Critical Issues in Suicide Intervention, *FBI Law Enforcement Bulletin*, August.

Laqueur, W. (1996) *Fascism: Past, Present, Future*, Oxford University Press, New York.

Macdonald, A. (1978) *The Turner Diaries*, National Alliance, Arlington, Virginia.

Noesner, G. (2010) *Stalling for Time*, Random House, New York.

Santayana, G. (1905) John Bartlett, *Book of Familiar Quotations*, Little, Brown and Company, Boston, 1960, p. 703.

Schlossberg, H. (1980) Crisis Negotiation Teams, *Annals of the New York Academy of Sciences*, Vol. 347, pp. 113–116.

Shirer, W. L. (1960) *The Rise and Fall of the Third Reich*, Simon & Schuster, New York.

Strentz, T. (1981) A Terrorist Organizational Profile. In Y. Alexander and Gleason (Eds.) *Behavioral and Quantitative Perspectives on Terrorism*, Pergamon Press, New York.

Strentz, T. (1983) Negotiating with the Inadequate Personality as a Hostage-Taker, *Journal of Police Science and Administration*, April.

Strentz, T. (1986) Negotiating with the Hostage-Taker Exhibiting Paranoid Schizophrenic Symptoms, *Journal of Police Science and Administration*, January.

Strentz, T. (1988) A Terrorist Psycho-Social Profile, Past and Present, *FBI Law Enforcement Bulletin*, April.

Strentz, T. (1990) Radical Right versus Radical Left Terrorists, Their Theory and Threat to Law Enforcement, *The Police Chief*, LVII.

Strentz, T. (1991) Thirteen Indicators of Volatile Negotiations, *Law and Order*. September, pp. 135–139.

Strentz, T. (1995) The Cyclic Crisis Negotiations Time Line, *Law and Order*, March, pp. 73–75.

Webster, M. (1996) Address at California Association of Hostage Negotiators Annual Conference, May 10, Monterey, California.

Appendix A

Chart of U.S. Domestic Terrorist Group Differences

Issue	Right Wing	Left Wing
Legitimate political parties	Republicans	Democrats
Radical expression	Nazi/Fascist	Communist/Socialist
Government	Retain or revive	Replace
	Perfect	Perfectible
	Limit	Expand
View of those opposed to establishment	Illegitimate	Honorable
Social change	Reactionary	Revolutionary
Social class	Lower/middle	Middle/upper
Leadership	Male dominated	Male/female egalitarian
Sexual orientation	Heterosexual	Homosexual
Sexual roles	Established/rigid	Unspecified
Marital status	Married	Single
		Divorced
		Separated
Group dynamics	Family/cults	Single
		Co-equals
Age	16–76	25–45
Member's education	Limited/high school	University
Leader's education	High school/university	University
Religion	Fundamental-Protestant	Agnostic/atheistic
Locality	Rural	Urban
Criminal planning	Impulsive	Meticulous
Criminal activity		
Robbery, bomb, shoot, kidnap	Yes	Yes
Crimes on board aircraft	No	Yes

Terrorism and the Tenets of Islam

18

Introduction

It is not the intent of this chapter to excuse those engaged in terrorism in the name of Islam, or any other faith. It is my hope to shed some light on the history, tenets, thinking, tactics, and practices of this minority of Moslems so we in the West can better understand them.

The reason for this information in a negotiations text is simple. Over the years, law enforcement has faced several hostage sieges where the subjects claimed to be Islamic terrorists. Their logic, if you would call their distorted thought process logical, was their intent to frighten law enforcement into letting them go. That never happened. What did happen was that the negotiators contacted people and agencies that were well versed in the Islamic belief system, the Moslem religion, The Tenets of Islam, to determine the veracity of the subjects' claims. Therefore, this chapter is designed to provide a quick study of Islam so negotiators can ask intelligent questions to determine the veracity of those claiming to be of that faith.

In all fairness to those interested or engaged in this divisive and very emotional issue, calling all Moslems terrorists would be the same as casting all Roman Catholics as members of the Irish Republican Army (IRA) or Protestants as members of the Ku Klux Klan (KKK). In each case we focus on a radical few who, by their criminal acts, cast dispersions on the faith and reputation of the majority. To further clarify matters, I define *terrorism* as politically or religiously motivated criminal activity.

The Middle Eastern Mind

To best understand where a person or a nation is headed or why they believe what they do, it helps to know where they have been. In this regard, the Arab mind is in many ways transfixed on what was, what should be, and if Allah wills it, will be again (Lewis, 2002). This orientation remains today in a very turbulent part of the world where Internet access and a very large youthful population have begun to revolt against dictators who have ruled using the Tenets of Islam to control their people and in the process blame the West for all their ills.

I have never lived in the Middle East. I have taught hundreds of students from that part of the world, lived with a Moslem family in Kosovo, and recently spent time teaching in the United Arab Emirates (UAE). With this background, I have come to understand the fatalism they share. However, most Moslems do not share a love of, or dedication to, terrorism. Those I met, taught, lived, and worked with in Kosovo were recent victims of Christian terrorism.

Past as Prologue?

Early in the last century George Santayana (1905) said, "Those who do not study their history are condemned to repeat it." In this regard, let me remind you of our Christian past that is a possible prologue for those of the Islamic faith. Most people in and from the Middle East have a strong sense of history. By way of example, a few years ago I was teaching a negotiations course in New England. We were discussing some current events in Iraq that included the killing of civilians. One student, whose family had immigrated from Syria in 1917, said with some strong emotion, "You must remember that King Richard did the same thing." He was referencing the Third Crusade of 1189 to 1192 as if it happened yesterday.

Insurrections and Islam

Islam has bloody borders. There are those of the Islamic faith who are fighting the Jews in the North, the Hindus in the South, and the non-Moslem minority in Indonesia to the East plus Christians everywhere and anywhere they can find them. Islam extends its influence and is the only recognized religion in dozens of countries from Morocco to Malaysia and beyond. They have yet to battle the Buddhists in China or Tibet. However, I think that is just a matter of time. To make matters worse, they are fighting among themselves as Sunni kills Shia and Shia kills Sunni throughout the world. All of this killing is in the name of Allah and their version of Islam.

Shia versus Sunni

The Shia versus Sunni split in Islam dates back centuries, and like many separations, time tends to aggravate the differences. The basic difference relates to the question of who should have succeeded Mohammed in 680. To the Western mind 680 AD is ancient history. To most Moslems it is as recent as last week.

The Shia say Abli ibn Abi Talib is the lawful successor while the Sunni say it is Umar ibn al-Kattab. I purposely used "is" rather than "was" because this reflects their current thinking. The Shia constitute about 15 percent of the Moslem faithful and tend to be more mystical and inclined toward martyrdom. The Sunni are the majority and more oriented on the law and rationalism (Gabriel, 2005). As a modern matter, Iran is mostly Shia while Iraq and the rest of the world is heavily Sunni.

The question is why? Why are so many members of the Islamic faith at war with their own and with the rest of the world? Perhaps it is because Mohammad is the only leader of a major religion who was a warrior. Certainly the history of Islam and the behavior of Mohammad are violent. But, is Islam inherently insurrectionary or is this a phase of its religious development?

Is the Christian Past Islamic Prologue?

Are religious wars a phase through which the faithful must pass as they grow into maturity?

Certainly one can see a Middle Ages parallel between present-day Islam and mid-Christianity when Catholics and Protestants fought and killed each other across Europe. If one remembers that Islam is approximately 750 years younger than Christianity and then looks at the warlike state of Christianity during the 13th through 15th centuries, some 700 years ago, one can see many parallels. The Crusades lasted from 1095 until 1250. Today viewed by many in the Middle East as recent Christian behavior and clearly indicative of current Christian conspiracies and intent.

Currently and internally within Islam, and especially in Iraq, Shia and Sunni are killing each other. Remember the Spanish Inquisition, 1478 to 1834, when the Roman Catholic Church in Spain killed thousands of Protestants, Gypsies, Jews, Moslems, and others who did not adhere to their view of God.

Violence is not inherent in Islam and certainly not all Moslems adhere to violence. The Moslem family with which I lived in Kosovo when I taught at the police academy in Visshtria was as far from being violent as any Buddhist monk or Baptist minister. One could not find a more peace-loving and caring family in any Christian community. They are alive today because the local Christian Chief of Police and his men warned them and helped them leave Kosovo for Europe when radical Christians moved across that part of Europe killing thousands of Moslems. Again, the Irish Republican Army does not represent most and mainstream Catholicism any more than the Covenant, Sword, and Arm of the Lord or the Ku Klux Klan represent most and mainstream Protestantism.

Having said that, remember Mohammad was a warrior. Moses, Buddha, and Christ were not. One can easily divide the early history of the development of the Islamic faith into two distinct phases of the life of Mohammad. His years as a prophet are followed by his years as a warrior.

Phase 1 is his life and times in Mecca. Phase 2 reflects his exploits after he gained power and settled in Medina. With this remarkable difference in his behavior as a frame of reference, the saying, "Power corrupts and absolute power corrupts absolutely," comes to mind.

The immigration of Mohammad from Mecca to Medina in 622 was a defining time in his life and therefore in the history of Islam. This move changed Islam from a religious and spiritual revolution to a political movement. A quick summary of the differences include the following:

Mecca
>   He invited converts by preaching.
>   He was a priest.
>   He had one wife.
>   He preached against idol worship.

Medina
>   He converted by force of arms.
>   He was a warrior.
>   He had over 10 wives.
>   He fought and killed Christians and Jews. (Gabriel, 2002, pp. 69–70)

Once Mohammad established himself politically and militarily in Medina he had political and thus military power. He used, or perhaps abused, that power to bring the unbelieving to the fold. When he moved to Medina he, unlike Christ, was no longer a man of peace. He had his opponents murdered. Unlike the Twelve Apostles of Christ, the early followers of Mohammed, like some of those today, were not adverse to homicide (Gabriel, 2002, pp. 104–111).

Fast forward to more modern times and the Ottoman Empire. It lasted about 600 years from the 1300s into early 1900, was centered in Turkey, and at its zenith stretched across and around the Mediterranean Sea and well east into what is now Tibet. When it collapsed in 1924, a far-sighted Turkish military leader, Mustafa Kamal Ataturk, established a thoroughly secular state in what is now Turkey. By so doing, he ended the rule, influence, and power of Islamic clerics in Turkey and other evolving Middle Eastern States. He adopted a Western and more democratic system of rule. Turkey is the center for a Sunni sect known as Hanafi Muslims.

This did not go over well with the deposed and displaced Islamic fundamentalists. Among them was Sheikh Hassan al-Banna who began the Muslim Brotherhood Movement (MBM) in Egypt. He aggressively taught that Islamic law should be followed with no tolerance for government interference. He sought a return to Islamic law and government. Like his followers today, they want a return to the rule of a theocracy as practiced by Mohammad. This, of course, is a fundamental difference between Christianity and Islam.

Remember the statement of Christ, "Render unto Caesar that which is Caesars and unto God that which is God's" (Mark 12:17). In other words political entities are not a union but a strict separation of church and state.

The Middle Eastern mind-set and reasoning reflects their history. Remember their part of the world gave us our numbering and writing system. Further, the streets of Damascus were lit by gas lamps long before they were used in Europe. Most institutions of higher learning were in "their" part of the world. In short, those were the Golden Years of Islam to which they yearn to return. Many believe they have fallen behind because they have drifted away from the fundamentals of what Mohammad taught. Therefore, to return to glory they must return to fundamental Islam and the Seventh Century way of life. To accomplish this, the West must be destroyed.

Because of the radical MBM views, speeches, and practices that included the killing of Egyptian Prime Minister Mahmoud Nokrashy Pasha in 1948 and later the killing of Supreme Court Judge Moustashar Ahmad El-Kazendari, they are considered a radical and outlaw Islamic group. In 1954 and again in 1965 they attempted to kill Egyptian President Gamal Abdel Nasser and placed bombs in Egyptian police stations that killed many law enforcement officers.

The Egyptian government cracked down and many members of the brotherhood ended up in jail where they died. Their foremost leader, Sayyid Qutb, was executed. Unfortunately, this had the effect of granting him martyrdom and dramatically increased the sales of his books that proclaim the justification for armed conflict to advance Islam across the waters and around the world (Gabriel, 2002, pp. 115–116).

Tenets of Islam

The five basic tenets of the Islamic religion are as follows:

1. There is only one God and Allah is his name.
2. One must pray five times a day.
3. One must give alms to the poor.
4. One must fast during Ramadan.
5. One must travel to Mecca during his or her lifetime.

There is an entire chapter in the Koran entitled "Spoils of War"; there is no chapter called "Peace." These are the words of Omar Abdel Rahman, a former lecturer, some say radical cleric, on Islam, at Al-Azhar University in Cairo, the oldest university in the world. Note, the oldest university in the world is not in Europe, it is in Cairo. He is now in an American prison for masterminding the 1993 attack on the World Trade Center. Recent terrorist acts in the United States, Spain, and Great Britain involved men of very diverse sociocultural, economic, and educational backgrounds. Their commonality is the influence of the same radical cleric (Sageman, 2005).

Thinking

Remember, most Middle Eastern countries were established in the salons and drawing rooms of Europe with little attention paid to ethnic, linguistic, racial, and religious differences. In fact, many of these differences were used by European powers to keep their subjects fighting each other rather than uniting and fighting them. Europe has nations within which there are many religions. In the Middle East there is one religion within which there are many nations (Lewis, 2002).

Therefore, most people in that part of the world do not think in national terms. Their first loyalty is to their family, then their tribe, then Islam, and then somewhere down the road some may think of themselves as members of a political entity.

According to *Time* magazine:

> Karzai, (The president of Afghanistan.) is not incompetent. He is acting according to his own priorities of his family, his tribe, his nation, in that order. (Klein, 2010)

The word *Islam* means "submission to the one true God, Allah." The words of Allah, as spoken to Muhammad over a period of 20 years as he meditated in Mecca, are recorded in the Koran. There is a second set of sacred writings. These are the Books of Hadith that record the things Muhammad did and said as recorded by his friends and wives.

External versus Internal

The thinking process of Moslems is closely allied with their religion. The practice of total submission to the will of Allah means one is not in control of his or her life and times. That is a significant factor in their mind-set. It clearly defines the attitude of the faithful. In addition, this orientation carries over into, and has a great influence upon, their personal, professional, political, and parochial lives.

Psychologists call people with this orientation "External." In other words, their basic belief is "what happens, happens." Remember the 1960s Doris Day hit "Que Sera, Sera?" "Whatever will be will be. The future's not ours to see …" Like the words of this song, they believe they have no control over their life or fate. Allah will decide what is to be, they are totally in his hands and at his mercy. This is a fatalistic and a very external orientation.

As an example, I recall one student from the Middle East who commented on the inevitable and eventual end of their control of most of the world's oil and the billions in revenues from this resource they have recently acquired and many are quickly spending. He said, "My grandfather rode a camel, as will my grandson. In the meantime, I am enjoying life." This mind-set is quite different from folks in Norway and the United Arab Emirates where their oil production revenues are going to ensuring the continuance and enhancement of basic services, education, and the infrastructure of their countries.

Another example is the typical response from Middle Eastern students when asked how they expect to use crisis negotiation training upon their return home. Typically, the response is, "That is up to my commander" or "Allah will use me as he sees fit."

Inshallah or Fatalism

There is a story told in Moslem circles that very accurately depicts their fatalistic attitude as it identifies its lack of logic.

According to the story, Abdul was shipwrecked on a remote island. He knew Allah would rescue him so he prayed daily. One day he looked out from his hilltop cave and saw that a ship had sailed into the bay of his tiny island. It anchored and those on board fished and swam. However, no one walked up the hill to his cave. The next day the ship left. Abdul said to himself, I guess Allah did not send that ship for me, and he continued to pray.

A few months later another ship arrived, anchored, and some came ashore. But once again, no one walked up to his cave, and the ship departed. Again Abdul rationalized saying I guess that Allah did not send that ship for me.

A few years later a third ship sailed into the bay. Like the other two it anchored, people swam; some came ashore to collect seashells and coconuts. But no one walked up the hill to his cave. Again, Abdul rationalized his fate and continued praying.

Finally he died. He met with Allah and reminded him how fervently he had prayed for rescue, yet he lived out his lonely life on that remote island. To this sentence Allah remarked, what do you mean? I did not ignore your prayers. I sent three ships.

Internal

Psychologists say the other extreme is represented by a person who is classified as "Internal." An example is the petroleum policy of Norway. Internals consider themselves as masters of their fate—they are in control. They believe God helps those who help themselves. By way of example, when Western students are asked how they expect to use the crisis negotiation training, their response is quite different from Middle Eastern officers. Most of them state what they will do to start or command a team, or some other statement of their intent and their role on the team or in the program.

This, I believe, is the mind-set of most Westerners, but not so with most Moslems. To them, Allah is in control and what he wills will happen and there is nothing any mere mortal can do about that.

And so it goes, "Que Sera, Sera, whatever will be, will be, the future's not ours to see ..."

In addition, and seemingly in contradiction, is the fact that Islam is a religion of works more than faith. Yet, work as you will, entry into paradise is up to Allah. Inherent in the religious beliefs of Islam is this sense of fatalism. One may live a life during which he or she strictly follows the basic tenets of Islam and so earn one's way into paradise. Ultimately, however, entry into paradise is up to Allah. There is one exception to this rule—it is Jihad. About 60 percent of the Koran discusses Jihad (Gabriel, 2002). Basically, Jihad means "inner struggle." It has been extended to mean struggling against or fighting nonbelievers who block the extension of Islam.

Practice

Jihad

When judgment day comes Allah will weigh the good works versus bad and decide the fate of every Moslem. So, your fate, entrance into paradise, is in his hands. The exception to this rule is when one dies during a fight with an infidel, now known as a Jihad. In that case, entry into paradise is guaranteed. In other words, Jihad is a contract between Allah and the faithful. If one dies fighting to spread Islam, Allah guarantees entry into paradise. Unfortunately for the world, this battle has been more broadly defined by some Moslem clerics to include the suicide bombing of innocent civilians and children. Excuse my digression here, but remember the end of IRA violence occurred when one of their bombs in a shopping center killed schoolchildren. This form of "collateral damage" is not an international transgression.

We turn back to the Middle East. The funeral service for a person who dies during a Jihad is different. In the case of death from illness or accident, the body is washed and dressed nicely. In the case of death in a Jihad, the body is not washed or given clean clothes. The person is placed in the coffin just as he or she died. Their blood is proof to Allah of death in a Jihad, and entry to paradise is immediate.

While most in the West view suicide bombers as probably insane, one need only spend time in most Middle Eastern countries where the lifestyle is impoverished, expectations for improvement nonexistent, and most people live at a standard and in conditions of centuries past.

Living in such conditions while watching the good life in the West on TV or via the Internet probably serves as a strong motivation for prospective suicide bombers to move from this veil of tears into paradise via Jihad. Such is the contrast seen daily by Palestinians. There is ample room in Middle Eastern countries for these poor people. However, to relocate them would take the pressure off Israel and dramatically diminish the terrorist applicant pool.

Wahhabi Movement

As previously stated, Islam is at least as segmented as Christianity. The Wahhabi "order" of the Islamic faith deserves special attention because they are quite fundamental in their belief system, and as such are more violent than most. They date back to the early 18th century. Their early leader, Muhammad ibn Abd al-Wahhab (1703 to 1792), founded the Islamic state now known as Saudi Arabia. It is so named because what is now Saudi Arabia was sewn together by Abdul Aziz al Saud. The current ruling family of Saudi Arabia is the direct descendant Abdul who worked closely with Abd al-Wahhab, and as such, they reign over some very violent Moslems and about one quarter of known petroleum reserves (Rossi, 2008). Ask anyone who has visited that country about the powers of the Religious Police who patrol and beat anyone in violation of their view of Islam. All this is going on while Saudi Arabia remains one of the strongest allies of the West in that part of the world. As an example, it was one of their agents who warned of the bombs on FedEx and UPS cargo planes headed for the United States which were found in London.

The rulers of Saudi Arabia, the Saud family, are sitting on a powder keg. As an aside, I cannot think of any other country that is named after the ruling family. On one hand the Saud family is very cooperative with the West, on the other they are home to the Wahhabis who are the most violent of Anti-Western Moslems. As an example, of the 19 September 11, 2001, hijackers, 15 were from Saudi Arabia. Eight others who were to engage in similar acts but were deterred were also from Saudi Arabia (Commission Report, 2004). Along these same lines Saudi Arabia is mostly Sunni. As such it is religiously at odds with its neighbor across the Persian Gulf, Iran, which is Shi'ite. In case you missed it, Saudi Arabia is engaged in a cold war with Iran that mirrors the European Cold War of the last century.

Conclusion

Finally, I am more than a little concerned about the all too frequent synonymous use of Islam and terrorism. I am reminded of the "Communist Menace" of the last century. In fact, every Communist country was a dictatorship, a totalitarian regime that used Communist ideology to justify its domineering demeanor. The parallels today are obvious. How many Islamic countries are democracies versus the number that are dictatorships?

How many of them have a free press? Only a few, like Turkey, have achieved some separation of church and state. A few have a legislature. However, most of these bodies are simply a rubber stamp for the dictator as was the Supreme Soviet. The press in most Islamic countries is as free today as was Tass in the Soviet Union.

All this is by way of saying that while we should know something about the beliefs, history, thinking, and practices of our adversary, we must be realistic and recognize that it may be nothing more than a deft disguise for despotism.

In the meantime, we should remember that some of them are at war with us. As a military tactic, they have chosen terrorism, criminal acts. It is a cost-effective way for a minority to wage war against a powerful nation. Democracies, by their very nature, are more easily targeted by terrorists than are dictatorships. They use our freedoms and modern methods, like computers, and commercial aircraft against us in an attempt to return the world to the ideal life of Mohammad in the 7th century.

We are at war. More diplomatically, there are those in the Moslem world who are at war with us. However, we should remember that as violent as they are, they are not representative of most Moslems.

In this regard I am reminded of a good friend who is a judge in a Domestic Relations Court. She deals daily with couples at war with each other. She says to them, "If the two of you do not come to a decision on custody and a division of your property, I will make those decisions and I guarantee my decisions will not please either of you."

The *Bible* says, "Vengeance is mine says the Lord" (Deuteronomy 32:35). However, humans, being as frail as we are, believe that if those within the Moslem world do not effectively deal with their violent minority, the West will and our dealings will not please any of them.

Finally, and ever the optimist, I view the current unrest among the downtrodden in countries like Egypt, Tunisia, Libya, Syria, and other dictatorships as a good sign. Their moves toward democracy have increased the price of gas but in the long run will bring stability and an end to state-supported or protected terrorists from that part of the world.

Also, we have the identification of the bombs on the UPS and FedEx flights and their maker by the government of Saudi Arabia. Further, the young "would be" bomber in Portland, Oregon, Mohamed Osman Mohammad and his Baltimore soulmate, Antonio Martinez, were identified early in their planning by members of the Islamic faith who reported them to the FBI.

Law enforcement and our military can defeat terrorists. However, the defeat of Islamic terrorism is in the hands of Moslem countries that tend to be dictatorships. Until and unless they make life more enjoyable, more free, and worth living for their citizens, the recruiting efforts of the radical Moslem minority will continue to draw from a large pool of willing and eager applicants.

In the meantime, crisis negotiators must deal with less than brilliant subjects who, in an attempt to frighten us into capitulation, feign Islamic religious beliefs. With the material presented in this chapter you can ask intelligent questions of them and make an educated decision of their religious affiliation and in so doing make more realistic recommendations to the on-scene commander.

References

Commission Report (2004) *The 9/11 Commission Report*, W.W. Norton, New York.

Gabriel, M. A. (2002) *Islam and Terrorism*, Charisma House, Lake Mary, Florida.

Gabriel, M. A. (2005) Personal interview, Florida Association of Hostage Negotiators Annual Training Conference, Altamonte Springs, Florida, June 5.

Klein, J. (2010) Obama's Afghan Dilemma, *Time Magazine*, p. 20.

Lewis, B. (2002) *What Went Wrong? The Clash between Islam and Modernity in the Middle East*, Oxford Press, New York.

Lewis, B. (2002) *The Crisis of Islam, Holy War and Unholy Terror*, Random House, New York.

Rossi, M. (2008) *What Every American Should Know about the Middle East*, Plume of The Penguin Group, New York.

Sageman, M. (2005) Understanding Terror Networks, *International Journal of Emergency Mental Health*, Vol. 7, No. 1, pp. 5–8.

Santayana, G. (1905) In John Bartlet, *Book of Familiar Quotations*, Little, Brown & Co., Boston, 1980.

Crisis Resolution Indicators

3

Indicators of Subject Surrender

19

Introduction

In Jacksonville, Florida, John M. Knight, 45, took an attorney, Christopher Hazelip, hostage, and demanded that a Duval County judge, Sharon Tanner, appear on local TV and announce her resignation from the bench. She made the appearance and Knight surrendered (Wood, 2004). Over March 17 to 19, 2003, in a pond between the Washington Monument and the Lincoln Memorial, in Washington, DC, Dwight Wade Watson sat in his tractor where he claimed to have explosives and told the U.S. Park Police about how he, and other tobacco farmers, had been maltreated by the tobacco companies (Stefansson, 2004). On July 2, 2002, in Edmonton, Alberta, Canada, Victor Ray Leland, age 50, took a Crown prosecutor hostage so someone would listen to his rambling concerns about his public assistance payments. The police arrived, and the negotiator sympathetically listened to Leland's rambling. When he finished telling his story, he surrendered (Hayden and Callioux, 2004).

As a general rule, hostage takers, subjects, who have expressive needs are easier and less dangerous to deal with than those who have instrumental demands. More simply stated, hostage takers who have a story to tell are easier to control and placate than those who want something. This assumes the negotiator has told the on-scene commander that what is necessary in this case is let him talk until he is tired, then he will surrender and we can all go home (Noesner, 2010).

It is not the intent of this chapter or the author to trivialize crisis situations or the law enforcement response to them. The difficulty and dangerousness of police work has been known for generations. To quote Gilbert and Sullivan, "the policeman's lot is not a happy one." The point of this material is to provide some subject/behavioral assessment tools to enable the on-scene commander and the negotiation and special weapons and tactics (SWAT) teams to better understand the potential for violence and prepare and react accordingly. In other words, there are a dozen common indicators during crisis negotiations that the subject will surrender, just *when* is usually a separate issue. Let us not make this crisis more dangerous than it is. Let us not unnecessarily go to the "action imperative"—that is, shoot or assault, and snatch defeat from the jaws of victory. *Remember our primary goal in a crisis is to save lives, not save time or save money.* The mind-set I find most useful during a hostage crisis is to assume that I am being *paid by the hour not by the job.*

It is with this in mind that many years ago, while I was an instructor in the Special Operations Unit at the Federal Bureau of Investigation (FBI) Academy, I began a research project to predict subject surrender versus those that indicate the need for the action imperative. Indicators of the need for an assault will be addressed in Chapter 20. Since my retirement from the FBI, I have remained active teaching, consulting, and responding to hostage crises around the country. Through these efforts and activity, I have kept the indicators current. As one indication of some of the differences that my ongoing research has identified, one need only compare the indicators identified in this chapter with those that I published some 10 years ago (Strentz, 1995).

The Indicators

As a group, the indicators of surrender are more easily prioritized than are those that predict violence. Therefore, the following ranking is compiled with the behavior and activity of the subject that is most predictive of surrender listed first. The exception is the last entry that deals with the types of threats. The types of threats—unconditional or conditional offensive and defensive—may change during the siege. A move from unconditional to conditional offensive to defensive is a very good sign that the subject will surrender. A better sign of surrender is a subject who only engages in defensive threats.

1. It is imperative that a *trusting relationship* be developed and maintained between the negotiator and the subject. The hostage taker must view the negotiator as a person who cares and can be relied upon to help him in this dilemma. This relationship lays the foundation for a discussion of what is really on the mind of the subject. It is truly the basis for successful negotiations. This means that the negotiator must not be caught in a lie. Therefore, negotiators should strive to be as truthful as possible. When in doubt be vague or ambiguous.

2. The second best indicator that the subject will surrender is his talking about *personal needs* and issues and less about demands. In other words, he is talking about *expressive* concerns. He has a need to tell someone in authority about his troubles. Like Mr. Knight in Florida, Mr. Watson in Washington, DC, or Mr. Leland in Alberta, across our continent from the southeast to the northwest, each had a story to tell. Once his story was finished, each surrendered without incident. Often, in the course of his diatribe, the subject may

identify some demands. However, they are *secondary* to his need to tell society that he is *the victim* of some grievous miscarriage of justice. As an aside, subjects typically view themselves as victims. I recall an incident in Washington, DC, where the subject claimed that the police forced him to take hostages. It was his intent to rob the bank. The quick police response forced him to the desperate act of hostage taking. In any case, this is the mind-set of the subject so listen and sympathize. The best indicator of surrender is the subject talking about personal issues that will include his being the victim.

3. The next best indicator that builds on the first two is the *subject talking* for longer periods of time, about expressive demands, and calling the negotiator. These two acts, talking more about personal or sensitive issues and *calling the negotiator,* are crucial and quite predictive of his eventual surrender. Just think of the opposite to see the contrast: a subject who is talking on and on about money, car, escape, and so forth, and one who lets the phone ring on and on each time the negotiator calls. Talking longer and calling a person with whom he has a trusting relationship are crucial.

4. Nonviolent subject. They say that the best predictor of future behavior is past behavior. In that regard, the courts, beginning with *Downs v. United States,* have said that the best indicator negotiations are working is that "no one has been killed or injured by the subject since negotiations began" (*Downs*, 382 F. Supp. at 752). Certainly, the lack of violent behavior by the hostage taker is laudable. How predictive this lack of violence is may be another matter and may be motivated by intentions or thoughts other than his plan to surrender.

5. The subject's expectations have been reduced. In other words, he is now more concerned with his personal safety than with any initial instrumental demands for a car, aircraft, money, or other items. One example of this was an incident where the subject who was holding hostages in a bank and had access to a calculator demanded several thousand dollars, a car, and a helicopter. In the course of negotiations, he also demanded a cup of coffee with cream and sugar. In this situation, it took well over 2 hours to safely deliver the coffee. By the time it arrived, it was cold and someone had forgotten to put cream and sugar in the mix. Shortly after the coffee arrived the subject announced his desire to surrender. During a postincident interview he said he began to understand that if the FBI could not deliver "the right kind of coffee" in a timely manner, how would they ever get him the money he demanded. Further, since it took about 2 hours to get the coffee, at a cost of about 50 cents, his calculations revealed that it would take several months for the FBI to deliver all the money he wanted.

6. A decrease in threatening behavior or words by the subject is always a welcome change. I recall that on the second day of the Hanafi Moslem siege in Washington, DC, there was a dramatic change in the demeanor of the lead hostage taker. Early in the siege, he issued a conditional threat to decapitate hostages if his demands were not met. He said this over and over with a good deal of conviction in his voice. By the second day, he was uttering similar threats, but he was saying them without emotion. He was exhausted. The crisis managers were then faced with the challenge of arranging an honorable surrender. This was achieved by employing the verbal skills of the ambassadors from Egypt, Iran, and Pakistan.

7. The subject is talking about the hostages as *people*. This sounds simple enough. An example would be him referring to those with him by their names rather than "that bastard so and so" or "that bitch." This type of behavior suggests the formation of the Stockholm Syndrome discussed in Chapter 24.

8. The *passing or extension of a deadline* without incident is always refreshing. However, it may be more predictive of the subject's level of exhaustion than anything else. Very few hostages have been killed or injured at a deadline in the United States. Considering the tens of thousands of incidents we have had, I can think of only two where the hostage taker killed a hostage at a deadline. One can never predict all human behavior. However, history suggests that the vast majority of nonsuicidal hostage takers will not do anything reckless at a deadline.

9. The *release of hostages* is always a good sign, or is it? It depends upon who is released and why. During any such crisis the negotiating team should have a list of hostages and prioritize them in terms of who they want out first, second, and so forth, and why. Certainly, matters such as the health of each hostage should be considered. Other factors include the role of the hostage and his or her relationship to the subject. There are those hostages who serve to calm a situation, while others do not, like the press attaché Abbas Lavasani during the Iranian Embassy siege in London, who engaged in countless arguments with the hostage takers and aggravated everyone (Eddy et al., 1980).

10. A *routine of exchanging material* goods for hostages is a goal of every crisis negotiations team. However, and in all reality, we usually start the process by providing the subject with something he wants in exchange for a promise to answer the phone on the first ring, or refer to the people in the room by their given names, or some other limited activity on his part. Early in the siege, it is not important what we exchange. What counts is that we begin a *pattern of exchanging*. It is during this process that the negotiating team can enhance the trustful relationship with the subject that will lead to

a peaceful conclusion. In addition, the use of the tactical team in making deliveries acquaints them with the location as the subject becomes accustomed to routine movement.

11. *Threats* are frequently factors that create a great deal of concern for negotiating and tactical teams as well as the incident commander. To more effectively evaluate a threat, it is important to differentiate between unconditional versus conditional offensive, and defensive threats and statements.

Unconditional: An unconditional threat is the most dangerous. It is a direct statement of harm. There is no action or inaction required on the part of the authorities or a hostage for the subject to implement his threat. An example of an unconditional threat is, "I am going to kill this SOB!"

Conditional:

Offensive: An example of a conditional offensive threat is a statement like, "If the money is not delivered in 15 minutes, someone is going to die!" Though action is intended, the logical question is who is going to die? Does the subject intend on shooting a hostage, at police, or himself?

Defensive: The more common conditional defensive threat is quite different and might be a statement like, "If you come in here I will shoot a hostage." This threat, contingent upon action on the part of authorities, though a threat, is quite different from the first two.

We have three threats. However, they are as different as day and night. When assessing the potential for a subject to surrender the most predictive type of threat heard is defensive. This usually means he is buying time to tell the world how he has been victimized. During this time, his adrenaline flow is gradually subsiding as he is searching for an honorable or face-saving solution.

It is the intent of this chapter to provide crisis negotiators with the judgments and experience of others across the country and around the world. Certainly, this is and remains a work in progress. I am certain that over the next 10 years additional predictors will emerge to assist the crisis management team in achieving our goal of the preservation of human life, responding officers, hostages, and even that of the hostage taker.

Crucial Conclusion

Finally, what good are these indicators if the negotiating team does not appraise their relief team, command, and tactical of them? Therefore, timely and regular situational assessments known as negotiation position papers

(NPPs) are vital (Dalfonzo and Romano, 2003). Each report should be sequentially numbered and include the date and time. Obviously, items in the NPP are likely to change for the better or worse over time. These reports consist of three simple parts: status, assessment, and recommendations.

Status

This is an overall description of the situation that typically includes weapons, dwelling, subject and hostage information, demands, deadlines, and current issues like the subject is refusing to come out or subject and hostage health or temperament problems.

Assessment

Is this a hostage siege? A barricaded gunman? Are there mental health issues? This includes background information on the subject and hostages, the level and indicators of the threats, if any, against hostages, law enforcement, or self. Is the threat level low, moderate, or high? Use examples of actions, words, or history to substantiate this rating. Note subject suicidal ideation and risk level. An evaluation and indicators of subject/negotiator rapport are also important to relay to command and the incoming negotiating team.

Recommendations

Use active listening skills (ALS), encourage surrender, use third-party interme-diaries (TPIs), ensure deliveries of various items, decide on high or low SWAT profile, plan the negotiation strategy, and specifically plan for subsequent con-tacts. Is this a negotiable situation or is a tactical rescue more likely?

A few years ago I taught this process to a group of police officers from India. That nation is known for its reliance on structure and bureaucracy. Because of their experiences back home they added a twist to the NPP that involved a person in the command post signing for each NPP as it was deliv-ered. I will leave it to you to sort out why they thought this was necessary.

References

Dalfonzo, V. A., and Romano, S. J. (2003) Negotiation Position Papers: A Tool for Crisis Negotiators, *FBI Law Enforcement Bulletin*, October, pp. 27–31.

Downs v. United States, 382 F. 2nd, 990, Supp. 752 (1975).

Eddy, P., Gillman, P., Connell, J., Ball, J., and Smith, J. (1980) *Siege*, Hamlyn Press, London.

Hayden, C., and Callioux, S. (2004) Edmonton Standoff, CAHN Annual Training Conference, Monterey, California, June 4.

Noesner, G. (2010) *Stalling for Time*, Random House, New York.

Stefansson, K. (2004) Tractor Man, CAHN Annual Training Conference, Monterey, California, June 4.

Strentz, T. (1995) The Cyclic Crisis Negotiations Time Line, *Law and Order*, March, pp. 73–75.

Wood, R. (2004) Judge Fakes Resignation to End Standoff, *The Baton Rouge Advocate*, p. 26A.

Indicators of Volatile Negotiations

20

Introduction

The first version of this material appeared in the September 1991 issue of *Law and Order* (Strentz, 1991). During the intervening 20 years, many additional indicators have been identified. Interestingly, the original 13 remain as valid today as they were in 1991. However, the Federal Bureau of Investigation (FBI) has instituted a process called "Crisis Site Assessment" that enables the negotiating team to evaluate about two dozen indicators to help predict the behavior of the hostage taker (subject). A copy of this form appears in Appendix A. It should be noted that this effort remains a work in progress.

It is the intent of this chapter to acquaint law enforcement and corrections with predictors of violence during a hostage crisis. Various behaviors, like a weapon tied to the subject, violence before or during an incident, multiple weapons, targeted hostages, and evidence of a planned siege, are obvious indicators of a potentially dangerous situation. Let us learn from the experiences of others and remember the axiom of Santayana, "Those who cannot remember the past are condemned to repeat it" (Santayana, 1905).

It is not the intent of this chapter to second-guess law enforcement actions during the incidents that will be referenced. Today, we have the benefit of looking back over 40 years at several situations from many departments. We have information available to us that the police at those incidents had no way of knowing or comprehending. Hindsight is always 20/20.

The focus of this chapter is to acquaint the crisis/hostage negotiator and the on-scene commander with early indicators of more serious problems developing during a hostage or suicidal siege. It is suggested that the negotiator and the commander measure the volatility of the situation against these criteria and make their tactical decisions accordingly. This list will help the negotiator identify those areas of hostage taker activity, behavior, and discussion upon which he or she should focus. With this list, the negotiator can be more realistic in his or her appraisal of the difficulty of a situation. The commander will have a better idea if an option other than negotiations will have to be exercised in this crisis to achieve the goal of the preservation of the greatest number of human lives. Since 1977, research has been conducted into many domestic and several foreign hostage situations (Strentz, 1983). These efforts have identified several early indicators of hostage taker violence.

The listing of these predictors of violence does not suggest that numbers one, two, or three are more predictive of hostage taker, or subject, violence than numbers 21, 22, or 23. Such a quantitative analysis of the hostage taker threat level reflects a degree of sophistication that is still in the developmental stages. Research has shown that most hostage takers are males who operate alone. Thus the pronoun *he* will be used rather than *she* or *they*.

Suicidal Subjects

1. A Depressed Hostage Taker Who Denies Thoughts of Suicide

This issue is at the heart of successful negotiations and suggests a lack of trust through untruthful behavior on the part of the subject. If the hostage taker sounds depressed to an experienced police officer, depressed enough to have taken hostages and initiated a potentially fatal confrontation with the authorities, then he has or is considering suicide. If he denies this, he is a very dangerous person. As noted in Chapter 19, the single best indicator that a subject will surrender is a trusting relationship between him and the negotiator. Until this exists, he is unlikely to surrender. If he is lying about suicidal thoughts that means he does not trust the negotiator. He is lying to the negotiator and to himself and may be trying to lure law enforcement into a suicide-by-cop scenario. He is a homicide looking for a victim.

2. No Rapport

This indicator is closely related in value to the previous predictor. After a few hours of negotiations, the negotiator should have developed a sense of rapport with the subject. The subject should make the transition from talking about money, a car, and other material demands to more personal points. If this transition has not been made, the chance of surrender is less likely.

It is especially difficult to develop rapport with an angry adolescent. There have been several recent hostage situations that involved youthful offenders. In Sacramento, the hostage situation involved several adolescent Asian hostage takers who were immature, impulsive, and antisocial juveniles. It is interesting to note that just as the Sacramento County Sheriff's negotiator Bob Currie was developing rapport with one subject and was convinced he and the others were about to surrender, the leader of the group took over negotiations and announced, "Call me number one." Before this siege ended several people and most of the subjects were dead.

There are several problems that emerge when an adult tries to convince a teenager to do something he or she may not want to do. School counselors, teachers, parents, and police officers generally have problems with this age group. Their cognitive process is quite different from adults. They are trying to prove themselves to the world. They may lack the ego strength to surrender. Therefore, trying to arrange a dignified or honorable solution will be more difficult. They tend to resent authority figures and usually consider themselves invincible. Their idea about danger is that old people and others die, not them. When one is faced with an adolescent hostage taker one should be aware that the common practices for successful negotiations may change. Time may no longer be our greatest ally. They may fear disfigurement more than death and are more prone to peer pressure than are most adults. They may be on drugs. Research has not yet been completed on how to effectively deal with this type of subject. Suffice it to say that an adolescent hostage taker is more dangerous than most other subjects. For a more detailed discussion of adolescent hostage takers, see Chapter 9.

3. Age of the Subject

It is well known that the most violent criminals faced by law enforcement are in the age range of 18 to 25. The FBI HOBAS research has found that most hostage takers are in the age range of 30 to 45. Common sense and research conducted during crisis negotiation courses suggest that younger hostage takers are more violent (Birge, 2004; Strentz, 2004). Therefore, when one is dealing with younger hostage takers, it is imperative that their tendency toward impulsive and violent behavior be kept in mind. For additional information on dealing with this age group see Chapter 9 that discusses adolescent hostage takers.

4. No Social Support System

This means that the hostage taker does not have an outlet for his anxiety, fears, and frustrations. He sees himself as facing the trials and tribulations of this life alone. He envisions himself as a man against the world. He may think that he has no one to turn to, so he has turned on society and may want to make them pay for his lonely life. In his mind, his problems are not his fault. This is called *projection* and is discussed in Chapter 1.

5. Subject Insists on Face-to-Face Negotiations

In this chapter, face-to-face negotiations means nose-to-nose. It is always dangerous for a negotiator to talk with the hostage taker out in the open. The concern is for the safety of the law enforcement negotiator who may be presenting himself to the hostage taker as a target for a person engaged in suicide by cop (SbC). The hostage taker may be thinking that the police will not kill him, as he desires, unless he provokes them by shooting a police officer. SbC is discussed in Chapter 15.

The negotiator should not converse from a position where he or she does not have adequate, approximate, and appropriate cover. Most hostage takers are leery about coming out into the open to talk with the negotiator. One who insists on face-to-face negotiations is an anomaly. In his mind, he is taking an unusual personal risk that most hostage takers refuse to take, unless they are about to surrender. A subject who insists that both parties meet in the open too *early,* or in the negotiator's mind *prematurely* in the negotiations process, should be viewed with suspicion.

6. Subject Sets a Deadline for His Own Death

This means that the hostage holder says this to the negotiator, or has told others, with the assumption that law enforcement will learn of his intent. This behavior was observed in Rochester, New York, by William Bradley Griffin, who left a diary. Sam Byke, who attempted to hijack Delta Flight 523 from Baltimore Washington International (BWI) airport in 1974, sent audiotapes that announced his suicidal plan to three public figures. This case is discussed in Chapter 13.

A more recent example is that of John Miranda who returned to his former place of employment, took several former coworkers hostage, tied a shotgun to his hand and the head of a hostage, and then walked in front of police as he counted backwards from 60. He told police that he intended to shoot his hostage when he got to one. It is interesting that he began counting at 60, not 10 or 5. One could speculate that he wanted to give the police ample time to shoot him. Fortunately, his hostage intervened and wrestled the shotgun away from his head as the police shot Miranda (Kakesako and Barayuga, 1996).

7. Verbal Will

A common tactic of people who are about to commit suicide, or force law enforcement to kill them, in a hostage/barricade siege is for them to talk about the disposition of their belongings. As an example, they may, during a conversation about surrender, say that they understand they will be incarcerated. Because of a past experience where they allege someone at the jail stole some of their valuables, they may ask the negotiator for assurances that specific relatives will get their belongings before someone has a chance to steal them (Bolz and Hershey, 1979, p. 57; Fuselier, Van Zandt, and Lanceley, 1991). The problem here is the negotiator may focus on the statement of surrender and not recognize the subject is giving him a layered message. The top layer is what the negotiator is hearing, surrender. The bottom layer, and the real meaning of the communication, is quite different. This is one case where the listening skills of the secondary negotiator are very important.

One way to deal with this hostage taker tactic is to change the subject of negotiations or confront his behavior (Bolz, 1979).

History of Violence

8. Subject Has a History of Violence

The one best predictor of future behavior is past behavior. Certainly, John Miranda, who had multiple arrests for assault and fighting with police, is a good example of this. In addition, he is suspected of killing his girlfriend just before the siege began. According to Fuselier, hostage taker preincident violence that indicates additional violence is usually very recent (Fuselier et al., 1991).

9. Prior Confrontations

There was a time when one could count the number of repeat hostage takers on one hand. However, that was long ago. Clearly, a person who repeatedly places himself in harm's way is sending a signal of suicidal ideation. It is well known among suicide hotline counselors that repeated suicidal threats and attempts are serious signs of severe problems. Although all threats are indicators of dangerous behavior, the person who attempts suicide again and again using the same method is probably seeking attention. However, the person who tries different methods is potentially much more likely to die. I suggest the same criteria might apply to hostage takers. There is always the chance that the repeat hostage taker may miscalculate and die when all he wants is attention. However, the hostage taker who employs the same tactics, over and over, is probably less dangerous than the repeater who experiments with different methods, weapons, or hostages (Fresno, 2004).

A history of hostage/barricade situations with the subject is not a good sign. Law enforcement agencies around the world are reporting an increase in repeat hostage takers (Birge, 2004). Because of the escalation in his threats, and his statement that he had a bomb, the FBI had to kill Glenn Tripp during his second hijacking of NWO 608. Taking hostages and forcing a violent confrontation with police is a dangerous act. Subconsciously, those who repeat this behavior may be trying to force the police to kill them. For a more detailed discussion of suicide by police, see Chapter 15.

10. Planned Siege

In any hostage crisis where it is clear that the subject is well prepared to defend himself, like Waco, Texas, or Ruby Ridge, Idaho, the prospect for violence is quite high. Evidence of planning can include the stockpiling of food, weapons, and ammunition. In addition, the potential for violence is greater if the subject is defending his home or returning to his place of employment where he takes former fellow coworkers hostage.

Negotiations Process

11. Refusal to Negotiate

One of the most frustrating experiences for a negotiator is when the subject does not answer the telephone. Clearly, one must make sure we have the correct phone number. Usually, the tactical team can verify the telephone is ringing. Although this type of behavior is troubling, the subject might not be ready to talk. Therefore, the negotiator should allow the phone to ring a reasonable number of times, hang up, log the attempt, and try again in a few minutes. Remember the courts have not ordered us to be successful at negotiations. However, we must make and in this case keep a record of that reasonable effort.

Almost as frustrating is the case where the subject insists that a hostage negotiate for him. This creates several problems. When we are forced to use an intermediary, we cannot accurately gauge the intelligence, mental health, emotional level, or reactions of the subject. It is important to determine why the subject will not come to the phone. Is it his idea that we negotiate through a hostage or has the hostage taken it upon himself or herself to undertake this responsibility? There are several tactics we can use to get the subject to the phone. We can try to convince the hostage that the siege will end more quickly and much more peacefully if we can speak directly to the subject. One of the problems the FBI faced in Waco was the refusal of David Koresh to regularly speak with the negotiators. Should that fail we may introduce some "errors" in what we deliver and blame the errors on our inability to deal directly with the hostage taker. We might also consider telling the hostage that the district attorney is considering charging him or her as an accessory. (See Figures 20.1 through 20.3.)

Subject–Victim Relationship

12. Targeted Hostages

Most hostages are people who just happened to be in the wrong place at the wrong time. Be it in an airplane, a liquor store, or a bank, they are the victims of circumstances. When a subject returns to his place of employment or school, or any setting where he has a grudge against the occupants, the potential for violence is greater. There may also be some psychological factors

Figure 20.1 We must negotiate from a position of strength provided by the tactical team.

Figure 20.2 All deliveries must be delivered through and with the approval of the tactical team.

at play. People who are victims at random are more likely to "play the role of a hostage" and follow the orders of the subject. Conversely, people who know the subject as a fellow or former employee, schoolmate, and so forth, may not acquiesce to his claim of control and authority. They may challenge his

Figure 20.3 The arrest plan of the tactical team must be followed. Any modifications must be cleared through them.

authority and thereby increase the potential for violence. These behaviors are discussed in Chapter 26.

13. Hostage Taker Insists That a Particular Person Be Brought to the Scene

This behavior, like that of tying a weapon to his hand, reflects premeditation. In most hostage situations the victims are pawns, innocent individuals who are trapped by an impulsive criminal. In most cases, the hostage taker is upset with the authorities who have, in his mind, "forced him to take people hostage." In this example, he has taken people whom he hates as his hostages. There are various versions of this behavior. One is his need for an audience for his eventual demise. Another includes the predicament where the held or requested hostage is the intended victim. This can be volatile and is common in domestic situations (Fuselier et al., 1991).

One way to gauge the emotional stability of the hostage taker is to determine the identity of his victims. Rational people do not take loved ones hostage and threaten to kill them.

This indicator extends to employers against whom the hostage taker has a grudge. In December 1987, a recently fired employee of Pacific Southwest Air, David A. Burke, commandeered PSA 1771. The man who had just fired him was a passenger on the ill-fated flight that Burke forced into the ground near Paso Robles, California. In his lust for revenge, Burke killed himself and 43 people.

An alteration of his behavior is the physical or psychological isolation of the hostages. During the PFLP hijacking of Air France 139 in July 1976 that ended up in Entebbe, the terrorists separated the Israeli passengers from the other hostages. After the dramatic rescue by the Israeli Defense Forces it was learned that the terrorists planned to kill all Jewish hostages. Even if Israel had complied with all of the terrorist demands, the terrorists had orders to kill their Hebrew hostages. To prepare for this massacre, they separated the hostages into groups of those who would live and those who would die.

14. Isolation and Dehumanization of Hostages

When the hostages are in the same room as the hostage taker, and they are conversing, the chance that the Stockholm Syndrome might take effect is much greater than when the hostages are isolated. In fact, isolated hostages, those in a different room, or in the same room with bags over their heads, or those with whom the hostage taker is having arguments are much more at risk. Therefore, it is important that the negotiating team assess the physical location of the hostages and their level and quality of interaction with the hostage taker. Along these lines, the hostages are at less of a risk when the subject calls them by their names rather than "that bastard" or "that bitch." This type of behavior is the exact opposite of indicator number seven of surrender discussed in Chapter 19.

A modification of this indicator is the situation where the subject dehumanizes his hostages. He does this by referring to them as "things" or to quote Jim Dutton in Las Vegas, "the girl." Dutton attempted to rob a savings and loan. He was trapped by a rapid police response and took one female teller as his hostage. Throughout the 6 hours of negotiations he referred to her as "the girl." He made threats against "the girl." During one exchange with the FBI negotiator he said that, "You are going to force me to do something we will both regret and you will have to explain to her children why their mommy is not coming home tonight." A psychological counselor said that given the slightest provocation, Dutton would probably kill his hostage. During an escape attempt, Dutton was killed by a police sniper. His hostage was not physically injured. She returned home to her husband and two children that night and is still employed by the bank.

Weapon(s)

15. A Weapon Is Tied to the Hostage Holder

This behavior demonstrates premeditation and suggests that we are dealing with someone who has given this drama some thought. He is going to be more difficult to deal with than the trapped armed robber or the deranged individual who, on an impulse, decides to take hostages. This behavior on the part of the subject is viewed as his intent that he remain a viable and visible threat to his hostages and law enforcement throughout the crisis. This weapon may be tied to his person, as we saw in the Griffin case, or may be tied to his hand. In the case of John Miranda, his shotgun was tied to his hand and the head of his hostage. Another example of this occurred during a bus hijacking in Jasper, Arkansas, in 1982. In this situation, two people who claimed to have been spoken of in the *Bible* in the book of Revelations, took a busload of people hostage and insisted that the police kill them. It was their plan to rise from the dead 3 days later. When the Arkansas State Police snipers only wounded them, this husband and wife team shot and killed each other (*Arkansas Democrat*, 1982).

16. Excessive Ammunition—Multiple Weapons

Due to his behavior in the bank, Griffin provided indicators of a high threat level by carrying two weapons, a shotgun and a revolver, along with excessive ammunition for both weapons. His pockets were filled with ammunition, and he had a bag of additional ammo. One could easily make the case for suicide by police when a person enters into a confrontation with law enforcement with excessive ammunition and multiple weapons. Common sense dictates that no matter how many weapons or ammunition a person may have, law enforcement has more. Therefore, the intent of the subject is more likely designed to provoke the authorities into a very one-sided fire fight rather than win the confrontation.

17. Explosives

A minor modification of this behavior includes the subject who has or claims to have a bomb. Glenn Tripp hijacked NWO 608 for the second time in 1983. He changed his behavior to be more of a threat. During his first hijacking of NWO 608 at SEATAC International airport located between Seattle and Tacoma, Washington, in 1980 he was arrested by the FBI and was tried and convicted for his crime. In 1980 he was young, inexperienced, and impulsive. He announced the hijacking while the aircraft was still at the gate. The aircraft never left Seattle. He was captured by the FBI. It was then discovered that he was a juvenile. The court allowed him to serve only a few years for his crime. Less than 2 months after his release from prison he returned to SEATAC, boarded the *same* flight, and waited until the aircraft was airborne to announce the hijacking. This repetitive, compulsive, and dangerous behavior is common in some types of mentally ill individuals. In this case, those who remember their past may choose to repeat it. He said that he wanted to fly to San Diego or Afghanistan. In those days the destination of

NWO 608 was San Diego. He settled for Portland. The aircraft landed, and FBI negotiators attempted to talk with the hijacker who claimed to have a bomb. He refused to negotiate and constantly threatened to kill everyone on the aircraft with his alleged bomb. Because of his intimidating behavior the decision was made to shoot. He was identified at the morgue.

Norman Mayer took the Washington Monument hostage in December 1982 and threatened the city of Washington, DC, with his truck he alleged was filled with explosives. During negotiations he was warned not to move his truck away from the monument. After his demands for a press conference were met he tried to drive his vehicle into the city. As he drove toward the White House he was killed by a police sniper. A search of his vehicle determined he did not have any explosives (Noesner, 1993). The presence of explosives—real, fake, or alleged—is guaranteed to peak the interest of law enforcement and is more likely to escalate the siege stress level.

It is important to note that the hostage taker may not have thought all this through as methodically as one might fear or imagine. He may be motivated by a subconscious desire to commit suicide and thus heavily arm himself to ensure a deadly confrontation.

Incident Behavior of Subject

18. Postnegotiations Violence

During a Sacramento siege known as "The Good Guys" after the name of the electronics store where the incident occurred, the subjects shot and wounded hostages after negotiations had begun. This type of behavior has long been recognized as a sign that negotiations were not going well. Similar behavior, shooting a hostage and shooting at the police during negotiations, was observed in Honolulu during February 1996 in an incident where the police were finally forced to shoot and kill the hostage taker, John Miranda (Kakesako and Barayuga, 1996). Of additional interest, Miranda had excessive ammunition, a weapon tied to himself and one hostage, a history of violence, multiple weapons, and had a history of drug use. In is now believed that he had just killed his girlfriend. He refused to negotiate with police or any relative and said from the outset that people were going to die during the siege (Kakesako and Barayuga, 1996). In brief, of the 23 indicators of violence, Miranda had 15 of them.

It is interesting to note that not all shooting is an expression of violence. One must differentiate between shooting at people versus a subject who shoots at objects. Miranda, Griffin, Byke, and other violent hostage takers shot at people or the police. In a Torrence, California, case, the hostage taker in a jewelry store shot at things. His hostages reported to the police that he had shot the clock, a TV set, and other inanimate objects. Although he fired over a hundred rounds, none of his shooting was at human targets. He was also careful that his bullets did not exit the store and accidentally hit someone outside. This subject, who eventually arranged for his own arrest, was very careful not to physically hurt his hostages or police during negotiations.

19. Negotiations Are Becoming More Volatile

In 1976, Dr. Clause Walter-Herbertz, the psychologist for the elite German counterterrorist force known as GSG-9, attended the FBI hostage negotiator's course. He had been studying hostage situations in Western Europe and noticed that as time passed most hostage takers became more tranquil. This gradual move toward tranquility may have its ups and downs, but overall, the move in hostage situations that ended peacefully was toward more amicable negotiations. Measures of this change toward tranquility first noted by him have been expanded upon by the hostage negotiations instructional staff at the FBI and New South Wales Police academies. This expansion is designed to give the negotiator some solid indicators of change. They include (1) an evaluation of the subject's tone of voice; (2) fewer threats to harm the hostages; (3) deadlines missed and not reestablished; (4) a general decrease in his demands; (5) a gradual switch from *instrumental* (car, money, and escape) to *expressive* (fears, feelings, and frustrations) demands (Noesner, 1993; O'Brien, 1988). With this insight, there is an ongoing study of American situations that include interviewing experienced law enforcement negotiators (Strentz, 2004).

In those very few situations where violence erupted late in the siege, the negotiator reported that after some initial progress toward tranquility, the subject became more aggressive. This was evident during a prison siege in Tennessee where an inmate took his female correctional counselor hostage with a knife. After hours of negotiations and progress toward a peaceful solution, his behavior changed. It became clear to the negotiators that the subject, who had a history of violence toward females, was beginning to enjoy the terror he was creating for his hostage. Early in the siege she did not appreciate the peril of her situation. As her defense of denial began to abate, it was replaced by a growing appreciation of the danger she faced, and she started to throw up. The more anxious she became, the more she regurgitated. The more she regurgitated, the more belligerent he became. The situation was finally resolved by an assault that rescued her and neutralized him (Denton, 1985).

A modification of this occurred at The Good Guys appliance store in Sacramento, California, where the negotiator was making progress with one subject who was beginning to show signs of surrender. After several hours of negotiations he was replaced by another hostage taker who was violent and intransigent.

Multiple hostage takers are rare in the United States. Thus the effect of this phenomenon on volatile negotiations can only be speculated. It is the impression of most police negotiators that the presence of multiple hostage takers increases the chance of violence (Birge, 2004).

An example of a more typical movement was that of the Hanafi Muslim takeover of three buildings in Washington, DC, in March 1977. The leader of this group, Ernest Timothy McGee, was a Negro male age 55 who had a history of violent confrontations with other Muslims. After a break with the Chicago-based Black Muslims, he formed his own group. He took the Muslim name of Hammas Abdul Khaalis and assumed the leadership of the Washington, DC, group. In 1973 several members of the Philadelphia chapter came to Washington, DC, and brutally murdered his family and followers. The killers were identified, tried, and convicted for their crimes. He was convinced that their actions were sponsored by a Jewish conspiracy. Four years later, he sought revenge. He did not want them detained; he wanted them dead. He and his followers took hostages at B'nai B'rith, a Jewish service organization, the Washington, DC, city hall known as the District Building, and at a local Mosque and Islamic shrine. Before negotiations began, one person was killed at the District Building and several were injured at the other sites. Via the telephone, Khaalis conducted the negotiations and commanded his group at all three sites. His initial demands were vocal and vicious. He wanted the killers of his family brought to him for a televised decapitation. He wanted Cassius Clay, then known as Muhammad Ali, also brought to him. His other demands included the removal of a movie, *Mohammed the Messenger of God*, from American theaters as well as other less significant demands. He repeatedly threatened to decapitate his hostages and throw their heads out the windows of his multistory stronghold. This created a tough tactical problem for law enforcement. At that time the skills did not exist within the police or the FBI to simultaneously assault three multistory sites with enough precision and surprise to prevent the killing of hostages. As time passed and negotiations continued, his threats became less brutal and his tone of voice became more moderate. By the second day it was clear to the negotiators that the key to a successful resolution to this dilemma was to help Khaalis find an honorable solution. His demands, tone, and threat levels were clearly moving down to more normal levels. A reasonable resolution was found. Khaalis went home and his followers went to jail. The next day when Khaalis appeared in court he was arrested and retained. He and his group were convicted and most remain incarcerated for the homicide and hostage taking. He died in federal prison.

20. After Hours of Negotiations, the Subject Has No Clear Demands, His Demands Are Outrageous, or They Are Changing

Griffin was unclear about his demands, and Sam Byke did not talk, he just shot at the police. Griffin had already told his story in a handwritten diary. His diary, like the audiotapes of Byke, were discovered after his death.

In addition, there are two slight modifications of this behavior. One is the subject who insists that negotiations be conducted through the hostages. This normally occurs in the siege because the subject fears being identified by the police. However, this behavior should cease after a few hours. If it does not, then this indicator becomes predictive of violence.

A closely related behavior pattern is that of a subject who does not negotiate. Griffin, Byke, and Glenn Tripp never negotiated with the authorities. This reluctance by a hostage taker to negotiate was also observed during the siege at the Harbor Island Travelodge in San Diego, California, in August 1990. In this case, the subject Randy Dolf, insisted that his hostage do most of the initial talking for him. Dolf had escaped from a prison in Colorado. He departed a day before he was scheduled to complete his sentence and be released on parole. He burglarized a home near the prison, stole a car and a shotgun, and drove to San Diego. He said that he wanted to kill himself by jumping from the Coronado Bridge. He could not find the bridge so he took a motel employee hostage in a ninth-floor room. Ultimately, his hostage was rescued by the San Diego Police Department SWAT team. Dolf was arrested. When the police searched the tear-gassed motel room they found a suicide note as well as a statement from Dolf that was his version of a will (LaBore, 2004).

Another indicator of a high potential for violence is subjects who have outrageous demands. An example of this is the situation at the Good Guys appliance store when the adolescent subjects wanted, among other things, head-to-toe bulletproof vests, and a helicopter to transport them and their hostages to Thailand. John Miranda wanted the police to throw $20,000 from a nearby roof into the wind. Psychologically speaking, these outrageous demands may be a form of projection. When the authorities fail to meet the demands the subject then blames them for his killing of hostages. His reasoning, if you want to call it that, is the action or inaction of the authorities forced him to kill. This was the thinking process of Donald Dunn in Seattle, when he killed his hostage because the deputies from King County did not deliver the cell phone he wanted within his time frame. This case is discussed in Chapter 10.

Subject Stress

21. Multiple Stressors

Like the polydrug abuser, the hostage taker who has a multitude of problems is probably more dangerous than one who is facing fewer frustrations. Burke, the hijacker of PSA 1771, was fired that day from the company for which he had worked for many years. He had fathered many children by several women and was suspected of drug dealing and theft from PSA. He had taken his recent girlfriend hostage and threatened to kill her and was heavily in debt. The multiple-problem hostage taker is a greater challenge for the negotiator than one who is in an emotionally less chaotic state.

22. Alcohol or Drug Use by Subject or Hostage during the Siege

It is said that alcohol is a solvent for the superego (Hassel, 1977). Some people find it easier to engage in antisocial behavior when they are drunk. This is especially true when the subject has a history of violence when intoxicated. Just as alcohol and gasoline do not mix, alcohol and gunpowder make an equally volatile combination. These dangerous combinations are so well known to police that case cites are not necessary. The connection between alcohol and suicide is also well established. It is well known that alcohol and drug abuse tend to decrease impulse control or precipitate a psychotic break (Shea, 1999). Because of the potential volatility of this combination, airlines advise their crews to lock up the alcohol during a hijacking.

23. Threat Analysis

Types of Threats

Threats are frequently factors that create a great deal of concern for negotiating and tactical teams as well as the incident commander. To more effectively evaluate a threat, it is important to differentiate between unconditional, offensive, and defensive threats and statements.

1. *Unconditional*: An unconditional threat is the most dangerous. It is a direct statement of harm. There is no action or inaction required on the part of the authorities or a hostage for the subject to implement his threat. An example of an unconditional threat is, "I am going to kill this SOB!"
2. *Offensive*: An example of an offensive threat is a statement like, "If the money is not delivered in 15 minutes, someone is going to die!" Though action is intended, the logical question is who is going to die? Does the subject intend on shooting a hostage, at police, or himself?
3. *Defensive*: The more common defensive threat is quite different and might be a statement like, "If you come in here I will shoot a hostage." This threat, contingent upon action on the part of authorities, though a threat, is quite different from the first two.

As delineated above, we have three threats. However, they are as different as day and night. When assessing the potential for a subject to surrender, the most predictive type of threat heard is defensive. This usually means he is buying time to tell the world how he has been victimized. During this time his adrenaline flow is gradually subsiding as he searches for an honorable or face-saving solution.

Conclusion

It is the intent of this chapter to provide law enforcement negotiators with a listing of some factors that have been associated with violence in American and Australian hostage situations. If we in law enforcement do not study our past and strive to learn from our experiences, then we may be condemned to repeat our errors. If we do not learn from what has been, then we will have forsaken our primary objective, the preservation of human life.

Crucial Conclusion

Finally, what good are these indicators if the negotiating team does not appraise their relief team, command, and tactical of them? Therefore, timely and regular situational assessments known as NPPs are vital (Dalfonzo and Romano, 2003). Each report should be sequentially numbered and include the date and time. Obviously, items in the NPP are likely to change for the better or worse over time. These reports consist of three simple parts: *status*, *assessment*, and *recommendations*.

Status

This is an overall description of the situation that typically includes weapons, dwelling, subject and hostage information, demands, deadlines, and current issues like the subject is refusing to come out or subject or hostage health or temperament problems.

Assessment

Is this a hostage siege? A barricaded gunman? Are there mental health issues? This includes background information on the subject and hostages, the level and indicators of the threats, if any, against hostages, law enforcement, or self. Is the threat level low, moderate, or high? Use examples of actions, words, or history to substantiate this rating. Also note subject suicidal ideation and risk level. An evaluation of and indicators of subject/negotiator rapport are also important to relay to command and the incoming negotiating team.

Recommendations

Use active listening skills (ALS), encourage surrender, use third-party inter-mediaries (TPIs), note deliveries of various items, decide on high or low SWAT profile, plan the negotiation strategy, and have a specific plan for subsequent contacts. Is this a negotiable situation or is a tactical rescue more likely?

A few years ago, I taught this process to a group of police officers from India. That nation is known for its reliance on structure and bureaucracy. Because of their experiences back home they added a twist to the NPP that involved a person in the command post signing for each NPP as it was delivered. I will leave it to you to sort out why they thought this was necessary.

References

Arkansas Democrat (1982), Bus Hijacking Ends with Death of Two, July 4, p. 1A.

Birge, Raymond (2004). Personal interview at the San Jose State University Hostage Negotiators Course, Pacific Grove, California, June 6.

Bolz, F., and Hershey, E. (1979) *Hostage Cop*, Rawson Wade, New York, p. 7.

Dalfonzo, V. A., and Romano, S. J. (2003) Negotiation Position Papers: A Tool for Crisis Negotiators, *FBI Law Enforcement Bulletin,* October, pp. 27–31.

Denton, J. (1985) Personal interview, FBI Academy, Quantico, Virginia, March 16.

Downs v. United States, 382 F. 2nd, 990, Supp. 752 (1975).

Eddy, P., Gillman, P., Connell, J., Ball, J., and Smith, J. (1980) *Siege,* Hamlyn Press, London.

Fresno County Sheriff's Department (2004) Discussions with Officers during the Basic Hostage Negotiations Course, Pacific Grove, California, April.

Fuselier, G. D., Vanzandt, C. R., and Lanceley, F. J. (1991) Hostage Barricade Incidents: High-Risk Factors and the Action Criteria, *FBI Law Enforcement Bulletin*, Vol. 60, No. 1, pp. 6–12.

Hassel, C. V. (1977) Personal interview, Crisis Management Conference, Evian, France, May 30.

Hayden, C., and Callioux, S. (2004) Edmonton Standoff. CAHN Annual Training Conference, Monterey, California, June 4.

Kakesako, G. K., and Barayuga, D. (1996) Hostage Drama Grips City, *Honolulu Star Bulletin*, February 8, p. A-1.

LaBore, H. (2004) Personal conversation with SDPD Sgt., August 17.

Noesner, G. (1993) Personal interview, FBI Academy, Quantico, Virginia, October 6, 1993.

O'Brien, M. (1988) Personal interview, New South Wales Police Academy, Goulburn, December, 1988.

Santayana, G. (1905) In John Bartlett, *Book of Familiar Quotations*, Little, Brown and Company, Boston, 1980, p. 703.

Shea, S. C. (1999) *The Practical Art of Suicide Assessment*, John Wiley and Sons, New York.

Strentz, T. (1983) A Statistical Analysis of American Hostage Situations, Unpublished handout, FBI Academy, Quantico, Virginia.

Strentz, T. (1988) A Terrorist Psycho Social Profile; Past and Present, *FBI Law Enforcement Bulletin*, Vol. 57, No. 4, pp. 13–19.

Strentz, T. (1991) Thirteen Indicators of Volatile Negotiations, *Law and Order*, pp. 135–139.

Strentz, T. (2004) Discussion with negotiators from Fresno County Sheriff's Department, Pacific Grove, California, April 6.

Appendix A

FBI Crisis Negotiations Unit Crisis Site Assessment II

Type of Incident
Hostage
Nonhostage
Barricade
Barricade with victims

Threats
Unconditional
Offensive
Defensive
None

Person Held
Selected
Romantic relationship
Family member
Stranger

Hostage/Victims Out
Yes   No

Initiation of Incident
By subject
By hostage/victim
911 call
Other

Preparation
Planned
Prepared for
Spontaneous

Demands
Unrealistic
Changing
Nonsubstantive
Substantive
None

Crisis Site
Subject's residence
Subject's employment

Timing of Violence
After contact
Relative to demand
History of violence
Initially
Type

Degree of Violence
Death
Injury
Random

Bomb
Real
Fake
Alleged
Unknown
N/A

Weapons
Shoulder
Handgun
Knife
Other

Weapon Tied to Subject
Yes   No

Subject's Demeanor
Angry/aggressive
Yes   No

Deadlines
Specific
Uncertain
None

Passed
With incident
Without incident

Psychiatric History
Yes   No   Unknown

Criminal History
Yes   No   Unknown

Degree of Communication
Noncommunicative
Brief exchanges
Lengthy exchanges
Willing to talk

Escape
Desire to escape
Not mentioned

Calm/Controlled
Sad/depressed
Confused/incoherent
Other

Suicide
Suicide by cop
Stated
Desire to live

Loss
Health, job, relationship
Status/self-esteem
Money
Freedom

Drugs and/or Alcohol
During
Prior
History
Type
Quantity

**Has Your Assessment
Changed?**
Yes   No
Why, how, when, suggesting
what?

Source: Adapted from Voss, C. (2004) FBI Crisis Negotiations Unit Crisis Negotiations Site
Assessment, Presentation to the Louisiana Association of Crisis Negotiators Annual
Training Conference, March 6, Gonzales, Louisiana.

Group Dynamics 4

Group Think

21

Executive Summary*

The underlying behavior, or lack of action, that allows the error of "group think" to occur in the group decision-making process can be traced to the 18th century political theoretician, Edmund Burke, who said, "All that is necessary for the triumph of evil is that good men do nothing." It is the purpose of this chapter to identify common pitfalls in the group decision-making process and provide a remedy for this problem. Perhaps a more modern version of this problem would be, "Don't rock the boat, let it sink." When group think takes over, boats do sink and men die. The eight factors that contribute to group think are listed in this chapter as are the five steps a good leader can take to prevent this decision-making disaster from occurring. It is clear that the problem in this process lies in the leadership style of the commander.

There is no denying the fact that the actions of the federal law enforcement agencies at Mount Carmel in Waco, Texas, during the spring of 1993 were monumental failures. How could honorable and intelligent men make such massive mistakes? Similar questions were asked of Admiral Kimmel and his staff in 1942 as well as President Kennedy and his advisors after the Bay of Pigs.

Unfortunately, we in the United States are not alone in our blundering. Our British friends, under Field Marshall Bernard L. Montgomery, made similar errors during World War II in their ill-fated attempt to take the bridge at Arnhem, *The Bridge Too Far.* In this operation, the British and Polish paratroopers suffered over 80 percent killed and captured (Ryan, 1974). Commanders would do well to remember the statement, "Those who do not study their history are condemned to repeat it" (Santayana, 1905).

The European Front Fall of 1944

During the summer of 1944, the Allied Armies under Eisenhower were advancing quickly across Europe on a broad front. So fast was this thrust that several well-planned allied airborne assaults designed to take and hold key

---

* The earlier versions of this material appeared in the April 1997 issue of *Law and Order.*

points until the infantry arrived had to be canceled because the infantry was already there. Additionally, the rivalry between the U.S. commander, General George S. Patton, and his British counterpart, Field Marshall Montgomery, was a major problem for Eisenhower. This friendly rivalry was voiced by the British in their saying that the Americans were, "Over paid, over sexed, and over here." The Americans countered saying the British were upset because they were "under paid, under sexed, and under Ike."

This sentiment, and the perceived pressure to use their elite airborne units, was a portion of the rationale that led Montgomery to press for a dramatic "one tank wide" assault—quite the opposite of the American-led assault across France. It was intended to traverse a narrow highway and cross several bridges through Holland to gain access to the Ruhr Valley. This would allow the allies to invade the German industrial heartland, destroy German industry, and ensure victory by Christmas. In their enthusiasm to win a quick victory the British ignored vital intelligence. They isolated their decision makers and silenced the opposition. Over 10,000 British and Polish paratroopers landed in the Low Lands. Two weeks later, less than 2,000 came out. Like Admiral Kimmel at Pearl Harbor, they fell into the same trap that was later identified by an American psychologist, Dr. Janis, and called *group think* (Janis, 1972).

Basic Human Nature Is to Go Along to Get Along

Simply stated, most people do not like arguments, disagreements, or fights. We are social animals and want to get along with others. This is especially true when the others include a charismatic leader, associates, or coworkers with whom one is bound by friendship. In a nutshell, friendship groups make poor decision-making teams because their priority tends to be the maintenance of their friendship and harmony, not the success of their decision. Other social and psychological dynamics impede good group decision making. Pressures to conform can be so strong that members may go along to get along. They may suppress self-doubts and other rational indicators of possible failure. This is especially true when the group leader is arrogant, dynamic, controlling, or charismatic.

These social/psychological obstacles can and have caused dysfunction in the decision-making process. This occurs when task-oriented group members become so obsessed with peer approval through unanimity that they negate their goal of finding a sound solution. Conformity pressures dominate and soon exclude the use of good judgment, attention to facts, and indicators of possible failure. They can result in defective judgment that arises in cohesive groups where concurrence seeking fosters over optimism. This process is aided and abetted by the need to conform. This need encourages members to moralize. The leader and members reward conformity. Thus, members tend to be less vigilant and ignore factual contraindicators of success. Among the well-known phenomena of group dynamics is the alacrity with which members of a cohesive in-group suppress deviant points of view by putting social pressure on members who express ideas that deviate from the desired consensus.

General Patton understood this when he addressed his staff as they were planning the counteroffensive to rescue Bastone and end the Battle of the Bulge. He said, "If all of us are thinking the same way then someone here is not thinking." Earlier that year, on May 15, 1944, during one of the final planning sessions for the invasion of France, Eisenhower also understood this problem when he more eloquently said:

> I will emphasize but one thing. I consider it to be the duty of anyone who sees a flaw in this plan not to hesitate to say so. I have no sympathy with anyone, whatever his station or rank, who will not book criticism. (D'Este, 1983)

Group Think

The group functions seeking concurrence with, *not* the correctness of, the decision. Their mind has been made up. They are not to be confused with the facts. Dr. Janis identified eight major factors that ensure a poor decision because of group think. When a preponderance of these factors is present the decision-making process is sufficiently flawed, and failure is almost certain. They are as follows:

1. Illusion of invulnerability creates excessive optimism leading to extreme risks.
2. A collective effort to rationalize in order to discount intelligence or warnings of failure.

   (*If 1 is true then 2 must logically follow.*)

3. Unquestioned belief in the group's inherent morality.
4. Stereotyped views of a weak or ignorant adversary.

   (*Because of 3, number 4 is a reasonable conclusion.*)

5. Direct pressure on members who express strong arguments against group stereotypes.
6. Self-censorship of members who go along to get along.
7. A shared sense of unanimity.

   (*Given the enthusiasm generated by 1 through 4, the decision-making process begins to generate so much enthusiasm that those who consider objecting are neutralized. Items 5 and 6 provide a false sense of 7.*)

8. Self-appointed members who protect the group from adverse information that might shatter their shared complacency about the effectiveness and morality of their decision.

This last factor serves to ensure a faulty process as it logically follows the previous seven (Janis, 1972).

A Bridge Too Far

To put these symptoms in perspective, let us look at the Allied airborne assault at and around Arnhem in September 1944 and then compare this event to Waco, Texas. By the late summer of 1944, the rapidly advancing allies had caused the cancellation of over a dozen allied airborne assaults. General George Patton had been successful in Africa, in Sicily, and after Normandy in the European theater. Field Marshall Montgomery who had lost for so long in Africa, took the wrong road in Sicily and was now bogged down in Europe. The British were anxious to prove their worth. The Allied Command was determined to use their elite Airborne Infantry. Thus, with only a few days notice, Montgomery presented Eisenhower with a plan to drop American, Polish, and British paratroopers along a narrow highway. They were to hold several bridges as the British Third Army raced 63 miles through enemy territory to Arnhem where they would turn east into the industrial heart of Germany and end the war by Christmas. It was a noble but unrealistic goal, and 8,000 British and Polish paratroopers paid for this mistake in death or captivity (Ryan, 1974).

Montgomery and his staff demonstrated all eight of the group think factors in their flawed decision-making process. These factors will be identified and discussed using examples from the European fall campaign of 1944 and the FBI fiasco at Waco in the spring of 1993.

Group Think in 1944

1. The British were convinced that their paratroopers were the best in the European Theater of Operations. This was based on the D-Day success of the British at Sword and Gold beaches versus the American difficulties around Omaha Beach.
2. One by one, contraindicators of success surfaced. Each in turn was ignored. (a) When it was learned that the radios they had used in North Africa would not work in the humidity around the trees and tall buildings of Arnhem they rationalized this by saying that they would not need radios. (b) It is sound practice to drop airborne

units as close to their target as possible. That translates into less than a mile. When a drop zone was found 8 miles from the target, the British decided that they would have to run faster. (c) It was learned that due to a shortage of aircraft, all of the men and equipment necessary for the mission would be dropped over 3 days rather than 1 day. It was decided that they probably did not need all that equipment immediately.

3. The attitude was that the mission was right. It would save lives and end the war by Christmas. They overlooked the mechanics of the mission to focus upon what success would mean.

4. The enemy was characterized as old men and young boys on bicycles. The most recent aerial intelligence photos showing a Panzer Division with a Field Marshall present were discounted as only one group of photos. Because the previous photos did not show tanks, those there now were said to be unserviceable.

5. The British Intelligence officer who pressed for the aerial photos to be given greater consideration was recommended for a psychiatric examination.

6. No one would tell Monty that their radios from North Africa would not transmit their maximum range of 8 miles in Europe. North Africa, like most deserts, was dry, flat, empty, and arid. Holland had humidity, hills, homes, and shrubbery. As a result, later air drops of men, supplies, and equipment fell into the hands of the Germans.

7. The attitude was, "We are the British Army. We can cover 63 miles in 2 days over the carpet of U.S. Airborne units." Those who asked if this carpet would consist of live or dead paratroopers were ignored (Ryan, 1974).

8. By all accounts, several British Army staff members isolated others who had doubts. The commander of the Polish paratroopers, General Stanislaw Sosabowski, voiced his concerns to the British Commander, General Browning, who did not pass them on to anyone. At Waco, Gary Noesner tried to communicate the disfunctioning of the FBI response to the on-scene commander who did not listen.

In the end, the Arnhem mission failed. The airborne units captured most of the bridges intact. Those the Germans destroyed were slowly replaced by pontoon bridges. Other obstacles, like thousands of cheering liberated Dutch civilians, delayed the 63-mile, 2-day dash. It took over a week. During this week, the Germans moved reinforcements into the corridor and shot down additional waves of paratroopers and their supplies. The British and Polish losses exceeded 8,000 men, 80 percent of their force. American losses were also very high and the war waged on until spring 1945 (Ryan, 1974).

What Went Wrong at Waco, Phase I

The material about the Bureau of Alcohol, Tobacco, Firearms and Explosives (ATF) at Waco has been drawn from their report and interviews of agents who participated in the investigation and the assault (Report of the Department of the Treasury, 1993). Not all of the eight symptoms identified by Janis were present among the ATF. However, enough were there to ensure failure of the decision-making process.

1. Their illusion of *invulnerability* was based upon the recent history of successful ATF raids against gun dealers around the South. They had spent a lot of money bringing the people from around the country. They trained for days at Ft. Hood. They had just solved the Twin Towers bombing.

2. The command staff rejected intelligence from their undercover agent Rodriguez who knew first hand of the telephone call to Koresh warning him of the raid. Rather than cancel the operation, they dealt with his information by moving faster; still Koresh had 40 minutes to prepare for the raid.

3. Because of the allegations about Koresh abusing children the attitude developed that his *immoral* behavior had to be punished. ATF was going to do this through their dramatic and newsworthy raid rather than quietly arresting him in Waco where he went regularly to dine and buy weapons.

4. A basic tenant of military operations is that the attacking force should outnumber the defenders by three to one. The ATF had 75 in their team. This was about equal the number of adults in the compound. The ATF believed that the women would not shoot. Even if they did, ATF believed that they were better shots, better armed, and still had the element of surprise.

5. Evidence of direct pressure on members who expressed strong arguments against group stereotypes was not reported in the findings of the investigators or during the interviews. However, enough is known about the other elements to suggest that the group think process had its effect.

6. Self-censorship was evident by the commander's rejection of intelligence from the lookout across the road from Mt. Carmel who reported that none of the men were working outside. Instead, everyone was inside. This information confirmed what Rodriguez had told them. Koresh knew something was up. Further, the on-scene commanders had specific orders from Washington to cancel the raid if they lost the element of surprise. All of these factors and orders were ignored.

7. Information on the issue of a shared sense of unanimity is not to be found in the report or participant interviews.
8. To make matters worse, the report states that those who were to lead the raid isolated themselves from intelligence that contraindicated the success of their plan. Like the British some 50 years before, they were so committed to the operation that they refused to consider the possibility of failure. No one asked the tough "why" questions.

On February 28, 1993, the ATF suffered a 43 percent casualty rate that included the deaths of four of their agents (ATF Report, 1993). They were relieved. The Federal Bureau of Investigation (FBI) inherited this failure and turned it into a disaster.

What Went Wrong at Waco with the FBI, Phase I

To fully understand how such a fine organization could err so badly, one must view the involvement of the FBI in 1993 against a backdrop of its crisis management history.

The FBI has been the premier law enforcement agency in the United States, if not the world, for many years. It has worked and solved major cases like the Lindbergh kidnapping. It tracked down John Dillinger and his peers to bring their reign of terror to an end. More recently the Ku Klux Klan (KKK) met its demise at their hands. These major cases were worked by using a management system that included a proven leader. This crisis manager was selected by, and reported to, FBI headquarters. He was supported by a staff from around the country. The local Special Agent in Charge (SAC) had the equivalent military rank of Major or Lieutenant General. He was subordinate to this headquarters crisis team. The SAC, in whose division the crime was being investigated, provided administrative support. This system worked so well that someone decided to change it. Someone decided that every FBI SAC was a crisis manager, they just needed some training. Crisis managers were selected by site and status and geography rather than aptitude and ability. This is as sound as stating that every general is a Pershing, Patton, or Chesty Puller, they just need some training.

To implement this change in the 1970s, crisis response teams from each field office came to the FBI Academy for special training. Typically, these teams trained in groups of four or five at a time. This training usually involved a few days of lecture followed by a command postexercise (CPX) where the SAC directed his team to resolve the CPX. It became apparent that members of the SWAT team could fulfill their responsibilities as could the crisis negotiators and others on the team. Time and time again, SACs, who may have been good administrators, made mistakes in the presence of their peers. Some mistakes were minor, others were major, but they all were embarrassing.

Given these training problems, one would think that when faced with a crisis the FBI would send a crisis manager from headquarters to assist or more effectively direct the local and imported talent. Instead the local, and possibly inexperienced or inept, SAC was given two sophisticated teams from headquarters to manage as the on-scene crisis managers.

The creation and fielding of a few dozen members of a super SWAT team from Quantico, known as the Hostage Rescue Team (HRT), to deal with the crisis has aggravated this leadership vacuum. The SAC now had the commander of the HRT to assist him. This person has the military rank equivalent of a Brigadier General. The FBI also sends a smaller negotiations team that is composed of experienced negotiators from Quantico and field offices. It is called the Crisis Negotiations Team (CNT). The leader of this team is the equivalent of a Lt. Colonel.

FCI Talladega, Alabama, 1991

When this mix was tried during the hostage siege at the Federal Correctional Center at Talladega, Alabama, it seemed to work well. In the final moments of the crisis, as the HRT made its approach, the CNT kept the inmates on the phone. When an inmate lookout saw the HRT approaching he alerted his leader who asked the FBI negotiator about this. As Scotland Yard did with the terrorists at the Iranian Embassy during spring 1980, so did the FBI at Talladega in 1991. In both cases, the negotiator told their adversaries that no tactical move was being made. They continued negotiating. Like the London Model of the Special Air Service and Scotland Yard, the HRT and CNT also succeeded. The siege ended without injury to a hostage or FBI responder. Unfortunately, the leadership of the HRT saw this as a victory for the CNT over the HRT rather than a victory for the FBI team. The role of the CNT was ignored or negated and an attitude developed within the leadership of the HRT that unless they could prove they could resolve a stand-off without the assistance of the CNT element, their continued funding was in jeopardy.

As every negotiator knows, to be effective we must negotiate from a position of strength. That position is provided by an on-site, well-positioned, and professional tactical element.

Ruby Ridge, Idaho, 1992

In August 1992 dozens of agents from the HRT one negotiator from Quantico with assistance from four field office negotiatiors responded to the siege at Ruby

Ridge where Bill Degan, a Deputy U.S. Marshall, had been killed by right-wing radicals. Typical of right-wing confrontations with the law, the initial violation was minor when compared to the consequences. What began as a federal firearms act violation over the sale of a sawed-off shotgun by Randal Weaver turned into the killing of Deputy Bill Degan, and the deaths of two members of the Weaver family at their cabin on Ruby Ridge in far northern Idaho.

After the killing of Degan, the FBI was called in. It made a bad situation worse. Without giving Weaver the opportunity to surrender, snipers from the HRT were positioned and told that they had the authority to shoot any male who appeared outside of the cabin with a weapon. Randy Weaver and his associate Kevin Harris soon appeared outside the cabin with weapons. Weaver went to examine the body of his dead son Samuel whom he had placed in a small berthing shed on the property. He was shot and wounded by the HRT. As he ran toward the cabin a second shot was taken. This round wounded Kevin Harris, went through Harris, and killed Vicky Weaver, the wife of Randy Weaver. Now wounded, with his son and wife dead, Randy Weaver was contacted by the negotiator. The initial contacts by the negotiator were fruitless. As the siege continued, it was learned that Weaver regularly listened to the radio commentator, Paul Harvey, and respected a colorful former Army Colonel named Bo Gritz. The FBI used Harvey and Gritz as intermediaries who convinced Weaver that he could surrender without being shot (Strentz and Barzelatto,1996). Unfortunately, as at Talladega, the leadership of the HRT saw this as a victory for the CNT rather than a victory for the FBI. They again negated the effectiveness of negotiations or the negotiators.

An internal investigation into this incident was initiated by the FBI. A cover-up followed. However, it was not discovered until the summer of 1993. It resulted in several indictments and many early retirements from the FBI. But, before the cover-up was discovered and the problems could be corrected, the leadership of the HRT, their attitude toward negotiations, and the ill-conceived crisis management process of the FBI responded to the ATF failure at Waco, Texas, in February 1993.

What Went Wrong at Waco with the FBI in 1993, Phase II

Some suggest that the concept of group think is not an appropriate explanation for the management decisions at Waco. They said, and told the Senate Committee, that one must add the effect of arrogant on-scene and headquarters leadership that initially ignored and eventually eroded or isolated opposition to their action-oriented solution (Dennis, 1993; Heymann, 1993; Smerick, 1996; Stone, 1993). Like the allied command in fall 1944, they were determined to deploy the elite force that was waiting in the wings. Any statements or suggestions to the contrary were disregarded.

The performance of the FBI leadership at Waco was a disgrace. Inept, arrogant, and ignorant commanders caused the HRT and the CNT to work against each other rather than coordinate their efforts as a crisis management team (U.S. Congress House Committee on Government Reform and Oversight, 1996). This rift devastated the morale of the FBI and continues to haunt the agency (Shannon, 1996).

The dynamic effect of group think was played out against the background of the earlier incidents at Talladega and Ruby Ridge.

1. *The illusion of invulnerability* clouded the thinking of the leadership of the HRT. The HRT has an esprit de corps that, though commendable, exceeded reality. They believed they were the elite of the elite. They were the American ninjas. This spirit led to excessive optimism and an attitude that they could do no wrong.

2. *Reliable indicators of failure* went unheeded. Weather forecasts in the United States are not a secret. They were not classified on April 19, 1993, in Waco. On the morning of the assault, an attack that relied heavily on the effect of tear gas, the U.S. Weather Service issued a warning that Waco would have 30-mile per hour winds. This warning went unheeded. Perhaps the HRT and crisis scene leadership believed that the wind would not affect FBI tear gas. Even if it were not for the wind, listening devices had revealed that the Branch Davidians had an ample supply of gas masks.

3. Koresh was a bad person who had killed federal agents. *The FBI is the most moral component* of the U.S. Department of Justice, if not the entire U.S. government. There was an unsubstantiated belief that Koresh was abusing children. He was immoral. Like the ATF before it, the FBI was determined to bring him to justice. The ATF search warrant alleged that he was manufacturing and selling drugs and making many illegal weapons. He and his followers had shot and killed four ATF agents. Vernon Wayne Howell, also known as David Koresh, was as bad a person as the FBI had encountered in a long time. On the other hand, the FBI is as good as people can get.

4. It was commonly believed that anyone who would follow an immoral person like David Korech had to be *ignorant, or physically and morally weak*. Because of their superior attitude, the on-scene and HRT leadership believed that when faced with the omnipotent power of the FBI the Davidians would immediately surrender. It was believed that the Davidians would run from the compound into the arms of, and follow orders from, the FBI.

Given items one through four and the fatigue of a 24/7 deployment during this 53-day siege, the following conditions developed.

5. Some of the negotiators were *pressured to agree* with a tear gas plan. Those who might have objected and others who stood up to the HRT leadership had been sent back to Quantico or to the prison riot in Ohio. Those from Quantico and other dissenters who remained were ignored. To ensure the failure of the negotiations process the leadership of the HRT induced the on-scene commander to allow them to undercut their progress. When hostages were released, the powder to the compound was turned off. When others came out, tanks were used to destroy Davidian property, their vehicles, boats, cars, motorcycles, and their home. Simply stated, when the negotiators succeeded in getting people out, in convincing Koresh to release innocent hostages, Koresh and his followers who arranged for the release were repeatedly punished.

6. Those frustrated negotiators, who like the HRT had been at Waco for 53 days, came under direct pressure from the condescending command presence of the HRT, haughty headquarters hierarchy, and on-scene command staff. Their doubts were censored. *Some went along to provide a united FBI front* and finally approved the use of tear gas. Disagreement continues on the issue of the CNT agreeing to "a" tear gas plan versus "the" tear gas plan that was eventually and tragically implemented.

7. With the opposition removed from the scene or neutralized, the tear gas plan was sent to Washington for approval of the Attorney General. *The leadership had achieved a sense of unanimity.*

8. Finally, the physical placement of the negotiators miles from the site with the HRT on scene created the impression that *the negotiators were not part of the FBI crisis management team.* When negotiators visited the forward command post they were subjected to shabby and very unprofessional treatment by their FBI tactical peers who wanted to teach the Davidians a lesson.

Given these factors, it is no wonder that on April 19th, the FBI commanders ordered tear gas during a windstorm against people they knew had gas masks and had little to gain by walking out. The initial tear-gas plan failed; the Davidians still refused to follow the FBI surrender script. The HRT command decided to use the tanks to open large holes in the building as they fired 400 ferret rounds into their home. It was thought by the commanders that the Davidians would run through the holes into the arms of the federal forces, those who had first tried to shoot them, later crushed their cars, then tried to gas them, and were now busy firing a tear gas ferret round each minute for 6 hours at them while destroying the home they had so lovingly constructed (U.S. Congress, House, 1996).

They knew the Davidians were desperately dedicated to a demigod who, like Jim Jones in Guyana, was ready, willing, and able to lead them to their deaths.

The FBI Studies Their History

The tragedy at Waco is compounded if we do not study and learn from our history (Santayana, 1905). Since Waco the FBI has changed its crisis response procedures. It now practices what we preached for so many years. The success that resulted from these changes was demonstrated during the Freeman standoff in Jordan, Montana, in the spring of 1996. You may recall that it lasted almost twice as long as the 1993 Waco siege. The only casualty was an FBI agent who was driving too fast on a dirt road when his vehicle overturned.

This reorganization involves a dozen FBI on-scene crisis commanders who have been selected for their leadership abilities rather than their geographic location or administrative assignment. They have been given special training, with regular updates, in the interdisciplinary practice of crisis command and control functions. Other changes include the rotation of *all* personnel during a crisis callout. In addition, and at long last, the CNT and the HRT have been enlarged and are under the same commander, assigned to headquarters, and working at Quantico.

Janis identified the social-psychological phenomena of group think and laid out a process by which leaders can avoid this predicament. His recommendations are much shorter than the symptoms.

Avoiding This Disaster

Listed below are remedies, identified by Janis, that can and should be considered by a group leader, as well as group members, to help prevent evil and encourage "Good men to do or say something."

1. In an effective problem-solving group, each member, including the leader, must respect the others' competence. An open climate must be encouraged and rewarded. Rank must be ignored.
2. The group's priority should be a critical appraisal to achieve a solid solution not group cohesion to achieve unanimity. The group must not be isolated from facts and constructive criticism.
3. Like a Supreme Court decision, a minority view is respected, *written*, and should accompany the final decision. Critical observers must be appointed. Someone must ask, the tough why questions. "Why won't this plan work?" "Why are we doing this?" Their views must be given an open and objective hearing.
4. A good leader must be mature and secure enough to *suspect not reward* unanimity. (Remember General Patton: "If we are all thinking the same way then someone isn't thinking.")
5. Loyal group members rock the boat rather than stand idly by and allow it to sink.

An appropriate model to avoid the disaster of group think is discussed by Janis as he describes the work of the Kennedy Cabinet, when the men who erred during the 1961 Bay of Pigs decision-making process succeeded a year later in the Cuban Missile Crisis (Janis, 1972).

Kennedy encouraged a loyal opposition. To avoid pressuring the working group into making a recommendation that they might believe he wanted, he absented himself from many of the meetings. Rank was ignored to favor an open climate for peers to present their views and challenge the ideas of others.

The group objectively reviewed all of the available facts. Each member was asked to play the role of an objective critical observer. Contraindicators of success were impartially examined. In fact, members of the opposition, Republicans, were invited to share their views (Janis, 1972).

When managers involve a knowledgeable group in the decision-making process, they will make better recommendations than when they work alone (Covey, 1990; Draft, 1986, 1991; Drucker, 1986; Gerloff, 1985; Haimann, 1970; Stone, 1993). Managers must keep their eyes on the objective, a good decision. Personal friendships and pressures to conform must be put aside. The coming years are sure to bring more crises like Ruby Ridge and Waco. It is not a matter of if they will happen, but where, and when.

Remember what General Dwight D. Eisenhower said to his staff on May 15, 1944:

> I will emphasize but one thing. I consider it to be the duty of anyone who sees a flaw in this plan not to hesitate to say so. I have no sympathy with anyone, whatever his station or rank, who will not book criticism. (D'Este, 1983)

His style of leadership and words of wisdom ensured the success of the greatest invasion in the history of man. His attitude toward subordinate participation is as valid today as it was in 1944. The question for decision makers today is, Do you want to emulate Patton and Eisenhower or follow the lead and example of Field Marshal Montgomery?

Another crisis is coming and it will bring changes. These changes will be peaceful if we are trained. They can be positive if we are prepared. We can alter the character and effects of the crisis, but we cannot alter its inevitability (Kennedy, 1964).

Today, as in Colonial times, it is necessary for good men to do something to avoid the triumph of evil. Good and honorable men rock the boat—they do not let it sink.

References

Covey, S. (1990) *Seven Habits of Effective Leaders*, Simon and Schuster, New York.
Dennis, E. S. G. (1993) Evaluation of the Handling of the Branch Davidian Standoff in Waco, Texas, February 28 to April 19, U.S. Department of Justice, Washington, DC.

D'Este, C. (1983) *Decision at Normandy*, Konecky and Konecky, Old Saybrook, Connecticut.

Draft, R. (1986) *Organizational Theory and Design*, West, St. Paul, Minnesota.

Draft, R. (1991) *Management*, Dryden Press, Ft. Worth, Texas.

Drucker, P. (1986) *The Frontiers of Management: Where Tomorrow's Decisions Are Being Shaped Today*, Truman Talley Books, New York.

Gerloff, E. (1985) *Organizational Theory and Design: A Strategic Approach to Management*, McGraw-Hill, New York.

Haimann, T. (1970) *Management in the Modern Organization*, Houghton Mifflin, Boston.

Heymann P. (1993) Lessons of Waco: Proposed Changes in Federal Law Enforcement, U.S. Department of Justice, Washington, DC.

Janis, I. L. (1972) *Victims of Group Think*, Houghton Mifflin, Boston.

Kennedy, R. F. (1964) Speech before U.S. Senate.

Recommendations of Experts for Improvements in Federal Law Enforcement after Waco (1993) U.S. Department of Justice, Washington, DC.

Report of the Department of the Treasury (1993) Investigation of Vernon Wayne Howell, U.S. Government Printing Office, Washington, DC, September.

Report on the Events at Waco, Texas, February 28 to April 19, 1993 (1993) The Department, Washington, DC.

Ryan, C. (1974) *A Bridge Too Far*, Simon and Schuster, New York.

Santayana, G. (1905) *John Bartlets' Book of Famous Quotations*, Little, Brown and Company, Boston, 1980.

Shannon, E. (1996) In the Loneliest Spot, *Time*, Vol. 148, No. 24, p. 42.

Smerick, P. (1996) Personal interview, Manassas, Virginia, November 15.

Stone, A. A. (1993) Report: To Deputy Attorney General Philip Heymann, Report and Recommendations Concerning the Handling of Incidents Such as the Branch Davidian Standoff in Waco, Texas.

Strentz, T. (2006) *Psychological Aspects of Crisis Negotiations*, CRC Press, Boca Raton, Florida.

Strentz, T., and Barzelatto, V. (1996) Negotiating with Extremists, *Law and Order*, October.

U.S. Congress, House Committee on Government Reform and Oversight (1996), Investigation into the Activities of Federal Law Enforcement Agencies toward the Branch Davidians: Thirteenth Report, U.S. Government Printing Office, Washington, DC.

U.S. Department of Justice (1993) Evaluation of the Handling of the Branch Davidian Standoff in Waco, Texas, U.S. Government Printing Office, Washington, DC.

Creative Criteria for Constructive Deviation from Crisis Negotiation Guidelines

22

THOMAS STRENTZ AND RAY BIRGE*

Introduction

All hostage situations involve varying degrees of crisis; some are clearly more dangerous than others and expose hostages, the negotiators, the tactical team, and innocent bystanders to myriad levels of peril. The greater the threat, the greater is the need for the authorities to perform error free. One of the most dangerous hostage situations involves a hostage taker who is mentally ill, has a history of violence, and is armed with a bomb (Strentz, 1986, 1991). Because he has a bomb the possibility of an accidental explosion is always a concern. This was the issue with the hostage taker, James Lee, at The History Channel in Silver Spring, Maryland, on September 1, 2010. As a hostage taker, he fit all three of the categories listed above. Response to these types of incidents, whether they have been resolved successfully or unsuccessfully, has resulted in the development of guidelines on how to react during these crisis situations.

The following will provide an overview of the development of crisis negotiations in the United States. In the past, some of the guidelines hostage negotiators were taught were thought by many to stifle any improvisation when the necessity arose. This chapter will provide commanders and negotiators with some criteria and guidelines so they can "creatively" deviate from established crisis negotiation guidelines when absolutely necessary.

The profession of crisis negotiations is more an art than a science. It is dynamic and in a constant state of modification. Like other professionals, we learn new techniques and daily modify old tactics (Birge, 2010).

Landover Mall

In Maryland, Leonard Thomas Dunmore (known as Lennie), was a young, dangerous Paranoid Schizophrenic who had been arrested and institutionalized for threatening to kill the President of the United States. He fit the profile

* Ray Birge, MA, NA, Retired/Captain from the Oakland Police Department (California).

of being one of the most dangerous types of hostage takers when he "held" several hostages in the offices of the Maryland Employment Commission and then told authorities he had a bomb. Again, we have this dangerous triad.

He was in the reception area, on the second floor of the Landover Mall, on the Beltway that surrounds Washington, DC. Dunmore could not see his hostages, but he knew he had people trapped in the back offices. He completely controlled normal access to, and exit from, this location.

During the standoff, police interviewed Dunmore's neighbors. They had recently reported several small explosions in nearby vacant lots. The police concluded that Dunmore had been practicing with his bombs. A search of his home produced bomb paraphernalia consistent with his claims. They determined his device was probably real. They later learned it was and detonated it in the parking lot.

During this incident, officials in charge made a critical decision that violated "normal" hostage negotiation guidelines. While the tactical team helped the hostages escape, the negotiator went "face-to-face," in an unprotected position in a hallway, with Dunmore, who was holding his bomb.

Part of the plan was for the negotiator to distract Dunmore as they sat, drank coffee, and talked. Dunmore could not see or hear the hostages from this position. While he and the negotiator talked about the Communist menace, the hostages escaped (Spaulding, 1993).

Eventually, Dunmore came to trust the negotiator enough to deactivate the bomb and surrender. In this case the ploy worked: as the negotiator talked, the hostages walked. Although the goal of resolving the siege without the loss of human life was achieved, many people asked the question, "Was it due to good procedure, or blind luck?" In this case, the highly skilled negotiator accurately assessed the subject and made his own good luck.

One thing is known, the decision was made after considerable discussion, and with the benefit of experience. It may have succeeded because the commanders, special weapons and tactics (SWAT) team, and the negotiator, then Corporal William Hogwood of the Prince Georges County, Maryland, Police Department, followed "logical" procedures. These were based on specific elements unique to this incident and suspect, even though they deviated from the normally accepted hostage negotiations practices (Hogwood, 2010).

Long Ago and Far Away

The cataclysmic event that spawned police crisis management teams, including tactical and negotiations teams, can be traced to the 20th Olympiad held in Munich, Germany, in September 1972. The Federal Republic of Germany intended this Olympiad to be in stark contrast to the 1936 games, also hosted by Germany under the Nazi regime of Adolph Hitler.

Tragically, the Palestine Liberation Organization (PLO) had other ideas for the 20th Olympiad. Their barbaric behavior during the sacred and peaceful games cast a shadow upon, and significantly altered our perceptions of, and relations with, many Middle Eastern nations.

This crime left one German police officer, nine Israeli Olympic athletes, and eventually all eleven Middle Eastern Terrorists dead (Fulton, 1976).

According to the police officer in charge of the German response:

> Nothing worse can happen to a Chief of Police than to have a highly politically motivated terrorist attack take place before the eyes of the world during a peace festival of the youth of the whole world. (Schriber, 1973)

It is difficult, if not impossible, for those who were developing policies and practices during these years to convey our complete and total revulsion to this act of terrorism. The world had been tricked. Some very inadequate adversaries made us look foolish. We were caught napping.

The reaction of the free world to this event was dramatic and effective. It was the law enforcement equivalent of the sneak attack on Pearl Harbor, the Australian experience at Gillapoli, and the British disaster at Scapa Flow.

Aside from Pearl Harbor, almost 50 years earlier, and more recently September 11, 2001, no single event in the recent history of the United States so welded the resolve of our nation to exact revenge as did the terrorist acts in Munich in September 1972. Law enforcement personnel from around the world were psychologically devastated and professionally motivated to ensure those responsible would be punished. Even more significantly, we were motivated to ensure such an event could never, and would never, happen again.

A New Direction

Americans worked with the English, the Australians, and other allies in war. Now, law enforcement joined with forces across the seas and around the world to challenge and defeat international terrorism. Prior adversaries, the Germans, Japanese, and Italians, became allies against the Middle Eastern menace.

Within this historical perspective, programs to teach police new methods in special tactics were developed. New terms, such as SWAT and HNT (Hostage Negotiation Team), became the "buzzwords" of the times.

Judicial Hindsight

In 1975, the Federal Bureau of Investigation (FBI) was reminded that we live in a litigious society. Four years earlier, on October 4, 1971 (1 year before

Munich), the FBI became involved in a domestic dispute in Nashville, Tennessee, that turned into an aircraft hijacking. It ended with a double homicide and suicide in Jacksonville, Florida. As a result of their role, the FBI became a defendant in a wrongful death suit. The plaintiff alleged that the "chief FBI agent had been negligent in handling the situation and had thereby caused the deaths" (*Downs v. United States*, August 8, 1975).

In 1975, 3 years after Munich, a federal judge awarded damages to the plaintiffs. In doing so he said, "the FBI was clearly unreasonable in turning what had been a successful waiting game, during which two persons safely left the plane, into a shooting match that left three persons dead" (*Downs v. United States,* 1975). He took little note, nor did he care to remember, that the technique of utilizing time, now a common ploy with hostage negotiators, had not been developed in 1971. The court held us responsible for tactics developed after the event but before their decision. How much more logical is it to hold us responsible today for current policy of other departments?

At the beginning of every Police Hostage Negotiators' Update Course for senior negotiators held in San Jose, California, the students are asked to share crisis incidents, including outcomes and any resulting lawsuits. Typically, the policies and practices of police departments that have been sued are more progressive than those that have not. It is interesting to hear students remark, "We have not been sued so our policy is not as well developed as that of..." Or better yet, "Our boss still thinks the best way to resolve a crisis incident is to cut overtime and send in the SWAT team" (San Jose, 2010).

It seems to be a matter of pay now or pay later. Or more accurately, train now or pay later. Training police crisis management personnel is like buying insurance. While one hopes never to need the protection, it can be invaluable and will save lives at the scene and dollars before the docket (Spaulding, 1993). The assumption is that you are training the right people in the right tactics (Birge, 2010).

The Spanish philosopher Santayana said "Those who do not learn from their history, are condemned to repeat it" (Santayana, 1905). Have we learned from Munich, and the several hundred less visible but equally critical crisis incidents that have followed? Since Munich, many effective guidelines for crisis negotiators have been developed. Not every police department has decided to implement basic and updated training programs.

In the Beginning

In the beginning of American hostage negotiations, the New York City Police Department inscribed the fundamental dogma of the value of human life upon the decision-making process for crisis incident commanders. The work done by then Lt. Frank Bolz and Sgt. Harvey Schlossberg was based upon the tenant that our purpose is to "save lives." They formulated the foundation for all subsequent negotiator training programs to follow (Bolz, 1979; Schlossberg and Freeman, 1974).

The foundation for negotiations, formulated in New York City, was modified to fit local needs for New Scotland Yard, New South Wales Police Department, the Royal Canadian Mounted Police, the Special Operations and Research Staff (SOARS) Unit of the FBI, and many others. With experience it grew into a series of training programs presented around our nation. On the West Coast, the San Francisco and Oakland Police departments, assisted by Dr. Harvey Schlossberg, developed their own programs. San Jose State University became the primary host for hostage negotiation training with Dr. Schlossberg as the primary instructor. These programs grew and have undoubtedly saved hundreds of lives, thousands of careers, and millions of dollars.

We've Come a Long Way, Baby

Initially, there were about a dozen basic principles, some based upon experience, others based upon "common sense." These tenets included imperative injunctions like "never" do certain things, or "always" do others. Additionally, not all the players subscribed to the same doctrines. For example, some agencies taught that one should never go face-to-face with the hostage taker. Others taught that face-to-face was both practical and effective. Some taught one, then because of a negative experience, changed their minds. Dr. Schlossberg has never forgotten an experience with an armed suspect in a residence that forever changed his perspective about going face-to-face. He now says face-to-face is a dangerous and undesirable tactic (Schlossberg, 1988).

After two decades of crisis negotiation experience, we have learned some new guidelines. Perhaps the most significant, and the very essence of this chapter, is that we "never say never" and we do not say "always." We are far more likely to express guidelines in terms of "avoid" or "try." We have also learned it is absolutely necessary to have well-defined guidelines from which commanders can approve negotiators' deviations in a very deliberate and well-thought out manner. When operating under stress without a "yardstick," it is easy to lose track of our very basic guidelines.

Making the Decision to Deviate

The decision to deviate from guidelines sounds a bit ominous as it should. It places a heavy burden on command that may cost lives and place organizations in serious financial jeopardy. Deviation from policy does not imply capricious or whimsical decision making. It must be made thoughtfully, rationally, and objectively. It is imperative that the decision to deviate be made within the structure set out below and without the effect of group think (Chapter 21).

Well-thought-out policy, based upon experience and the current "standard of care," is everyone's best friend. It sets in motion a procedure to minimize the stress and chaos inherent in every crisis. It would be ideal if agencies could ensure their best-trained personnel were always immediately available in every incident. Reality and Murphy's Law suggest the initial responding personnel will seldom be the most qualified (the specialist) to handle the incident. Policy gives everyone a starting point. These critical early decisions will often dictate the direction of events for hours to come (Dolan and Fuselier, 1989; Sacramento, 1991; Strentz, 2011).

The Decision to Deviate

Every policy must provide a structured process to modify or violate the guideline when sufficient intelligence indicates the guideline is not working or may exacerbate the situation. There are five steps that should be required in that process:

1. All decisions to deviate must be ratified by the commander. Decisions made at a lower level invite liability (Franscell, 1991).
2. Input from trained specialists, both tactical and negotiators, should be solicited and considered.
3. The experts must be required to be detailed in "articulating" their reasons for the creative solution that will cause them to deviate from accepted guidelines and policy. They must also specifically detail the desired alternative and the expected results. The required response categories should be structured and practiced routinely in training exercises prior to "real world" application.
4. The decision, and the reasons for the decision, should be recorded for future review. If recording the decision causes concern for the commander, perhaps it is the wrong choice (Birge, 2010). In law enforcement, if it is not written down, it did not happen.
5. Before any policy is implemented or taught, the agency's legal advisors should review and sanction its content (Franscell, 1991).

Decisions, particularly tactical decisions, must be governed by policy. Sound policy should include an acceptable method for deviation. Investing in training for crisis personnel is critical insurance. A key portion of that insurance policy is ensuring that agency policy demands any deviation from sound practices not be taken lightly. Experience suggests decisions to deviate from policy should, when possible, only be made by the commander and the specialist, and then after sufficient time has elapsed to allow significant intelligence gathering and evaluation.

Procedures for Creativity in Deviation

We have learned that not all situations lend themselves to standard negotiations procedures (Strentz, 1991). The following criteria should be considered as part of the "expert responses" to the commander in recommending any deviation from the guidelines:

1. *Identify the guideline that applies.* The history of the guideline and why it exists should be articulated. In the case of face-to-face negotiations, a long line of bad experiences like Butte, Montana; Ottawa, Ontario; and other suicide-by-cop scenarios should be recalled. Experience has led most instructors in the field to recommend strongly against exposing negotiators to that level of danger. We do this, knowing face-to-face negotiations occasionally may be the only available means, or the better way, of communication.

   Never forget, no matter how well-intentioned a specific police agency is, if the procedure violates practice commonly applied by law enforcement in general, any negative outcome leaves the agency and the negotiator open to liability. The higher-level, more commonly practiced procedure will likely be the "standard of care" used by the courts to determine liability (Fenton, Ruud, and Kimbell, 1991).

2. *Prove why the guideline is not working or will not work.* One of the critical factors in the Lennie Dunmore case was an immediate need to rescue hostages. Because of the physical conditions of the building, a distraction was needed. While other options may have been available, one thing is certain, without a distraction the hostages remained at severe risk. Utilizing the normal telephonic communication link would not have served this purpose.

3. *Take the time to list the reason(s) why and how this ameliorated approach that deviates from standard practice will help ensure the preservation of life.* Remember the foundation for crisis negotiations is to preserve human life above all other considerations. If this modification will save time or money but raise the level of risk to hostages or our officers, it should be suspect. Again, in the Dunmore incident, the risk to the negotiator was raised. However, the trade-off was the safety of the rescuing officers and the hostages. Difficult decisions may involve dangerous options.

4. *Time, why won't waiting awhile be better?* After-action critiques often disclose that decisions to deviate have been made prematurely. A succinct explanation of the reason for the deviation should be required from the experts. Although there are several situations where time is not on our side, experience has demonstrated these situations are in the minority. The process of explaining the reasons can often prevent premature action that cannot be later undone. Sometimes while the experts verbally articulate their reasons for deviating, the commander may decide that the reasons are not so sound after all (Noesner, 2010).

5. *Specific details of the plan and what it will accomplish should be articulated.* This should involve very detailed information articulated in behavioral terms. It should include the short-term goal and identify behavior and events that will indicate success. At Landover Mall they wanted to, and succeeded in, removing innocent civilians from harm's way. They turned a hostage crisis into a barricaded gunman siege.

6. *How will we exploit our success?* The plan should include several options for exploiting any success, no matter how slight. Do not settle for one success. Have a plan to build on each small success to increase trust to further diffuse the crisis. After the successful face-to-face meeting with Hogwood, Lennie felt more confidence in his ability to trust the police. He did not realize it was only a ruse to rescue hostages. The negotiator built upon this experience to convince Lennie it was "safe" to surrender.

7. *What are the risks, and will the results be worth the danger?* This is a decision that only command can make. A team member, due to courage or personal involvement, may not be objective in the assessment of the situation. Common questions include: Are there options? Who and what is being exposed to danger? How high is the risk? Is success worth the risk? This is a case where "brain-storming" on a "situation board" may be of great value.

   During the Landover Mall incident, one fear was that the negotiator could be killed by a bomb blast. A SWAT back-up was available, with questionable capability against a bomb. The overriding factors were the need to save several hostages and the rapport developed by the negotiator.

8. *How dangerous is this crisis?* Throughout the incident, there must be a continuous assessment of the level of potential violence. With levels of emotion and new factors constantly changing the dynamics, threat levels may change throughout the incident. One key function of the negotiation team is to constantly monitor and report the level of threat.

If the hostage taker exhibits "normal" patterns that indicate the process is working, this must be communicated to command. Conversely, if the hostage taker is engaged in behavior consistent with the deterioration of the situation, command must be alerted and deviations, particularly tactical options, must be considered; see Chapters 19 and 20 (Strentz, 1991). It is during these times that negotiators are often asked to implement significant deviations from normal negotiation procedures to complement tactical efforts.

9. *What are the indicators of failure?* How quickly can a miscalculation be identified? What words or deeds will tell us our tactic is not working? This is a two-part test:
   a. What specific words or deeds will indicate failure?
   b. What specifically can we do to diffuse the mistake and get back on track?

Had Dunmore exhibited behavior that indicated a deterioration in trust, or worse, an inclination to detonate the bomb, how could they distract him long enough to save Hogwood's life?

10. *If the plan fails, what do we do next?* This is a business of "playing the odds." It most surely is not an exact science. It is unfortunate, but given the nature of the job, we know we are dealing with people in crisis, as well as some very sick minds. Sooner or later we will experience tragedy. What do we do then? This is part of the plan, but greater than the parameters of this chapter.

A final critical factor is having a plan for the mental health of your officers, all members on scene or involved, other agency personnel, the hostages, their families, and, yes, the community (Conroy, 1990; Mitchell, 1991). This is as much a part of preparation as the actual tactical plan. Those agencies that have done this have reaped great rewards (Sacramento, 1991).

Conclusion

The purpose of this chapter has been to set forth some guidelines for modifying established procedures for successfully resolving a hostage crisis. These procedures are very effecting in assisting the decision makers to so structure the changes as to avoid the trap of group think as discussed in Chapter 21. Another purpose is to reaffirm that crisis negotiation guidelines are just that—guidelines—and not set in concrete. It is equally important to instill the need for serious, structured thinking before agencies depart from lessons of the past, decisions from the courts, and large awards to plaintiffs.

It is my hope that police departments will establish policies and procedures and incorporate them in training programs. We must learn and practice proper policies, procedures, and tactics to successfully negotiate crisis situations before someone is killed and the courts force the department to pay damages now and do tomorrow what they should have done yesterday.

For every police department, a crisis negotiation incident is coming, and it will bring change. The change can be constructive, only if we are wise enough. The crisis can make us stronger, only if we care and prepare. We can plan now and affect its character, but we cannot alter its inevitability (Kennedy, 1971).

References

Birge, R. and Birge, A. (1993) Criteria for the Selection of Police Crisis Negotiators. *U.S. Negotiator*, pending publication.

Birge, R. (2010) Modification of Lecture to Post Certified Command and Hostage Negotiators Update Course, San Jose, California.

Bolz, F., and Hershey, E. (1979) *Hostage Cop,* New York, Rawson Wade.

Conroy, R. J. (1990) Critical Incident Stress Debriefing, *FBI Law Enforcement Bulletin*, February, pp. 20–22.

Dolan, J. T., and Fuselier, G. D. (1989) A Guide for First Responders to Hostage Situations, *FBI Law Enforcement Bulletin,* April, pp. 9–13.

Downs, Brent et al. v. United States of America (August 8, 1975) U.S.C. 6th Circuit, #74-1660.

Fenton, J., Ruud, W., and Kimbell, J. (1991) Negligent Training, *Labor Law Journal*, June, pp. 351–356.

Franscell, G. (1991) Modification of Lecture to California Association of Hostage Negotiators in San Diego, California.

Fulton, A. B. (1976) Countermeasures to Combat Terrorism at Major Events. Paper presented at the 18th Session of the Senior Seminar in Foreign Policy, U.S. Department of State, Washington, DC.

Hogwood, W. (2010) Personal interview with the primary police crisis negotiator of the Prince Georges County Crisis Negotiating team during the Landover Mall siege, Monterey, California.

Kennedy, R. F. (1971) Speech before the United States Senate on crisis and revolutions coming in South America.

Mitchell, J. (1991) *Emergency Services Stress*, Chevron Publishing, Ellicott City, Maryland.

Murphy's Law (Origin obscure).

Noesner, G. (2010) *Stalling for Time*, Random House, New York.

Sacramento, California (1991) Personal interviews with team leader, Lieutenant Harry Machen, and primary negotiator Bob Curry of the "Good Guys" hostage incident occurring April 4, 1991, in Sacramento, South Lake Tahoe, Nevada.

San Jose, California (2010) Tabulated and articulated responses from advanced hostage negotiators attending the Post Certified Advanced Hostage Negotiators Course(s) from 1986 to 2004.

Santayana, G. (1905) John Bartlett, *Book of Familiar Quotations*, Little, Brown and Company, Boston, 1980, p. 703.

Schlossberg, H., and Freeman, L. (1974) *Psychologist with a Gun*, Coward, McCann and Geoghegan, New York.

Schlossberg, H. (1988) Modification of lecture to Basic Hostage Negotiators Course, San Jose, California.

Schriber, M. (1973) Personal interview at the FBI Academy, September.

Spaulding, W. (1993) Personal interview with the leader of the Prince Georges County Special Weapons and Tactics Team during the Landover Mall siege, Vienna, Virginia.

Strentz, T. (1986) Negotiating with the Hostage Taker Exhibiting Paranoid-Schizophrenic Symptoms, *Journal of Police Science and Administration*, Vol. 14, No. 1.

Strentz, T. (1991) Thirteen Indicators of Volatile Negotiations, *Law and Order,* Vol. 39, September, pp. 135–139.

Strentz, T. (2011) First Responder Issues and Answers, *Crisis Negotiator,* Vol. 12, No. 3, Summer, pp. 6–9.

Hostage Issues

5

Phases of a Hostage Crisis

23

Introduction

In contrast to dictatorial governments, most Western democracies value human life well above anything else. This is an obvious by-product of a form of government whose structure and strength are dependent upon votes cast in a free and secret electoral process. This fact was clearly manifest to the world in the spring of 1980 when the Iranian Embassy in London was taken and held for 6 days by six Iraqi-sponsored terrorists. While this drama was being played out in Great Britain, a similar scenario was in its sixth month in the Middle East. The reactions of these embassies' mother countries, one a Western democracy and the other a Middle Eastern theocracy, were markedly different.

The United States

When the American Embassy in Tehran was wrested from our control and 52 American citizens became long-term prisoners, threatened with death by a domestically embattled Ayatollah, the American public was shocked. During those 444 days, a dominant thought in our lives was the fate of 52 fellow Americans who came to be called "our hostages." Churches included them in their prayers, politicians argued strategy, and Americans of every political and religious persuasion were united in their concern for the welfare and safe return of the hostages.

The Government of Iran

Our attitude stood in stark contrast to the proclamations of the Ayatollah when his London Embassy and most of its staff were taken. He announced to them that they should welcome this opportunity to die for their faith and flatly refused to negotiate on their behalf. Ultimately, the British Special Air Service and New Scotland Yard rescued these hostages.

The value we place on human life has left us open to victimization by those who do not share, but seek to exploit, our belief system. A human hostage has become a valuable asset in foreign and domestic confrontations. The victimization of the United States and other democracies has increased over the years with the problem in Tehran as the most dramatic incident. The hijacking of Kuwait Airlines Flight 422 in April 1988, provides evidence of the continued and more sophisticated use of this weapon against the airline industry and countries that seek to combat terrorism through their judicial processes.

Problem

An increase in the number of incidents, or at least an increase in the reporting of both targeted and randomly perpetrated hostage situations, has underscored the need for those who may be so victimized to prepare themselves for this ordeal. Proper training can improve one's chances for psychological as well as physical survival should one become a hostage. The studies conducted thus far on hostage survival have answered some questions but have raised others. For instance, how should victims behave to best protect their lives? What psychological strategies and training might be employed before an incident to assist potential victims in their attempts to cope with this psychologically stressful and life-threatening situation? Who are the hostage takers? Does one ever recover from this trauma (Jenkins, Johnson, and Ronfeldt, 1977; Ochberg, 1979, 1980; Strentz, 1986b; Strentz and Auerbach, 1988; U.S. Congress, 1975)?

A major problem encountered when instructing people in hostage survival is the ambiguous nature of the major variables. In many training settings, one may not know the psychological or physical strengths or weaknesses of the students. Additionally, the personality of the captor is unknown as is the setting of the captivity. The political climate may also be a factor. This chapter will deal with those variables that are known or about which something is known. Each individual must decide for himself the setting in which he is most vulnerable and in what political climate he is most likely to be involved as a hostage. Regardless of the physical or political setting, certain behaviors and roles can be generalized as usually successful. A review of hostage situations reveals what types of individuals are most commonly involved as the hostage takers. An additional limitation of this chapter is the fact that hostage survival is a skill. Thus while one can read about survival, to perfect this behavior for physical and psychological survival, one should practice these skills and understand the role to be played. The military does this very well. I lectured to the U.S. Navy Survive, Evade, Resist, and Escape (SERE) students in California and had the opportunity to spend time with several former prisoners of war (POWs) to include my uncle who was a POW after the Allied catastrophe at Arnhem, discussed in Chapter 21.

Evidence of the value of preparation for potential victims is growing. American law enforcement and banks have learned that tellers who have been trained to cope with the trauma of a robbery or a hostage situation survive with fewer resulting problems and provide better information to investigators than their untrained peers. Employees not so trained tend to become distraught and are frequently traumatized by the experience (Moore, 1980; Turle, 1981).

The challenge for trainers, and the focal point of this chapter, is to implement appropriate programs to enable potential hostages to learn how to more effectively cope with the stress of captivity.

Individual Differences in Response to Stress

The study of individual differences in anxiety level as a response to various stress situations has received considerable attention in recent years. A general finding has been that even though individual differences in trait anxiety (A trait) successfully predict who will develop excess anxiety in situations involving ego threat or threat to self-esteem or loss of control, such differences are generally unsuccessful predictors in situations involving physical dangers (Auerbach, 1973; Johnson, Dabbs, and Leventhal, 1970; Katkin, 1965; Kendall et al., 1976; McAdoo, 1971).

Studies involving physical danger have largely focused on specific situational stress (Hodges and Spielberger, 1966; Martinez-Urrutia, 1975). In all of its training simulations with potential prisoners of war, the U.S. military has not identified any individual personality factor that may predispose persons to success or failure (Nardini, 1952).

How does the prisoner of war (POW) adjust to the stresses and psychological forces of imprisonment, and are these survival skills transferable to the shorter-term civilian hostage experience? Nardini (1952) analyzed the qualities of the emotional stresses and physical factors associated with POW survival versus death. It was his opinion that emotional shock and reactive depression contributed heavily to the massive death rate early in captivity. Physical disease and the shortages of food, water, and medicine were at their highest during this period and exacerbated the psychological stress. Most men experienced bouts of apathy as do civilian hostages. These ranged from slight to prolonged, deep depressions where there was a loss of interest in living and lack of willingness or ability to marshal the powers of will necessary to combat depression and disease. One of the most disturbing features was the stress of an indeterminate incarceration. Though this has been a factor in the Middle East and was a problem when our hostages were held in our Tehran embassy, it is uncommon in the civilian setting. Equally troublesome to the civilian hostage, versus the prisoner of war, is the thought that the forces that are intent on their rescue may hasten their demise. Though this is extremely rare, it did happen on May 15, 1974, during the rescue at Ma'Alot in Israel (Jenkins et al., 1977) and on November 23, 1985, in Malta during the Egyptian military assault on the hijacked Egypt Air Flight 648 during which two-thirds of the passengers were killed. It is always on the minds of the rescuing force and a constant fear of those held hostage.

Nardini also pointed out that survival depended on the effectiveness of psychological defenses in preserving the strength of the ego and feelings of self-esteem. It was important that the survivors thought of themselves as better than their captors (Nardini, 1952). Successful defenses in this area included persistent recollections that one was an American, a Westerner, a soldier, an officer, a father, or some other acceptable ego-supporting role; many of these POW defenses apply to hostages.

The Role of Hostage

The best adjusted prisoners of war and civilian hostages survive by keeping busy and productive in nonthreatening activities. These activities constitute a role to ensure survival. The role of a hostage is one of subordinate status to the abductor. Though subordinate, it can be one of dignity, and it should be comfortable to keep stress within certain limits.

We spend our lives engaging in dignified, socially prescribed behaviors. These are called social roles, and each of us plays a variety of them daily. We do not interact with a peer the way we do with strangers. Each society directs how one interacts with parents, pilots, peers, partners, Popes, and police. Each role carries certain responsibilities and expectations. The role of son may be different from the role of daughter, even though each share the role of child, family member, citizen, and a score of other prescribed behaviors. When interacting with a parent, one must play the role of child to ensure healthy communication and respect. If a child fails to play his or her role when interacting with a parent, we say he or she is disrespectful and administer appropriate punishment. Similarly, hostages have a role, a role they must play to allow the captors their role and thus avoid unnecessary conflict. Failure to play a subordinate role in the presence of an authority figure is insubordination and will lead to conflict. I learned and played this subordinate role as a young Marine. When I interviewed our Marines who had been held hostage in Tehran, I learned their experience in "Boot Camp" contributed heavily to their psychological survival in Iran.

Hostage survival skills should be practiced to be perfected. One can give the dilemma some consideration and perhaps think of situations where one was called upon to change roles to adapt. Think of the role played as a new employee or a military recruit or a college freshman. During our lives, we all must interact with people who are different, those who choose to control, manipulate, or exploit us. We can build upon these experiences and generalize our success in these situations to that of being a hostage.

Two Campers

Consider the story of two people camping in the wilderness who hear a bear—a hungry bear—outside their tent and fear for their lives. In this high-stress situation, one frets and gives up hope while the other begins to put on a pair of tennis shoes. The first questions this activity and says, "Why bother? You cannot outrun that bear." The second responds, "I don't have to outrun that bear; I only have to outrun you." A fairly heartless story that nevertheless points out that any kind of preparation will improve one's chances of survival—and potentially will help one improve others' chances as well. If we as professionals are prepared to survive, we are in a better position to help others who have not considered survival tactics.

When dealing with hostage takers, one must recognize that they have placed themselves in the role of authority. One may not agree with this self-proclaimed status, but in this instance, might makes right. They are in the role of parent, and, as their hostage, one is placed in the role of child. Therefore, one must play a subservient role—that is, defer to their authority and play the role of hostage even while within oneself one is maintaining an awareness of one's superiority and employing coping reactions that will reduce the stress of the situation. As Shakespeare wrote, "All the world's a stage/And each of us a player on it." In a hostage situation, one is cast in the subservient role of hostage and would do well to learn the part and play it well. Proper acting means survival; improper acting could end one's career.

In interviews and books, many former hostages speak of their ability to escape mentally from the hostage experience by engaging in fantasy (Asencio and Asencio, 1983; Fly, 1973; Hargrove, 2000; Hearst, 1982; Jackson, 1980; Neihouse, 1973). Some speak of building homes in their heads, while others plan trips to various places. Some reduce stress by daydreaming the hours away, others by withdrawing into sleep. All agree that occupying the empty hours and thus dealing with the real enemy of boredom is the major problem of their ordeal (Derrer, 1985; Rahe and Genender, 1983).

Keeping to normal, everyday routines will greatly relieve stress. I have interviewed hostages who found great consolation by doing sit-ups, push-ups, or running in place. Flight attendants speak of exceptionally clean galleys while engineers take pride in navigating a perfect course. These activities, which are nonthreatening to the captor, help one escape mentally from captivity into a fantasy life or activity in which they can exercise some control. With the return of even a small measure of control to their life, their stress level decreases.

London Syndrome

Thus, the role of hostage is similar to the role of child in a family, a recruit in a training company, or a recently hired employee. Although these roles include subservience to a socially approved superior, the role of hostage is that of subservience to a social outcast. This role includes subservience but it is not limited to such behavior. Though one is subservient, one must maintain a sense of dignity, but not defiance. When Lufthansa Airlines Flight 181 was hijacked to Mogadishu, Somalia, in October 1977, the commander of that aircraft, Captain Shuman, died because he could not change roles. He could not make the switch from captain to pilot. He could not defer to the self-proclaimed authority of the lead terrorist, Zuhair Mousot Akkash, who called himself Captain Mahmould. Akkash could have been an inadequate personality who took the title of captain as a compensation for his feelings of inferiority. This inadequacy may have been sensed and exploited by Captain Schuman. Because Akkash had a weapon and could not tolerate the competition from the real captain of the aircraft, he murdered Schuman at Dubai. Schuman died, his crew was deprived of his leadership, and his family was deprived of his love. This was a tragic waste of life, a tragedy that is compounded if we do not learn from his errors. As difficult as it may be, hostages must accede to the authority of the captor and play the role of child to survive.

Since then, during the Iranian Embassy siege in the spring of 1980 in London, an embassy staffer, Abbas Lavasani, refused to compromise his dedication to the Ayatollah and continuously and passionately argued the righteousness of the Islamic revolution. Intent on martyrdom, he prolonged political discussions despite the pleas from fellow hostages for silence and was ultimately killed by his captors. This mutually antagonistic hostage–captor relationship is now called the London Syndrome. It is the opposite of the Stockholm Syndrome, a positive reciprocal relationship that was identified during a weeklong siege in the basement of a bank in Stockholm in 1973 (Strentz, 1979). This hostage coping tactic will be discussed later and in Chapter 24.

Hostage hostility, as stated above, is counterproductive. Although most people can readily understand the problems that might result from hostile behavior, moving too far in the other direction is not recommended. Diego Asencio, the U.S. Ambassador to Colombia, survived many weeks of captivity and advises that one must "Try to maintain your dignity and don't become too passive" (Asencio and Asencio, 1983). Thus, the activity of the hostage to endure survival with dignity seems simple. One must retain one's dignity but not antagonize the captors. Being too cooperative or overcompliant is also counterproductive. During a 1981 bank robbery in Rochester, New York, the only hostage ever to be shot at a deadline in the United States by the hostage taker was overcompliant. She cried, held her hands high over her head while her peers walked with their arms at their sides, said "yes sir!" while others said, "okay." Further, she answered the phone for the hostage taker and was the first to respond to his many other requests for order and obedience. He interpreted this behavior as a sign of weakness. The more she did, the more he demanded. He was playing a game with her while she was seeking to survive. Ultimately, he sent her out the door carrying a message for the police. As she cleared the door he shot her through the glass and watched her fall in the parking lot. He was then shot and killed by a Rochester police sniper.

Stockholm Syndrome

One way to survive with dignity is to understand, use, and control, a survival tactic known as the Stockholm Syndrome. This tactic draws its name from a bank robbery that turned into a 131-hour hostage siege in Stockholm, Sweden, in September 1973, in which the bank employee hostages and the bank robbers became good friends. Like this ordeal, most hostage situations include many empty hours. You should do what you are told, and do it slowly to ensure personal safety while not conveying a sense of extreme fear or enthusiasm. Do not volunteer to help, avoid hostile eye contact, and, if possible, engage the hostage takers in friendly conversation. Do not allow yourself to become a symbol of a government or a philosophy your abductors may dislike. Humanize yourself. Talk about your personal life, your role as a family member, and why you must return home to care for an ailing father, mother, child, or aunt, even if you have no relatives. During this process, you may experience the Stockholm Syndrome, a positive reciprocal relationship that develops between the hostage and hostage taker during a siege. Other publications contain a more detailed discussion of this behavior (Strentz, 1979, 1984, 1988). For the purpose of this discussion, it is important to know that this is a normal stress-induced reaction that will enhance survival. Hostage survival is enhanced by a controlled version of this relationship. The hostage who is not aware of this bonding process may engage in behavior he may later regret. If the positive feeling expressed by a hostage toward a captor is reciprocated, obviously the victim will be better off. The outcome of an incident may be affected if the reciprocation occurs without manipulation; that is, if there is subconscious genuineness to the relationship. If a victim attempts to encourage a captor to feel some attachment, it is important to allow the necessary feelings of natural warmth, empathy, and understanding to occur over time. Here again, the importance of the dictum "be yourself" is obvious (Ochberg, 1979). For a more detailed account of this phenomenon, see Chapter 24.

U.S. Marines in Tehran

The U.S. Marine Corps Embassy Guards who were held for 444 days by followers of the Ayatollah were able to improve their morale by exploiting a perceived weakness of their captor. Though this behavior can be dangerous, successful exploitation can improve hostage morale. The Marines in Tehran were threatened with immediate execution by their captors. The Marines soon learned that this threat was a bluff and began to tell their captors where they wanted to be shot. During several interviews they told me, in brief, they harassed their captors as they had been harassed in boot camp. They exploited weaknesses in their captors as their drill instructors had exploited weaknesses in them. This behavior enabled them to improve their morale, make their captivity more tolerable, and promote survival without benefit of the Stockholm Syndrome (U.S. Marines, 1981).

According to McClure (1978), other arrogant hostages were Dr. Claude Fly and Sir Geoffrey Jackson, who were so proud and influential that terrorist organizations found it necessary to remove guards who were falling under their influence. Dr. Fly was an American agronomist who was held by the Tupamaros for 208 days in 1970. The British Ambassador, Jackson, was held for almost as long. However, most hostages are not individuals of the strength of character of Fly, Jackson, or the captured Marines, and thus cannot retain an aura of aloofness during their ordeal.

The Hostage Takers

While it is difficult, if not impossible, to predict who will take hostages, certain generalizations can be drawn from previous situations. A review of aircraft hijackings reveals that those planes taken in the United States tend to have one captor while those taken overseas tend to have two or more. Further, while domestic hijackings have evolved from the early politically motivated into those who were intent on personal gain to those who were mentally ill, most foreign hijackings have been initiated by politically, religiously, or socially motivated groups or individuals.

We have seen hijackers who fit into one of several psychological categories. The politically motivated hostage taker has been rare in the United States. Those who claim political, social, or religious motivation and think they must take hostages to voice their views in a democracy tend to be mentally deranged. In those groups where mental illness is not a problem, there are a variety of motivations, levels of expertise, and degrees of dedication. One should attempt to determine the level of sophistication, education, language skills, mechanical skills, dedication, and motivation of one's abductor. While it is dangerous to underestimate the sophistication of your abductor, going to the other extreme is also unwise. Over the years, we have faced hijackers who could not find the cockpit, others who wanted the plane to land in the ocean and taxi to the airport, and some who did not know their mission because of a communications breakdown between takeoff and take-over. Remember the 2001 AA 63 "Shoe Bomber" Richard Reid who was unable to ignite his shoe.

Regardless of the type of hostage taker or the location of the siege, hostage takers have a need to talk about how they are the real victims. This psychological phenomenon is discussed in Chapter 1 in the section "Defense Mechanisms."

Types of Hostage Takers

One way to prepare for the ordeal of being a hostage is to know something about those who take hostages and thus be better prepared to cope with the demands they may make.

The Criminal Subject

1. *The Antisocial Personality*: This individual is usually the armed robber who, because of rapid police response, is trapped at the crime scene. When he learns that the police have him cornered, he takes hostages to secure his escape. He may bargain with police in an attempt to keep the money or goods from the robbery, to gain additional funds, and to find a way out of this dilemma and reach freedom. This subject can be identified by the logical nature of his demands, for example, money, food, and freedom. His hostages are usually employees and customers of the establishment and are generally unknown to him. Research has shown that he is an experienced felon and has above average education for a criminal (Graves and Strentz, 1977). He is articulate and wants to control, if not dominate, those with whom he is involved. He tends to blame others for his problems and to ratio-nalize his transgressions. As discussed in Chapter 1, he is never at fault; others cause him to hurt or rob. Furthermore, they do not need the money he has taken from them as much as he does. Some go so far as to believe that they are not stealing, they are taking what is rightfully theirs; the previous owner was just holding it for them. His behavior in a hostage situation is discussed by Lanceley in his article, "The Antisocial Personality as a Hostage Taker" (Lanceley, 1981) and in Chapter 11.

2. *Borderline Personality*: In the past, this individual was known as the inadequate personality, a term that is much more descriptive of the disorder than its present name. I prefer inadequate but the American Psychological Association (APA) did not check with me before they made the change. This is the armed felon who, because of poor or

inept planning, has seriously miscalculated his ability to rob an establishment or hijack an aircraft. His errors are almost childlike; his demands, such as a million dollars in gold or $5 bills, border on the impossible. Frequently, those he has taken hostage feel sorry for him and may negotiate for him in an attempt to help him out of this dilemma. This character was well portrayed by Tim Robbins in the movie *Cadillac Man*. He has a history of getting into difficult situations that exceed his coping ability. Generally, others feel sorry for him and provide assistance out of compassion. Left to his own devices, he can be dangerous. He does not really appreciate the inherent danger of holding hostages nor does he comprehend the logical and legal consequences of his actions. Additional information on him as a subject in a hostage situation can be found in the article, "The Inadequate Personality as a Hostage Taker" (Strentz, 1983) and in Chapter 10.

The Mentally Ill Subject

1. *The Paranoid Schizophrenic*: This is one of the more common forms of serious mental illness. His demands are frequently bizarre: a bank robber in California demanded that a truckload of bird seed be delivered to every bank in Los Angeles, another bank robber demanded that the moon be turned off. This type of individual generally suffers from hallucinations and delusions. These symptoms are discussed in Chapter 1. Verbal examples of these symptoms can take the form of bizarre and incoherent statements. He may believe he has special supernatural powers or that he is being tormented. His senses may be seriously distorted. He may hear, feel, smell, taste, or see things no one else can. Generally, he wants to tell people about his mission or his problems. The single best way to cope with this individual is to listen and be as comforting as possible without agreeing with him. This individual is probably responsible for more hostage situations, on and off aircraft, than any other captor. His behavior as a hostage taker is discussed in an article entitled "Negotiating with the Hostage-Taker Exhibiting Paranoid Schizophrenic Symptoms" (Strentz, 1986a) and in Chapter 12.

2. *Depressed Individuals*: Another mentally ill captor is the deeply depressed individual who may be suicidal. He can be identified by his quiet tones, slow speech pattern, negative outlook, and inability to see any other solution to his problem. He may kill a hostage to force the police to shoot him. His demands are generally mixed with

statements of depression and death. He talks at length about how good things were and how hopeless the future seems. His hostages may be known to him. By taking hostages he is crying out for help; he wants to be punished, but he is often willing to be talked out of his plan. Like the schizophrenic, he needs a good listener. This type of person is discussed in Chapters 14 and 15.

The Politically, Socially, or Religiously Motivated Subject

Although these individuals are rare in the United States, we see them in greater numbers elsewhere in the world. As a general rule they have carefully selected the time and place of the confrontation as well as those to be taken hostage. They want an audience to listen to their proclamations. Frequently, their hostages are tokens to be used to secure their demands. As individuals, their hostages are not important; it is what they represent or will allow them to achieve that is important. Thus, one should endeavor to listen to their claims, ask intelligent questions, and try to humanize oneself. Become a human being, not a symbol. Additionally, one should not assume they are all of the same level of intelligence, expertise, or dedication. Frequently, they are a collection of individuals who are very different. Although one of these hostage takers may be very hostile, another may be friendly and talkative. Thus, it behooves the hostage to get to know them as individuals and be as friendly as reason will allow to ensure survival with dignity. Remember that those who belong to such organizations are not necessarily similarly motivated, educated, or come from the same levels of society (Hacker, 1976; Russell and Miller, 1977; Strentz, 1981, 1988). A review of prison incidents, as discussed in Chapter 16, serves as another example of how inmates have a need to project blame onto others and portray themselves as the victims. Other types of extremists are discussed in Chapter 17.

Is It Ever Over?

Just as running a marathon results in physical exhaustion, being a hostage results in a similar level of psychological exhaustion. The stress of this experience may continue for several days and may not be resolved until the former hostage has worked through the many conflicting feelings and emotions of this ordeal. A very effective tactic used by many former hostages is to sit with a friend, a person with whom one can cry, and talk freely about the situation, one's emotions, and secret fears. This process of ventilation works for most people.

Frequently, one will experience some posttraumatic stress symptoms. These may be mild like avoiding certain places, being hypersensitive to people who resemble one's captors, insomnia, or more severe like reexperiencing or reliving the trauma. One may have symptoms of an adjustment reaction, an anxiety disorder, or the more severe posttraumatic stress disorder. According to the American Psychiatric Association, the essential feature of this disorder is the appearance of symptoms after a psychologically stressful event such as a hostage situation (APA, 2000). The most common symptoms include reexperiencing of the traumatic event; avoidance of things associated with the event, such as flying after being hijacked; the numbing of responses; increased arousal; sleeplessness; nightmares; startle responses; and a general sense of fearfulness. Also, one may feel a new sense of guilt over past psychological conflicts. Just as the running of a marathon may cause old physical injuries to act up, so the psychological stress of being a hostage may rekindle old fears and unresolved conflicts.

The best course of action for any and all former hostages to follow is to seek some professional help. Take some time to talk with someone who cares and has the professional training to help one work through the conflicting feelings of this stress.

Some former hostages expressed considerable antagonism toward their former captors and were very enthusiastic participants in the debriefing conducted by Special Agents of the FBI. They knew that by providing information on their captivity to the FBI they were taking a step toward getting even, exacting some revenge, upon those who had abused them. They were not getting mad, they were getting even. Others felt animosity toward a fellow hostage and affection for the captor. Such feelings are normal as are antagonistic attitudes toward law enforcement or others one may feel let one down and allowed this tragedy to cause such trauma. These examples are not meant to be totally inclusive but should serve to suggest the wide variety of feelings that might seem ridiculous to someone who has not been a hostage, yet they are within the common range of reactions for those who have been held.

Finally, one should recognize that being a hostage is stressful. So, the normal person will experience some postincident discomfort. It is important that the former hostage has the opportunity to build upon this trauma and emerge a stronger person from the challenge of being held rather than suffer for the rest of one's life from the aftereffects of the ordeal.

"Remember, it's not what the hostage taker does or did to you but what you do about what he does or did to you" (Rahe, 1985). Make the experience a test that was passed, not an ordeal that has condemned one to a life of suffering from the trauma. Determine now, while you are calm and unstressed, what kind of person you are. Imagine, based on your experience, how you think you will react in a hostage situation. How effectively have you played the role of a subordinate? Can you shift into that role in the future? If you habitually are fatalistic in your daily actions, plan to blend with your peers and concentrate on not standing out in the crowd. If you are one who strongly believes in controlling your own fate, think of what kinds of things you might do as a leader that will help you help yourself and your fellow hostages. Be the camper who wears running shoes so you are better prepared to assist others in the process of hostage survival.

Conclusion

It is the author's hope that this chapter and the articles referenced will enable the reader to do something positive to prepare and cope with the stress of captivity. With proper preparation one can emerge with a stronger sense of dignity and self-worth after successfully dealing with the stress of captivity. The ordeal of captivity will be a test that one has passed, not a trauma that has inflicted long-term psychological damage.

References

American Psychological Association (2000) *Diagnostic and Statistical Manual of Mental Disorders*–4th Edition Revised, APA, Washington, DC.

Asencio, D., and Asencio, N. (1983) *Our Man Is Inside*, Little, Brown and Co., Boston.

Auerbach, S. M. (1973) Trait-State Anxiety and Adjustment to Surgery, *Journal of Consulting and Clinical Psychology*, Vol. 40, pp. 264–271.

Derrer, D. (May 1985) Terrorism, Proceedings/Naval Review, 185.

Fly, C. (1973) *No Hope But God*, Hawthorn, New York.

Graves, B. J., and Strentz, T. (1977). The Kidnapper: His Crime and His Background. Unpublished research paper, Special Operations and Research Staff, FBI Academy, Quantico, Virginia.

Hacker, F. J. (1976) *Crusaders, Criminals, Crazies: Terror and Terrorism in Our Time*, Norton, New York.

Hargrove, T. R. (1980) Personal interview, CAHN conference, San Diego, California, June 2.

Hargrove, T. R. (2000) *Long March to Freedom*, Ballentine, New York.

Hearst, P. C. (1982) *Every Secret Thing*, Doubleday, New York.

Hodges, W. F., and Spielberger, C. D. (1966) The Effects of Threat of Shock on Heart Rate for Subjects Who Differ in Manifest Anxiety and Fear of Shock, *Psychophysiology*, Vol. 2, pp. 287–294.

Jackson, G. (1973) *Surviving the Long Night*, Vanguard Press, New York.

Jenkins, B. M., Johnson, J., and Ronfeldt, D. (1977) *Numbered Lives: Some Statistical Observations from Seventy-Seven International Hostage Episodes*, The Rand Corporation, Santa Monica, California.

Johnson, J. E., Dabbs, J. M., and Leventhal, H. (1970) Psychological Factors in the Welfare of Surgical Patients, *Nursing Research*, Vol. 19, pp. 18–29.

Katkin, E. S. (1965) The Relationship between Manifest Anxiety and Indices of Autonomic Response to Stress, *Journal of Personal and Social Psychology*, Vol. 2, pp. 324–333.

Kendall, P. C., Finch, A. J., Auerbach, S. M., Hooke, J. F., and Mikulka, P. J. (1976) The State-Trait Anxiety Inventory: A Systematic Evaluation, *Journal of Consulting and Clinical Psychology*, Vol. 44, pp. 406–412.

Lanceley, F. (1981) The Antisocial Personality as a Hostage Taker, *Journal of Police Science and Administration*, Vol. 9, pp. 28–34.

Martinez-Urrutia, A. (1975) Anxiety and Pain in Surgical Patients, *Journal of Consulting and Clinical Psychology*, Vol. 43, pp. 437–442.

McAdoo, W. G. (1971) The Effects of Success, Mild Failure and Strong Failure Feedback on A-State for Subjects Who Differ in A-Trait, *Dissertation Abstracts International*, Vol. 31, No. A, p. 21.

McClure, B. (1978) Hostage Survival. In M. H. Livingston, L. B. Kress, and M. G. Waneck (Eds.) *International Terrorism in the Contemporary World*, Greenwood Press, Westport, Connecticut.

Moore, J. D. (1980) Spokane's Robbery Education Training Program, *FBI Law Enforcement Bulletin*, Vol. 49, No. 11, pp. 1–5.

Nardini, J. E. (1952) The William C Porter Lecture. Psychiatric Concepts of Prisoners of War Confinement, *Military Medicine*, Vol. 7, pp. 299–307.

Neihouse, W. (1980) *Prisoner of the Jungle*, Vanguard Press, New York.

Ochberg, F. M. (1979) The Victim of Terrorism: Psychiatric Considerations, *Terrorism: An International Journal,* Vol. 1, No. 2, pp. 147–168.

Ochberg, F. M. (1980) Preparing for Terrorist Victimization. In Y. Alexander and R. A. Kilmarx (Eds.) *Political Terrorism and Business*, Prager, New York.

Rahe, R. H. (1985) Coping with Captivity, Unpublished manuscript, Uniform Services, University of the Health Sciences, Bethesda, Maryland.

Rahe, R. H., and Genender, E. (1983) Adaptation to and Recovery from Captivity Stress, *Military Medicine*, Vol. 148, pp. 557–585.

Russell, C. A., and Miller, B. H. (1977) Profile of a Terrorist, *Terrorism: An International Journal*, Vol. 1, pp. 17–34.

Strentz, T. (1979) The Stockholm Syndrome: Law Enforcement Policy and Ego Defenses of the Hostage, *FBI Law Enforcement Bulletin*, Vol. 48, pp. 1–9.

Strentz, T. (1981) A Terrorist Organizational Profile: A Psychological Role Model. In Y. Alexander and J. M. Gleason (Eds.) *Behavioral and Quantitative Perspectives on Terrorism*, Pergamon Press, New York, pp. 86–104.

Strentz, T. (1983) The Inadequate Personality as a Hostage Taker, *Journal of Police Science and Administration*, Vol. 11, pp. 363–368.

Strentz, T. (1984) Preparing the Person with High Potential for Victimization as a Hostage. In J. T. Turner (Ed.) *Violence in the Medical Care Setting*, Aspen Press, Rockville, Maryland, pp. 183–208.

Strentz, T. (1986a) Negotiating with the Hostage Taker Exhibiting Paranoid Schizophrenic Symptoms, *Journal of Police Science and Administration*, Vol. 14, pp. 12–16.

Strentz, T. (1986b) A Hostage Psychological Survival Guide, *Proceeding: Third Annual International Aircraft Cabin Safety Symposium*, Los Angeles, University of Southern California, pp. 310–321.

Strentz, T. (1988) A Terrorist Psychosocial Profile Past and Present, *FBI Law Enforcement Bulletin*, Vol. 57, pp. 13–19.

The Stockholm Syndrome

24

The Bank Robbery

At 10:15 A.M. on Thursday, August 23, 1973, the quiet early routine of the Sveriges Kreditbank in Stockholm, Sweden, was destroyed by the chatter of a submachine gun. As clouds of plaster and glass settled around the 60 stunned occupants, a heavily armed, lone gunman called out in English, "The party has just begun" (Lang, 1974).

The "party" was to continue for 131 hours, permanently affecting the lives of four young hostages and giving birth to a psychological phenomenon subsequently called the Stockholm Syndrome.

During the 131 hours from 10:15 A.M. on August 23rd until 9:00 P.M. on August 28th, four employees of the Sveriges Kreditbank were held hostage. They were Elisabeth, age 21, then an employee of 14 months working as a cashier in foreign exchange, now a nurse; Kristin, age 23, then a bank stenographer in the loan department, today a social worker; Brigitta, age 31, a loan officer at the bank; and Sven, age 25, a new employee, today employed by the national government (Lindroth, 1978). They were held by a 32-year-old convicted thief, burglar, and prison escapee named Jan-Erik Olsson (Lang, 1974). Their jail was an 11 × 47 foot, carpeted bank vault that they came to share with another convicted criminal and former cell mate of Olsson, Clark Olofsson, age 26. Olofsson joined the group only after Olsson demanded his release from Norrkoping Penitentiary (Lindroth, 1978).

This particular hostage situation gained long-lasting notoriety primarily because the electronic media exploited the fears of the victims, as well as the sequence of events. Contrary to what had been expected, it was found that victims feared the police more than they feared the robbers. In a telephone call to Prime Minister Olaf Palme, one of the hostages expressed these typical feelings of the group when she said, "The robbers are protecting us from the police." Upon release the hostages puzzled over their feelings, "Why don't we hate the robbers" (Lang, 1974).

For weeks after this incident, and while under the care of psychiatrists, some of the hostages experienced the paradox of nightmares over the possible escape of the jailed subjects and yet felt no hatred toward their abductors. In fact, they felt the subjects had given them their lives back and were emotionally indebted to them for their generosity.

Some History

Machiavelli, when writing *The Prince* in 1513, said:

> And since men, when they receive good from whence they expect evil, feel the more indebted to their benefactor. (Machiavelli, 1948)

Hostages expect their captors to abuse them. Instead their abductors give them the impression that they care for them and are protecting them from the police.

In American history we have seen ample evidence of this phenomenon. The earliest account I found occurred during the infamous raid of John Brown in October 1859. Briefly, Brown and his 21-man "Army of Liberation," that included three of his sons and five free African Americans, seized the Armory and several other strategic buildings in Harpers Ferry, Virginia. Thirty hours after the raid began most of his men had been killed or wounded. Brown, his few surviving followers, and some 30 of his original 40 hostages, remained in the fire engine house. During the course of this siege, many exchanges of food and medicine for wounded hostages took place. One exchange included hostages, Joseph Brua and the Acting Superintendent of the armory, A. M. Kitzmiller, who exited the infamous engine house to assist in the transport of wounded to safety. Upon the successful completion of this movement, Kitzmiller escaped. Brua returned to the engine house and took his place with his fellow hostages where he remained until he was rescued (Everhard and Sullivan, 1974).

Thirty-six hours after the raid began and following some 20 hours of negotiations conducted by J.E.B. Stuart for the On-Scene Commander, Col. Lee, the engine house was attacked by a dozen of the 90 U.S. Marines from the Washington, DC, Navy Yard. Because of his concern for the preservation of human lives, Lee ordered the Marines to unload their rifles and "fix" their bayonets. During the rescue, Brown was stabbed by Lt. Israel Green, USMC, and captured. All of the hostages survived the rescue (Green, 1885). One of the Marines, Private Quinn, was mortally wounded; a second, Private Rupert, was injured (Shriver, 1859).

Brown and his men were tried in Charles Town, Virginia, on charges of murder, conspiring with slaves to rebel, and treason against the State of Virginia. The attorneys for Brown put his hostages on the stand. Each reported that he had been treated well (Scott and Scott, 1988). The trial lasted 5 days. The jury found Brown guilty on all charges. The penalties assessed were life in prison for murder and treason and death for conspiring with slaves.

The Phenomenon

The Stockholm Syndrome seems to be an automatic, probably unconscious, emotional response to the trauma of becoming a victim. It dates back through many years of human reactions to the stress of captivity. Though some hostages may think it through, this is not a rational choice by a victim who decides consciously that the most advantageous behavior in this predicament is to befriend his captor. This syndrome has been observed around the world and includes a high level of stress as participants are cast together in this life-threatening environment where each must achieve new levels of adaptation or regress to an earlier stage of ego development to stay alive. This phenomenon, this positive bond, affects the hostages and the hostage taker. This positive, reciprocal emotional bond, born in, or perhaps because of, the stress of the siege environment, serves to unite its victims against the outsiders. A philosophy of "it's us against them" tends to develop. To date there is no evidence to indicate how long the syndrome lasts. Like the automatic reflex action of the knee, this bond seems to be beyond the control of the victim and the subject.

One definition of the Stockholm Syndrome takes into account three phases of the experience and describes it as follows:

> The positive feelings of the captives toward their captor(s) that are accompanied by negative feelings toward the police. These feelings are frequently reciprocated by the captor(s). To achieve a successful resolution of a hostage situation, law enforcement must encourage and tolerate the first two phases so as to induce the third and thus preserve the lives of all participants. (Ochberg, 1978a)

Though this relationship is new in the experience of law enforcement officers, the psychological community has long been aware of the use of an emotional bond as a coping mechanism of the ego under stress.

Many years ago, Sigmund Freud forged the theory of personality and conceived three major systems, calling them the *id*, the *ego*, and the *superego*. The id is man's expression of instinctual drive without regard to reality or morality. It contains the drive for preservation and destruction, as well as the appetite for pleasure (Hall, 1954).

In the well-adjusted person the ego is the executive of the personality, controlling and governing the id and the superego and maintaining commerce with the external world in the interest of the total personality and its far-flung needs. When the ego is performing its executive functions wisely, harmony and adjustment prevail. Instead of the pleasure principle, the ego is governed by the reality principle (Hall, 1954).

The superego dictates to the ego how the demands of the id are to be satisfied. It is in effect the conscience and is usually developed by internalization of parental ideals and prohibitions formed during early childhood (Hall, 1954).

Coping with reality is one function of the ego. The ego in the healthy personality is dynamic and resourceful. One of its functions is the use of defense mechanisms, a concept developed by Sigmund Freud in 1894 when he wrote "The Neuro-Psychoses of Defense." Freud conceived the defense mechanisms as the ego's struggle against painful or unendurable ideas or their effects (Freud, 1974). Since Freud, the defense mechanisms have been discussed, explained, examined, and defined repeatedly. They vary in number depending upon the author. However, they all serve the same purpose— to protect the self from hurt and disorganization (Coleman, 1995).

When the self is threatened, the ego must cope with a great deal of stress. The ego enables the personality to continue to function even during the most painful experiences, such as being taken hostage by an armed and anxious stranger. The hostage wants to survive, and the healthy ego is seeking a means to achieve survival. One avenue open is the use of defense mechanisms. The mechanism used most frequently by hostages interviewed by the author has been regression, which Norman Cameron defines as a return to a less mature, less realistic level of experience and behavior (Bellak, Hurvich, and Gediman, 1973). Several theories have been advanced in an attempt to explain the observable symptoms that law enforcement and members of the psychiatric community have come to call the Stockholm Syndrome.

In her book, *The Ego and the Mechanisms of Defense*, Anna Freud discusses the phenomenon of identification with the aggressor. This version of identification is called upon by the ego to protect itself against authority figures who have generated anxiety (Freud, 1974). The purpose of this type of identification is to enable the ego to avoid the wrath, the potential punishment, of the enemy. The hostage identifies out of fear rather than out of love (Hall, 1954). It would appear that the healthy ego evaluates the situation and elects from its arsenal of defenses that mechanism which best served it in the past when faced with trauma. The normal developing personality makes effective use of the defense mechanism of identification, generally out of love, when modeling itself after a parent.

Identification often takes place during imitative learning, as when a boy identifies with his father and uses him as a model (Coleman, 1995). Some authors have called this type of identification introjection and use the Nazi concentration camps as an example of people radically altering their norms and values (Bluhm, 1948).

According to James C. Coleman in his book, *Abnormal Psychology and Modern Life*,

> Introduction is closely related to identification. As a defense reaction it involves the acceptance of others VALUES AND NORMS as one's own even when they are contrary to one's previous assumptions. (Coleman, 1995)

He goes on to discuss the common occurrence of people adopting the values and beliefs of a new government to avoid social retaliation and punishment. This reaction seems to follow the principle, "If you can't beat 'em, join 'em" (Coleman, 1995).

Though identification with the aggressor is an attractive explanation for the Stockholm Syndrome, and may indeed be a factor in some hostage situations, it is not a total explanation for the phenomenon. This reaction is commonly seen in children at about the age of 5 as they begin to develop a conscience and have resolved the Oedipal complex. They have given up the dream of being an adult and now begin to work on the reality of growing up. This is usually done by identifying with the parent of the same sex and is generally healthy. However, when this parent is abusive, we see the identification serving the dual purpose of protection and as an ego ideal.

The Stockholm Syndrome is viewed by this author as regression to a more elementary level of development than is seen in the 5-year-old who identifies with a parent. The 5-year-old is able to feed himself, speak for himself, and has locomotion. The hostage is more like the infant who must cry for food, cannot speak, and may be bound. Like the infant, the hostage is in a state of dependence and fright. He is terrified of the outside world, like the child who learns to walk and achieves physical separation before he is ready for the emotional separation from the parent.

This infant is blessed with a mother figure who sees to his needs. As these needs are satisfactorily met by the mother figure, the child begins to love this person who is protecting him from the outside world. The adult is capable of caring and leading the infant out of dependence and fear. So it is with the hostage—his extreme dependence, his every breath a gift from the subject. He is now as dependent as he was as an infant—the controlling, all-powerful adult is again present—the outside world is threatening once again. The weapons the police have deployed against the subject are also, in the mind of the hostage, deployed against him. Once again he is dependent, perhaps on the brink of death. Once again there is a powerful authority figure that can help. So the behavior that worked for the dependent infant surfaces again as a coping device, a defense mechanism, to lead the way to survival.

On a more current note, most law enforcement officers have seen this phenomenon in the battered spouse. I recall a 1964 psychology class where the professor, Marie Emil, said people deal with difficult relationships by fight, flight, or paring. In other words, they fight with their abuser, run away, or identify with the abuser. This was well before the infamous Stockholm bank robbery. All this basically means the Stockholm Syndrome has been around for at least 100 years. We just did not recognize it until 1973.

Domestic Hostage Situations

Since 1973, law enforcement has been faced with many hostage situations. The subject–hostage bond is not always formed, yet case studies show that it is frequently a factor. As such, the Stockholm Syndrome should be kept in mind by police when they face such a situation, plan an attack, debrief former hostages, and certainly when the subjects are prosecuted.

Hostage situations seem to be on the increase. Today more than ever, police are responding to armed robberies in progress in a fraction of the time it required a few years ago. This increased skill in incident response unfortunately promotes a perpetrator's need to take hostages. Previously, the armed robber was frequently gone before the employees felt safe enough to sound the alarm. Today silent alarms are triggered automatically. Computerized patrol practices place police units in areas where they are more likely, statistically, to encounter an armed robbery. An analysis of past armed robberies dictates placement of patrol units to counter future attempts. Progress in one phase of law enforcement has created new demands in another.

The vast majority of hostage incidents are accidental. In cases such as these, it is likely the robber did not plan to take hostages. However, the police arrived sooner than anticipated and as a new form of flight, a method of escape, the now-trapped armed robber takes a hostage so he can bargain his way out.

In his desperation, the armed robber compounds his dilemma by adding kidnapping and assault charges. These considerations are initially minimal to him. His emotions are running high; he wants to buy time, and in this succeeds. Research has shown that the leader of the abductors usually has a prior felony arrest (Graves and Strentz, 1977). Therefore, though desperate, the hostage taker is not ignorant or inexperienced in the ways of the criminal justice system and realizes the consequences of his new role.

The trapped subject is outgunned and outnumbered, and with each fleeting moment, his situation becomes less tenable. Perhaps he takes hostages as a desperate offensive act, one of the few offensive acts available to him in his increasingly defensive position. Whatever his motivation, the subject is now linked with others, usually strangers, who will come to sympathize and in some cases empathize with him in a manner now recognized and understood.

The stranger—the victim—the law-abiding citizen—is forced into this life-and-death situation and is unprepared for this turn of events. Suddenly, his routine world is turned upside down. The police, who should help, seem equally helpless. The hostage may feel that the police have let him down by allowing this to happen. It all seems so unreal.

Stages of Hostage Reaction

Many hostages seek immediate psychological refuge in denial. According to Anna Freud, "When we find denial, we know that it is a reaction to external danger, when repression takes place, the ego is struggling with instinctual stimuli" (Freud, 1974, p. 42).

Hostages, in interviews with this author, frequently discuss their use of denial of reality. The findings of denial are not limited:

> As I continued to talk to victims of violence, I became aware that the general reactions of these victims were similar to the psychological response of an individual who experiences sudden and unexpected loss.
>
> Loss of any kind, particularly if sudden and unexpected, produces a certain sequence of response in all individuals. The first response is shock and then denial. (McClure, 1978, pp. 21–48)

Hostages have also repressed their feelings of fear. Frequently, these feelings of fear are transferred from fear of the hostage taker to fear of the police. Research has shown that many hostages die or are injured during the police assault phase (Jenkins, Johnson, and Ronfeldt, 1977). This is not to say that the police kill them.

Denial is a primitive, but effective, psychological defense mechanism. There are times when the mind is so overloaded with trauma that it cannot handle the situation. To survive, the mind reacts as if the traumatic incident is not happening. The victims respond, "Oh no," "No, not me," "This must be a dream," "This is not happening" (Hearst, 1987). These are all individually effective methods of dealing with excessively stressful situations.

Denial is but one stage of coping with the impossible turn of events. Each victim who copes effectively has a strong will to survive. One may deal with the stress by believing he is dreaming and will soon wake up, and it will be all over. Some deal with the stress by sleeping; this author has interviewed hostages who have slept for over 48 hours while captive. Some have fainted, though this is rare.

Most hostages gradually accept their situation but find a safety valve in the thought that their fate is not fixed. They view their situation as temporary, sure that the police will come to their rescue. This gradual change from denial to dreams of reprieve reflects a growing acceptance of the facts. Although the victim accepts that he is a hostage, he believes freedom will come soon (U.S. Congress, 1975).

If freedom does not immediately relieve the stress, many hostages begin to engage in busywork, work they feel comfortable doing. Some knit, some methodically count and recount windows or other hostages, and some reflect upon their past life. This author has never interviewed a former hostage who had not taken stock of his or her life and vowed to change for the better, an attempt to take advantage of a second chance at life. The vast majority of hostages share this sequence of emotional events—denial, dreams of reprieve, busywork, and taking stock. The alliance that takes place between the hostage and the subject comes later.

Time

Time is a factor in the development of the Stockholm Syndrome. Its passage can produce a positive or negative bond, depending on the interaction of the subjects and hostages. If the hostage takers do not abuse their victims, hours spent together will most likely produce "positive" results. Time alone will not do so, but it may be the catalyst in nonabusive situations.

In September 1976, when five Croatian hijackers took a Boeing 727 carrying 95 people on a transatlantic flight from New York to Paris, another incident of the Stockholm Syndrome occurred. Attitudes toward the hijackers and their crime reflected the varying exposures of those involved in the situation (TWA, 1976) (Alpern, 1976). The hostages were released at intervals. The first group was released after a few hours, the others a day later. The debriefing of the victims in this situation has clearly indicated that the Stockholm Syndrome is not a magical phenomenon but a logical outgrowth of positive human interaction.

TWA Flight 355, originally scheduled to fly from New York City to Tucson, Arizona, via Chicago, on the evening of September 10, 1976, was diverted somewhere over western New York State to Montreal, Canada, where additional fuel was added. The hijackers then traveled to Gander, Newfoundland, where 34 passengers deplaned to lighten the aircraft for its flight to Europe via Keflavik, Iceland, with the remaining 54 passengers and a crew of seven. The subjects, primarily Julianna Eden Busic, selected passengers to deplane. She based her decision to release or retain on the age and family responsibilities of each hostage. The remaining passengers, plus the crew of seven, were those who were single, married with no children, or those who had volunteered to remain on board, such as Bishop O'Rourke. After flying over London, the aircraft landed in Paris where it was surrounded by the police and not allowed to depart. After 13 hours, the subjects surrendered to the French police. The episode lasted a total of 25 hours for most of the passengers and about 3 hours for those who deplaned in Newfoundland.

During the months of September and October 1976, all but two of the hostages and all of the crew were interviewed. The initial hypothesis before the interviews was that those victims released after only a few hours would not express sympathy for the subjects, while those released later would react positively toward their abductors. In other words, time was viewed as the key factor.

The hypothesis was not proven. Instead, it seemed that the victims' attitudes toward the subjects varied from subject to subject and from victim to victim regardless of the amount of time they had spent as captives. Initially this seemed illogical; interviews with the victims revealed understandable reasons. It was learned that those victims who had negative contacts with the subjects did not evidence concern for them, regardless of time of release. Some of these victims had been physically abused by the subjects; they obviously did not like their abusers and advocated the maximum penalty be imposed.

Other victims had slept on and off for 2 days. This could be a form of defense mechanism of denial, a desperate ego-defensive means of coping with an otherwise intolerable event (Laughlin, 1970). These victims had minimal contact with the subjects and also advocated a maximum penalty. They may not have had distinctly negative contact, but they had experienced no positive association. Their only contact with the subjects was on the occasions when hostage taker Mark Vlasic awakened them in Paris and ordered all of the passengers into the center of the aircraft where he threatened to detonate his explosives unless the French government allowed them to depart.

The other extreme was evidenced by victims, regardless of time of release, who felt great sympathy for their abductors. They had positive contact with the subjects, which included discussing the hijackers' cause and understanding their motivation and suffering. Some of these victims told the press that they were going to take vacation time to attend the trial. Others began a defense fund for their former captors. Some recommended defense counsel to the subjects, and others refused to be interviewed by the law enforcement officers who had taken the subjects into custody (TWA, 1976).

Perhaps one of the most self-revealing descriptions of the Stockholm Syndrome was offered by one of these hijack victims:

> After it was over and we were safe, I recognized that they (the subjects) had put me through hell and had caused my parents and fiancé a great deal of trauma. Yet, I was alive. I was alive because they had let me live. You know only a few people, if any, hold your life in their hands and then give it back to you. After it was over, and we were safe and they were in handcuffs, I walked over to them and kissed each one and said, "Thank you for giving me my life back." I know how foolish it sounds, but that is how I felt. (TWA, 1976)

Yet, this feeling of affection seems to be a mask for a great inner trauma. Most victims, including those who felt considerable affection for the subjects, reported nightmares. These dreams expressed the fear of the subjects escaping from custody and recapturing them. Dr. Ochberg reports similar findings, as did the psychiatrist in Stockholm in 1973 (Ochberg, 1978b).

Again, the hostages aboard the plane developed a personal relationship with the criminals. The feelings of one hostage were expressed when she said, "They didn't have anything (the bombs were fakes), but they were really great guys. I really want to go to their trial" (TWA, 1976). This is a very different view from that of New York City Police Commissioner Michael Codd, who said in an interview, "What we have here is the work of madmen—murderers" (Newsweek, 1976). The interview with the commissioner followed an attempt to defuse a bomb left by the hijackers; the bomb killed one officer and seriously injured three others (New York Times, 1976).

By June 2008, some 34 years after the incident, all five were deported to Croatia.

The situation in 1973 in Stockholm was not unique. These same feelings were generated in the Croatian aircraft hijacking, and during the Japanese Red Army hijacking of JAL Flight 472 in the fall of 1977, and also in the hostage situation that took place at the German Consulate in August 1978 (Stoulgas, 1978). Similar reactions were observed in some passengers on TWA 847 in June 1985 where one person was slain and during the April 1988 hijacking of Kuwait 422 in which two passengers were murdered.

Isolation

But the Stockholm Syndrome relationship does not always develop. Sir Geoffrey Jackson, the British Ambassador to Uruguay, was abducted and held by the Tupamaro terrorists for 244 days. He remained in thought and actions the ambassador, the Queen's representative, and so impressed his captors with his dignity that they were forced to regularly change his guards and isolate him for fear he might convince them that his cause was just and theirs foolish (Jackson, 1973). Others, such as the American agronomist Dr. Claude Fly, held by the Tupamaros for 208 days in 1970, have also avoided identification with the abductor or his cause. He accomplished this by writing a 600-page autobiography and by developing a 50-page "Christian Checklist," in which he was able to create his own world and insulate himself against the hostile pressures around him (Fly, 1973).

According to Brooks McClure,

> In the case of both Dr. Fly and Sir Geoffrey Jackson, and other hostages as well, the terrorist organization found it necessary to remove the guards who were falling under their influence. (U.S. Congress, 1975)

Usually, the Stockholm Syndrome is a two-way street. However, most victims of terrorist or criminal abductors are not individuals of the status of Dr. Fly or Ambassador Jackson, and as such do not retain an aura of aloofness during their captivity. As yet, there is no identified personality type more inclined to the Stockholm Syndrome. The victims do share some common experiences, though.

Positive Contact

The primary experience that victims of the syndrome share is positive contact with the subject. The positive contact may be generated by lack of the expected negative experiences (i.e., beating or physical abuse), rather than by an actual positive act on the part of the abductors. The few injured hostages who have evidenced the syndrome have been able to rationalize their abuse.

They have convinced themselves that the abductor's show of force was neces-sary to take control of the situation, that perhaps their resistance precipitated the abductor's force. Self-blame on the part of the victims is very evident in these situations. Many think that bad things do not happen to good people; therefore, I must have done something to deserve this trauma.

Stockholm Syndrome victims share a second common experience. They sense and identify with the human quality of their captor. At times, this quality is more imagined than real, as the victims of Fred Carrasco learned in Texas in August 1974 (*Houston Post*, 1974).

On the afternoon of July 24, 1974, at the Texas Penitentiary in Huntsville, Fred Carrasco and two associates took approximately 70 hostages in the prison library. In the course of the 11-day siege, most of the hostages were released. However, the drama was played out on the steps of the library between 9:30 and 10:00 on the night of August 3, 1974. It was during this time that Carrasco killed the remaining hostages (*Houston Post*, 1974). These murders took place in spite of his letters of affection to other hostages who were released earlier due to medical problems (House, 1975).

Some hostages expressed sympathy for Carrasco. A Texas Ranger who was at the scene and subsequently spoke to victims stated to the author that there was evidence of the Stockholm Syndrome (Burks, 1975). Though the hostages' emotions did not reflect the depth of those in Sweden a year before, the hostages admitted affectionate feelings toward a person they thought they should hate. They saw their captor as a human being with problems similar to their own. Law enforcement has long recognized that the trapped armed robber believes he is a victim of the police. We now realize that the hostage tends to share his distorted opinion.

When a robber is caught in a bank by quick police response, his dilemma is clear. He wants out with the money and his life. The police are preventing his escape by their presence and are demanding his surrender. The hostage, an innocent customer or employee of the bank, is also inside. His dilemma is similar to that of the robber—he wants to get out and cannot. He has seen the arrogant robber slowly become "a person" with a problem just like his own. The police on the outside correctly perceive the freedom of the hostages as the prerogative of the robber. However, the hostages perceive that the police weap-ons are pointed at them; the threat of tear gas makes them uncomfortable. The police insistence of the surrender of the subject is also keeping them hostage. Hostages begin to develop the idea that, "If the police would go away, I could go home. If they would let him go, I would be free," and so the bond begins.

Hostage Taker Reaction

As time passes and positive contact between the hostage and hostage taker begins, the Stockholm Syndrome also begins to take its effect upon the subject. This was evident at Entebbe in July 1976. At least one of the terrorists, the one who had engaged in conversations with the hostages from Air France Flight 139, elected at the moment of the attack to shoot at the Israeli commandos rather than kill hostages (Stevenson, 1976).

A moving account of this relationship is presented by Dr. Frank Ochberg as he recounts the experience of one hostage of the South Moluccans in December 1975. Gerard Vaders, a newspaper editor in his 50s, has related his experience to Dr. Ochberg:

> On the second night they tied me again to be a living shield and left me in that position for 7 hours. The one who was most psychopathic kept telling me, "Your time has come. Say your prayers." They had selected me for the third execution .... In the morning when I knew I was going to be executed, I asked to talk to Prins (another hostage) to give him a message to take to my family. I wanted to explain my family situation. My foster child, whose parents had been killed, did not get along too well with my wife, and I had at that time a crisis in my marriage just behind me .... There were other things, too. Somewhere I had the feeling that I had failed as a human being. I explained all this and the terrorists insisted on listening. (Ochberg, 1978a)

When Vaders completed his conversation with Prins and announced his readiness to die, the South Moluccans said, "No, someone else goes first" (Ochberg, 1978a).

Dr. Ochberg observed that Vaders was no faceless symbol anymore. He was human. In the presence of his executioners, he made the transition from a symbol to be executed to a human to be spared. Tragically, the Moluccans selected another passenger, Bierling, led him away, and murdered him before they had the opportunity to know him (Ochberg, 1978b).

Vaders goes on to explain his intrapsychic experience, his Stockholm Syndrome:

> And you had to fight a certain feeling of compassion for the Moluccans. I know this is not natural, but in some way they come over human. They gave us cigarettes. They gave us blankets. But we also realize that they were killers. You try to suppress that in your consciousness. And I knew I was suppressing that. I also knew they were victims, too. In the long run they would be as much victims as we.
>
>   Even more. You saw the morale crumbling. You experienced the disintegration of their personalities. The growing of despair. Things dripping through their fingers. You couldn't help but feel a certain pity. For people at the beginning with egos like gods—impregnable, invincible—they end up small, desperate, feeling that all was in vain. (Ochberg, 1978a)

Most people cannot inflict pain on another unless their victim remains dehumanized (Aronson, 1972). When the subject and his hostages are locked together in a vault, a building, a train, or an airplane, a process of humanization apparently takes place. When a person, a hostage, can build empathy while maintaining dignity, he or she can lessen the aggression of a captor. The exception to this is the subject who is antisocial, as Fred Carrasco demonstrated in August 1974. Fortunately, the Fred Carrascos of the world are in a minority, and in most situations the Stockholm Syndrome is a two-way street. With the passage of time and the occurrence of positive experiences, the victims' chances of survival increase. However, isolation of the victims precludes the forming of this positive bond.

In some hostage situations, the victims have been locked in another room, or they have been in the same room but have been hooded or tied, gagged, and forced to face the wall away from the subject (Dozier, 1992). Consciously or unconsciously, the subject has dehumanized his hostage, thereby making it easier to kill him. As long as the hostage is isolated, time is not a factor. The Stockholm Syndrome will not be a force that may save the life of the victim.

Individualized Reactions

Additionally, it has been observed that even though some hostages responded positively toward their captors, they did not necessarily evidence Stockholm Syndrome reactions toward all of the subjects. It was learned, logically, that most victims reacted positively toward those subjects who had treated them, in the words of the victims, "fairly." Those hostages who gave glowing accounts of the gentlemanly conduct of some subjects did not generalize to all subjects. They evidenced dislike, even hatred, toward one hostage taker whom they frequently call an "animal."

A hypothetical question was posed to determine the depth of victims' feelings toward their captors. Each former hostage was asked what he or she would do in the following situation: A person immediately recognizable as a law enforcement officer, armed with a shoulder weapon, would order them to lie down. At that same instant, one of the former captors would order him to stand up. When asked what they would do, the response varied according to the identity of the captor giving the "order." If a captor who had treated them fairly hypothetically yelled, "stand up," they would stand up. Conversely, if they thought it was the command of the subject who had been verbally abusive, they would obey the law enforcement officer. This would indicate that the strength of the syndrome is considerable. Even in the face of an armed officer of the law, they might offer themselves as a human shield for an abductor. As absurd as this may seem, such behavior has been observed by law enforcement officers throughout the world.

Whether the incident is a bank robbery in Stockholm, Sweden, or in the Philippines, a hijacking of an aircraft over Western Australia, New York, or in the Middle East, a kidnapping in South America, or an attempted prison break in Texas, there are behavioral similarities despite geographic and motivational differences. In each situation, a relationship, a healthy relationship (healthy because those involved were alive to talk about it), seems to develop between people caught in circumstances beyond their control and not of their making, a relationship that reflects the use of ego defense mechanisms by the hostage. This relationship seems to help victims cope with excessive stress and, at the same time, enables them to survive—a little worse for wear, but alive. The Stockholm Syndrome is not a magical relationship of a blanket affection for the subject. This bond, though strong, does have its limits. It has logical limits. If a person is nice to another, a positive feeling toward this person develops, even if this person is an armed robber, a hijacker of an aircraft, a kidnapper, or a prisoner attempting to escape.

The victim's need to survive is stronger than his impulse to hate the person who has created his dilemma. It is the ability to survive, to cope, that has enabled man to survive and claw his way to the top of the evolutionary ladder. Our ego is functioning and has functioned well and has performed its primary task of enabling the self to survive. At an unconscious level, the ego has activated the proper defense mechanisms in the correct sequence—denial, regression, identification, or introjection to achieve survival. The Stockholm Syndrome is just another example of the ability of the ego, the healthy ego, to cope and adjust to difficult stress brought about by a traumatic situation.

The application for law enforcement is clear, though it does involve a trade-off. Our first priority in dealing with hostage situations is the survival of all participants—each hostage, the crowd that has gathered, the police officers, and the subject. To accomplish this, various police procedures have been instituted. Inner and outer perimeters are longstanding procedures designed to keep crowds at a safe distance. Police training, discipline, and proper equipment save officers' lives. The development of the Stockholm Syndrome may save the life of the hostage as well as the subject. The life of the subject is preserved because it is highly unlikely that deadly force will be used by the police unless the subject makes a precipitous move. The lives of the hostages are also saved by the Stockholm Syndrome, the experience of positive contact, thus setting the stage for regression, identification, and introjection. The subject is less likely to injure a hostage he has come to know and on occasion to love (Aronson, 1972).

It is suggested that the Stockholm Syndrome can be fostered while negotiating with the subject: By asking him to allow the hostage to talk on the telephone, asking him to check on the health of a hostage, or discussing with him the family responsibilities of the hostage. Any action the negotiator can take to emphasize the hostage's human qualities to the subject should be considered by the negotiator. One way to do this is to avoid the use of the term *hostage*. In its place use the names of those being held. However, the negotiator must not overemphasize the value of the hostages. In so doing we run the risk of raising the value of those we are trying to save and in the process weakening our bargaining position. We must phrase our discussion of the hostages in such a way as to make it clear to the subject that it is to his advantage not to mistreat the hostages.

The police negotiator may pay a personal price for this induced relationship. Hostages will curse him as they did in Stockholm in August 1973. They will call the police cowards and actively side with the subject in trying to achieve a solution to their plight, a solution not necessarily in their best interest or in the best interest of the community.

Unfortunately, it may not end there. Victims of the Stockholm Syndrome may remain hostile toward the police after the siege has ended. The "original" victims in Stockholm still visit their abductors, and one former hostage is engaged to Olofsson (*Washington Post*, 1976).

Some victims visit their former captors in jail. Others have begun defense funds for them (TWA, 1976). A hostile hostage is a price that law enforcement must pay for a living hostage. Antilaw-enforcement feelings are not new to the police. But this may be the first time it has been suggested that law enforcement seek to encourage hostility, hostility from people whose lives law enforcement has mustered its resources to save. However, a human life is an irreplaceable treasure and worth some hostility. A poor or hostile witness for the prosecution is a small price to pay for this life.

Perhaps Machiavelli, in 1513, encapsulated this psychological phenomenon best when he said: "Men, when they receive good from whence they expect evil, feel the more indebted to their benefactor" (p. 28).

All that said, since September 11, 2001, we are seeing fewer sympathetic hostages. Perhaps the public is more aware of the fact that law enforcement and correctional crisis response teams are really on their side or they have had their fill of self-serving subjects who are using them as pawns to satisfy their egos.

The only exception I have seen has been in children who are abducted and come to believe their abductor's version of events that includes a story of saving them from a greater harm.

References

Alpern, D. M. (1976) A Skyjacking for Croatia, *Newsweek*, September 20.

Aronson, E. (1972) *Social Animal,* W. H. Freeman, San Francisco.

Bellak, L., Hurvich, M., and Gediman, H. K. (1973) *Ego Functions in Schizophrenics, Neurotics and Normals,* John Wiley and Sons, New York.

Bluhm, H. O. (1948) How Did They Survive? Mechanisms of Defense in Nazi Concentration Camps, *American Journal of Psychotherapy,* Vol. 2.

Burks, G. W. (1975) Personal interview, Austin Texas, December 2.

Coleman, J. C. (1995) *Abnormal Psychology and Modern Life*, Scott Foresman, Glenview, Illinois, p. 122.

Cooper, L. (1974) Hostage Freed by Carrasco Aided Prison Officials in Assault Plan, *Houston Chronicle*, August 5, p. 1.

Dozier, J. C. (Brigadier General U.S. Army retired) and Judy (1992) Personal interview at National Academy Retraining, Albuquerque, New Mexico, July 17.

Everhard, W. C., and Sullivan, A. L. (1974) John Brown's Raid Washington, DC. National Park Service history series, Supt. of Docs. no. 129-2:J61/4. U.S. Government Printing Office, Washington, DC, p. 37.

Fly, C. (1973) *No Hope But God,* Hawthorn, New York.

Freud, A. (1974) *The Ego and the Mechanisms of Defense,* rev. ed. International Universities Press, New York, p. 42.

Graves, B., and Strentz, T. (1977) The Kidnaper: His Crime and His Background, research paper, Special Operations and Research Staff, FBI Academy, Quantico, Virginia.

Green, I. (1885) The Capture of John Brown, *North American Review,* December, pp. 565–569.

Hall, C. S. (1954) *A Primer of Freudian Psychology,* World Publishing, New York, p. 34.

Hearst, P. C. (1987) Personnel interview, FBI Academy, Quantico, Virginia, October 12.

House, A. (1975) *The Carrasco Tragedy,* Texian Press, Waco, Texas.

Houston Post (1974) Murder Suicide Found in Huntsville Case, September 4.

Jackson, G. (1973) *Surviving the Long Night,* Vanguard, New York.

Jenkins, B. M., Johnson, J., and Ronfeldt, D. (1977) Numbered Lives: Some Statistical Observations from Seventy-Seven International Hostage Episodes, The Rand Corp., Santa Monica, California.

Lang, D. (1974) A Reporter at Large, *New Yorker,* November, p. 56.

Laughlin, H. P. (1970) *The Ego and Its Defenses,* Appleton-Century-Crofts, New York.

Lindroth, K. (1978) Personal interview, FBI Academy, Quantico, Virginia, November.

Machiavelli, N. (1948) *The Prince,* Appleton-Century-Crofts, New York, p. 28.

McClure, B. (1978) Hostage Survival, in *International Terrorism in the Contemporary World,* Westport CT, Greenwood Press, pp. 21–48.

Newsweek (1976) Skyjackers Are Charged with Murder, September 20, p. 25.

New York Times (1976) Skyjackers Are Charged with Murder, September 12.

Ochberg, F. J. (1978a) The Victim of Terrorism: Psychiatric Considerations, *Terrorism: An International Journal,* Vol. 1, No. 2, 147–168.

Ochberg, F. (1978b) Personal interview, Acting Director, National Institute of Mental Health, November 2.

Scott, J. A., and Scott, R. A. (1988) *John Brown of Harper's Ferry,* Facts on File, New York, p. 154.

Shriver, E. (1859) Report to Brigadier General James M. Coale, 9th Brigade, Maryland Militia.

Stevenson, W. (1976) *90 Minutes at Entebbe,* Bantam, New York.

Stoulgas, O. (1978) Personal interview, German Consulate, Chicago, Illinois, August 19.

TWA 847 (1976) Personal interviews with crew, New York City, September 13.

U.S. Congress, Senate (1975) Committee on the Judiciary, Terrorist Activity; Hostage Defense Measures, Hearings before a subcommittee to investigate the administration of the Internal Security Act and other internal security laws Part 5, 94th Cong., 1st session.

Washington Post (1976) Swedish Robin Hood, *Parade* magazine supplement, November 14.

What Do You Say to a Hostage?

25

What do you say to a naked person? It all depends ...

Introduction

If this chapter was easy to write, others would have done it long ago. However, since I earned my doctorate, at the expense of the Federal Bureau of Investigation (FBI), taking flight attendants hostage and training them to deal with the stress of captivity, it seems appropriate that I should comment on this potentially volatile topic and sometimes necessary tactic.

There are several caveats the negotiator must consider and within which he or she should work when communicating with a hostage. These include but are not limited to the following:

1. Are there any hostages?
2. Are we really speaking with a hostage?
3. Is the subject listening?
4. Does the hostage want to talk or listen to us?
5. We must not pay too much attention to a hostage.
6. Will the hostage believe what we are saying?
7. Will the hostage tell the subject what we told them?
8. What is the mental or legal status of the hostage?

Time

An accurate analysis of hostages to determine if and how a negotiator can and should speak with them takes time. Time is to a hostage negotiator what an anesthetic is to a surgeon. Without its beneficial effects, the most mundane medical maneuver may be fatal. Take the time to identify the hostages before any specific or intelligence-gathering communications are attempted.

They may have been forced to make the physical transition from freedom to fetters more quickly than their minds made the transformation. They may be in a mild form of shock or denial.

Do's

Initial contacts should be limited to reassuring statements that may or may not be accepted. Expect hostility. Expect the hostages to blame you for their plight. Assess their stress level. Their attitude may be that if the police would leave, they would be free. They do not care about our policies. Their needs are understandably very selfish. They want to live. They do not care that giving in to all the demands of a hostage taker will encourage others. They want to live. They could care less that, if allowed to leave, their abductor may injure others. They want to live.

Repeatedly acknowledge their plight and fears. Ask them if they are okay. Assure them that you are doing everything in your power to ensure their safety and the safety of everyone in their location. Say things like, "I can assure you that we are doing everything we can to end this situation as quickly as possible without anyone getting hurt. Are you okay?" Expect anger and blame.

Contact their families and significant others. Bring a representative to the site to gain intelligence on the hostages. Use this person as an initial recontact for the hostage upon release before your intelligence-gathering interview. Say things like, "Through your employer, friends, neighbors (or whomever you have contacted), we have located your…and they are here with us." Do not lie to the hostages unless you believe that your misrepresentation is in their best interest.

Don'ts

Do not say, "Be calm" or "relax." If this were possible for them to achieve, they would not be in complete control of their senses. They are and should be frightened. They are looking to you for help while harboring the thought that you are the cause of their plight. They may believe that if you would go away they would be free. They are in fear for their lives. They are not particularly concerned with the long-range political or legal consequences of allowing a hostage taker to go free. Their goals are short sighted, self-serving, and survival oriented—they want out. Now!

Do not attempt to gather intelligence until you are certain that you are speaking to a reliable person. Intelligence from an emotional hostage is a secondary consideration and may be of marginal value or totally wrong. Your primary concern is to keep them calm. Prevent them from making a bad situation worse. Do not allow them to become their own worst enemy by aggravating the already frightened and hostile hostage holder. Remember, our primary goal is the preservation of life.

Have a Plan

What do you want to achieve by talking with a hostage? Is the subject listening? Is this person a resource for valuable information, or must you limit your contacts to reassuring statements?

One way to help identify the veracity of the information one gets from a hostage is to determine if the hostage was targeted or a victim chosen at random. Is there a previous hostile relationship between them? If so, the chances are that their information may be reliable. The hostages may be more likely to blame the subject rather than the police for their plight.

Who Are the Hostages?

Is the hostage a police officer from whom you can expect reliable information? As we all know, Constable Treavor Locke provided Scotland Yard with valuable intelligence during the spring of 1980 Iranian Embassy siege. He was decorated for his valor by a grateful government.

Are we fortunate enough to have a trained hostage like an airline, bank, or embassy employee upon whom we can rely for information? Conversely, is the hostage a stranger to, and possible adversary of, law enforcement?

A Litany of Legendary Animosity and Misinformation

What guarantee do you have that the hostage taker is not listening? During a bank robbery in Las Vegas, Nevada, the hostage taker took time to listen on an extension during every telephonic conversation the negotiator had with the lone hostage. Fortunately, he asked her mundane questions and reassured her repeatedly during his conversations.

In a siege at the Travelodge in San Diego, California, the hostage told the subject everything the negotiator said to him.

On a more positive note, the Memphis (Tennessee) Police Department was able to gather good information from doctors who were held hostage by a deranged father of a former patient. They fully understood the gravity of the situation. They knew that police were doing the best they possibly could. They were intelligent enough to understand that the subject was deranged. They knew the constraints of the police and their own vulnerability.

Conversely, during the Chula Vista, California, Redi-Care City Medical Clinic siege in February 1992, an adolescent male who was a part-time law student was an antagonistic hostage. When he finally learned that the hostage taker had killed one person and wounded a police officer, his attitude changed. However, during most of the siege, he was a serious problem for the police and could not be reasoned with or trusted. He appeared on a TV talk show and now recognizes the error of his ways and the effect of the Stockholm Syndrome on his behavior.

More positively, during the Sacramento, California, The Good Guys April 1991 siege, the sheriff's office negotiator used a store employee who always wanted to be a police officer. They obtained excellent intelligence from him.

However, a few months before, in October 1990, at Henry's Pub in Berkeley, California, a male hostage filtered information and did not allow the hostage taker to talk.

Conversely, during a Torrence, California, jewelry store robbery that turned into a hostage siege, the adolescent female hostages taunted the police by saying, "Are you cowards? Why don't you come in here," and so forth.

On a totally different note, the Bank of America in Placentia, California, was robbed on New Year's Eve 1991. The police believed that there were two subjects. One had left and was shot and killed at a freeway off-ramp traffic jam. Back at the bank, other officers were negotiating with hostages in a situation where they believed the subject had left a bomb. In addition to these complications, they ended up negotiating with a person who, though a hostage, was a wanted felon from Florida.

Finally, there is the infamous incident in September 1973 in Stockholm, Sweden. Some of the hostages were romantically involved with the subjects, another was aloof, and a fourth hostage was verbally and physically abused by the subjects.

The Role of the Hostage in the Surrender

Avoid snatching defeat from the jaws of victory. Be sure to prepare the hostages for their role in the surrender scenario. They want to live. They may see the surrender scenario as the end of their nightmare and the realization of their fondest dreams. They must understand that this process, like that of their ordeal, will not happen as quickly as they might wish. To ensure their safety, it will take time. Ease them into the role change from fetters to freedom. Let them know that they will be searched, questioned, and treated like a subject until they are positively identified. Advise them of other aspects of the surrender process that you do not want to startle them. Consider telling them the names of the police officers who will meet and process them prior to the release to their families. Consider using your psychologist to ease them back and consider scheduling a postcritical incident stress debrief for them.

Conclusion

Every negotiator should remember that when dealing with a hostage one is talking to an unknown commodity. We all know that one negotiates differently with an antisocial hostage taker versus a person who is suffering from Paranoid Schizophrenia or is the leader of a cult. We listen to the subject, gather intelligence from several sources, make an assessment, and direct our dialogue accordingly. Similarly, each hostage is unique. It takes time to evaluate them. We need intelligence to determine the direction of our dialogue. The only constant is their need to believe that we understand their plight and are doing our very best to ensure their personal safety. Our goal remains *the preservation of human life*, not the expeditious ending of a siege to save money.

A Hostage Psychological Survival Guide

26

Introduction

Tough times don't last, tough people do. There are hundreds of books written by former hostages and prisoners of war (POWs). The majority of them did not think of themselves as tough people. However, they were and have shared their story of survival with our free society. Freedom is not free. These survivors are living proof of that axiom.

The topic of my dissertation was the creation of a training program for hostages to ensure their survival. In my research I had the opportunity to interview dozens of former Korean and Vietnam POWs when I spoke at the U.S. Navy Survive, Evade, Resist, Escape (SERE) course in California. In addition I have interviewed dozens of civilian hostages who survived terrorist and criminal abductions. In every case it was clear to me that the person I was interviewing was much stronger than his or her adversary. It was true of them and it is true of law enforcement and correctional staff. If the person who is holding you had your strengths and ability, they would be gainfully employed and not engaging in criminal activities.

The only time I was taken hostage is when I enlisted in the U.S. Marine Corps (USMC). I was reasonably certain their intent was to remake me into a Marine, not to destroy me. However, there were times when I harbored some doubts.

However, there was an incident on the Malaysian–Thailand border when I was detained and I thought I was a hostage. I was removed from the train by a young Thai soldier who did not speak English. However, he communicated his commands well and moved me to a holding area in the station. I considered trying to escape into the jungle. However, I grew up in Chicago and urban areas of California so I knew the jungle was filled with cobras, tigers, lions, quicksand, and probably a tribe or two that practiced cannibalism. I had seen *The Bridge on the River Kwai* but did not consider myself as lucky as Bill Holden was to find a friendly tribe. So I waited. My stomach turned and I suffered some serious sadness when the train left the station. I took some comfort in my guards' compassion and the possibility of survival when through sign language I indicated I had to urinate and he led me to a bathroom in an adjoining room. My ordeal ended when his commander arrived and verified the validity of my passport, was impressed with my Federal Bureau of Investigation (FBI) credentials, and told me his job was to make sure I had valid documentation, a round-trip ticket, and enough money to live in Thailand until my return date. Further, he had relatives in San Francisco.

The bottom line is there is ample literature on how to survive the ordeal of captivity. The fact is that, in my judgment, most people who have a difficult time as a hostage do things that make a bad situation worse. One example is a person who was one of our hostages during a training exercise in California.

As part of our preparation for the Olympics, the FBI conducted many field training exercises (FTX) in areas of our nation where Olympic events were scheduled. Typically, the week-long FTX included terrorists taking hostages. My job was to train our volunteer hostages to cope with the stress of captivity and then evaluate their performance, the negotiations process, and the rescue. Initially, we used law enforcement staff as volunteer hostages. However, one of them sneaked a derringer into the FTX. So we switched to the military; they brought knives.

I was discussing this problem with a friend from United Airlines (UAL) with whom I was making some training films. She said that UAL would provide the FBI with hostages and would fly them anyplace in the country, put them up for free, and then fly them back. I knew the FBI would like the free aspect, and I was certain that FBI SWAT and Hostage Rescue Team (HRT) personnel would prefer to rescue flight attendants rather than cops or military types.

During one of these FTX that involved terrorists holding hostages on a small vessel in Long Beach harbor, we had a problem. Our two dozen female flight attendant hostages were fitted with blindfolds made from protective goggles that had tape over the lenses. The terrorists were muscular military types. It was hot so the terrorists wanted to remove their masks. They ordered one group of hostages to sit in a circle with their heads bowed and another group to face the bulkhead. One hostage was a very slight female whose goggles did not fit as tightly as they should have. She tried to sneak a peek at the terrorists. To do this she had to twist her head in such a way as to make her attempt obvious to all. The terrorist ordered her to bow her head. She did so briefly but peeked again. They threatened to throw her overboard. She bowed her head briefly but peeked again. They picked her up and carried her to the deck. She was screaming and promised not to peek. She peeked again. This scenario ended with the terrorists holding her by her ankles as they dipped her head into the bay. She screamed, then gurgled, then screamed over and over. Rather wet from the shoulders up, she was brought back to the holding area. She peeked again. She was removed from the problem. The next night the hostages were rescued. The following day, during the group critique she commented on how well she had done using the survival techniques I had taught them prior to the FTX. The other hostages and I did not understand her logic. Later, LCDR Doug Derrer, the Navy psychologist who ran the SERE program, reminded me that some people have a need to be the center of attention even when it is negative attention. Perhaps this is one explanation for the London Syndrome discussed in Chapter 23.

Reacting to the Terrorist/Criminal/Inmate Episode

Coping with Abduction

The most dramatic and dangerous phase of any hostage siege is the moment of abduction when victims must make an instant choice and correct decision regarding resistance (Derrer, 1985). Without exception, resistance is dangerous. The abductors may have planned this well and have tried to choose circumstances favorable to them. Certainly they have the element of surprise. They will be tense: their adrenaline will be rushing to muscle groups. They will be physically and verbally abusive. If anyone tries to escape, their action must be swift, fierce, and effective. Effective resistance or quick escape requires strength, knowledge of vulnerable parts of the body, a willingness to apply this strength to those parts, and the skill to succeed. Any half-hearted or ill-conceived defensive measures will only make a bad situation much worse. Any attempt at escape should not be made unless you possess the above qualities in the right setting. Victims who resist heavily armed abductors may needlessly die or be injured, and they may cause others to be harmed.

For unprepared, law-abiding citizens this initial phase is traumatic. With your world so suddenly turned around you may experience near paralyzing fear (Nardini, 1952). Unexpected, rapid reversals will cause you to feel abandoned and unreal. Because the mind cannot accommodate radical change quickly, it uses the automatic defense mechanism of denial to make the transition (Ochberg, 1979, 2010). Consciously, you will react as perceiving the situation as a dream, a nightmare that is not really happening. When Patricia Campbell Hearst was abducted by the Symbionese Liberation Army (SLA) and dragged past the unconscious and bleeding body of her boyfriend, she screamed amidst the shooting and shouted, "No, not me! No, not me!" (Hearst, 1982, 1987). These words and her reaction were conscious manifestations of her denial, her subconscious hope that someone else, not her, was the victim of this terror. Every day feelings of omnipotence and invulnerability are quickly replaced by the opposite extremes of confusion and complete defenselessness (Rahe and Genender, 1983).

Control

Playing the role of a hostage is a difficult adjustment for everyone. It is especially hard for authority figures like law enforcement and correctional staff. The reason is control. I am not suggesting that either group has any pathology regarding control. The fact is both, as part of their job, are in control. The nature of your job is such that all of you tell people what to do, when, where, and how to do it. As a hostage, you lack a lot of control. A lot of, but not all, control is beyond your grasp. When you review survivor behavior suggestions listed below, think about how many of them involve control issues. Granted, the amount of control, in some cases, is slight. However, it is there. A major factor in stress reactions is the real or perceived loss of control. So as a hostage, try to regain as much control as possible and in the process reduce stress and enhance your chances of survival.

Preparing for Psychological Reactions

Research has shown that stress-related trauma can be minimized by preparation (Strentz, 1984). One can learn to expect certain reactions and to assume consciously certain roles that will minimize the stress and maximize one's chances of surviving the hostage siege. Abductors, however, are counting on severe reactions and may have practiced routines that will increase victim trauma.

Remember the story of the two campers from Chapter 23. One can only prepare himself or herself in advance for the trauma of abduction and siege survival.

Studies on hostage sieges have examined the roles played by hostages. They compare and contrast those who survived with those who succumbed. These studies defined *survivors* as those who returned to a meaningful existence with strong self-esteem and went on to live healthy and productive lives with little evidence of long-term depression, nightmares, or serious stress-induced illnesses. They defined *succumbers* as those who either did not live through the siege, or upon release or rescue required extensive psychotherapy to deal with real or imagined problems. Almost without exception, these studies found that survivors reacted one way while succumbers acted in another.

Hostage Psychological Reactions

Survivors	Succumbers
Had faith	Felt abandoned
Contained hostility	Acted out aggression
Maintained a superior attitude	Pitied self
Fantasized	Dwelled on situation
Rationalized situation	Despaired
Kept to routines	Suspended activities
Controlled outward appearance	Acted out of control
Sought flexibility and humor	Behaved obsessive compulsively
Blended with peers	Stood out as overcompliant or resistant

Roles for Survivors

I am not suggesting that abductors think things through as discussed below. However, hostages, having thought things through, will see that certain behaviors are logical and survival oriented. The basic strategy for survival is to play a subordinate role. Control yourself. I certainly did this when I joined the USMC and everyone has done it when they were new on the job. We spend our lives engaging in socially prescribed behaviors. These are called *social roles*, and each of us plays a variety of them daily.

We do not interact with a peer the same ways in which we act toward strangers. Our society directs how one interacts with parents, pilots, peers, partners, the police, and Popes. Each role carries certain responsibilities and expectations. The role of son may be different from the role of daughter, even though they share the role of child, family member, citizen, and a score of other prescribed behaviors. When interacting with a parent, one must play the role of child to ensure healthy communication and respect. If a child fails to play this role when interacting with a parent, we say he or she is disrespectful and administer appropriate punishment. Similarly, hostages have a role they must play to allow the hostage takers their role and thus avoid unnecessary conflict. Failure to play a subordinate role in the presence of an authority figure is called insubordination and will lead to conflict. Again, we all learned that when we were new on the job. Granted, the authority of our boss was legitimate while the authority of the hostage taker is not. However, that is a legal point to be dealt with in court, not during the crisis.

When dealing with hostage takers you must recognize they have placed themselves in an authoritarian role. You may not agree with this self-proclaimed status, but in this instance might makes right. Therefore, on the surface, you must act subservient—that is, defer to their authority and play the role of hostage while within your mind you are maintaining an awareness of your superiority and employing coping reactions that will reduce the stress of the situation. As Shakespeare wrote, "All the world's a stage and each of us a player on it." In a hostage siege, you are cast into the role of a victim and would do well to learn the part and play the role well. Proper playing means survival; improper playing could abruptly end your acting career and cause others to die.

Sucessful Coping Strategies

Have Faith in Yourself and Your Government

As a captive, depression is a common affliction and sometimes seems like an insurmountable obstacle. To survive an abduction and a siege, a positive mental attitude is absolutely necessary. Fortunately, there are many reasons for hostages to have faith in their country and themselves. An American hostage at home or overseas is never alone. He or she can always be certain that their government at many levels is monitoring the flight or their plight while working toward a negotiated release or rescue. The recent actions in the Indian Ocean bear witness to this. The FBI and the U.S. Navy are just two of several government agencies that have and will respond. Many other nations have similar response capability as has been demonstrated by the Indians and the government of Thailand. The message is clear. Responsible governments of the free world will allow no citizen to be abandoned.

Contain Your Hostility toward Your Captors

Hostile reactions toward your captors can and must be masked and under your control. Most often the psychological defense mechanism called "suppression and isolation of affect" arises naturally as a check on emotions. This reaction helps hostages keep aggressive feelings inside rather than letting them burst out as hostile words and deeds or as demands for more comfortable conditions. The London Syndrome, as discussed in Chapter 23, must be avoided. The opposite of this syndrome was demonstrated by those Americans and Philippine military and civilians who survived the Bataan Death March in World War II (Nardini, 1952).

Maintain a Superior Attitude

A superior attitude will help you rise above your hostage status and siege as long as you do not use this attitude to justify hostile words or actions toward your captors. Indeed, hostages have every reason to feel superior: after all, they have been taken because they are of value to their government. No matter how the abductor(s) may try to demean you, you can and must remain secure in the knowledge of your value to your government. Remember the time and resources expended to resolve previous prison and other sieges like the recent dispatch of the U.S. Navy that included several ships, a team of SEALs and FBI negotiators. Those Somali pirates who survived are now in American prisons where they belong and will stay for years. Obviously, if you did not have any value, you would not be a hostage.

Fantasize to Fill Empty Hours

In writings and interviews, many former hostages reflect on the ability to escape mentally from their trauma by engaging in fantasy (Fly, 1973; Jackson, 1973; Neihouse, 1973). They take control of the time by escaping into a fantasy. Some speak of building homes in their imagination while others plan trips to various places. Some reduce stress by daydreaming the hours away and others by withdrawing into sleep. All agree that occupying empty hours, and thus dealing with the real enemy of boredom, is one of the major problems of their experience. By withdrawing into the pleasures of the imagination you will gain some sense of control. Correctional officers know well how much time inmates spend engaging in an escape fantasy.

Rationalize the Abduction

No matter what the circumstances of the abduction, you must never blame yourself or dwell on what you should have done. You must force yourself to rationalize and accept your actions. You must focus on the fact that you are alive and a hostage. Avoid engaging in 20/20 hindsight to rationalize how you could have avoided the situation. Except in the minds of the fanatics, you are clearly better off as a live hostage than as a dead martyr. You must accentuate the positive, give thanks for being alive, and resolutely adjust to the demeaning hostage status. Hostages can learn to play mental games with themselves and each other. Think about how things could be worse. Remember, you could be dead or disabled. Do not dwell on how much better off you would be if you had gone to work for the railroad.

When all is said and done, hostages must recognize and accept that they cannot change their status immediately. They must instead adjust to the circumstances and make the best of a difficult situation. The most dangerous phase of a siege is the abduction. Having survived that trauma you are now on the road to rescue or release.

Keep To or Establish Routines

Keeping to normal everyday routines will greatly relieve stress. I have interviewed flight attendants who found great consolation as hostages by cleaning the galley, and other hostages have deliberately written letters and kept logs. Some flight engineers have navigated their most perfect course as pursers speak of achieving a perfect accounting of items served and money received while pilots detail the variables of smooth flights and landings.

Captives should use routine activity to occupy their minds because it helps them escape mentally from the stress of captivity. But, they must be careful not to threaten their captors by inadvertently gazing fixedly in their direction or practicing martial arts.

Physical exercise like dynamic tension activities provide a multitude of benefits. It occupies time, keeps you healthy, and allows you to function better physically and mentally. It also enables you to sleep better and gives you a sense of goal setting and accomplishment. Sir Geoffrey Jackson paced around his cell and marked off the daily distance as he mentally moved closer and closer to home (Jackson, 1973). Set goals you can control like the number of sit-ups rather than a goal beyond your control like the date of rescue or release. When that very artificially identified day passes without release, depression and despair quickly follow.

Other important routines involve service and care for others. Survivors who have a strong sense of obligation to others are so occupied with helping or caring for them that they have little time to dwell on their own misery. This was especially true for medical doctors who were POWs (Nardini, 1952). The doctors not only engaged in comfortable behavior but helped others and in the process took some control away from their captors.

Control Your Outward Appearance

A mature, stable, and controlled appearance, no matter what the inner turmoil, conveys a sense of self-confidence that may help settle things down. When you project a sense or façade of mature professional and decisive behavior chances are good that your abductors will respond with a degree of respect or at least without anxiety. The Australian, Leon Richardson, on the other hand, controlled his outward appearance in an unconventional but highly effective way by artificially projecting extreme depression. He manipulated his captors into cheering him up for fear his suicide would diminish if not eliminate his value to them. When he was too cheerful they would try to put him down. So, each day he decided which role he would play. Granted, this did not win his immediate freedom, but it made the time pass and gave him some sense of control (Richardson, 1985).

Strive to Be Flexible and Keep Your Sense of Humor

Our POW servicemen in Vietnam who were routinely tortured learned that physical conditioning and flexibility are crucial in captivity. The Marine Security Guards who were held in Tehran remained physically active through exercise. The problem was their diet was too poor to sustain vigorous exercise. They did maintain a healthy sense of humor as evidenced by their answer to a question from one of the guards who asked, "Is it true that to become a Marine you must first strangle your sister?" To which the young Marine answered that he was a Sergeant and therefore had no living female relatives. This story spread to the other Marines via a communications system they devised. Then everyone relished in telling their versions of acceptance into the Corps and subsequent promotions earned through intrafamily violence.

Blend with Your Peers

My last recommendation is that of blending which requires some teamwork. Although some situations may call for a role of leadership to be taken, some abductors routinely select leaders for abuse. If you are comfortable in a leadership role or have skills that can improve the situation, you may choose to lead. The medical doctors mentioned earlier certainly served as leaders. They were generally left alone because they, in their caring for their peers, made life easier for the captors. Flight attendants and cabin crew have also served well as leaders. Certainly Uli Derickson, the lead flight attendant on TWA 847, is credited with saving the lives of many hostages by intervening for them after the terrorists killed Jim Stetham. It is believed that they selected him not because of anything he did but because *sailor* translated into *Marine* and the terrorists feared Marines, plus he, as a Navy hard hat diver, was a big and strong guy who presented a physical threat to them.

Quite honestly, it is the extreme of standing out too much that invites trouble. Crying or being overly polite or helpful by doing more than the abductor(s) require is setting yourself up as an easy mark to be exploited. Most people understand that being hostile is not good, and neither is the other extreme. I recommend you do what you are told, but do it slowly to ensure safety and not convey a sense of extreme fear or enthusiasm. Doing more than what your captors order is not a good survival tactic. If asked why you are doing it slowly, explain saying something like, "What you asked me to do is important so I want to make sure and do it right." By doing it slowly you are taking some control. By telling your captor that what he wants done is important is also telling him that he is important so you gain additional control by lying to him, her, or them.

Conclusion

Now, while you are calm and unstressed, ask yourself, "What kind of a person am I?" Remember, the initial strategy is to play a subservient role, the new hire or private in boot camp as you evaluate your abductors. Remember, if they were superior to you they would not be abductors. While we never want to underestimate our adversary, neither do we want to make him into a superman.

Imagine, based on experience, how you think you will react in a hostage siege and play your survival strategy accordingly. If you are habitually fatalistic in your daily actions, plan to blend in with your peers and escape into fantasy. If you strongly believe you are in control of your fate, think now of the kinds of things you might do as a leader that will help yourself and other captives. Most hostages do a little of both. The good news is that hostages who die do things listed under Succumbers. Remember, it is not what the abductor does to you and your fellow captives, it is what you do about what they do to you and your peers that counts (Rahe and Genender, 1983). Tough times do not last, but tough people do.

References

Derrer , LCDR (1985) Terrorism Proceedings Naval Review, May, p. 185.

Fly, C. (1973) *No Hope But God*, Hawthorne, New York.

Hearst, P. (1982) *Every Secret Thing*, Doubleday, New York.

Hearst, P. (1987) Personal interview, FBI Academy Quantico, Virginia, October 12.

Jackson, G. Sir (1973) *Surviving the Long Night*, Vanguard, New York.

Nardini, John E. (1952) Survival Factors in American Prisoners of War of the Japanese, *The American Journal of Psychiatry*, October.

Neihouse, W. (1973) *Prisoner of the Jungle*, Vanguard, New York.

Ochberg, Frank (1979) Preparing for Terrorist Victimization. In Y. Alexander and R. Kilmarx (Eds.), *Political Terrorism and Business*, Prager Special Series, New York.

Ochberg, Frank (2010) Personal conversation, Montross, Virginia, April 25.

Rahe, R. M. Capt., and Genender, E. (1983) Adaptation to and Recovery from Captivity Stress, *Military Medicine*, Vol. 148, pp. 577–585.

Richardson, L. D. (1985) in B. M. Jenkins (Ed.), Surviving Captivity: One Hundred Days, Terrorism and Personal Protection, Butterworth, Stoneham, Massachusetts.

Strentz, T. (1984) Preparing the Person with High Potential for Victimization as a Hostage. In J. T. Turner (Ed.), *Violence in the Medical Care Setting: A Survival Guide,* Aspen Press, Rockville, Maryland.

Strentz, T. (1987) A Hostage Psychological Survival Guide, *FBI Law Enforcement Bulletin*, November.

Index

A

Accidental hostage incidents, 296
ACL; *See* Adjective Check List
ACLU; *See* American Civil Liberties
        Union
Active listening skills, 9, 222
    bipolar hostage taker, 137
    correctional setting, 184
    mechanics of, 10–12
        emotional labeling, 10
        minimal encouragers, 10
        open-ended questions, 10
        repeat last few words, 10
        summarize or paraphrase, 10
        tolerate silence, 10
    subject surrender, 222
Active listening stages, 81–82
    reflecting emotional level, 82
    repeating words, 82
    say nothing, 82
    summarize, 82
Adjective Check List (ACL), 23
Adolescent hostage taker, 87–95
    adolescent crisis resolution skills, 91
    adult role models, faulty, 91
    common clinical conditions, 91–93
        antisocial personality, 92–93
        anxiety/inadequacy, 92
        depression, 91–92
        psychotic, 93
    crisis mind-set, 90–91
    defining adolescence, 88–89
        phase 1, 88–89
        phase 2, 89
        phase 3, 89
    executive part of the brain, 87
    guidelines for negotiating with
            adolescent hostage taker, 94–95
    immediate crisis, getting past, 88
    negotiating guidelines, 93
    negotiation tactics, 93
    normal adolescents, 90
    peer pressure, 89
    rejection, 92

    role of negotiator, 88
    scenario, 87
    school systems, 90
    social criteria, 88
AFL/CIO, 129
Airline industry, "The Common Strategy,"
        xxvi
Alcohol
    impaired judgment and, 141, 167
    as solvent for superego, 239
ALS; *See* Active listening skills
American Civil Liberties Union (ACLU),
        185
American Psychiatric Association (APA),
        3–17, 110–113
    Antisocial Personality Disorder hostage
        taker, 110–113
    axioms of negotiations process, 9–16
        active listening, 9–12
        defense mechanisms, 13–16
        listening, 9
        no, 13
        role change, 12
        time, 13
        tone of voice, 12
        victimization, 12
    Bad hostage takers, 8
    Bipolar Disorder and, 132–133
    body language, 12
    confidentiality, 7
    delusional disorder, 8
    denial, definition of, 13
    empathy, communication of, 12
    ethical conflict, 7
    KISS axiom, 8
    Mad people, 8
    mental health negotiators, 6–8
    mental health professionals, 4
    multiaxial evaluation, 5–6, 131–132
    paranoia, 8
    patient-centered therapy, 9
    patient–doctor privilege, 7
    posttraumatic stress disorder, 286
    projection, 14–16
    psychiatric nurses, 4

rationalization, 14
Sad people, 8
social workers, 4
Sour Grapes, 14
types of disorders typically encountered
      by crisis negotiators, 8–9
typical symptoms of psychosis, 16
Anti-Sniper Survival Training (ASST),
      49
Antisocial Personality Disorder (ASP), 6,
      107, 132
Antisocial Personality Disorder hostage
      taker, 107–115
   American Psychiatric Association,
      110–113
   Antisocial Personality Disorder,
      108–110
      law enforcement version, 110
      movie version, 109
   cause of disorder, 109
   children with disorder, 109
   elusiveness of cure, 115
   faking success in treatment, 112
   hostage takers, 113
   impulsiveness, 111
   it's all about me, 108
   junior therapist, 112
   labels, 107
   negotiating guidelines and their
      rationales, 113–115
   psychopathic liar, 109
   self-indulgence, 108
   statistics, 111
   Stockholm Syndrome, 114
   trust, 108
APA; *See* American Psychiatric Association
ASP; *See* Antisocial Personality Disorder
Assistant Special Agent in Charge (ASAC),
      xxvii, 47, 52
ASST; *See* Anti-Sniper Survival Training
ATF; *See* Bureau of Alcohol, Tobacco,
      Firearms and Explosives
Attica, 181
Avoidant personality Disorder, 98

B

Behavioral Science Unit (BSU), xxii, xxiv
Bipolar hostage taker, 129–138
   adult adolescent, 132
   American Psychiatric Association
      multiaxial evaluation, 131–132

Antisocial Personality Disorder, 132
audiotapes, 129
Bipolar Disorder and American
      Psychiatric Association,
      132–133
Bipolar Disorder and Hollywood,
      133–135
changes in mood, 133
countdown, 130
excessive mood swings, 133
hostage takers, 135
law enforcement encounters, 129–131
manhunt, 130
Manic-Depressive Psychosis, 132
medications, 136
most dangerous time, 134
negotiating guidelines and their
      rationale, 135–138
   active listening skills, 137
   follow-up, 137
   involvement in process, 136
   keeping busy, 136
   nonpolice negotiators, 137
   off meds, 137
   publicity, 137
   reality oriented negotiations, 136
   sharing information, 136
outstanding people who suffered from
      Bipolar Disorder, 130
work-a-holic, 131
"Black Jesus," 119
Body language, 12
Booby-trap mechanism, xxvi
BoP negotiators; *See* Bureau of Prison
      negotiators
Borderline personality, 283
Brown Shirts, 197
BSU; *See* Behavioral Science Unit
Bureau of Alcohol, Tobacco, Firearms and
      Explosives (ATF), 252
Bureau of Prison (BoP) negotiators, 182

C

California Association of Crisis
      Negotiators, xxviii
California Association of Hostage
      Negotiators (CAHN), 54
California Psychological Inventory (CPI),
      22
Carbolith, 136
Central Intelligence Agency (CIA), xxvi

Characteristics of hostage/crisis negotiators;
        See Effective hostage/crisis
        negotiators, characteristics of
Chlorpromazine, 123
CIA; *See* Central Intelligence Agency
CINT; *See* Crisis Incident Negotiations
        Team
CISD; *See* Critical Incident Stress
        Debriefings
City of Winter Haven v. Allen, 28
Civilian suicide, 146
CNT; *See* Crisis Negotiations Team
Combat fatigue, 69
Communication with hostage, 307–311
    caveats, 307
    conclusion, 311
    don'ts, 308
    do's, 308
    gathering intelligence, 308
    have a plan, 309
    initial contacts, 308
    litany of legendary animosity and
        misinformation, 309–310
    reassuring statements, 308
    role of the hostage in surrender, 310
    Stockholm Syndrome, 310
    time, 307
    who the hostages are, 309
Community hotline services, 142, 168
Confidentiality, 7, 70
Correctional setting, crisis negotiations in,
        175–193
    daily experience, 178–179
    hostage survival, 179–180
    institutional crisis negotiations,
        186–189
        formal face-saving surrender ritual,
            187
        negotiator progress, measurement of,
            186
        story to tell, 186
        telling the truth, 186
        threats, 187–189
        time, manipulation of, 186
        violence, 187
    manipulative parolees, 179
    prison population, 180
    scribe
        information recorded by, 189
        wearing headphones, 188
    some sieges, 180–186
        Attica, New York, 181–182

federal correctional facility in
        Atlanta, 182
federal correctional institution in
        Talladega, Alabama, 182–183
    lessons learned, 184–186
    Lewis Penitentiary in Buckeye,
        Arizona, 183–184
    Lucasville, Ohio State Prison, 183
    Oakdale Correctional Facility,
        Oakdale, Louisiana, 182
street versus the institution, 175–178
    decisions made in chain of
        command, 177
    immediate response plans and
        capabilities, 175–176
    personalities of players, 176
    prison staff knowledge of incident
        location, 176
    prison subcultures, 177
    staffing of institutional negotiating
        teams, 177
systems approach to crisis management,
        191–192
    accountability, 191
    call-back system, 192
    checklist, 192
    communication, 191
    first response, 191
    mutual aid, 192
    staging areas, 191
CPI; *See* California Psychological Inventory
Crisis Incident Negotiations Team (CINT),
        51, 53
Crisis negotiations, goal of, xxv
Crisis Negotiations Team (CNT), 254
Crisis negotiation team, 47–61
    Downs v. United States, 51–53
    FBI Crisis Negotiations Unit crisis site
        assessment, 61
    perishable skills, 50
    process of crisis negotiations, 53–54
    successful approach (teamwork), 58
    team concept, 49–51
    team roles, 48
    team structure, 54–58
        behavioral science experts, 57–58, 59
        chronographer, 57, 59
        CINT commander, 55, 59
        guard, 56–57, 59
        intelligence, 55–56, 59
        messenger, 56, 59
        primary negotiator, 55, 59

radio operator, 57
secondary negotiator, 55, 59
tactical liaison, 57, 59
technical resource person, 57, 59
think tank, 56, 59
transition to, 54
Crisis negotiator stress, 63–75
ambiguities, 70
arousal response mechanisms, 68
combat fatigue, 69
Critical Incident Stress Debriefings,
68–71
debriefings, 69–70
defusing, 70–71
demobilizations, 71
denial, 64
general personality traits of emergency
personnel, 64–65
Holmes–Rahe stress scale, 73
International Critical Incident Stress
Foundation, Inc., 73
life change indicators and disease risk
patrol (school version), 74–75
lip service, 63
negotiating and negotiators' stress, 65–68
incident, 66–67
postincident, 67–68
preincident precautions and
preparation, 65
recognition of problem, 63–64
shell shock, 69
Critical Incident Stress Debriefings (CISD),
68–71
debriefings, 69–70
defusing, 70–71
demobilizations, 71
postincident, 67
process, 70
Cross-cultural communications
extremist, 199
non-law enforcement/correctional crisis
negotiators, 39
Cross-training, cross-qualifying versus,
27–30
communication, 29
Crisis Resolution Team, 29
difference of opinion, 27
Group Think, 27
Renaissance Men, 28
Ruby Ridge, Idaho, 27
SWAT team, 27
Waco, Texas, 27

D

Defense mechanisms, 14–16
automatic, 315
denial, 315
identification, 294
projection, 14, 111
rationalization, 14, 111
suppression and isolation of affect, 318
Delusional disorder, 8
Delusions, 16, 123
Denial
definition of, 13
occurrence of, 64
Stockholm Syndrome, 297
Depakane, 136
Depakote, 136
Dependent Personality Disorder, 98
Diagnostic and Statistical Manual (DSM),
3, 4, 143
Downs v. United States, 29, 31, 45, 51–53,
180
Drug use, 239
DSM; See *Diagnostic and Statistical Manual*
Dynamic inactivity, 32

E

Effective hostage/crisis negotiators,
characteristics of, 19–26
Adjective Check List, 23
early incidents, 19–20
emergency assault option, 20
Entebbe raid, 19
ineffective negotiators, 24
international hijackings, 20
Iranian hostage drama (1980), 20, 21
Munich Olympics (1972), 19
negotiations team, most effective
weapon of, 19
past tactics, 20
preservation of human life, 19
recommendations, 20–21
Ruby Ridge, Idaho, 25
social-psychological traits of negotiators,
21–24
method, 23
results, 23–24
Waco, Texas, 25
Emergency assault option, 20
Emotional labeling, 10
Empathy, communication of, 12

Entebbe raid, 19
Escalith, 136
Executive Officer (XO), xxv
Explosives, 234
Extremist, negotiating with, 195–202
　　brief case studies from 1980, 198–199
　　constitutional rights, 197
　　cross-cultural communications, 199
　　extremist, 197
　　FBI categories of hostage holders, 196
　　intermediaries, 198
　　media coverage, 197
　　political orientation, 196
　　right-wing radicals, 197
　　role of third-party intermediaries, 199
　　terrorist mystique, 198
　　time is on our side, 199
　　types of hostage holders, 196–197
　　U.S. domestic terrorist group
　　　　differences, 202

F

FBI; *See* Federal Bureau of Investigation
FCI; *See* Federal correctional institution
Federal Aviation Administration (FAA),
　　xxvi, 52
Federal Bureau of Investigation (FBI), xxi
　　Academy, xxi–xxiv
　　　　Behavioral Science Unit, xxii
　　　　father of behavioral Science, xxiii
　　　　FBI director, xxi
　　　　firearms training, xxi
　　　　identification of KGB and GRU
　　　　　　agents, xxii
　　　　legends, xxiii
　　　　location, xxiv
　　　　Mainside Quantico, xxiii
　　　　nicknames for, xxiii
　　　　noncommissioned officers, xxii
　　　　Quantico, xxi
　　　　relationship with field agents, xxiv
　　Anti-Sniper Survival Training, 49
　　categories of hostage holders, 196
　　credentials, 313
　　Crisis Negotiations Unit crisis site
　　　　assessment, 61
　　difference of opinion, 27
　　HOBAS research, 227
　　Hostage Negotiations program,
　　　　instruction, xxx
　　interpreters, 41

Philadelphia Field Office, 122
Special Operations Unit, 47
version of hostage (crisis) negotiations
　　exchange program, xxxi
　　　　FBI Hostage Negotiations program,
　　　　　　instruction, xxx
　　　　hijackings, xxx
　　　　interview of officers and agents,
　　　　　　xxix–xxx
　　　　mental disorders among hostage
　　　　　　takers, xxx
　　　　New Scotland Yard, xxx
　　　　therapy guidelines, xxx
Federal correctional institution (FCI), 175;
　　　　See also Correctional setting,
　　　　crisis negotiations in
Field Training Exercise (FTX), 102
First responder guidelines, 31–35
　　credibility, 34
　　dynamic inactivity, 32
　　factors, 31–32
　　good opening, 33
　　hearsay, 33
　　life and crime scene analogy to crisis
　　　　scene first responder, 31
　　listening, importance of, 32
　　lying, 34
　　negotiation process, 32
　　noncorrectional negotiators, 34
　　past findings, 32–33
　　peaceful resolution, 32
　　some good guidelines, 33–35
　　suicidal suspect, 35
　　suicide by cop, 33
"The Foundation of Ubiquity," 102
Freemen, 45
FTX; *See* Field Training Exercise

G

Global Assessment of Functioning, 5
Group think, 27, 247–260
　　Allied Armies, 247
　　avoiding this disaster, 258–259
　　basic human nature is to go along to get
　　　　along, 248–249
　　bridge too far, 250
　　European front fall of, 1944, 247–248
　　executive summary, 247
　　FBI studies their history, 258
　　FCI Talladega, Alabama (1991), 254
　　group think, 248, 249–250

group think in 1944, 250–251
Hostage Rescue Team, 254
Ku Klux Klan, 253
"one tank wide" assault, 248
Ruby Ridge, Idaho (1992), 254–255
super SWAT team, 254
what went wrong at Waco (phase I),
    252–253
    arguments about group stereotypes,
        252
    attacking force, 252
    contraindicated intelligence, 253
    illusion of invulnerability, 252
    immoral behavior, 252
    intelligence from undercover agent,
        252
    self-censorship, 252
    shared sense of unanimity, 253
what went wrong at Waco with the FBI
    (phase I), 253–254
what went wrong at Waco with the FBI
    (phase II), 255–257
    FBI morality, 256
    frustrated negotiators, 257
    illusion of invulnerability, 256
    morally weak followers, 256
    pressure to agree, 257
    reliable indicators of failure, 256
    sense of unanimity, 257
    tear-gas plan, 257
    treatment of negotiators, 257
GSG-9, 236
Guidelines
    adolescent hostage taker, 93
    Antisocial Personality Disorder hostage
        taker, 113–115
    bipolar hostage taker, 135–138
        active listening skills, 137
        follow-up, 137
        involvement in process, 136
        keeping busy, 136
        nonpolice negotiators, 137
        off meds, 137
        publicity, 137
        reality oriented negotiations, 136
        sharing information, 136
    constructive deviation from, 261–271
        art of crisis negotiation, 261
        beginnings, 264–265
        buzzwords, 263
        danger, 268–269
        decision to deviate, 266–267

        experiencing tragedy, 269
        how to exploit success, 268
        identify guidelines that applies, 267
        indicators of failure, 269
        judicial hindsight, 263–264
        Landover Mall, 261–262
        logical procedures, 262
        making the decision to deviate,
            265–266
        Munich (1972), 262–263
        Murphy's Law, 266
        new direction, 263
        procedures for creativity in
            deviation, 267–269
        progress, 265
        prove why guideline is not working,
            267
        risks, 268
        specific details of plan, 268
        standard of care used by courts, 267
        SWAT back-up, 268
        timing, 268
        why approach deviates from standard
            practice, 267
first responder, 31–35
    credibility, 34
    dynamic inactivity, 32
    factors, 31–32
    good opening, 33
    hearsay, 33
    life and crime scene analogy to crisis
        scene first responder, 31
    listening, importance of, 32
    lying, 34
    noncorrectional negotiators, 34
    past findings, 32–33
    peaceful resolution, 32
    some good guidelines, 33–35
    suicidal suspect, 35
    suicide by cop, 33
inadequate personality, 105–106
normal people, negotiating with, 82–84
    clarify the situation, 84
    do not lie, 83
    introduction, 82
    offer hope, 83
    play down events, 83
    stalling for time, 83
    substitute for no, 83
paranoid schizophrenic hostage taker,
    124–126
    confrontation, 125

distance, 125
family members, 126
indicators, 126
listening, 124
medication, 125
publicity, 126
questions, 125
sexual concerns, 126
sincerity, 124–125
stalling for time, 124
Stockholm Syndrome, 126
trust, 124
suicidal hostage holder, 147–149
CPR acronym, 148
evaluate preincident behavior,
147–148
negotiating guidelines and rationale,
147–149
negotiating techniques, 149
postincident considerations, 149
suggested officer (negotiating team
activities) behavior and strategies,
148

H

Haldol, 123
Hallucinations, 16, 121, 123
Haloperidol, 123
Hanafi Muslims, 206
Harper's Ferry, xxviii
Health maintenance organizations (HMOs),
4
Hijacking
explosives, 234
heyday of, xxx
international, 20
Lufthansa Flight 181, 47
Stockholm Syndrome, 298
HMOs; *See* Health maintenance
organizations
Holmes–Rahe stress scale, 73, 85, 151
Hostage crisis, phases of, 275–289
antagonism toward captors, 286
apathy, 277
"be yourself" dictum, 281
Boot Camp, 278
ego-supporting role, 278
hostage hostility, 280
hostage takers, 282–285
Antisocial Personality, 283
Borderline Personality, 283–284

criminal subject, 283–284
depressed individuals, 284–285
mentally ill subject, 284–285
paranoid schizophrenic, 284
politically, socially, or religiously
motivated subject, 285
types, 283
individual differences in response to
stress, 277–278
intelligence, 285
Iran, 275–276
Iraqi-sponsored terrorists, 275
London Syndrome, 280–281
mental escape, 279
motivation, 282
New Scotland Yard, 275
"our hostages," 275
posttraumatic stress, 285
prisoners of war, 276, 277
problem, 276–277
psychological exhaustion, 285
role of hostage, 278–279
socially prescribed behaviors, 278
social roles, 278
Stockholm Syndrome, 281
two campers, 279
United States, 275
U.S. marines in Tehran, 282
ventilation process, 285
Hostage/crisis negotiations (introduction),
xxiv–xxviii
baptism of fire, xxv
booby-trap mechanism, xxvi
difficult decision, xxv
Executive Officer, xxv
goal of crisis negotiations, xxv
hijacking, xxv
Hostage Rescue Team, xxvii, xxviii
improvised explosive devices, xxvii
SOARS, xxvii
Special Agent in Charge, xxvii
TRAMS, xxvii
Hostage negotiations (introduction),
xxviii–xxix
California Association of Crisis
Negotiators, xxviii
early instance of U.S. hostage
negotiation, xxviii
Harper's Ferry, xxviii
hijacking, xxviii–xxix
New York City Police Department,
xxviii

Pearl Harbor syndrome, xxviii
Quantico, xxix
world's largest negotiator's association, xxviii
wrongful death suit, xxix
Hostage psychological survival guide, 313–322
    automatic defense mechanism, 315
    defenselessness, 315
    group critique, 314
    insubordination, 317
    literature, 314
    London Syndrome, 318
    omnipotence, feelings of, 315
    paralyzing fear, 315
    physical exercise, 319
    reacting to terrorist/criminal/inmate episode, 315–317
        control, 315–316
        coping with abduction, 315
        preparing for psychological reactions, 316
        roles for survivors, 317
    social roles, 317
    successful coping strategies, 317–321
        blend with your peers, 320–321
        contain your hostility toward your captors, 318
        control your outward appearance, 320
        fantasize to fill empty hours, 318–319
        have faith in yourself and your government, 317–318
        keep to or establish routines, 319–320
        maintain superior attitude, 318
        rationalize the abduction, 319
        strive to be flexible and keep your sense of humor, 320
    succumbers, 316
    suppression and isolation of affect, 318
    survivors, 316
Hostage Rescue Team (HRT), xxvii, 254
Hostage taker
    adolescent; See Adolescent hostage taker
    Antisocial Personality Disorder; See also Antisocial Personality Disorder hostage taker
    bipolar; See also Bipolar hostage taker
    emotional state of, 37
    paranoid schizophrenic; See also Paranoid schizophrenic hostage taker
    suicidal; See also Suicidal hostage holder
HRT; See Hostage Rescue Team

I

ICISF; See International Critical Incident Stress Foundation
ICs; See Incident commanders
Ideas of reference, 120
Improvised explosive devices, xxvii
Inadequate personality, 97–106
    American Psychiatric Association version, 98–99
    Avoidant personality Disorder, 98
    congenital personality disorders, 97
    cults, 102
    family of overachievers, 97
    Field Training Exercise, 102
    "The Foundation of Ubiquity," 102
    Inadequate Personality Disorder, 97, 98
    incidence in society, 97–98
    joint exercise, 101
    K-9 unit, 104
    law enforcement version, 101–104
    media event, 100
    military version, 99–100
    Miranda Warning, 103
    movie version, 100
    negotiating guidelines and their rationales, 105–106
    poor judgment, 102
    public circus, 100
    shoe-shining seminar, 99
    Stockholm syndrome, 103
Inadequate Personality Disorder, 97, 98
Incident commanders (ICs), 177
Insubordination, 217
Intelligence
    gathering, communication with hostage, 308
    team structure, 55–56, 59
    undercover agent, 252
Internal Revenue Service audit, 79
International Critical Incident Stress Foundation (ICISF), 73, 168
Introjection, 294
Iranian hostage drama (1980), 20, 21, 280
Islam, tenets of; See Terrorism and tenets of Islam

J

Jihad, 210
Junior therapist, 112

K

KISS axiom, 8, 81
Ku Klux Klan (KKK), 205, 253
K-9 unit, 104

L

LASD; *See* Los Angeles Sheriff's
        Department
Lewis Penitentiary in Buckeye, Arizona,
        183–184
Life change indicators and disease risk
        patrol (school version), 74–75
Listening, 80; *See also* Active listening skills
Lithium, 135, 136
Litigation
        City of Winter Haven v. Allen, 28
        Downs v. United States, 29, 31, 45, 51–53,
                180
        Moon v. Winfield, 28
        State v. Sands, 30
        United States v. Crosby, 30
London Syndrome, 280–281, 318
Los Angeles Sheriff's Department (LASD),
        157
Lucasville, Ohio State Prison, 183

M

Manic-Depressive Psychosis, 132
Marine Corps Recruit Depot (MCRD), 99
Marriage and Family Therapists (MFTs), 4
MBM; *See* Muslim Brotherhood Movement
MCRD; *See* Marine Corps Recruit Depot
Mental disorders, negotiator classification
        of, 8
MFTs; *See* Marriage and Family Therapists
Minnesota Multiphasic Personality
        Inventory (MMPI), 22
Miranda Warning, 103
Mood changes, 133
Moon v. Winfield, 28
Multiaxial system, 5
Munich Olympics (1972), 19, 262
Muslim Brotherhood Movement (MBM),
        206

N

NCOs; *See* Noncommissioned officers
Negotiation position papers (NPPs),
        221–222, 240
New Scotland Yard, xxx, xxxi, 275
New York Police Department (NYPD), xxvi
Noncommissioned officers (NCOs), xxii
Non-law enforcement/correctional crisis
        negotiators, 37–46
        control of non-law enforcement/
                correctional interpreters, 43–45
                interpreter cannot be allowed to
                        improvise, 44
                third-party intermediators do not
                        guarantee success, 44–45
        cross-cultural communications, 39
        dialects, 39
        Freemen, 45
        hostage taker, emotional state of, 37
        legendary linguistic lapses, 38–39
        listening, 38
        maintaining control of crisis, 37
        misinterpretation, catastrophic example
                of, 38
        potential problems, 39
        Potsdam terms, 39
        professional models, 42–43
        psychologist, 42
        role of third-party intermediaries, 37–38
        search and seizure, 44
        time is on our side, 40
        typical third-party problems, 40–42
                risks, 40
                some simple solutions, 41–42
                translator problems, 40–41
Normal people, negotiating with, 79–85
        active listening, 81–82
                reflecting emotional level, 82
                repeating words, 82
                say nothing, 82
                summarize, 82
        credibility, 83
        every call for service means stress for
                someone, 80–81
        Holmes–Rahe stress scale, 85
        institutions, circumstances existing
                within, 80
        IRS audit, 79
        KISS, 81
        mind-set, 80
        mission statement, 79

negotiating guidelines, 82–84
  clarify the situation, 84
  do not lie, 83
  introduction, 82
  offer hope, 83
  play down events, 83
  stalling for time, 83
  substitute for no, 83
  stress is personally defined, 79
NPPs; *See* Negotiation position papers
NYPD; *See* New York Police Department

O

Oakdale Correctional Facility, Louisiana,
    182
Omnipotence, feelings of, 315
Open-ended questions, 10

P

Paranoia, 8
Paranoid Schizophrenia, 118, 284
Paranoid schizophrenic hostage taker,
    117–128
  barricaded persons off meds, 123
  "Black Jesus," 119
  definition, 120–121
  etiology, 119–120
  ideas of reference, 120
  incidence in society, 121–122
  law enforcement exposure, 121–122
  major symptoms, 122–123
    delusion, 123
    hallucinations, 123
  movie version, 120
  negotiating guidelines and rationale,
      124–126
    confrontation, 125
    distance, 125
    family members, 126
    indicators, 126
    listening, 124
    medication, 125
    publicity, 126
    questions, 125
    sexual concerns, 126
    sincerity, 124–125
    stalling for time, 124
    Stockholm Syndrome, 126
    trust, 124
  preliminary tasks, 118

prescription drugs, 123
rapport, developing, 124
Shannon Street Siege, 119
SWAT team, 117
ventilation, 118
voices, 123
Patient-centered therapy, 9
Patient–doctor privilege, 7
Pearl Harbor, 263
Pearl Harbor syndrome, xxviii
Perishable skills, 50
Personality disorders, 97, 143; *See also*
    specific disorder
Personally defined stress, 79
Philadelphia Cohort Studies, 111
Police-assisted suicide, 157–174
  alcohol, 167
  American Indians, 158
  backup plan, 168
  case, 157
  community hotline services, 168
  diagnostic criteria for suicide by cop,
      172–173
  diagram of grounds, 159
  Golden Gate Bridge, alcohol, judgment,
      and doubt, 165–167
  historical examples, 158
  identification, 167–168
  impaired judgment, 167
  indications, 174
  law enforcement as mental health
      professionals, 160–163
  less than lethal alternative, 168–170
    CPR acronym, 169
    negotiating techniques, 170
    postincident considerations, 170
    preincident behavior, 169
    suggested officer (negotiating team
        activities) behavior and strategies,
        169
  Los Angeles Sheriff's Department,
      157
  methods, 163–165
  negotiator safety, 166
  off meds, 163
  Short Doyle Clinics, 163
  snakes with and without venom,
      163–165
  subject on grounds, 159, 160, 161
  suicide-by-cop scale, 173
  victims of crime, 163
  Web resources, 171

Police Officers Standards and Training (POST), 23
Posttraumatic stress disorder (PTSD), 68–69, 285, 286
Prison; *See* Correctional setting, crisis negotiations in
Prisoners of war (POWs), 276
Projection, 14–16, 111, 227
Psychiatrist, definition of, 3
Psychological survival; *See* Hostage psychological survival guide
Psychopathic liar, 109
Psychosis, typical symptoms of, 16
    delusions, 16
    excellent idea, 16
    hallucinations, 16
PTSD; *See* Posttraumatic traumatic stress disorder

Q

Quantico
    Crisis Negotiators class taught at, xxxi
    FBI negotiators from, 183
    Mainside Quantico, xxiii
    "Nuts and Bolts," xxix

R

Rationalization, 14, 111
RCMP; *See* Royal Canadian Mounted Police
Reality oriented negotiations, 136
Rejection, 92
Renaissance Men, 28
Respirdol, 123
Respiridone, 123
Role change, 12
Royal Canadian Mounted Police (RCMP), xxvi, 44
Ruby Ridge, Idaho, 25, 45, 50, 195

S

SAC; *See* Special Agent in Charge
SAS; *See* Special Agent Supervisor
SbC; *See* Suicide by cop
Shannon Street Siege, 119
Shell shock, 69
Short Doyle Clinics, 163
Skin Heads, 197
SLA; *See* Symbionese Liberation Army

SOARS; *See* Special Operations and Research Staff
Social roles, 278, 317
Solo suicidal subject; *See* Suicidal hostage holder
Somali pirates, 318
Sour Grapes, 14
Special Agent in Charge (SAC), xxvii
Special Agent Supervisor (SAS), xix
Special Operations and Research Staff (SOARS), xxvii
Special weapons and tactics (SWAT) team, 20, 27
    commander, 47
    constructive deviation from guidelines, 264
    messenger, 56
    paranoid schizophrenic hostage taker, 117
    San Diego Police department, 238
    subject surrender, 217
State v. Sands, 30
Stockholm Syndrome, 103, 114, 281, 291–306
    accidental hostage incidents, 296
    affection, 299
    bank robbery, 291
    common experience of victims, 301
    communication with hostage, 310
    coping with reality, 293
    defense mechanisms, 294
    denial, 297
    domestic hostage situations, 295–296
    ego, 293
    hijacking, 298
    history, 292
    hostage taker reaction, 301–303
    id, 293
    identification, 294
    individualized reactions, 303–305
    introjection, 294
    isolation, 300
    notoriety, 291
    original victims, 305
    phenomenon, 292–295
    positive contact, 300–301
    regression, 295
    stages of hostage reaction, 296–297
    superego, 293
    time, 298–300
    volatile negotiations, 233
Stress; *See* Crisis negotiator stress

Subject surrender, indicators of, 217–223
  crucial conclusion, 221–222
    assessment, 222
    recommendations, 222
    status, 222
  indicators, 218–221
    calling the negotiator, 219
    decrease in threatening behavior, 220
    expressive concerns, 218–219
    hostages as people, 220
    nonviolent subject, 219
    passing or extension of deadline, 220
    pattern of exchanging, 220–221
    personal needs, 218–219
    reduced expectations, 219
    release of hostages, 220
    routine of exchanging material goods
      for hostages, 220–221
    subject talking, 219
    threats, 221
    trusting relationship, 218
  negotiation position papers, 221–222
Suicidal hostage holder, 139–155
  alcohol, 141
  asking the difficult question, 140–141
  chemical imbalance, 144
  chemically depressed person, 145
  civilian suicide, 146–147
  community hotline services, 142
  depression, types of, 143
  depression in *DSM-IV*, 143–145
  Golden Gate Bridge, doubt, alcohol, and
    judgment, 141–142
  Holmes–Rahe stress scale, 151
  impaired judgment, 141
  jailer, 139
  less than lethal alternative, 142–143
  mental health professionals, 147
  methods, 145–146
  negotiating guidelines and rationale,
    147–149
    CPR acronym, 148
    evaluate preincident behavior,
      147–148
    negotiating techniques, 149
    postincident considerations, 149
    suggested officer (negotiating team
      activities) behavior and strategies,
      148
  personality disorders, 143
  phrases that work, 152
  police and solo suicidal subjects, 143

    snakes with and without venom,
      145–146
    solvent for the superego, 141
    some effective answers, 152
    suicide-by-cop subject, 145
    suicide intervention flowchart, 152–155
    Web resources, 150
Suicide by cop (SbC), 145, 157, 227; *See also*
    Police-assisted suicide
Surrender; *See* Subject surrender, indicators
    of
SWAT team; *See* Special weapons and
    tactics team
Symbionese Liberation Army (SLA), 315

T

Talladega, Alabama, 182–183
Taylor Manifest Anxiety Scale, 22
Team; *See* crisis Negotiation team
Teenagers; *See* Adolescent hostage taker
Terrorism and tenets of Islam, 203–213
  Allah, 203, 208
  Christian past as Islamic prologue,
    205–207
  collateral damage, 210
  dictatorships, 212
  Egyptian government, 207
  external versus internal, 208–210
    inshallah or fatalism, 209
    internal, 209–210
  Hindus, 204
  inner struggle, 210
  insurrections and Islam, 204–205
  Ku Klux Klan, 205
  Middle Ages, 205
  Middle Eastern mind, 203–204
  past as prologue, 204
  practice, 210–211
    jihad, 210–211
    Wahhabi movement, 211
  Saudi Arabia, 211
  Shia versus Sunni, 204–205
  tenets of Islam, 207–208
  thinking, 208
  violence, 205
Terrorist Research and Management Staff
    (TRAMS), xxv, xxvii
Think tank, 56
Third-party intermediaries (TPIs), 185, 222
Thorazine, 123
Threats, 187–189, 239

conditional defensive, 189, 221, 239–240
conditional offensive, 189, 221, 239
unconditional, 187–189, 221, 239
Topomax, 136
TPIs; *See* Third-party intermediaries
Training; *See* Cross-training, cross-qualifying versus
TRAMS; *See* Terrorist Research and Management Staff

U

United States v. Crosby, 30

V

Valborate, 136
Ventilation, 118, 285
Verbal will, 228
Vietnam POWs, 320
Volatile negotiations, indicators of, 225–243
  crucial conclusion, 240–241
    assessment, 240
    recommendations, 241
    status, 240
  deliveries, 231
  "The Good Guys," 235
  GSG-9, 236
  incident behavior of subject, 235–238
    after hours of negotiations, subject has no clear demands, his demands are outrageous, or they are changing, 237–238
    negotiations are becoming more volatile, 236–237
    postnegotiations violence, 235–236
  Muhammad Ali, 237
  negotiations process, 230
  on-scene commander, 225
  projection, 227
  refusal to negotiate, 230
  revenge, 232
  Stockholm Syndrome, 233
  subject has history of violence, 229–230
    planned siege, 229–230
    prior confrontations, 229
  subject stress, 238–239
    alcohol or drug use by subject or hostage during siege, 239
    multiple stressors, 238–239

subject–victim relationship, 230–233
  hostage taker insists that particular person be brought to scene, 232–233
  isolation and dehumanization of hostages, 233
  targeted hostages, 230–232
suicidal subjects, 226–229
  age of subject, 227
  depressed hostage taker who denies thoughts of suicide, 226
  history of violence, 229
  no rapport, 226–227
  no social support system, 227
  subject insists on face-to-face negotiations, 227–228
  subject sets deadline for his own death, 228
  verbal will, 228–229
suicide by cop, 227
switch from instrumental to expressive demands, 236
threat analysis, 239–240
types of threats, 239
Washington Monument, taking of, 235
weapon(s), 233–235
  excessive ammunition (multiple weapons), 234
  explosives, 234–235
  weapon tied to hostage holder, 233–234

W

Waco, Texas, 50, 195; *See also* Group think
  cross-training, 27
  effective hostage/crisis negotiators, 25
  size of FBI team, 178
Washington Monument, taking of, 235
Web resources
  police-assisted suicide, 171
  suicidal hostage holder, 150

X

XO; *See* Executive Officer

Z

Zyprexa, 136